WITCHCRAFT
AND
BLACK MAGIC

MONTAGUE SUMMERS

DOVER PUBLICATIONS, INC.
Mineola, New York

Bibliographical Note

This Dover edition, first published in 2000, is an unabridged republication of *Witchcraft and Black Magic,* originally published ca. 1946 by
Rider & Co., Ltd., London and New York.

Library of Congress Cataloging-in-Publication Data

Summers, Montague, 1880–1948.
    Witchcraft and black magic / Montague Summers.
       p. cm.
    Originally published: London ; New York : Rider, 1946.
    Includes index.
    ISBN 0-486-41125-7 (pbk.)
      1. Witchcraft. 2. Magic. I. Title.

BP1566 .S86 2000
133.4–dc21

                                                 99-053054

Manufactured in the United States of America
Dover Publications, Inc., 31 East 2nd Street, Mineola, N.Y. 11501

CONTENTS

CHAPTER I

CHAPTER II

CHAPTER III

CHAPTER IV

CHAPTER V

CHAPTER VI

CHAPTER VII

LIST OF ILLUSTRATIONS

7

INTRODUCTION

"The most interesting and instructive work that could be written," said Dr. Johnson, "would be a History of Magick."

It has been observed that "it is quite impossible to appreciate and understand the true and inner lives of men and women in Elizabethan and Stuart England, in the France of Louis XIII and during the long reign of his son and successor, in Italy of the Renaissance and the Catholic Reaction—to name but three European countries and a few definite periods—unless we have some realization of the part that Witchcraft played in those ages amid the affairs of these Kingdoms. All classes were affected and concerned from Pope to peasant, from Queen to cottage girl."

It is hardly surprising, then, that during the last five-and-twenty years the history of witchcraft should have engaged the particular attention of a large number of writers, some of whom, scholars, after devoting to the subject much preparative thought and ripe reflection, and as the result of long and patient research, have enriched the literature of demonology with contributions, which, however divergent, maybe, the angles of approach and hence the logical conclusions arrived at, are of permanent and essential value.

On the other hand, witchcraft has proved an irresistible lure to not a few freakish and facile pens, and there have appeared far too many books made of paste and scissors, which are either the veriest rag-bag of folk-lore, or else bold and rather blatant paraphrases from the work of recent authorities.

For the history of English Witchcraft the material collected and so ably commented with ample annotations by Mr. C. L'Estrange Ewen in his *Witch Hunting and Witch Trials* (1929), *Witchcraft and Demonianism* (1933), and the privately printed *Witchcraft in the Star Chamber* (1938), is of the very first importance. A useful reprint with an excellent Introduction is Dr. G. B. Harrison's *The Trial of the Lancester Witches, A.D. MDCXII* (1929). To Dr. Harrison we are also obliged for a reprint of the *Dæmonologie* (1597) of King James I, and *Newes from Scotland* (1591) in "The Bodley Head Quartos". *The Age of Arsenic* (1931), by Mr. W. Branch Johnson, is a good survey of witchcraft as practised in Paris under Louis XIV, the infamies of La Voisin and her gang. Two very scholarly studies by the Rev. Joseph J. Williams, S.J., *Voodoos and Obeahs* (1932), and *Psychic Phenomena of Jamaica* (1935), are our authority for the gruesome workings of the Black Man's witchcraft in the West Indies.

Poltergeists (1940), by Mr. Sacheverell Sitwell, examines at considerable length and most masterly these extraordinary happenings, which are often so nearly allied to satanic supernaturalism.

The late Professor George Lyman Kittredge's *Witchcraft in Old and New England* (1928) to some extent suffers, in my opinion at least, from the fact that it presents a series of unconnected essays, their unity being that the eighteen chapters one and all relate to the same subject. Nevertheless it is a notable piece of work, although curiously unsympathetic and even sceptical in its survey, a bias which can hardly fail to lead to error, or at any rate misunderstanding, in some important details.

It were ungenerous and unfair to animadvert upon the late Dr. Henry Charles Lea's *Materials Toward a History of Witchcraft*, a book left incomplete and unrevised by the author. These three volumes, published in 1939, must necessarily remain and be regarded as a collection of synopses and excursuses, references and notes, material often of much value, but on account of the circumstances of the case in some essential features lacking and inchoate. This is all the more to be regretted since a redaction must, I think, have led the author not unseldom to modify his judgements, when both facts and deductions would doubtless have been marshalled in correcter and clearer perspective.

Long and intensive inquiry into the subject of witchcraft has fully convinced me that if one is endeavouring after a more intelligent and wider comprehending of this universal and darkly intricate cult, it is necessary to study the wisdom of the days of old, to turn to the masters for guidance and direction. For example, as a mere preliminary, the serious student must read carefully and digest that noble treatise, the *Malleus Maleficarum*. Nor can he be considered even initially equipped unless he has something more than an acquaintance with the work of such high authorities as Guazzo, Anania, Remy, de Lancre, Delrio, Thyraeus, Sinistrari, Glanvil, Boulton, Romanus, Brückner, Görres, Baumgarten.

It is no mere academic question upon which he engages. Professor Burr, of Cornell University, is of opinion that certain of my writings on witchcraft savour too much of theology. But, with rarest and very special exceptions, it is only the theologian who is competent to treat the subject, and who is best able to diagnose the essential malice of witchcraft. The very problems of evil and man's essay to put himself in touch with and in some sense to control wicked spirits at once enter into the domain of theology, and cannot be divorced from it. The authors of the *Malleus Maleficarum*, James Sprenger and Henry Kramer, were trained theologians, Thomists. Two hundred years later a divine of a very different school, a learned and acute mind, the Rev. Cotton Mather, defines witchcraft in almost exactly the same terms. Guazzo, Delrio, Thyraeus, Sinistrari, were theologians of the first rank. In fact, it is unusual to find an authority on demonology who has not been thus specially trained, unless, indeed, he be a jurist, treating the crime purely from a legal standpoint.

It should, perhaps, be mentioned here that there are not the least grounds for the very empty suggestion that Sinistrari's important treatise, *Demoniality*, was disapproved "by an ecclesiastical censor". The work has, in fact, been carefully read by two professed theologians, the one a regular, a Capuchin, and the other a secular of much experience. Both pronounce it to be a good book, and without grave error. There may be some slight and superficial corrigenda, but nothing of moment.

It is my pleasurable duty to thank the Rev. Fr. Gregory Raupert, O.P., for his kindness in allowing me to quote from his admirable account of the life of his father, the famous psychic investigator, *A Convert from Spiritualism, J. Godfrey Raupert, K.S.G.*

I also have to add my grateful obligation to Mr. Arthur Machen for a similar favour, permission to quote from *The House of Souls.*

MONTAGUE SUMMERS.

2 July, 1945.
   In Visit. B.M.V.

CHAPTER I

What is Witchcraft?—How does One become a Witch?—The Essential Pact.

"Your Covenant with Death, your Agreement with Hell."—*Isaiah* xxviii, 18.

AN old and experienced Oxford tutor throughout nearly half a century was wont to give the men who had read with him and attended his lectures, when they had finished their residence and came to say good-bye, a very precious parting legacy which consisted of just three simple words of advice—"Define your terms". So, at the outset, in writing about and examining into witchcraft we can hardly do better than inquire precisely what witchcraft is, in what sense we are going to use the word, what ground it covers, what were and are the aims and objects of the members of this horrid craft.

In the first place, for our present general purpose, it is mere waste of time and hair-splitting to attempt to draw minute and cavilling distinctions, to chop up words and quibble and subdivide, to argue that technically and etymologically a sorcerer differs from a witch, a witch from a necromancer, a necromancer from a satanist. In actual fact and practice all these names are correlative; in use, synonymous. Thus, although originally and in its first implication a sorcerer strictly means one who casts lots, and is derived from the late Latin *sortiarius*, *sors* being a lot or chance, our standard authority, *The Oxford English Dictionary* has: "Sorcerer, One who practises sorcery; a wizard, magician", whilst Sorcery is "The use of magic or enchantment; the practice of magic arts; witchcraft". Necromancer comes through the Greek, and means one who can reveal future events or disclose secrets by communication with the dead. There has in this word been some confusion of the Greek prefix *Nekros*, a corpse, with the Latin *niger*, *nigr—*, black; and in Middle English, that is to say roughly from 1200 to 1500, we have the form "nigromancer", one skilled in the black art. (*Mancer* is the Greek *Manteia*, foretelling, divination.) Satanist, as is plain, means a devotee of Satan, a person who is regarded as an adherent and follower of Satan. It is significant, however, and worth remembering, that when first employed the word Satanist was equivalent to an atheist, and it is used in this sense by John Aylmer, who was Bishop of London under Queen Elizabeth. In his political pamphlet, *An Harbour for Faithful and True Subjects*, published in 1559 at Strassburg, where he was then living, he speaks of Satanists, implying infidels and unbelievers generally. Later the word became more restricted and changed its complexion, since, whatever else, the witch is certainly no atheist. In *The Life of Mrs. Lynn Linton*, published in 1901, the following passage occurs: "There are two sects, the Satanists and the Luciferists—and they pray to these names as Gods." This is a distinction without a difference, Satan and Lucifer being identically the same entity and power. Dr. Charles H. H. Wright, sometime Grinfield lecturer on the Septuagint, Oxford, may say of Lucifer, "the word in Scripture has nothing to do with the devil", but he is wrong. In English, all accepted understanding and ordinary use are against him, and we parallel the words of Isaiah (xiv, 12), "How art thou fallen from heaven, O Lucifer, son of the morning!" with the gospel (*St. Luke* x, 18): "I beheld Satan as lightning fall from heaven."

To sum up, sorcerer, witch, necromancer are essentially all one, so it is convenient, as well as—what is unusual with convenience—perfectly correct to employ the word "witch" to cover them all, whilst witchcraft is the cult, together with the practices, of a witch.

A well-known Elizabethan writer, a preacher and theologian of some note in his day, George Giffard, the minister of Maldon, Essex, understands a witch to be "one that worketh by the Devil, or by some devilish or curious art, either hurting or healing, revealing things secret, or foretelling things to come, which the Devil hath devised to entangle and snare men's souls withal to damnation. The conjuror, the enchanter, the sorcerer, the diviner, and whatsoever sort there is, are in deed compassed within this circle."

Incidentally, it may be noted that the word "witch", although now popularly and almost exclusively intended to denote a woman, can be used of a man, and in some remoter country places it may still be heard with its old meaning: "He's a feaw (foul) witch." Actually "witch" is from the Old English masculine noun-substantive *wicca*, "A man who practises witchcraft or magic; a magician, sorcerer, wizard"—a pretty comprehensive definition.

In a Latin Glossary of about 1100, King Henry I's reign, the two words *augur* and *ariolus* are translated by *wicca*.

Lewis and Short in their Latin Dictionary derive the word *augur* from *avis*, a bird, and the Sanscrit *gar*, to make known. They define the word as: "an augur, diviner, soothsayer; at Rome, a member of a particular college of priests, much reverenced in earlier ages, who made known the future by observing the lightning, the flight or notes of birds, the feeding of the sacred fowls, certain appearances of quadrupeds and any unusual occurrences". That copious but rather arid rhetorician, Cicero, in the most interesting of his treatises, *On Divination*, has a good deal to say with regard to the sacred birds. He is rationalistic, and entirely unconvincing in his explanations, but happy in his examples. Thus in 217 B.C. the consul Flaminius, when facing the Carthaginians, was warned by the keeper of the sacred chickens not to give battle, as the birds refused to eat. "A pretty kind of omen!" jeered Flaminius. "Suppose they never ate, what then?" "You would do well to refuse to enter into action," was the reply. Upon this, with fine bravado, mocking Flaminius gave the signal for attack, and in the ensuing battle at Lake Trasimene he was defeated by Hannibal with the loss of 15,000 men, himself falling on the field. Unusual occurrences were generally held to include monstrous births, of which there are many recorded, and which are believed to announce the especial wrath of the Deity. Such abortions all nations have held in horror, and there are warning instances chronicled throughout all history. In his day, when a girl was born with two heads, Cicero notes, this shocking omen was followed by seditions and troubles of every sort. At Ravenna in the year 1512 was born a strange creature with a kind of wings instead of arms, and marked with extraordinary signs. Another monster, of the male kind, represented a hairy child of hideous deformity. It was born in the year 1597 at Arles, in Provence, and lived but a few days, terrifying all who beheld it.

> Where children thus are born with hairy coats
> Heaven's wrath unto the kingdom it denotes.

Thus runs the old distich, truly exemplified in that unhappy region, in which men to each other were more like brute beasts than human beings. Another monster was born at Nazara in the year 1581. It had four arms and four legs. In Flanders, in a village between Antwerp and Mechlin, a poor woman was delivered of a child which had two heads and four arms, seemingly two girls joined together. "Likewise in the reign of Henri III of France (1574-1589) there was a woman delivered of a child having two heads and four arms, and the bodies were joined together at the back; the heads were so placed that they looked contrary ways; each had two distinct arms and hands. They would both laugh, both speak, and both cry, and be hungry together; sometimes the one would speak and the other keep silence, and sometimes both speak together. They lived several years, but one outlived the other three years, carrying the dead one (for there was no parting them) till the survivor fainted and expired with the burden, and more with the stench of the dead carcass." These examples are mentioned in the work known as *Aristotle's Problems* or *Aristotle's Masterpiece*, a curious volume, which has, of course, nothing to do with the great Greek philosopher, although erroneously passing under his name. The earliest edition in Latin was printed in Rome, 1475, under the title *The Problems of Aristotle*. As it went through many editions, various contemporary happenings were added. There are translations into nearly all modern languages. Thus in 1597 there was published in London *The Problems of Aristotle with other Philosophers and Phisitions*. An almost identical version had appeared in Edinburgh two years before. In 1710 we have "The Twenty-Fifth English Edition", and there are innumerable reprints.

Ariolus (or *hariolus*), from the Sanscrit *hira*, entrails, is explained by Lewis and Short as "a soothsayer, prophet", and given as the equivalent of *augur*. The word has a grim complexion, for the *ariolus* was introduced among the Romans from the Etruscans, masters of dark mysteries. Well might Cicero write that the Etruscans were soaked in superstition, and that no folk were more skilled in splanchnomancy, which is to say the Etruscan diviners foretold future events from the inspection of the warm and palpitating entrails of victims, sometimes animal, sometimes human, and these horrid sacrifices were clandestinely offered in Rome itself, especially under the Emperors. Strange and awful gods are named in the ancient mythology of Etruria, "where once stood the proud city of Tarquinii, which gave kings to Rome, when Rome itself was but a thing of yesterday, sprung from an upstart settlement of outlaws and robbers". There were Teramo, and Fufluns, and Lord Tinia, who has writhing serpents for legs, and who with frowning face and outstretched wings grasps the red thunderbolt of destruction to hurl it forth furiously and far. It is whispered even today that among the hamlets and farms where Marta runs from Lake Bolsena to the sea there are still those descended from the old stock who worshipped Tinia a long time before the she-wolf suckled twin Romulus and Remus in her Sabine lair. With bated breath men tell how an immemorial tradition has been handed down from that race whose history and tongue are alike forgotten in the dust of ages, that still a few initiates, skulking, secret and close, are all too well versed in nameless liturgies and practise ghostly conjurations, accursed rites, fearfully banned by Mother Church. Three centuries ago, during his brief reign of little more than a couple of years, Pope Gregory XV, no unenlightened pontiff, was so appalled by what he learned of these carrion creeds of corruption and gods of the grave that by special mandate and by word of mouth he ordered the Holy Office to make sharp inquisition without delay and purge of its rot and foulness the infected countryside.

Actually in the days of Hadrian (A.D. 117–138), when Rome eagerly embraced every hoodoo, every superstition, however grotesquely debased, however gloatingly obscene, when there was a "divine invasion" from exotic Egypt, from Syria, from furthest Asia and the East, whilst the decadent devotee demanded the most frenzied delirium of the dervish and the faquir, when Caesar himself was more than suspect of midnight magic and sortilege, for very shame a law was passed strictly forbidding human sacrifice; but none the less many of the later Emperors, particularly Commodus, the sadistic Caracalla, the mad Maxentius, resorted to these horrible rites to learn what fate held in store. On 25 May, A.D. 385, Theodosius I, a Christian ruler, prohibited absolutely any sort of magic sacrifice of any kind, and decreed that the punishment for diviners attempting such abominations, especially the ritual inspection of human viscera, was a painful, lingering, and ignominious death. Yet, as there will be occasion to note, these bloody immolations have persisted throughout all, and are not unknown in demon worship even today.

As has just been mentioned, the Old English word *wicca* is explained by the dictionaries as, "A man who practises witchcraft or magic". What is magic?

Whilst a much-talked-of case was being heard before Mr. Justice Swift in the King's Bench Division during April, 1934, the Judge* asked the plaintiff "the shortest, and at the same time comprehensive, definition of magic which he knew". *Answer:* "Magic is the science of the art of causing change to occur in conformity with the will. White Magic if the will is righteous, and Black Magic if the will is perverse." *Mr. Justice Swift:* "Does that involve the invocation of spirits?" *Answer:* "It may do so. It does involve the invocation of the Holy Guardian Angel, who is appointed by Almighty God to watch over each of us." *Mr. Justice Swift:* "Then it does involve invocation of spirits?" *Answer:* "Of one spirit. God is a spirit, and they that worship Him must worship Him in spirit and in truth." *Mr. Justice Swift:* "Is it, in your view, the

---

* From contemporary newspaper reports: the *Daily Telegraph*, Friday, 13 April, 1934. "Judge asks: 'What is Magic?'"

ABOMINATION DES SORCIERS

Est il rien qui soit plus damnable,   Ils tirent de leurs noirs mysteres·   C'est la que ces maudites ames
Ny plus digne du feu d'enfer,   L'horreur, la hayne le debat,   Se vont preparer leur tourment
Que cette engeance abominable   Et font de sanglans caracteres   Et quelles attisent les flammes,
Des ministres de Lucifer?   Dans leur execrable Sabat.   Qui bruslent eternellement

THE BLACK MYSTERIES OF WITCHCRAFT
An Engraving by Jaspar Isaac (1614)

SADUCISMUS TRIUMPHATUS (1681)

art of controlling spirits so as to affect the course of events?" *Answer:* "That is part of magic, one small branch." *Mr. Justice Swift:* "If the object of the control is good, then it is White Magic?" *Answer:* "Yes." *Mr. Justice Swift:* "If the object of the control is bad, then it is Black Magic?" *Answer:* "Yes." *Mr. Justice Swift:* "When the object of the control is bad, what spirits do you invoke?" *Answer:* "You cannot invoke evil spirits. You must evoke them, and call them out." *Mr. Justice Swift:* "When the object is bad, you evoke evil spirits?" *Answer:* "Yes. You put yourself in their power. In that case it is possible to control evil spirits or blind spirits for a good purpose, as we might if we use the dangerous elements of fire and electricity for heating and lighting, etc." This last reply is very sophistical, since anyone evoking evil spirits would never want to employ them for a good purpose, and even if it were seemingly good, this would only be in order that eventually the greater mischief might be wrought. When the plaintiff, in reply to the Judge's question, "Then it [magic] does involve invocation of spirits?", answered, "Of one spirit. God is a spirit . . ." he was quoting a mistranslation, and in consequence a good deal of confusion must have arisen. The correct translation of *St. John* iv, 24, is "God is spirit", a vastly different thing. To say "God is *a* spirit" is bad metaphysic and worse theology. In fact, it makes no sense.

I very much doubt whether this drawing the line, this talk of "white" magic and "black" magic, is anything other than verbal emptiness, and in effect a purely artificial (and rather perilous) discrimination between the Good and the Bad. All magic, all witchcraft, depends on the Devil, and is fundamentally evil. It is true that we speak of "natural magic", which the dictionaries define as "that which did not involve recourse to the agency of personal spirits", but the phrase is no better than a vulgarism and metaphor. It were a good thing, if possible, to get rid of these ambiguities and misnomers from our common everyday speech. A recent writer (1929) goes so far as to speak of "white witchcraft for the cure of disease and other purposes innocent in themselves". Although what he means is abundantly clear, actually there cannot be such a thing as "white witchcraft". The very words are contradictory, and little wonder that a wiser age condemned this art, under whatever pretext it was practised, as "heathenish and diabolical". Ancient spells and charms, a knowledge of herbs and planetary influences—these are neither witchcraft nor magic, but leechdom. No conjuration, the evoking of demons and malign spirits, is involved.

George Giffard, sometime minister of Maldon, Essex, uncompromisingly condemns the "white witch". His *Dialogue Concerning Witches*, published in 1593, was reissued in 1603, three years after the writer's death. "These cunning men and women with charms, seeming to do good, ought to be rooted out" is his verdict.

William Perkins, the eminent Elizabethan divine, in his posthumous *Damned Art of Witchcraft*, published in 1608, lays down that all Witches "convicted by the Magistrate" should be executed. He allows no exception, and under his condemnation fall "all Diviners, Charmers, Jugglers, all Wizards, commonly called wise men and wise women". All those purported "good Witches, which do not hurt but good, which do not spoil and destroy, but save and deliver" should come under the extreme sentence. "The blessing Witch" is "the right hand of the Devil". Men shun and abhor the sorcerer, the necromancer, but they will fly to the white witch in any necessity, and thus thousands of heedless folk are carried away to their final confusion. "Death therefore is the just and deserved portion of the good Witch." The very terms "good witch", "white witch", are self-contradictory.

In 1684 Richard Bovet, who came of an old West of England family, thus sums up the matter in his *Pandæmonium, or The Devil's Cloyster*. "Being a further Blow to Modern Sadduceism, Proving the Existence of Witches and Spirits. In a Discourse deduced from the Fall of the Angels the Propagation of Satan's Kingdom before the Flood: The Idolatry of the Ages after greatly advancing Diabolical Confederacies. With an Account of the Lives and Transactions of several Notorious Witches. Also a Collection of several Authentick Relations of Strange Apparitions of Daemons and Spectres, and Fascinations of Witches, never before Printed", "By a Witch is commonly understood a Female Agent, or Patient, who is become Covenant with the Devil; having in a literal sense sold herself to work Wickedness, such whose chief Negotiation tends to the spoiling their Neighbours' persons or goods. They have commonly certain excrescencies, like Teats or Nipples, in private parts of their Bodies which their Familiars often suck. Sometimes personally, and sometimes in a Dream or Trance they revel with the evil Spirit in Nightly Cabals and Consults. Those particularly intended here are those such as are commonly called Black Witches; there is beside another sort termed White Witches; These by a Diabolical Complaisance, or good-nature, are to uncharm and give ease to those the other have afflicted: but sometimes it so happens that one or other of the Witches dies by force of the Counter-charm. Both these are condemned to death by the Divine Law, *Exodus* xxii, 18. The Suasion of such hath been sometimes sought unto, and used to entice young Maids to unclean folly. But Witches are themselves imposed upon as well as they impose on others. The Grand Impostor, the Devil, deceiveth them, as they deceive those that seek unto them." All are "Black Scholars" learned in that "Hellish Science of Sorcery, Necromancy, and Witchcraft".

In everyday use for a male witch, "wizard" is perhaps the commonest word. Now, "wizard" merely means "a wise man", the termination "ard" being added to the adjective "wise", and so it did not necessarily carry any very sombre or unholy signification. "Warlock" is a far more impressive and ill-sounding term, with all sorts of eeriness lurking in the background. A north-country and Scottish vocable, it has become familiar through Sir Walter Scott's poems and romances, and is highly appropriate, since the Old English *wærloga* is a traitor, a deceiver, an oath-breaker, and the warlock is a traitor and an oath-breaker, since he has transferred his allegiance from God, to Whom it is due, unto God's enemy, Satan, the arch-deceiver. Such picturesque and precisely accurate phrases as "men-witches", "he witches", "witch-man", "witch-woman", "witch-maid", are fast dying out, although even these linger in dusty odd corners, and among village grannams whose pure speech is that of their forbears a century and two centuries ago.

> A witch is a slave self-sold and dedicate to Satan.
> Witchcraft is completest homage paid to a Power—The Power of Evil.

The Clash of Good and Evil. It is the Eternal Conflict, that vital question which cannot be burked by any one of us, to which we cannot shut our eyes in easy contentment. Sooner or later it will find the joint in the best-fitting armour of the most complacent self-satisfaction. Whether we like it or not, it continually, remorselessly, inevitably thrusts itself in upon us every day, every hour of the day. It disturbs us, and raises important issues in the narrow circle of our own little lives, within the consciousness of our own limited experience, and as the problem faces us again and again and presses hard upon us we have to answer, in action as well as by word of mouth (more pregnant than action, maybe), and sometimes we answer rightly, and oftener perhaps we answer amiss, knowing that each decision we arrive at, each step we take, must bring its unavoidable and logical consequence, but right or wrong our reply on our own responsibility has to be given every time, and seldom is there much space allowed for deliberation, consult, or delay, and it is this which all the while is moulding man's character, which is, bit by bit, as the tiny coral-polyp works, shaping his destiny for weal or for woe. Unless we are mere humbugs and hypocrites, few indeed are there who would dare to bind themselves by the vow Teresa of Avila vowed— at any cost in every action always to do what seemed to be the most perfect thing.

The existence of evil surely needs no argument, no proof; it is self-evident, a vivid and terrible reality. The power of evil—who can look out upon the world today, a world shattered and wounded and rent, and not recognize its cruel tyranny?

Masquerade the essential realities of life in pseudo-scientific terms, pose as a modern philosopher, affect a polite but icy indifference, scoff with the sceptic, deny outright with the hoodwinked materialist, adopt whatever rôle the man who is afraid to face truth may be pleased to play, the fact remains that there are two principles only at work in the world, Good and Evil, White and Black, God and the Devil.

"The *Devil*," says Richard Baxter, "is a *Do-Evil*. And if he do Good it is to greater Hurt."

> And oftentimes, to win us to our harm,
> The Instruments of Darkness tell us Truths,
> Win us with honest Trifles, to betray us
> In deepest Consequence.

There is the Supreme Good.

There are also fearful forces of Evil, forces of power which seem almost illimitable, which only too often seem to triumph, to exult in victory. Some think, or affect to think, that evil is merely a blind, vagrant, undetermined force, not regulated, irresponsible, wandering and random energy. Surely it must be apparent to the shallowest mind that the evil of the world is too masterly marshalled, too subtly planned, too skilfully directed, too logically remorseless, for any such facile explanation. There is design; there is diplomacy; there is cunning; there are stratagems and campaign.

Faber, when speaking of "the extraordinary versatility of human wickedness"—a fine phrase—significantly adds: "The empire of the demons abounds in fearful intelligence, backed by no less fearful power."

At the back of it all there is for a certainty an intellect far greater than any mind of man, a vast intellect, a superb genius which is wholly and entirely evil, which works and plots patiently, tirelessly, everlastingly, for sheer evil and the enjoyment of evil, employing with the utmost adroitness and deceit, when the chance is given, human talent and wisdom and wit, as the middleman, so to speak, as the medium, but in plain truth as the driven subject and abject slave. That Evil Intellect, a spiritual being, we know by various names: the Devil, Satan, Lucifer, and many more.

But, let us never forget, there is the Supreme Good, the Almighty Good. I do not propose to discuss here the obvious question which at once arises, and which perhaps has seldom been poised in such commonplace, matter-of-fact terms as by old Daniel Defoe. Robinson Crusoe had been telling his man Friday how the devil was God's enemy and used all his malice and skill to defeat the good designs of Providence. "Well," says Friday, "but you say God is so strong, so great; is He not much stronger, much might as the devil?—yes, yes, says I, Friday, God is stronger than the devil, God is above the devil. . . . But, says he again, if God much stronger, much might as the devil, why God no kill the devil, so make him no more do wicked?" And Crusoe gives a very excellent and, in its degree, satisfying answer, although perhaps his reasoning is not quite according to Augustine or Aquinas, for, as he confesses, "I was but a young doctor."

Of the First Rebellion in the spirit world, the primal eldest revolt ere time was, we are not told much, and indeed speculate as we may, the mystery must in its essence be beyond human understanding. How profoundly significant, yet how deeply mysterious, for example, are the few words we meet in Sacred Writ. In transcendental vision the seer of the Apocalypse cried: "There was war in heaven; Michael and his angels fought against the dragon: and the dragon fought and his angels. And prevailed not; neither was their place found any more in heaven. And the great dragon was cast out, that old serpent called the Devil, and Satan, which deceiveth the whole world: he was cast out into the earth, and his angels were cast out with him." Isaiah, poet and prophet, in some extraordinary rapture, some moment of sublime ecstasy, exclaimed in accents broken with sorrow: "How art thou fallen from heaven, O Lucifer, son of the morning!" And above all, upon the return of the seventy who had been sent forth, and who declared with wonder and joy, "Lord, even the devils are subject unto us in thy name," the Divine Teacher replied this much and no more: "I beheld Satan as lightning fall from heaven."

What was the cause of this fall? We cannot, I think, within human limits, go far astray if in answer we follow Joachim, the Abbot of Fiore among the lonely hills of Calabria, a monk who had spent much of his youth in learned Byzantium, who had travelled in Syria and companioned with the wise old Saracen imaums, who had passed one whole Lent in solitary communion with the unseen upon Tabor, the very Mount of Transfiguration, who had journeyed from country to country, gleaning curious knowledge, and sifting the wheat from the chaff. Joachim, whom the historian Salimbene of Parma names with Merlin; with Amalthæa, the Sibyl of Cumae; with the famous Michael Scot. Incidentally, too, we have to the same effect the authority of Cornelius à Lapide, the most voluminous and perhaps the most learned of all biblical exegetes since the days of St. Jerome. *Pride* was the cause of the fall of him who had been called Lucifer—"The Light Bearer". *Pride*, the most corrupt and corroding, the most hideous, of all sins. Pride and Lust for power. If we would gauge the horror of these, look out upon the misery of the world today. For the spawn of pride is war.

The dragon fell, "and with his tail drew the third part of the stars of heaven, and did cast them to the earth". A third part of the hierarchy of heaven became the hierarchy of hell, the dragon's angels. The word *Angel* literally means a *Messenger*, and as there is a "voice of many angels round about the throne" of heaven, so there is a voice of many angels round about the throne of hell, hosts upon hosts, ministers that do the bad pleasure of the Lord of Hell, and they rest not day nor night.

One third part of the stars of heaven, bright angels once, the messengers of God, are now black angels of the pit, demons, the dark messengers of woe.

Their numbers are infinite. There are few more striking incidents in Sacred History than the healing of the "exceeding fierce" man, "which had devils long time", the dweller among the tombs in some lone, haunted spot outside the city of the Gadarenes. So vast a number of unclean spirits possessed him that when commanded to declare their name they yelled in chorus: "Legion, for we are many". There is not a writer on occultism in any age or country who is not agreed concerning the huge multitudes and tireless activities of the demon hosts. It would be both tedious and superfluous to quote a long list of authors' names who have emphasized these points, and one or two may stand for many. Richalm, Abbot of Schönthal in the Neckar Valley (about 1218-1219), has much to say in his discourses about demons, to whom he justly attributes all the ills, public and domestic, great and small, that fall to the lot of man. We recognize, of course, as King James I so shrewdly remarks in his *Dæmonologie*, that "there are three kinds of folks whom God will permit" thus to be tempted and troubled by the devil, "the wicked for their horrible sins, to punish them in the like measure; the godly that are sleeping in any great sins or infirmities and weakness in faith, to waken them up the faster by such an uncouth form: and even some of the best, that their patience may be tried before the world, as Job's was. For why may not God use any kind of extraordinary punishment, when it pleases Him; as well as the ordinary rods of sickness or other adversities?"

Abbot Richalm explains how evil spirits are everywhere: "they swarm like motes in the sunbeam; they are scattered all over like particles of dust; they shower down on the world like drops of pelting rain; their numbers fill and crowd out the whole world; the very air we breathe is infected thick with devils". After all, there is nothing startling in this. What are demons but foul spiritual bacilli engendered of the pestilence breathed from hell?

The same truth is repeated in almost the same words by masters and doctors of every race, of every school. Manasses Ben Israel and other learned rabbis declare that myriad demons hover round men, clustered as motes in the sunbeam. Paracelsus wrote that ever and always demons, invisible, intangible, are swarming about us as thick as a cloud of gnats or whirring mayflies on a sultry summer noon. The grave and solid François Perreaud, a Huguenot minister of Gex, in Burgundy, in his *Demonologie* (1653) observes: "There are verily and actually devils and evil spirits, truly a very great and countless number."

Cotton Mather in his *The Devil Discovered* (1692) avers: "The *High Places* of Our Air are swarming full of those *Wicked Spirits* whose Temptations trouble us; they are so many, that it seems no less than a *Legion* . . . maybe spared for the Vexation of one miserable man. But those Apostate Angels, are all *United* under one Infernal Monarch, in the Designs of Mischief."

There are few more familiar passages in Milton than the lines (*Paradise Lost*, I, 301–3) in which he speaks of the fallen angels as Legions

> Thick as Autumnal Leaves that strow the Brooks
> In *Vallombrosa*, where th' *Etrurian* shades
> High overarch't imbowr.

A little later the poet compares them to

> a pitchy cloud
> Of *Locusts*, warping on the Eastern Wind.

Nor are these armies a mere chaotic mob. The Platonist, Michael Psellus, most erudite of Byzantine writers, whose works were reputed to have covered every department of knowledge, and than whom none was riper in occult lore, in his dialogue *On the Operation of Demons*, written about 1050, very precisely divides the infernal battalions into six great ordered sections. The celebrated ascetic author John Cassian in earlier days had spoken of the disciplined organization of the demon hosts. Following Psellus, Vincent of Beauvais, librarian to St. Louis of France (1215–1270), at whose royal bidding he compiled his huge encyclopaedia, notes the various hierarchies of devils, their grades, stations, and individual employment. Such things are the veriest commonplaces to a scholar like Abbot Guibert of Nogent, and to Meffrat, the famous fifteenth-century preacher of the diocese of Meissen, who spoke with authority to crowded congregations. Johann Weyer, again, disciple and intimate of Cornelius Agrippa, has much to tell us of the kingdom of the demons, of their ranks and stations, their princes and dominations and powers.

It is not impossible that he learned this from Johannes Faustus, with whom he had conversed and whom he describes as a mighty scholar, but most impious and profane.

That very great and very wise book the *Malleus Maleficarum* (*The Hammer of Witches*) has: "It is Catholic to maintain that there is a fixed order of interior and exterior actions, and a degree of preference among devils. Whence it follows that certain abominations are committed by the lowest orders, from which the higher orders are precluded on account of the quality of their natures. . . . For sin does not take away their nature, and the devils after the Fall did not lose their natural gifts: . . . and the operation of things follow their natural conditions. Therefore both in nature and in operation devils are various and multiple. . . . Since some are believed to have fallen from every order, it is not unsuitable to maintain that those devils who fell from the lowest choir, and even in that held the lowest rank, are deputed to and perform the foulest and beastliest acts. . . . Moreover, the names of the devils indicate that order there is among them, and what office is assigned to each" (Part I: Question 4).

In 1847 there appeared in the popular *London Journal* a series of articles entitled "A Few Chapters on Astrology and Magic", by W. E. Hall. The circulation of this penny journal, published by George Vickers, 3 Catherine Street, Strand, was very great, and these articles did much to increase its already huge circulation. Hall had evidently read up his subject with considerable care, and he writes with a vivid, facile pen. He gives one article to "Satan, the Personification of the Evil Principle", the following article to "Inferior Demons", and a third to "Familiar Spirits". His researches led him rightly to differentiate between the varying grades and ranks of evil spirits.

At the same time we should not forget that, as the pious Franciscan Jerome Menghi so lucidly explains, although one and united in their hatred of mankind, demons, by the very essence of their wholly wicked nature, loathe and detest one another, and are ever at strife with their fellows, raging and brawling, full of malice and wrath. So in the Gospels the Devil is spoken of as a wolf, and St. Peter describes him as "a roaring lion" who "walketh about, seeking whom he may devour".

Although the demons, many as the sands of the shore, are ever at enmity each with another, they are, says St. Basil, marvellously united and agreed in one thing, their blind and murderous hatred of the human race.

In a terse telling phrase St. Gregory the Great calls demons *latrunculi*, gangsters.

Cotton Mather, in his *Discourse on the Wonders of the Invisible World*, 1692, published "a most awful and solemn Warning for our selves at this day; which has four *Propositions* comprehended in it", with some weighty sentences, and his words are as true and necessary for us today as they were when he uttered them two hundred and fifty years ago. His Propositions briefly are: (1) "That there is a *Devil*, is a thing Doubted by none but such as are under the Influences of the *Devil*. There are multitudes of devils. 'Tis to be supposed that there is a sort of Arbitrary, even

Military *Government* among the Devils. Some *Devils* are more peculiarly *Commission'd*, and perhaps *Qualify'd*, for some Countries, while others are for others. (2) There is a Devilish *Wrath* against *Mankind*. (3) The *Devil*, in the prosecution, and the execution of his *wrath* upon them, often gets a *Liberty* to make a *Descent* upon the Children of Men. (4) Most horrible *woes* come to be inflicted upon Mankind, when the *Devil* does in *great wrath*, make a *descent* upon them." I am convinced that the Devil has been permitted to make such a descent today, and I echo Mather's cry: *"Woe to the world, by reason of the wrath of the Devil!"*

To scoff at the existence and activities of evil discarnate intelligences, that is to say demons, is not merely to reject the Christian religion, it is to deny all religion. For, from the very dawning of the world, in no land, however barbarian and remote, is to be traced any form of religion which does not recognize evil spirits. And the older, the more learned, the tradition, the firmer is the belief.

The Jews held that God often employed demons to punish and avenge, and so the Psalmist, when he has sung of the plagues of Egypt, sacred Nile turned to blood, the devouring locust on the wing and black swarms of noisome flies, the fair vineyards laid waste with hail, the fruit-crop ruined with hoarfrost, exulting proclaims: "And he sent upon them the wrath of his indignation: indignation and wrath and trouble, which he sent by evil angels." (Douai, *Psalm* lxxvii, 49; A. V. *Psalm* lxxviii, 49). "There are spirits that are created for vengeance, and in their fury they lay on grievous torments"; so writes Ben-Sira, the "Wise Man" (*Hakam*), in *Ecclesiasticus* (xxxix, 33).

We cannot, of course, exactly map out the world of spirits, and many persons believe that alleged spirit communications, so often amazingly veridical and yet more often maliciously misleading and intentionally deceptive, proceed from discarnate intelligences, possibly human, possibly quite alien to earth. Sister Anne Catherine Emmerich tells us that there are "souls neither in heaven, purgatory or hell, but wandering the earth in terrible anguish", and there are also "planetary spirits, who are entirely different from devils, but who may yet have to be judged". This certainly agrees with the teaching of Sinistrari, who holds the possible existence of rational creatures having spirit and body (in the philosophical sense), and distinct from man. There may be creatures in existence endowed with a rational spirit and a corporeity less gross, more subtile than man's. Among these would rank the poltergeist.

None the less these considerations must not in any way persuade us to minimize the fact of the existence of the demon hosts and their activities and correspondence with wicked men and interference in human affairs.

In the Sermon on the Mount we are bidden: "After this manner, therefore, pray ye: Our Father . . . deliver us from evil." There are, I think, few who would dispute that Dean Inge must be regarded as an extremely advanced master of the modernist school. On Sunday, 6 March, 1932, when preaching at St. Mark's, North Audley Street, London, W., the Dean said: "Liberal theologians may jeer and philosophers scoff, but there it is. We cannot get rid of the Devil. 'Deliver us from the Evil

One' is the right translation. *I have not the slightest doubt that Christians are enjoined to believe in a positive, malignant, spiritual power.*"

At a congress of savants some years ago, one of the chief speakers put the rhetorical question: "Who in these days believes in a personal Devil?" He then paused a moment with a smile for effect. A voice, hitherto silent, was heard firmly and clearly to answer: "I do." It was the voice of the late Lord Acton, esteemed to be one of the most learned, if not the most learned, of scholars at that time in Europe.

In a letter to the Press (*Daily Telegraph and Morning Post*, Tuesday, 21 June, 1938) Mr. E. H. Blakeney, of Winchester, well known as an author of rare erudition and elegance, put the matter quite plainly: "For people 'who profess and call themselves Christians' to deny the actuality and presence of demonic powers is altogether futile. The facts are given with unmistakable clearness in the New Testament. . . . Christians—the genuine ones—are bound to believe in the existence of devils; otherwise how could their Master have cast them out? The pages of the New Testament are full of instances indicating that its writers were perfectly sure that 'demonism' is no fond thing vainly invented, but a terrible truth."

John Wesley, in 1768, wrote in his *Journal*: "It is true likewise, that the English in general, and indeed most of the men of learning in Europe, have given up all accounts of witches and apparitions as mere old wives' fables. I am sorry for it, and I willingly take this opportunity of entering my solemn protest against this violent compliment which so many that believe the Bible pay to those who do not believe it. I owe them no such service. I take knowledge that these are at the bottom of the outcry which has been raised, and with such insolence spread through the land, in direct opposition, not only to the Bible, but to the suffrage of the wisest and the best of men in all ages and nations. They well know (whether Christians know it or not) that the giving up of witchcraft is in effect giving up the Bible. With my latest breath I will bear testimony against giving up to infidels one great proof of the invisible world; I mean that of witchcraft and apparitions, confirmed by the testimony of all ages." Thus John Wesley.

"I have no doubt but the greater part of my readers, and perhaps the bulk of mankind at this day, totally disbelieve the possibility of witchcraft, magic, or divination; . . . But, however incredulous the wisest critic may be, as to what has been related on this subject, certain it is that such spirits really do exist, and that confederacy and compact with them in former times was no uncommon thing. Blackstone seems to have established this fact in a very satisfactory manner, when he speaks of the laws formerly provided in this country against magicians and witches, and those who held confederacy with spirits; which to disbelieve, would not only be found to militate against numerous important passages of Scripture, but would cast in question the express words of our Saviour Himself, and give the lie to authors and attestators of the first reputation and character."

So wrote Dr. Ebenezer Sibly from his house, No. 1, Upper Titchfield Street, Cavendish Square. His *magnum opus* is a thick quarto of more

than eleven hundred pages, and carries a title not altogether out of proportion to the size of his great tome: *A New and Complete Illustration of
the Occult Sciences: or the Art of foretelling future Events and Contingencies,
By the Aspects, Positions, and Influences of the Heavenly Bodies. Founded on Natural
Philosophy, Scripture, Reason, and the Mathematics. In which the abstruse Doctrine
of the Stars, of Magic, Divination, Exorcism and Familiarity with Spirits,
vegetable, astral and infernal—the Calculation of Nativities—Horary Questions—
and the Astrological Prescience of Futurity—are clearly demonstrated and proved;
and the Ability of doing it made easy to the meanest capacity.* This work, now
an exceedingly uncommon book, was first published in 1790. I have
used the Tenth Edition, "By the late E. Sibly, M.D., F.R.H.S. London.
1807." It is in Four Parts. Of these, Parts I to III deal at great length
with the science of Astrology. Part IV, which is often missing or at least
has several pages and the plates torn out, is distinguished by a separate
title: "The Black Art. By Ebenezer Sibly. Astro. Philo." It comprises
"The Distinction between Astrology and the Diabolical Practice of Exorcism; in which the Methods used for raising up and consulting Spirits
are laid open, with various instances of their Compacts with wicked Men.
Account of Apparitions and Spirits, including a general Display of the
Mysteries of Witchcraft, Divination, Charms and Necromancy. Compiled from a Series of Intense Study and Application, and founded on real
Examples and Experience."

Sibly's reference to the authority of Blackstone is interesting. Sir
William Blackstone (1723–1780), Vinerian Professor at Oxford, was a
lawyer of the very first reputation. Solicitor-General to the Queen, he
declined such appointments as the Chief Justiceship of the Common
Pleas in Ireland, and in England the Solicitor-Generalship itself. His
Commentaries on the Laws of England, the first volume of which (soon to be
followed by three others) appeared in 1765, were regarded as an ultimate
authority. The considered judgement of so eminent a man we are bound
to respect. Very foolishly, the Act of King James I against witchcraft
was repealed in the ninth year of George II, 1736, and witchcraft ceased
to be a statutory or (under English law) an ecclesiastical offence. Writing
less than thirty years later, Blackstone was obliged to pick his words carefully; he could not offend by his criticism the Majesty of the Law, im-
pugning so recent a repeal, the work of statesmen and legislators, still
living, in high honour and venerable in years. All the same, it is
no hard matter to read between the lines what were his real con-
victions.

Addison had observed in *The Spectator* for 11 July, 1711, "I believe
in general that there is, and has been such a thing as Witch-craft; but
at the same time can give no Credit to any particular Instance of it."
This fine silky sentiment has often been quoted with huge admiration
as the creed "of a sensible man of the world", but it should be obvious,
surely, that Addison might have taken as his motto the Duke of Bucking-
ham's witty couplet:

Now Critiques do your worst, that here are met;
For like a Rook, I have hedg'd in my Bet.

To hedge in a bet is to stake on both sides of a wager so that there must be a certainty of winning. Addison says in effect: "I am not going to deny outright that such a thing as Witchcraft may have been and may be; but, mark you, I don't for a moment believe that such a thing ever existed." This adroit sitting on the fence is a very shallow trick, but it seems to have commended itself to an extraordinary number of writers. Again and again we meet with the same sleight, sometimes cleverly done, sometimes clumsily. It is an old crack, but it wears well. It is precisely the attitude, for example, of the late Father Herbert Thurston, S.J., of whom Monsignor Barnes so justly wrote: "No one will deny his scholarship or doubt his integrity. . . . But it is unfortunate all the same . . . that he should habitually approach all questions of this kind [supernormal phenomena] . . . in a spirit of intense scepticism. That scepticism has, I venture to think, on several occasions warped his judgement and led him to a conclusion not justified by the evidence before him." It is a pity that so many of these rationalizing performers appear wholly ignorant when they tumble pretty badly, whilst their gaping audiences, too, remain quite unaware that the maître has lost his balance and flopped.

Sir William Blackstone, as I believe shrewdly enough and of set purpose, makes particular reference to Addison, most elegant of essayists yet most facile of philosophers. But the matter does not end there. In his *Commentaries* (edition 1765, Vol. IV, p. 60) Blackstone lays down— and we may carefully weigh his words—"To deny the possibility, nay, the actual existence of witchcraft and sorcery, is at once flatly to contradict the revealed word of God in various passages both of the Old and New Testament, and the thing itself is a Truth to which every nation in the world, hath, in its turn, borne testimony, by either example seemingly well attested or by prohibitory laws, which at least suppose the possibility of a commerce with evil spirits."

The learned Pierre Mamor, who was a Canon of the Cathedral Chapter of St. Pierre, Saintes (Charente Inferieure), and Rector of the University of Poitiers towards the end of the fifteenth century, shrewdly remarks that it is at least significant how many of those who scoffingly deny the very existence of the Devil have themselves proved to be under the Devil's influence and are his ablest partisans. Indeed, it has been truly said that to persuade man he does not exist is the Devil's most glorious triumph.

A certain showy but very unsound preacher made himself conspicuous by continually proclaiming from the pulpit that there are no witches, no agents of darkness, and that witchcraft is a mere fable. Nobody can have been much surprised, I think, when it was discovered that this fellow was actually the chief companion and master of a brotherhood of sorcerers. He even confessed that he had bound himself by a solemn promise to an evil spirit always to sermonize in this atheist strain. Similarly, Abraham Palinghi acquired a very bad name as a great defender of witches, and his contemporaries more than suspected him of being a member of that horrid society. Our King James I was unquestionably in the right of it when in "The Preface to the Reader" before his

Dæmonologie, 1597, he summed up the sceptical Reginald Scot as a mere
arid Sadducee, "for the Sadducees say that there is no resurrection,
neither angel, nor spirit" (*Acts of the Apostles* xxiii, 8). Nor can the royal
author have been very far from the mark, again, when he did not hesitate
to declare that Johann Weyer, by making a public apology for witches,
"plainly betrays himself to have been one of that profession".

Where Ebenezer Sibly has gone a little astray is in the one point
that he far underestimates the numbers of those who from experience,
from experiment, or from plain common sense are heartily convinced of
and acknowledge not indeed the mere possibility, but the actuality and
very present terrible power, of witchcraft.

"The father of the English law", Sir Edward Coke (commonly
called My Lord Coke), defines a witch as "a person that hath conference
with the Devil to take counsel or do some act".

"A witch is one who by commerce and close confederacy with the
Devil has a deliberate and very determined intention of attaining his
own ends. I give this definition here, at the outset, because not only is it
vitally material to grasp it thoroughly for the full understanding of my
book, but also because it explains at once and supplies ample reason
for the divers laws which in all Christian countries have been directed
against witches, and furthermore because no precise definition has
hitherto been furnished by the many authorities who have written upon
witchcraft, whilst at the same time some such explicit definition is an
essential preliminary to any discussion and we must be quite clear as
to the use of our terms. If we examine our definition in detail it will be
remarked that I have emphasized the words 'deliberate and very determined'. The reason for this lies in the point that the witch of his own free
will and volition prepensed seeks communion with the Devil, entertains
and employs the evil spirit."

Thus Bodin begins his famous treatise *Demonomania*, first published
at Paris in 1580. Jean Bodin, who was born at Angers in 1530, died of
the plague at Laon in 1596. At Toulouse he occupied the Chair of Civil
Law, and so eminent a professor was soon invited to the capital. So far
from being a fanatic or bigoted, his opinions were notoriously tolerant
and easy, on which account it is said that he ran no small risk during the
disturbances of St. Bartholomew's Eve, 1572. Shortly after, indeed, he
withdrew for safety's sake into the provinces, where he prolonged his stay.
Gabriel Naudé, the proto-bibliothecarius of Cardinal Mazarin's magnificent library, does not hesitate to speak of Bodin as "the first man in
France (*Ce premier homme de la France*)". Hallam ranked Bodin as a political
philosopher with Aristotle and Machiavelli. As a historian, Buckle judged
him to be superior to Commines, and fully equal to, if indeed not to be
placed above, Machiavelli.

To speak of "Bodin and Danæus and Institoris [*sic*]" as "bookish
witchmongers", as a fairly recent writer, applauded by some as an
authority, has airily written, is sheer nonsense. The author in question
adroitly leaves himself a loophole, it is true, and if challenged would no
doubt have retorted that the three names he cites are those of professed
scholars, deep read in occult lore. But the whole tenor of his argument

is quite another thing. He is dwelling at length upon what he calls the "developed system" of witchcraft, a "superstructure" reared "by the ingenuity of jurisconsults, philosophers, theologians, and inquisitors". There is no such artificial "superstructure". Witchcraft, of course, may have many facets and can be discussed from many angles, but the essential element—be it English or continental witchcraft in question—is the same. That element is confederacy and intercourse with evil spirits, whence follow the fulfilment of wicked ends, and the satisfaction of wicked desires—revenge, luxury, avarice, power—and these ends are directly brought about and accomplished by the medium and ministry of the said evil spirits, in which transactions must be inevitably involved the working of harm to fellow men, injuring body and goods alike, such harms being the destruction of sailing vessels, houses, harvests; the laming of cattle and other animals; incendiarism; enmities and strife; the moulding of food; the souring of drink; domestic jars and quarrels; or, more nearly, the afflicting of men with unusual ailments; hurts to life and limb; infections; poisonings; wasting diseases or consumptions; and even death.

As we shall see in detail a little later, the dark and horrid confederacies are sealed and confirmed by some kind of impious pact or solemn bargain, which not only (as in common law) presupposes a consideration on the side of either party, but necessarily entails such murderous malice, such apostasies and blazing blasphemies, such outrageous sacrileges and pitiless cruelties, such fornications and foulness, that so judicious and impartial a writer as Paul Laymann in his treatise, *A Corpus of Statutes touching Witches and Poisoners*, roundly declares: "This offence of Witchcraft is so great and comprehensive that it includes in itself almost every other felony and crime."

To suppose that Jean Bodin, Lambert Daneau, and Heinrich Kramer (Institoris) were mere theorizers with no practical experience, is to labour under a gross error, and such a mistake could only be made by one who had not been at the trouble to acquaint himself with the lives and careers of these eminent men. Of Bodin, sufficient mention has already been made. Lambert Daneau, who died in 1595, was a French Huguenot pastor, who exercised his functions at various important centres, at Gien, which is thirty-nine miles south-east of Orléans; at Orthez, in Navarre, twenty-five miles from Pau; and at Castres, on the Agout, in the Department of Tarn. Among Daneau's works are a treatise on the poisons commonly employed by witches, and a dialogue *Les Sorciers*, 1574, which ran into more than one edition and was translated into English in the following year as *A Dialogue of Witches*. It cannot be doubted that Daneau was present at and very closely followed in every detail not a few witch-trials. He even transcribed (in greater part, at any rate) two trials from the official documents entrusted to him for this purpose by the clerk of the court. Albert Caillet in his encyclopaedic *Manuel Bibliographique* names Daneau as one of the most learned Protestant divines of the sixteenth century. Such a man was assuredly no empty unpractical theorician.

Heinrich Kramer (Institoris) is a far weightier and more important name. He was born about 1430, and died in 1508. In early youth he joined the Order of St. Dominic, and the acknowledged authorities, Quétif and Echard, in their great work, *The Writers of the Order of Preachers* (i.e. the Dominicans), list him under the year 1500. Kramer was a Master of Sacred Theology, and Inquisitor-General for all the dioceses of the five metropolitan sees of Germany. For several years he lived at Salzburg, occupied with work of the first importance. Hence, in 1495–6, he was summoned to Venice as the fittest and most learned doctor to give a series of public lectures, and these so enhanced his already brilliant reputation that he was forthwith commissioned by the Pope to act as Censor of the Faith in Moravia and Bohemia. It was in this latter country he died, probably at the Priory of his Order in Prague. With his brother Dominican, the erudite James Sprenger, he was part-author ot *The Hammer of Witches* (*Malleus Maleficarum*), and there can be no question that he must have assisted at and presided over some hundreds of witch-trials. Judicature and prosecutions of this kind would inevitably fall to his share by reason of the high and honourable appointments he held, and we know that he was very zealous and faithful in the strict discharge of his duties.

It was a singularly unhappy hazard, then, which selected Bodin, Daneau, and Kramer as three salient examples of mere academic demonologists, authors whose knowledge of witchcraft was derived purely from books and libraries.

It has seemed necessary to emphasize—as I propose to do—this, and to lay particular stress upon Bodin's authority and the grounds for that authority if we are going to adopt his definition of a witch, and accept it as admirably expressed and hardly to be bettered.

It would be easy to give a long list of famous scholars who have approved and accepted Bodin's definition, whilst curiously enough (as he himself remarks) very few—Bodin says none—of the great writers on demonology, whose works preceded the *Demonomania* of 1580, have given the precise meaning they attach to the word "witch" in their pages.*
A hundred years later, too, we find that the learned Christian Stridtbeckh, of Augsburg, in his Dissertation entitled *Concerning Witches, and those Evil Women who traffic with the Prince of Darkness* (1690), which I have little hesitation in saying is, within its own limits, one of the ablest, most comprehensive, and most concise summaries of the subject known to me, after having as an enthusiastic philologist discussed the derivations and the subtle shades of meaning of the many and varied words in Hebrew, Latin, Greek, and German, which denote a warlock, a sorcerer, a magician, a witch, an enchantress, a sibyl, and so on, when he wishes to furnish a practical working definition of a "witch", at once quotes Bodin. It is true that Stridtbeckh expands a little what Bodin had to say, but this merely because he is detailing the activities of a witch. Incidentally, he remarks that eminent lawyers such as Benedict Carpzov (1595–1666), and profound theologians such as Theodore Thumm, in his work *On the*

---

* In the same way, a recent writer, Jean Baar, Fils, in *Le Malin*, "Essays on the devil, demons, warlocks and witches", Liége, 1927, whilst very copious but not very correct on the subject of "Satan et Compagnie", entirely omits to suggest any definition of a "witch".

Awful Wickedness of Witches (1667), have provided ampler and far more wordy definitions than Bodin, but he does not consider that they have either improved on the older writer or added anything of real moment.

Now, Bodin was only dealing with European witchcraft, but his definition is so complete and so universal that the Professor of Cultural Anthropology at Boston College Graduate School, Father Joseph J. Williams, S.J., in his *Psychic Phenomena of Jamaica* (1935), tells us: "Certainly we have this definition [of Bodin's] fully verified in the case of the Jamaica obeah-man as the direct descendant in theory and practice from the Ashanti *obayifo*." Captain R. Sutherland Rattray, who is the chief authority on the Ashanti, in his *Ashanti Proverbs* (Oxford, 1916, p. 48), notes that the Ashanti word Obayifo signifies "a wizard, or more generally a witch".

The obayifo has every characteristic of the European witch. "Men and women possessed of this black magic are credited with volitant powers, being able to quit their bodies and travel great distances in the night. Besides sucking the blood of victims, they are supposed to be able to extract the sap and juice of crops. Cases of coco blight are ascribed to the work of the obayifo. These witches are supposed to be very common, and a man never knows but that his friend or even his wife may be one."

The volitant powers of witches; their nocturnal transvections, whether actually in the body or psychically in a trance-state; the witches' pharmacopoeia of flying ointments; and many more details of these levitations are discussed by every demonologist. Thus the *Malleus Maleficarum* devotes one long and important chapter (Part II, Question 1, chapter 3) to *How Witches are Transported from Place to Place*.

Instances of the witches' malice in blighting crops and ruining the harvest occur again and again. The magicians of Egypt are able to wither and wreck the whole countryside by their words of power, and it will be remembered how fearfully they were paid in their own coin, so to speak, when Moses stretched forth his rod towards heaven and "there was hail, and fire mingled with the hail, very grievously such as there was none like it in all the land of Egypt since it became a nation. . . . And the hail smote every herb of the field, and broke every tree of the field . . . and the flax and the barley was smitten" (*Exodus* ix, 24–31). The Laws of the Twelve Tables of ancient Rome contain a particular statute penalizing any who has cast a spell on the fruits of the earth. Kramer and Sprenger in the *Malleus Maleficarum* (Part II, Question 1, chapter 15) record at length "an instance which came within our own experience". Two women, Agnes, a bath-attendant, and Anna von Mindelheim, by their incantations raised a violent hailstorm near Constance, which destroyed "all the fruit, crops and vineyards in a belt one mile wide, so that the vines hardly bore fruit for three years". Boguet in his *Examen of Witches* has a chapter (xxxiv): *How Witches do Hurt to the Fruits of the Earth*. The celebrated English divine, William Perkins, minister of St. Andrew's Church, Cambridge, in his *Discourse of the Damned Art of Witchcraft*, published posthumously in 1608, reckons among the six "wonders done by Inchanters" "Blasting of corne". I myself have known at least two cases, in Gloucestershire and Wiltshire villages, where the crops and orchards of a couple of farmers who had in some way given offence to certain reputed wise women in the respective localities were mysteriously mildewed and cankered, whilst the neighbours' harvests were rich and plentiful, their snowy apple-garths untouched by greenfly or early rime.

On Monday, 13 June, 1938, Dr. B. O. F. Heywood, Bishop of Ely, in an address to the diocesan conference held at Ely, commented upon the May frosts which had so sadly harmed fruit trees. His Lordship said: "To many people these late frosts present a perplexing problem. Nature, through the untimely frosts, appears to be destroying her own handi-work, and in doing so impoverishes a number of people. . . . Why, they ask, does God thus damage His own handiwork, and strike a blow at His servants? . . . It seems clear to me that nature does not perfectly express the will of God. We have the authority of the Bible for believing that something has happened and continues to happen in subhuman nature which might not unfairly be compared to the Fall in our human nature. Those who wish to pursue the subject would do well to read verses 18 to 23 of the eighth chapter of the Epistle to the Romans, in which St. Paul seems to suggest that not man only, but the whole creation, needs redemption. Discarnate rebellious spirits may have some temporary and limited power to exercise evil influences in the realm of nature as they apparently have in the realm of humanity. In endorsing disbelief in Angels and demons the members of the Doctrinal Commission seemed to me to be showing a certain lack of imagination, and to be creating rather than solving problems."

What the "Doctrinal Commission" may be I do not know, and, whether the personnel be permanent or temporary, I am entirely ignorant of the names of those who constitute this body, nor do I think it at all worth while to inquire into the matter, but this I do know: that if the "Doctrinal Commission" disbelieves in Angels and demons, the members who maintain such an opinion are, in so far as the simple gospel faith is concerned, grievously uninstructed in the very elements of Christianity. Since they thus frankly reject the confession of the Bible, the Fathers, the Church—nay, since they repudiate the teaching of Our Lord Himself —one can only suppose that the "Doctrinal Commission", although it seems a curious nomenclature in this connexion, is a non-Christian, secular association, in which case, of course, the findings on these heads of such a sederunt can have not the slightest interest for us who regard their doctrinarianism as frivolous, unsound, and ignorant.

Very timely the Bishop of Ely stated a fundamental religious truth. I would respectfully suggest that the words "may have" might with advantage be altered to "certainly have" and the word "apparently" should be deleted. When the Bishop's speech was duly reported in the Press a flood of correspondence followed. Several letter-writers gave a fine display of ill-temper and were—to judge by their language—exacerbated to the last degree. I subscribe to Mr. Blakeney, who put the position quite admirably: "A Christian Bishop is only doing his duty in laying stress on a much-overlooked element in the revelation which he was pledged at his ordination to uphold. Why should he be criticized for doing this duty I cannot imagine."

WITCHES ADORE THE DEMON

THE BAPTISM OF HELL

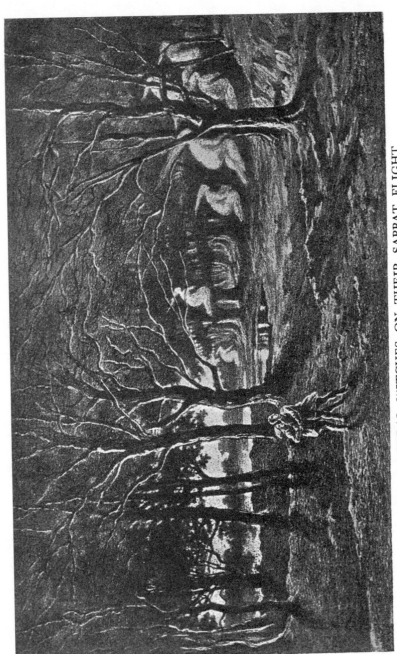

THE SPECTRAL WITCHES ON THEIR SABBAT FLIGHT

Sir William Pope, F.R.S., Professor of Chemistry, Cambridge, was pleased to be vastly facetious in a letter he contributed to the *Daily Telegraph and Morning Post* on Tuesday, 21 June, 1938, but his essay at bantering the Bishop proved extremely clumsy and fell flat.

A Mr. W. R. Davis was pained and rather whiningly aggrieved. (*Daily Telegraph and Morning Post*, Thursday, 16 June, 1938.) These letters were very competently and completely answered, and it was truly gratifying to note that the majority of—I might say very nearly all—the correspondents, amongst whom were thinkers and names of distinction, were wholly in sympathy with and stoutly defended Dr. Heywood's position.

The fact is that—galling as it must be in some quarters—the superstitions of science are outworn and dying fast. As Mr. Kevin Hayes wrote: "The last twenty years have seen the undermining of too many of the great Victorian theories of physical science." Probably Mr. W. R. Davis "will be appalled by the number of men of science who openly believe in the supernatural. As to evil spirits, the man who does not believe that they are abroad in the world today is forced into pessimism and misanthropy." (*Daily Telegraph and Morning Post*, Monday, 20 June, 1938.)

Their charms and cantrips may differ; their dark ceremonials in one land may be bloodier and more elaborate than in another; their powers may be greater here and seemingly less effectual there; gradations and degrees exist, no doubt, but the malice and mischief (the maleficium, as it was technically termed) of witchcraft will be found to be essentially the same in all lands and throughout all races, be it in the Minch-girt Hebrides or in sweltering Jamaica, in mediaeval Germany or ancient Greece, in Mexico or Madras, be it the frank diabolism and black mass of the Satanist in Parisian occult circles or the ghoulish carrion with which the Obi man is busy in his lonely forest cave; or the muttered age-old spells and eerie woven gestures, the touch of the hand, the glance aslant of some grizzled gammer in a hamlet of the Sussex Downs. It is the same service. All own the same allegiance. All are bound to the same master; all are vassals of hell.

In Mr. Arthur Machen's Prologue to his story *The White People* two of the interlocutors discussing deep philosophical problems converse as follows:

"On the whole, it is, perhaps, harder to be a great sinner than a great saint."

"There is something profoundly unnatural about sin? Is that what you mean?"

"Exactly. Holiness requires as great, or almost as great, an effort, but holiness works on lines that *were* natural once; it is an effort to recover the ecstasy that was before the Fall. But sin is an effort to gain the ecstasy and the knowledge that pertain alone to angels, and in making the effort man becomes a demon. . . . The saint endeavours to recover a gift which he has lost; the sinner tries to obtain something which was never his. In brief, he repeats the Fall."

The lowest depths of black mysticism are well-nigh as difficult to plumb as it is arduous to scale the heights of sanctity. The Grand Masters of the witch covens are men of genius—a foul genius, crooked, distorted, disturbed, and diseased.

The Catholic Church in her divine wisdom teaches us that in order to commit a sin in the full and completest sense of such an act, and therefore to incur the guilt of and entire responsibility for the sin, and hence reap the inevitable and logical consequences, there must be a deliberate intention as well as a clear consciousness of the nature of the act. These must be, in legal phraseology, *malice prepense*.

Sin in its essence is an intellectual act.

"When a soul is vehemently moved to wickedness"—to use the words of St. Thomas Aquinas—a man reprobate, of hardened heart and dead conscience, is beyond all question wholly disposed to colleague and cabal with the powers of darkness. Such a one calls evil good; and good, evil. He puts darkness for light, and light for darkness. Happily, it is neither so simple nor so sudden a matter to arrive at such a state of corruption. Conscience strives and will speak. Good will break through the bad. Yet a long and malignant obstinacy in evil may and does attain the supreme wickedness.

The majority of men are safeguarded because the average individual is *au fond* a weak and vacillating kind of creature. Comparatively few men can will anything very determinedly. Fewer yet are able to combine fixity of purpose with strength and undeviating resolve, factors necessary to perfect accomplishment. Most persons are indolent in their thought and tepid in their appetites. Enthusiasms genuinely great prove dangerous rather than pleasurable. They entail exertion, self-denial, asceticism almost. They do not admit of mental untidiness. "It is for this reason," says Bryce, "that a strenuous and unwearying will sometimes becomes so tremendous a power, almost a hypnotic force." In the realm of created intelligences a supreme exemplar of this intensive individual will is Satan, wholly set and bent upon evil, and his servants partake of his strength, the measure of their participation being in ratio to their devotedness and resolve.

In *The White People* Mr. Arthur Machen speaks of "the 'sorcerers' who use the material life, who use the failings incidental to material life, as instruments to obtain their infinitely wicked ends . . . our higher senses are so blunted, we are so drenched with materialism, that we should probably fail to recognize real wickedness if we encountered it".

"But shouldn't we experience a certain horror . . . in the mere presence of an evil man?"

"We should if we were natural: children and women feel this horror you speak of, even animals experience it. But with most of us convention and civilization and education have blinded and deafened and obscured the natural reason . . . and, as a rule, I suspect that the *Hierarchs* of Tophet pass quite unnoticed."

This was not so, of course, in the ages of faith, when the world was in agreement regarding the nature and actuality of true religion, and traitors or outlaws were almost immediately recognized in all their baseness and vile revolt.

There can be no question that a man who is determined is able to get intimately in touch with the dark shadow world, to companion with the demon, to become a witch by swearing fealty to Satan, the god of the witches.

There are, so the *Malleus Maleficarum* instructs us, "three necessary concomitants of witchcraft, which are the Devil, A Witch, and the Permission of Almighty God".

As I have said elsewhere, "Plainly, a man who not only firmly believes in a Power of evil but also that this Power can and does meddle with and (so far as is allowed) mar human affections and human destinies, may invoke and devote himself to this Power, may give up his whole will to this Power, demanding in exchange that his own bad wishes and wicked ends shall be accomplished, and so he will succeed in definitely and explicitly entering into a mysterious contract with evil whose master in some sort he may temporarily seem to be, whose bondslave and victim he will assuredly be throughout an eternity."

A contract presupposes a condition, the condition here being that the demon brings to pass the desires of the witch, and since the aims and purposes of the witch must obviously always be infamous, impious, and malign, this condition is invariably agreeable to and acquiesced in by the demon, for thus it opens a way for him to do yet more mischief and sharpen yet more keenly his hatred of the human race through the instrumentality of his besotted medium the witch.

Maître Maurice Garçon, one of the leaders of the French Bar today, and a high authority upon contemporary black magic and witchcraft, in the course of an address delivered before the Institut Métaphysique in Paris, September, 1929, stated, "The first step for novices in sorcery and witchcraft is to make a contract with the devil." Richard Bovet in his *Pandæmonium* says that once the witch has made the contract with the devil he "hath *Seisin* of her as his *Property*". The terms of these contracts are that the proselyte pledges his soul to the Evil One in return for power, wealth, revenge, or some other material object he craves for in this world. "I have not only held some of these contracts in my hand," said Maître Garçon, "but I actually witnessed one of these strange businesses not so very long ago." He related how it had come to his knowledge that a neophyte in demonianism intended to evoke the Devil in a haunted wood near Fontainebleau. Maître Garçon and a second witness concealed themselves behind the trees, whence under a full moon they had a clear view of the spot appointed for the rendezvous. The sorcerer arrived on the scene at midnight, and proceeded to enact in every detail the horrid ritual of blasphemy. He traced with meticulous care upon the ground the magic circle inscribed within and without with the seals and sigils of fallen angels and their awful names; he lighted two pitch-black candles, which, owing to the chemicals kneaded into the wax, flickered with a dull blue flame; he burned in a silver censer stolen from a church sacristy, and in bitter mockery broken and defiled, cold deadly nightshade, rank henbane, the prickly purpling capsules of thorn apple, and acrid myrrh; he paced widdershins about the circle, in the centre of which he next took his place, intoning meanwhile in raucous voice the litanies and conjurations of power that summon the Regents of Hell. At the climax, raising himself on tiptoe with frenzied gestures, the man threw out his hands in ghastly appeal, proffering to Satan the infernal charter scrawled and blotted with his own blood, and amid grim and grinding imprecations vowing that in addition to the forfeit of his own unhappy soul he would win the demon a votary for every wish that was granted, every lust that was satiate and fulfilled. That the fiend, who doubtless was hovering hard by, did not actually manifest himself is without question due to the fact that these goblin ceremonies were overseen by profane eyes, by secret watchers not of the warlock band.

For Satan loves secrecy, and dark mystery and lonely horror, and will not tolerate at his rites the presence of any who are not his worshippers and sworn slaves. If their assemblies are intruded upon by any accident, the members endeavour to kill the too curious stranger on the spot, which is very easily to be understood. So when Mr. Williams, of Cardrona, on the River Tweed in Peebles, Scotland, walking home late one evening, came upon the witches who were dancing on Minchmoor, the whole coven gave chase to him, and he was glad to escape alive. It is true that they were aware he had discovered and was filching the register or roll of the witches, but he was obliged to fling it away in the hurry of his flight. In the course of various trials it has not unseldom come to light how, when a witch has introduced to their impious orgies some candidate who sickened and appalled, it may be by some last spasm of conscience or some shudder of fear, has rejected the oaths and asked but to escape and be gone, the whole gang in an excess of fury have fallen upon the luckless wretch and murdered him, partly in rage at his revolt against their damnable mysteries, and partly to close his mouth lest he betray them.

That Satan should not always appear is in most cases probably because the demon wishes to draw the aspirant to black magic further and further into his net, to inveigle and irretrievably enmesh him in the coils of hell. Yet perhaps it is better not to go beyond the teaching on this point of that great theologian and philosopher Francesco Suarez, "the most distinguished doctor", as he is known, who in his treatise *On Superstition* instructs us that when no response is received from the demon "it is either because God does not permit it, or for some other reason we may not know". Yet, he proceeds to explain that the silence of the evil spirit does not in any way mitigate the guilt of the experimenter, who has at least dabbled in divination, although he may not have obtained the desired result.

At the end of the eighteenth century, in Madrid, Juan Perez, an artisan, vowed himself body and soul to Satan if he were only revenged on those whom he suspected of injuring him. According to his confession, after a long-continued steady run of ill-luck, convinced that in some way his misfortunes were being deliberately brought about by personal spite and malice, he lost all hope, and blasphemed furiously, crying: "If God won't help me, let's see whether the devil will!" He first consulted a gipsy "patrico" or beggarman, an ill-favoured fellow of very bad repute. This wretch, who for a few coppers was ready to aid and abet any mischief, in the words of the Highland ballad

> applied to an auld woman,
> Who had mair skill than he.

Acting upon the hag's instructions, Perez withdrew to a lonely spot a league or more from the city, and there, on three nights in succession, exactly at twelve o'clock, after declaiming certain mysterious rhymes which she taught him and which must be uttered with certain inflexions of the voice and a kind of intonation, he called upon Satan in a loud voice, profferring his soul to the Devil and renouncing God and religion. When nothing resulted, he angrily upbraided the witch. "There must be something which prevents the charm," she said; "let us see. Have you by chance any object of piety on you?" Perez replied that he had always worn a scapular, and carried a rosary in his pocket. "A murrain choke you for a fool," quoth she, "to go to meet Lucifer carrying along this gear. Now we must try by way of the pact." A piece of parchment was provided inscribed with curious signs, and Perez wrote his name in his own blood, devoting himself as a slave for ever to the Dark King whom he saluted as "Master and Lord". So horrible, however, were the terms of this self-oblation to evil that the neophyte, thoroughly alarmed, at break of day went to the Palace of the Holy Office and unburdened his guilty soul before a full tribunal. He was condemned to a year's imprisonment, but as it was considered he had offended partly, at least, through ignorance, he received absolution, and when he had served his sentence he was recommended to the particular care of his parish priest for instruction. Further, a friar was appointed to be his director, and a few easy rules of life and conduct were prescribed.

It might seem from this very light punishment that the Holy Office regarded the pact and all it involved as a minor offence, or at any rate as hardly ranking among the graver crimes. Nothing could be further from the truth. What the tribunal endeavoured to do, so far as the circumstances permitted, was to deal leniently with enormities of this kind, and if there was no obstinacy, but a frank and free acknowledgement of guilt, to reconcile and absolve all penitents. This is very remarkable, since in England a proof of any such pact would have meant the rope and gallows-tree. In Scotland the tar-barrel and the stake. In the face of such merciful treatment, such patience and understanding, we may very well—some of us, I think—begin to reconsider our ideas of the Spanish justiciaries.

The pact, tacit or explicit, with the powers of evil was regarded as the very foundation and basis of sorcery, so that in Spain the Inquisition disclaimed all jurisdiction in such cases unless the accused at the outset admitted having entered into a bond and covenant with the demon. Rightly judging this point to be of essential importance, in 1655 the Suprema—that is to say, the supreme executive and legislative head of the Holy Office—issued elaborately detailed instructions with regard to the conduct of examinations in all cases where demoniacal pacts were in question. The accused must be questioned whether there was in the first place a pact, and when, how, where, it had been made. When the familiar appeared in consequence of the initial conjuration, under what form did he manifest himself and what condition did he demand? If the accused had by chance employed remedies which healed, were the results dependent on the pact or had the drugs, herbs, lotions, employed a natural curative power? And so on, through a very large number of sections and sub-sections.

Stevenote de Audebert, a witch of the Pyrénées, who was executed in 1619, actually showed the judge, Pierre de Lancre, "the contract she had made and bond she had entered into with the demon. It was a foul piece of parchment, all crocked and grimy, scrawled with blood and feculent matter, enough to turn a man's stomach to see."

An English witch, Elizabeth Style, of Stoke Trister, Wincanton, Somerset, in 1664 confessed to the examining magistrate, Robert Hunt, J.P., that some ten years before the Devil "appeared to her in the shape of a handsome man", who promised, "she should live gallantly" and "have the pleasure of the World for Twelve years if she would with her own Blood sign his Paper which was to give her Soul to him . . . and with a drop or two of her Blood she signed the Paper" with her mark, since she did not know how to write. She was found guilty at the County Sessions, but died in gaol. In 1672 a Nottingham boy inscribed a formal agreement with the powers of evil.

The most notorious and most terrible of these written pacts with Satan is probably that drawn up and signed by the arch magician, Urbain Grandier, who was executed on 18 August, 1634, in the market of Loudun, Vienne. This holograph is preserved in the Bibliothèque Nationale at Paris. In the library at Upsala may be seen the contract by which Daniel Salthenius, a reckless young undergraduate, but in later life Professor of Hebrew at Königsberg, sold himself to Satan.

These formal and written pacts with the fiend are still made today, and there are, indeed, printed grimoires and manuals of sorcery (only sold clandestinely, and fortunately not to be found without the greatest difficulty) which set out the most efficacious formulas and ceremonies to be used in these horrid transactions.

It is said that there is preserved in the archivium of the Cathedral of Girgenti a written pact entered into between a canon of the Cathedral, of the eleventh century, and the demon. This document is traditionally supposed to be a holograph of the fiend, a thing in itself not at all impossible, and indeed the characters are ill-omened enough, and so extraordinary that nobody has ever been able to decipher the script. The only reproduction I have seen is dated 11 August, 1676, which is certainly not the eleventh century. This accompanies a few paragraphs slangily dished up in the worst possible taste as a journalistic stunt, and the whole description is obviously second-hand. The document is indifferently referred to as a pact made by a canon, and a letter addressed to a nun! From another and serious source of information I have learned that there is a mysterious writing of this kind kept very closely at Girgenti, but no details have been forthcoming. Until it is possible for some scholar and expert to examine the parchment and unfold its precise nature and history, one must be content with merely recording the fact of its existence.

About forty years ago, that is to say early in the present twentieth century, Dr. Jean Fauconney, of Paris, published a series of some twenty or more volumes all dealing with occult, curious, and unusual subjects, amongst which the arcana of black magic occupied a prominent place. Dr. Fauconney, who died in 1909 or 1910, wrote under several pseudonyms: Dr. Caufeynon, Dr. Eynon, Dr. X., and probably also Dr. Jaf. His studies of witchcraft and satanism were issued as by Dr. Caufeynon and Dr. Jaf, and although it is possible there may have been some collaborator, it is just as likely that—as it would appear merely for the sake of mystification—these two names really designate one and the same author. Be that as it may, in 1904 (actually the book is undated) there appeared *Les Secrets Merveilleux du Grand et du Petit Albert; Le Grand Grimoire et la Clavicule, ou le Secret de la Magie Noire Dévoilée*, par les Drs. Caufeynon et Jaf: *The Marvellous Secrets of Albert the Great and Albert the Less; the Great Grimoire and the Key [of Solomon], or The Whole of Mystery of Magic Revealed.* The word "grimoire", which is derived from the French, being an alteration of *grammaire*, Grammar, is defined by the great *Oxford English Dictionary* as "a magician's manual for invoking demons". The *Clavicula* or *Key* is a collection of incantations, spells, and charms of various kinds, rather vaguely associated with King Solomon, who, according to Talmudic and Oriental legend, was a magician of mickle might and commanded hosts of jinn or elemental spirits. Albert the Great is St. Albert the Dominican, who died in 1280, and whose complete works have been collected in twenty-one huge folio volumes. His immense learning, his recondite researches, and the treatises of profound mysticism which he wrote earned him among the common folk the name of the "magician", and in subsequent centuries there were fathered upon him all kinds of books of abracadabra with which, of course, he had nothing to do. Nor can we agree with Caillet's suggestion that some of these earlier occult opuscules may be from the pens of Albert the Great's disciples and immediate followers, such as the learned Benedictine monk Thomas of Cantimpré, who died at Louvain in 1263, or Henry of Saxony, a famous mediaeval scholar. Who Albert the Less may be is uncertain. Some think that "the Less" merely means a selection or excerpts from the larger works once popularly attributed to Albert the Great, but this seems a little far-fetched, especially as in some old editions this second Albert is called Albert Lewis the Less. Not to go too deeply into this rather obscure question, it may briefly be said that possibly Albert Lewis was a fictitious name deliberately adopted on account of the extraordinary reputation and authority of Albert the Great, but what writer assumed this title— whether it was Peter of Abano or Arnold of Villeneuve or Francesco Prelati, all profound occultists—there is no evidence to decide. As has just been remarked, Maître Maurice Garçon tells us he has actually held some of the diabolical contracts in his own hand. He also stated: "We have many ancient examples of these contracts in old French legal documents, and those which are being drawn up today are practically identical with these records. They are always written, or at least signed, in Blood. The substance of such contracts is that the novice agrees to sell his soul to the Evil One in return for power, money, revenge, or whatever else he desires." In his practice Maître Garçon has appeared in court in many cases involving the celebration of black masses. He declares that it is no exaggeration to say there hardly passes a week without some police proceedings in one district of France or another which bring to light the activities of the widespread cult and creed of the Satanists. As in England, sorcerers abound in France. "At this very time I am speaking to you," Maître Garçon said in his address (September, 1929), "a pastrycook of Fontenay-sous-Bois, a suburb of Paris, is prosecuting a neighbour of ill repute as a witch doctor for making his cream turn sour in midwinter." Maître Garçon had emphatically contradicted the idea that these sorceries were confined to the remoter mountainous provinces or to villages and hamlets off the beaten track. "I know," he affirmed, "a number of instances of highly intelligent individuals who have made pacts with the Devil, and, in particular, I know of a leading French banker of a famous Paris house who attributes all his success to such a contract. In return for various material benefits from the Devil during their lives on earth, these sorcerers agree to deliver their souls to Satan after death."

Great authorities, doctors and fathers of the Church have written of the formal contract with the demon. St. Augustine, for example, treats of it more than once in some detail. The learned Francesco Maria Guazzo in his *Compendium Maleficarum*, 1608 (English translation, 1929, pp. 13–19), discusses at length *The Witches' Pact with the Devil*. A famous Spanish Jesuit, Father Ricardo Cappa, in his study *La Inquisicion española* (Madrid, 1888, p. 242), tells us that of his own personal knowledge commerce and compacts with Satan are quite frequent, and deliberate preconcerted traffic with evil is in many quarters eagerly purchased and pursued.

A famous English Jesuit, but recently (1939) deceased, Father Herbert Thurston, of Farm Street, was obliged to admit that "in the face of Holy Scripture and the teaching of the Fathers and theologians the abstract possibility of a pact with the Devil and of a diabolical interference in human affairs can hardly be denied". I use the phrase "obliged to admit", since the late Father Thurston was notoriously one of the most sceptical of minds. Anything savouring of the uncommon, of the abnormal, of the miraculous, he regarded with unbounded suspicion and distaste, at once setting to work to explain it away in terms of some error in observation or record, some obscure morbid affection, or pithiatism otherwise called hysteria.

The question at once arises—are these compacts in any sense valid or binding? Here all authorities of all schools of thought are in agreement. Such abominations as a contract with the demon are in their very essence utterly null and void.

St. Alphonsus Liguori, in his *Moral Theology*, Book III, No. 28, instructs us how such impious intercourse with evil must be ended and dissolved. Four points are laid down:

1. Any formal or tacit contract entered into with demonic intelligences must be renounced and abjured. 2. All books, writings, talismans connected with the black art, charms, and the like must be burned and completely destroyed. 3. If the written contract be held by the person seeking to repent, it must be burned, but if this contract is believed to be held by the demon, there is no need to demand its restoration, since it is wholly annulled by sincere penitence and resolve to amend. 4. Any harm which has been done by the exercise of sorcery must as far as possible be made good. None the less it cannot but be acknowledged that anyone who is so rotted with evil as to deliver himself a bondslave to Satan and who signs this deed and charter of hell stands in fearful peril. For Satan will hardly let go, and, as Jules Bois says, the interior pact and consent of which the written paper is in some sense an outward sign and a symbol are not easily dissolved.

The infernal fetters welded with pains and perseverance and hate cannot lightly be broken; when a man has dipped so far and is quagmired it is a sore struggle and sweat for him to recover his traces. Almost invariably the cost of deliverance is a shattered nervous system; a wrecked life; even death, swift and premature. Notwithstanding, as numerous happy examples prove, the effort has been made, and so great a victory won that demonism has become sanctity. St. Basil, Bishop of Caesarea (370–379), wrested from the fiend a written contract whereby a besotted youth had bartered his salvation, demanding in return the love of a fair courtesan. It is no exaggeration to say that in every country in Europe and in every tongue for full a thousand years there was scarcely a history more familiar than that of Theophilus, first translated from Greek into Latin as early as the ninth century, sung in poem, sounded from the pulpit, told in stone—it is sculptured in Beverley Minster and in the Lady Chapel of Ely—pictured in the painted glass of more than one great Cathedral window, all crimson and blue and gold. Bitterly resenting a change in his good fortune, Theophilus bound himself to the Evil One by a written pact. Upon his repentance, after much suffering, the bond was recovered and annulled. The sorcerer Cyprian, of Nicomedia—the modern Izmid—a town of Asia Minor, sought by the Devil's aid to seduce the maiden Justina. When he failed the fiend was forced to avow: "She is protected by a Power greater than mine own." "Then," replied Cyprian, "I will worship that Power, and none other will I serve." In spite of the fact that, as Alban Butler says, he had been devoted from infancy to the devil, and "brought up in all the impious mysteries of idolatry, judicial astrology, and the black art", and had "stuck at no crimes, blasphemed Christ, and committed secret murders, to offer the blood and inspect the bowels of children, as decisive of future events", Cyprian underwent so complete a change that when the persecution of Diocletian broke out he was constant even unto martyrdom in the year A.D. 304, and on 26 September is kept the Feast of St. Cyprian, once a mage.

A Portuguese of noble birth, Giles, or Gil, whilst yet an undergraduate, joined a secret society at Toledo, and was presently persuaded to sign with his own blood a paper vowing himself to the demon in return for worldly honour and academic distinction. For seven years he absorbed himself in the dark study of necromantic sciences, but, warned by a vision, he repented of the evil and was able to halt on the very brink, as it were, of the abyss. It is doubtful, says the old chronicler, which had waxed the greater, the fame of his learning or the infamy of his wickedness. He abruptly quitted Paris, the scene of his professorial triumphs, and in the lowliest station sought admittance to a monastery of Dominicans, a new and obscure foundation at Palencia, on the River Carrion, in the north of Spain, where he was utterly unknown. The one regret which tortured him throughout the remorseful days and broken nights of penance and prayer was that obscure and execrable charter which still lay in the demons' hands. At long last there met him one evening in the cloisters a tall, ill-favoured man of frowning and horrible aspect, who threw down with a gesture of impotent fury the accursed paper, muttering in a hoarse voice, "Take the bond, for I am compelled to return it to you," and forthwith seemed to melt into the twilight shadows. Giles eagerly seized the horrid scroll, and tearing it to bits, burned them in the fire. But for all that his life was made miserable by a thousand vexations and mischiefs, all of which he endured so patiently that he attained great heights of sanctity. He died in the year 1265, amid the tears of his brethren and the lamentations of the whole countryside. He is buried at Santarem, which is on the River Tagus, about fifty miles north of Lisbon. Miracles of healing were worked at his tomb, and in the Dominican Order and many dioceses of Portugal his feast is kept year by year on 14 May.

When the pact is made, the witch confides in the devil, thinking that —poor fool!—he can command the Powers of Evil, and the devil pretends to acknowledge the witch's power. The demon, however, is merely mocking his federate, since, as the learned Abbot Johann Trithemius says: "Such pacts with the devil are vain and empty; for the devil never keeps faith, and scorns to be bound by any promise or pledge."

> *Nein, nein! der Teufel ist ein Egoist*
> *Und tut nicht leicht um Gottes willen,*
> *Was einem andern nutzlich ist.*
>
> Goethe: *Faust.*

> Nay, nay, the Devil is an Egoist,
> And doth but little for the love of God——
> Gratis he never grinds your grist.

CHAPTER II

The Familiar, in Human Shape and Animal—How Acquired—The Sacrileges of Witches—The Reward of Blood.

"They shall say unto you, Seek unto them that have familiar spirits, and unto wizards that peep and that mutter."—*Isaiah* viii, 19.

As has been pointed out in some detail, the huge hosts of demons, these foul but brilliantly alert intelligences, the rulers of the darkness of this world, are divided into ranks and grades and orders, into principalities and powers; there are lords and menials, aristocracies and plebs, we may say. When the pact has been struck it is not unusual that there should be assigned to the witch a familiar, that is to say an attendant demon or mysterious entity to obey the behests and serve in various bad ways the pleasure of the witch. The familiar or Astral spirit who companions with and carries out the directions of the witch is a demon—it may be of the higher orders, it may be of some lower grade. We find that the more hardened and resolute in evil is the witch, the more powerful and malignant, and therefore we may suppose the higher in rank is the familiar. These beings are often invisible to any save the witch, and often again they exhibit themselves in human or animal form, and are plainly manifest to everyone. It does not need any psychic perception to see them. Almost invariably their dark supernatural origin can be recognized by some hideously grotesque feature or deformity, and even when such blemish is hidden they carry with them an effluvium of evil which betrays them to the horrified spectator. It is seldom that the familiar can altogether conceal the features, blasted and seared by Divine Wrath, of the fallen angel, but such cases have been known. I suspect, however, that the dupe was only willing to be deceived. Familiars are employed by the witch for purposes of divination, and also for various hurtings and harms, for mischief generally, to destroy property, to afflict with illness, to

> raise jars,
> Jealousies, strifes, and heart-burning disagreements
> Like a thick scurf o'er life.

In his *Institute of the Laws of Scotland*, Edinburgh, 1722–1730, William Forbes writes that "to some [the Devil] gives certain Spirits or Imps to correspond with, and serve them as their Familiars, known to them by some odd names, to which they answer when called".

The horrid practice of employing spirits for divination, which is so prevalent today, is referred to many times in the Bible. The Mosaic law enjoins: "A man also or woman that hath a familiar spirit, or that is a wizard, shall surely be put to death" (*Leviticus* xx, 27). Again, we have: "There shall not be found among you any one that useth divination, or an observer of times, or an enchanter, or a witch, or a charmer, or a

consulter with familiar spirits, or a wizard, or a necromancer. For all
that do these things are an abomination unto the Lord" (*Deuteronomy*
xviii, 10–12). King Saul, who reigned over Israel about 1095–1055 B.C.,
in the first flush of zeal upon ascending the throne, "had put away those
that had familiar spirits, and the wizards, out of the land". But when,
distracted with sickness and fear, upon the eve of the battle of Gilboa,
"he consulted the Lord, and He answered him not, neither by dreams,
nor by priests, nor by prophets", in the extremity of his misery he said
to his servants, "Seek me a woman that hath a familiar spirit, that I may
go to her and inquire of her. And his servants said to him, Behold, there
is a woman that hath a familiar spirit at En-dor." In sorry disguise, with
only two to bear him company, at deep midnight hour, under the silent
watchful stars, the king stealthily made his way guided across the shadowy
plain, and striking up a lonely and deserted track, they came to the
northern slope of the hill, where huddled a few hovels builded and
botched with mud and natural clay, an aerie clinging to the rough caves
which honeycomb that rocky spur, veritable dens, squalid and filthy,
stenchy and ill-omened, which men knew as En-dor, fit home for the
necromancer and the witch. Rapping softly but urgent and quick, the
strangers beat upon the crazy door of one of these kraals, set a little way
apart from the rest, as if shunned even by its wretched companions.
Presently it is opened with care and caution, and in the naked flickering
flame of her earthern lamp a fearful hag peers from bleared, rheumy
eyes at her secret visitors. There is scant time for parley. The foremost
speaks abruptly and to the point: "Divine to me by thy divining spirit,
and bring me up him whom I shall tell thee." But the beldame is little
used to such peremptory command. Far other were her trembling clients
accustomed to approach the sibyl's bothy. She should be entreated and
besought, won with fair promises and ample fees of gold. Not so easily
would she be persuaded to exhibit her foul mysteries. Who was this
belswagger with his orders and his hests, this tall warrior, muffled in a
cloak, who bore himself as if he were a king?

Without flat denial, she temporized. "Behold, thou knowest all
that Saul hath done, and how he hath rooted out those that have familiar
spirits and the wizards out of the land: why then dost thou lay a snare
for my life, to cause me to be put to death?" That should answer the
spy, for a royal spy, an *agent provocateur*, he might well be.

His reply, however, set all doubt at rest and lulled every suspicion.
The stranger bound himself by a most solemn and awful oath, swearing
unto her in the very Name of God: "As the Lord liveth there shall no
evil happen to thee for this thing." To business. "And the woman said
to him: "Whom shall I bring up to thee?" and he said, "Bring me up
Samuel." The horrid rites began. The words of blasphemy and power,
the strong invocations, were muttered in mystic rhyme and with woven
spell. Through the acrid suffumigations the wreaths of smoke grew denser
and seemed to be taking the form of an old man wearing the sacred tallith
of the prophets and the seers. This was not the demon she looked for, this
was not her goblin familiar. Some force far, far greater than her own was
stirring now! Trembling and sore afraid, she called out with a loud voice

to the querent, "Why hast thou deceived me? for thou art Saul." She saw in a flash the whole truth. It was indeed the king, the relentless enemy of her infernal sisterhood. But he, scarcely less moved than the hag herself, reassured her quickly, "Fear not," and then in a hoarse, horrid whisper, "What hast thou seen?" "An old man cometh up, and he is covered with a mantle," she cried. "And Saul understood that it was Samuel, and he bowed himself with his face to the ground, and adored." Terrible was the message of doom, defeat and death that fell from the prophet's lips. Lost crown, lost kingdom, lost life! "And tomorrow thou and thy sons shall be with me", in the same state, in another world but —in the same place? "And forthwith Saul fell all along the ground" in a death-like swoon.

If Saul by his edicts drove the witches and charmers into holes and corners, and punished their divinations and sorceries with the utmost penalties, some at any rate of his successors in their day called forth the evil crew from their hiding-places and raised them to honour. Three centuries pass by and King Manasses of Judah "used enchantments and dealt with familiar spirits and wizards". He officially appointed pythons, that is diviners by spirits, and multiplied soothsayers and their schools. Only five-and-twenty years before, upon the capture of Samaria by Sargon of Assyria, the Ephraimite monarchy had come to an end with Hoshea, last of that line. It is recorded that for many a decade the Northern kingdom had openly encouraged, and indeed avidly practised, witch-crafts of every sort and kind. "They gave themselves up to divinations and soothsayings and used enchantments."

From the New Testament, to cite one example—but that is sufficiently striking—of divination by means of a familiar spirit will serve. When St. Paul and St. Silas were at Philippi (modern Bereketli), "as we went to prayer, a certain damsel possessed with a spirit of divination met us, which brought her masters much gain by soothsaying". This was a case of possession by a familiar rather than the evocation of a familiar, but it is in effect the same practice, divination by the aid of a demon.

It is both theologically and philosophically possible that an immaterial intelligence can be contained in materiality, that is to say a spiritual individual essence, an angel, either good or evil, can be invested with corporeity, and thus angels can exhibit themselves in place and time.

In the Canary Isles, before the natives were converted to Christianity, familiar spirits who had taken human forms might be seen walking about, accompanying and conversing with their wizard masters, and that not only under cover of darkness but in the broad light of day.

Mr. Wirt Sikes, who was the United States Consul for Wales, writes in his study *British Goblins* (1880): "The sort of familiar spirit employed by magicians in the eighteenth and preceding centuries was distinctly a demon."

In his *Discourse on the Wonders of the Invisible World*, 1692, Cotton Mather says: "The *Witches* which by their covenant with the Devil, are become Owners of *Spectres*, are oftentimes by their own Spectres required and compelled to give their consent, for the molestation of

some, which they had no mind otherwise to fall upon; and cruel depre-
dations are thus made upon the Vicinage. In the Prosecution of these
Witchcrafts, among a thousand other unaccountable things, the *Spectres*
have an odd faculty of cloathing the most substantial and corporeal
Instruments of Torture, with Invisibility, while the wounds thereby
given have been the most palpable things in the World; so that the
Sufferers assaulted with Instruments of Iron, wholly unseen to the
standers by, though, to their cost, seen by themselves, have, upon snatch-
ing, wrested the Instruments out of the *Spectres'* hands, and every one has
then immediately not only *beheld*, but *handled*, an Iron Instrument taken
by a Devil from a Neighbour. These wicked *Spectres* have proceeded so
far, as to steal several quantities of Money from divers people, part of
which Money, has, before sufficient Spectators, been dropt out of the Air
into the Hands of the Sufferers." This passage is extremely significant,
and to some extent at any rate it may be an explanation of the apports
which not infrequently materialize at séances today.

The familiar often appeared in human shape, and under this form
constantly companioned the witch. A Suffolk witch, Abre Grinset, alias
Thrower, of Dunwich, who died in April, 1667, confessed that she had
made a league with Satan and served him for twenty years. The Devil
first visited her "in the form of a Pretty handsome Young Man" who
spoke in a "hollow solemn voice". The famous Scottish witch, Isobel
Gowdie, of Auldearn, a village about two and a half miles south-east of
Nairn, at her examination in 1662 gave very full details of the familiars
who attended the several members of the coven. Thus Margaret Wilson,
of Auldearn, had a spirit called Swein, who was always clad in grass-
green; Bessie Wilson's spirit was Rory, who was clothed in yellow;
Jean Martin's familiar appeared like a young fellow scarcely twenty
years old and he wore grass-green. Her own familiar was invariably
clad in black. Dr. Eugenio Torralba, a very famous Spanish scholar and
physician, who for many years was highly esteemed both by the grandees
of Castile and at Rome itself, entertained a familiar, named Zequiel
(Ezechiel). He was, however, bound by no sort of pact to this spirit,
and when he was tried before the Inquisition on a charge of sorcery he
declared that Zequiel had never counselled a wrong thing, had never
suggested an evil thought, but on the contrary warmly encouraged him
in acts of piety, and especially in daily attendance at Mass, so that he
was fully persuaded that this spirit was an angel of light, his heavenly
guide. None the less, when judgement was given on 6 March, 1531, by
the tribunal of Cuenca, Torralba was required to swear on the Gospels
that he would hold no further communication with Zequiel. The sentence passed by the Holy Office was in effect a mere formality, mainly
consisting of a solemn abjuration of any form of magic or curious art.
From first to last the whole case is extremely puzzling, and indeed
assessors, masters in theology, were called in to advise and debate the
most intricate and riddling points. Zequiel appeared as a young man
of great comeliness, with fair hair, blue eyes, and a mild beautiful
countenance.

For the most part the familiar in human form is ugly and deformed, so full of menace in his bearing and so malign in his glances that he betrays his dark original. Robin, or Robert, Filius Artis (literally "Son of Art"), the familiar of Lady Alice Kyteler of Kilkenny (1324), appeared as a horrible black dwarf, and he was not unseldom accompanied by two goblins as foul and ill-favoured as himself. Pierre Croschard, of Couvet, Neuchâtel, renounced God and pledged himself to Satan and was served by a familiar, a lean swarthy man, who presented him and his father-in-law, Pierre Perret, a master sorcerer, with five sols apiece. The familiar of Oliver Cromwell, who had been initiated into the blasphemies of black magic by Menasses Ben Israel, a rabbi of Amsterdam, was a tall dark man with a sour frowning face. His name was Grimoald. The late Mrs. Violet Tweedale has described a not dissimilar, gruesome, and gashly familiar whom she saw at Nice. Her attention was rather unpleasantly attracted by a man in grotesque attire, who seemed to be the inseparable companion of a certain Prince Valori, a well-known figure in fashionable Riviera society. This strange shadow or satellite was preternaturally emaciated, and looked little other than a walking skeleton with very thin, spidery legs. "He was dressed entirely in chocolate brown—a sort of close-fitting coif or cowl was drawn over his head, and his curious long impish face was made more weird by small sharply pointed ears rising on each side of his head." He appeared to have "got himself up" to look like a satyr or some such mythical monstrosity. When Mrs. Tweedale saw Prince Valori at a magnificent *bal masque*, the tip-top event of the season, he was gorgeously costumed as a courtier of the reign of Louis XV with a fine flowing perruque and a coat of old silken brocade, the flower of Longchamps or Versailles. To her amaze, at his heels there glided the man in brown. The two came up to her, when she naturally supposed that the Prince was about to present his friend, an introduction from which, truth to tell, she shrank for some indefinable reason. She felt a natural repugnance to this atomy, and a cold shudder ran through her as he approached. After bending over her hand for a moment, Prince Valori seated himself on a tabouret at her side, and with a pretty compliment to her frock and her bouquet, began chatting of indifferent things: the decorations, the dancing, the music. As they talked, the brown satyr stood close behind them in perfect silence. Mrs. Tweedale says she felt a growing sense of apprehension, an uneasiness which almost amounted to terror. She was, indeed, on the point of rising with some hurried excuse, when fortunately her partner came up and claimed her for the next valse. A few days later she took the opportunity of asking a Russian lady, a clairvoyante, an old acquaintance of the Prince, who this ominous brown satyr was. "Why, don't you know?" was the reply. "It is his familiar, who constantly attends him. People say they became attached whilst he was assisting at a Sabbath in the Vosges, and he can't get free of his goblin. Sabbaths are still held at Lutzei, and each initiate receives a familiar. These beings have odd names—Minette, Verdelet, and so forth. One of my ancestors, Adalbert Laski, Count Palatine of Siradia, the Polish boyar who patronized Dr. Dee, owned a familiar called Sainte-Buisson." "How horrible!" exclaimed Mrs. Tweedale. "Then this satyr creature attached to Prince Valori is not real flesh and blood? Is he always there?" "Always. Anyone who is psychic sees him. I have often seen him myself with the Prince in Paris." A couple of mornings later, Mrs. Tweedale, meeting Prince Valori on the Promenade des Anglais, screwed up her courage and boldly inquired: "By the way, Prince, who is that tall man so quaintly dressed in brown I have seen with you lately?" The Prince's face fell: "Ah, you also . . ." he muttered. "My question was a thoughtless impertinence. I am so sorry to have hurt you. Pray forgive me, and don't answer." He shook his head sadly, and looking at her with gloomy eyes merely said: "I am not the only one in the world so afflicted."

Mrs. Tweedale knew General Elliot, who commanded the forces in Scotland, and was a distinguished social figure during the 'nineties. The General had a familiar, "Wononi", to whom in moments of abstraction he actually used to speak aloud in the middle of a dinner-party.

To some witches, wrote King James, the devil "will be a continual attender in form of a page".

At Oxford, not much more than ten years ago, one of the best-known figures in the University was commonly believed to entertain a familiar. The presumption seemed borne out by some curious facts and happenings. Myself, I never saw plainly any strange corporeal form going to and fro with the wizard—for wizard he undoubtedly was—but on several occasions in brilliant sunshine as he walked the streets there moved at his side a dark and quite distinct man's shadow other than his own, a shadow which could not possibly have been cast by any person in his proximity, and, what is more, if he happened to pass certain churches—for example, St. Aloysius or Blackfriars—this shadow would vanish completely away. It is significant that the witch Perrenon Megain of Boudry (1617) was invariably accompanied by a sombre shadowy form with which she used to converse, and which was entirely separate and distinct from the shadow cast by her own body. The familiar of Marie Leschott used to appear to her as a kind of smoky vapour of human shape, conveying news to her and advising her in mischief. In Marlowe's *Doctor Faustus* "shadow" is used as equivalent to "familiar". Faustus exclaims:

> 'Tis Magic, Magic, that hath ravished me.
> And I . . .
> Will be as cunning as Agrippa was,
> Whose shadow made all Europe honour him.

The allusion is to the famous Henry Cornelius Agrippa von Nettesheim (*c.* 1486–1537), who was traditionally supposed to be accompanied everywhere by a familiar under the form of a black dog, called Monsieur. It is probable that Milton had in mind the meaning of a familiar spirit implied by "shadow" or "shade" when, in *Paradise Lost*, Book X, 249–50, Sin says to the Goblin Death:

> Thou my Shade
> Inseparable must with me along.

An old English author writes: "The *Devil* is as really a Spirit, tho' a degenerated, fallen and evil Spirit, I say, he is as much a Spirit to all the Intents and Purposes of a Spirit that we are capable to judge of, as an Angel; and he is called the evil Spirit; He has Invisibility and Multi-presence, as a Spirit has; he can appear tho' the Doors be shut; and go out, tho' bolted and barred in; no Prison can hold him, but his last eternal Dungeon; no Chain can bind him, but the Chains fasten'd on him by Heaven, and the Angel of the bottomless Pit; no Engine or human Art can wound him; in short, he is neither to be seen, felt, heard, or understood, unless he pleases; and he can make himself be both seen and heard too, if he pleases; for he can assume the Shape and Appearance of Man or Beast, and in these Shapes and Appearances can make himself visible to us, terrify and affright us, converse in a friendly or in a frightful manner with us, as he thinks fit; he can be a Companion and Fellow-Traveller in the Day, an Apparition and a horrible Monster in the Night: In a word, he can be among us, and act upon, and with us, visibly or invisibly as he pleases, and as he finds for his purpose. Now if he does and can do thus, merely as he is a Spirit and by his spiritual Nature, we have a good deal of Reason to believe, that all Spirits may do the same. Any Kinds of Spirits may be reasonably supposed to be vested with the same Powers and may exert those Powers in the same or a like Manner."

In a communication to *Notes and Queries* (Vol. XI, p. 397), Mr. Thomas Q. Couch, who was living in Cornwall, said of his village, and indeed of the whole duchy: "The belief in witchcraft holds its ground very firmly. The notion that mysterious compacts are formed between evil spirits and wicked men has become almost obsolete. In the present day such a bargain is rarely suspected, and there are few found hardy enough to avow themselves parties to so unholy a transaction. One instance occurs to my memory of a poor unhappy fellow who pretended, in vulgar parlance, to have sold himself to the devil, and was accordingly regarded by his neighbours as a miracle of impiety. He was not, however, actively vicious, never being known to use his supernatural powers of ill-doing to the detriment of others, except, indeed (and they were the only occasions upon which he is said to have openly asked the foul fiend's assistance), when the depth of his potations had not left him enough to pay the reckoning. He was then accustomed to hold his hat up the chimney, and demand money, which was promptly showered down into it. The coin so obtained the landlord invariably refused with a shudder, and was glad to get quit of him on these terms. This compact with the spirit of evil is now but vaguely suspected as the secret of the witch's power."

Mr. Couch wrote some years ago, and it is natural that witches should be very secret about these pacts. None the less, as we have seen, this horrid practice is far from obsolete, as was once supposed.

Joan Rous, an old widow of Polstead, Suffolk, a district notoriously infested by witches, confessed that her familiars supplied her with money. The devil, "whom she called Bunne", of Jane Williford, of Faversham, Kent, brought her money as he had promised. A poor woman, Jane Wallis, of Keyston, Hunts, was also provided with ready money by familiars, and this she used to buy victuals. In one instance a purse was filched away for her by the spirit, which seems to be some poltergeist kind of teasing trick. In the annals of French witchcraft it is on record that Jehanneret Regnal-le-Boiteux, of Combre-Uldry, Neuchâtel (1481), made a pact with the demon, and was served by a familiar, Josaphat, who furnished him with money, on one occasion bringing him so large a sum as twenty gold florins. A sorceress of the Jura, Marguerite Aubert, received from her familiar a "sol de roi" as a reward for every piece of mischief she did, and Catherine Pingeon, of the same coven, was given by her familiar three "gros" on each occasion she harmed man or beast.

In England the witch's familiar or Astral Spirit went under many names. He was called a bunn or bunting; a dandiprat—terms of endearment; imp; spirit; devil; fiend; fury; angel; little master; maumet; puckril; nigget, and (particularly in New England) spectre.

The animal familiar, which in the British Isles was and is the commonest form as being the least likely to attract notice or arouse remark, the imp, or maumet, must be distinguished from the familiar in human shape, and probably belongs to a lower order of evil intelligences. The old English country name under which he may conveniently be known is "puckril". In his famous *Dæmonologie*, 1597, King James VI of Scotland (in 1603 James I of England) writes: "To some of the baser sort of them [witches] he [the devil] obliges himself to appear at their calling upon him, by such a proper name which he shows unto them, either in likeness of a dog, a cat, an ape, or such-like other beast; or else to answer by a voice only. The effects are to answer to such demands, as concerns curing of diseases; or such other base things as they require of him." It is true that witches can cure diseases, but one would surely have expected "as concerns afflicting with diseases". Yet a witch will do a seemingly good turn in order to entice the dupe farther into the toils.

The animal form ordinarily assumed by a familiar was that of a dog or a cat, but he was able to appear in almost any shape: as a bird, a chicken... a ferret, a hare, a hedgehog, a mole, a mouse, a polecat, a rabbit, a rat, a toad, a wasp, a spider, a beetle, or some other insect, and very many more. Examples of every one of these could be cited again and again from English trials, and multiplied yet again from the continental records. A very few instances must suffice. It is true that in other countries save the British Isles the domestic familiar is not so often remarked, and no very great stress seems to have been laid upon this detail, which in English law was regarded of the first importance and most damningly significant.

In the course of the trials at Chelmsford, March, 1582, of the St. Osyth witches many confessed how they entertained familiars. Ursula Kemp "had four spirits, whereof two of them were hes, and the other two were shes: the two he spirits were to punish and kill unto death, and the two shes were to punish with lameness and other diseases of bodily harm". The two he-spirits were Tittey, like a grey cat, and Jack, like a black cat. Elizabeth Bennet had a familiar, "called Suckin, being black like a dog". Alice Manfield had four imps, Robin, Jack, William, and

Puppet, two hes and two shes, all like unto black cats. Agnes Heard had six familiars, avices or blackbirds, white speckled and all black.

At a General Gaol Delivery, Essex Summer Sessions, Chelmsford, held in July, 1589, was put in the confession of Joan Prentice of the Almshouse, Sible Hedingham. This witch nourished a familiar "in the shape and proportion of a dunnish-coloured ferret, having fiery eyes". It answered to the name Bidd. Joan Prentice sent Bidd to sour and ruin the beer (then in brewing) of William Adam's wife, causing her great loss and injury, and she also commanded him to torment young Sarah Glascock. The child died in consequence of these devilments and sorceries. Two independent witnesses, Elizabeth Whale, a labourer's wife, and Elizabeth Mott, a cobbler's wife, gave testimony that they had often seen this mischievous ferret-imp, Bidd. Several members of the coven which was brought to light during the famous First Case of the Lancashire Witches (1612) confessed to harbouring and cosseting familiars. Elizabeth Sowtherns, generally known as old Mother Demdike, made a contract with "a spirit or a Devil in the shape of a Boy", whose name was Tibb. Later, "the said Spirit appeared unto her in the likeness of a Brown Dog". She employed him to molest any who fell out with her. Anne Whittle, generally known as old Mother Chattox, had "a thing in the likeness of a spotted Bitch", called Fancy.

When John Law, a pedlar, refused Alizon Device pins from his wares—the pin was then not only a useful but a costly article, especially for country folk to buy (compare the term "pin-money")—the witch became very angry, and set her Spirit at him to cripple "the poor distressed pedlar", who had a paralytic stroke, when "he saw a great Black Dog stand by him, with very fearful fiery eyes, great teeth, and a terrible countenance, looking him in the face". He had been "a very able sufficient stout man of Body, and a goodly man of Stature. But by this Devilish art of *Witchcraft* his head is drawn awry; his eyes and face deformed; his speech not well to be understood; his thighs and legs stark lame; his arms lame, especially the left side; his hands lame and turned out of their course; his body able to endure no travel; and thus remaineth at this present time."

Ellen Green, of Stathorne, Leicester (1619), had two familiars, one in the shape of a kitten called Puss, the other in the shape of a mouldi-warp—a dialect term for a mole—called Hiff, Hiff. They performed ugly tricks at her suggestion, and mortally injured several persons, even causing death. Jane Hott, a widow, of Faversham, Kent, entertained for about twenty years a thing like a hedgehog. Elizabeth Harris, a near neighbour, had a familiar who appeared in the shape of a large mouse. Mother Hott and two other notorious witches of the same infernal sisterhood were hanged at Faversham on Monday, 29 September, 1645.

A pamphlet of 1669, *Hartford-shire Wonder or Strange News from Ware*, tells in plain straightforward language of some very curious happenings which were taking place in the little town of Ware. The narrative, which is related without flourishes or fustian, commends itself as true by its very simplicity. An old man who lived at Ware, a wretch deeply versed (as it proved) in the black art and every foul mystery of the infernal sciences, upon some mischance picked a quarrel with a local wheelwright, one Thomas Stretton, an honest, peaceable fellow. At once the wizard set to work to revenge himself. His wife, in passing Wheeler's cottage, feigning to be very tired and thirsty, asked for a drink, which Wheeler's daughter Jane, who knew nothing of the tiff and was all unsuspecting, very readily and friendlily gave the woman. Shortly afterwards the girl fell sick with strange and sudden fits, although hitherto—she was twenty years old—she had been as healthy and happy as any maid in Hertfordshire. About a week later the woman returned and begged the loan of a pin, which Jane foolishly let her have. The illness increased, and for six months the doctors were sadly put to it to find a name for what was in fact a supernatural affliction. The wizard, whose malice was only whetted rather than satisfied by the mischief he had wrought, then set his familiars to torment even further the poor girl, who was haunted by half-human toads and mice, the evil spirits, so that her life became a very burden. As may be supposed, this business caused a great deal of talk, and not a few shrewd observers detected sorcery. Large numbers of people flocked to see the sufferer, for the most part out of merest curiosity. Many even came out from London, a journey of more than twenty miles. So distressing was the appearance of the invalid, fallen away in the course of a few months from a buxom comely wench with youth, a sweetheart, and all to make her content and gay, to a fevered skeleton tortured by a hacking cough and convulsed with unnatural epilepsies, that the idlest sightseer was lost in amaze and pitiful wonderment, whilst the sceptics and those who had disbelieved in the power and reality of witchcraft went back home convinced of their errors. This, which is fully attested, was in the days of Barrow, Isaac Newton, and Robert Boyle; of Etherege, Rochester, and Wycherley; of Evelyn and Pepys.

To come down to our own days, a resident of Horseheath, a village about fourteen miles from Cambridge, gave the following details of the sorceries of Mother Redcap, a local witch who died in 1926. "One day a black man called, produced a book and asked her to sign her name in it. The woman signed the book, and the mysterious stranger then told her she would be the mistress of five imps who would carry out her orders. Shortly afterwards the woman was seen out accompanied by a rat, a cat, a toad, a ferret, and a mouse. Everybody believed she was a witch, and many people visited her to obtain cures" (the *Sunday Chronicle*, 9 September, 1928).

It should be remarked that witches often keep some small animal, which they feed upon a particular diet, in order to assist them in their fortune-telling and divinations. No doubt these animals are tamed and taught tricks, which wonderfully impress the clients of the sorceress, those curious inquirers into the future who are willing to run sad, perilous risks to learn what is to come of weal or woe. The exact methods of this particular form of augury, which is very ancient, differ widely and cannot be precisely understood by any not initiated into the secrets of the mysterious society.

We learn from many passages in Latin and Greek authors that the wizard priests and priestesses who delivered the oracles of the gods were wont to divine by the aid of animals whose gait and actions they carefully observed, thence deriving their prognostications. These occult sciences were technically known by many names, such, for example, as Myomancy, divination by mice; Orniscopy, by birds; Ophiomancy, by fishes; Alectryomancy or Alectoromancy, by the manner in which a cock would pick up scattered grains. With anxious eyes the Roman auspex would watch the flight of birds across the cloudless sky; with keenest ear he would listen to the gentle cooing of the doves in their cote, or mark the harsh caw of the raven from the bough. There is truth in Southey's lines—and indeed they do no more than exactly paraphrase the very words of Matthew of Westminster—with which commences his ballad, "The Old Woman of Berkeley":

> The Raven croak'd as she sate at her meal,
> And the Old Woman knew what he said,
> And she grew pale at the Raven's tale,
> And sicken'd and went to her bed.

In his *Gypsy Sorcery and Fortune Telling* (1891) Charles Godfrey Leland says: "If you are a gypsy and have a tame toad it is a great assistance in telling fortunes, and brings luck." He also remarks: "The reader has often seen in London Italian women who have small birds, generally parrakeets or paraquitos, which will for a penny pick out for her or for him slips of paper on which is printed a 'fortune'." I can very well remember formerly to have noticed these amateur *Streghe*, so to speak, and their trained birds, paraquitos or yellow canaries, deftly picking out with their tiny beaks little billets from a heap; but of recent years these women, in their gaily striped petticoats and bodices, all adorned with mosaic jewellery, the white linen *cuffia* on their heads, their ears weighed down with heavy silver rings, veritable contandine of the operatic stage from the chorus of *Masaniello* or *L'Elisire d'Amore*, are no longer met with, and their picturesqueness seems completely to have disappeared. The fortune-telling was, of course, nothing more than a pretty pastime, and nobody took it as other than a jest, but none the less it was some far-off memory of the older traditional method which has persisted from time immemorial.

In France the familiar, *esprit familier*, was known by many names. This spirit was termed *esprit servant; ennemi familier, follaton* or *foulaton*, who generally appeared as a woman; *diable familier; mandragore; esprit de python*, "*pytho*" being the Latin for a familiar, or the demon possessing a soothsayer. In England familiars had the most grotesque names: Inges, Tewhit, Jarmara, Great Tom Twite, Jeso, Prickear, "Elemauzer, Pye-wacket, Peck in the Crown, Griezel Greedigut, which no mortal could invent", and many more. In France we find equally monstrous nomenclature: Carabin, Sulpy, Volan, Murguet, Rapha, Phrin, Rago, Piépla, Piquemouche, which is nothing else than another title for Beelzebub, Baal-zebub, the lord of flies, who was consulted by wicked King Ahaziah, *II Kings* i, 2–16.

A familiar, as has been remarked, was generally awarded to a witch upon the signing of the infernal pact, as a kind of gift from the Devil, but familiars could also be acquired in other ways. A familiar was in some mysterious way attached to the Château de Vauxmarcus, Béroche, Neuchâtel, and would serve any of the seigneurs de Vauxmarcus who dared to enter into an agreement with and bind themselves to this demon. Elizabeth Frauncis at her trial in July, 1566, confessed that she had been taught witchcraft at twelve years of age by her grandmother, Mother Eve, of Hatfield Peverel, a notorious witch, who presented her with a familiar in the shape of a white-spotted cat, Satan. After sixteen years she in her turn gave the cat Satan to the widow Waterhouse, a sister witch of Hatfield Peverel. In 1582 Margery Sammon, of the St. Osyth coven, when examined before Justice Brian Darcy, acknowledged she had two astral spirits which she had from her mother. When Ursula Kemp was apprehended, Margery Sammon hastily sent off her imps to Mother Pechey, an old sorceress who lived in a cottage hard by her own dwelling. Curiously enough, there is evidence that the familiar could be bought for money, small enough sums in specie perhaps, but, it is to be feared, in reality at a fearful price. A witch of Neuchâtel, Clauda Brunyé, bought a familiar named Cajy from a warlock, a valet of Captain Frölicher. For two ducats Jean Berger purchased the services of a familiar from a wandering astrologer and necromant, Zimerlé. In 1627 Jean-Jacques Bovet bought a *diable familier* at Lyons from the Grand Master of a witch society, whose rendezvous was in that city. These were all imps of the lowest kind, and the purchase was in fact symbolical. In the Suffolk trials of 1645 Mary Smith, of Glemham, confessed that he had received several imps from the demon, after she and her sister, Anne, solemnly covenanted with the darker power, and of these puckrils she sold two, which were employed in harming persons and killing cattle.

The familiar could also be obtained by certain magical ceremonies, a ritual of the most awesome blasphemy involving the desecration of the Host or Sacramental Bread, which appalling profanity seems to have been in some evilly mysterious way a handsel to confirm and ensure the readier and more willing services of the familiar. The words of Berthold von Regensburg (Ratisbon) are as true today as ever they were seven hundred years ago, when he spoke in his sermon of those "who do witchcraft with God's Body, that is the greatest of all sins that can be committed in the whole world". Not long before, Giraldus Cambrensis (Gerald of Wales), who lived *circa* 1146–*circa* 1220, in his work entitled *Gemma Ecclesiastica* has an emphatic warning to priests against allowing the Host to fall into the hands of sorcerers. Witches were always eager to purloin the Host, or to purchase it from abandoned wretches who pursued the horrid practice of making sacrilegious communions with that design. "This woman works magic spells with herbs," cries Berthold, "that woman with the holy oil of chrism, another woman with God's Holy Body. Out on it! No Jew would act thus, nay, no heathen . . . magic, magic, everywhere!"

The Host is often stolen by witches and horribly profaned, as there will be occasion to notice later when speaking of the Devil's Eucharist, the hideous black mass. It is also foully desecrated by being abused in dark ensorcelments of nearly every kind. Thus love-charms are confected with the Host, as the most powerful of all, which indeed it manifestly is. Paolo Grillando, of Castiglione Fiorentino, a learned lawyer and judge of the diocese of Arezzo, in Tuscany, who about the year 1525 published an important treatise dealing with sorceries, goety, divinations, and the arcana of witchcraft, writes: "In these love-potions and aids to venery there is oftenest some commixture of the Sacraments of Holy Church, ay, even of the consecrated Host." He relates in detail the cases —not a few—which have come before him of sorcerers, who gained an ample livelihood by peddling love-philtres and obscene amulets. In well-nigh every instance of this kind of charm the Host had been stolen or procured by bad means, and, generally broken up small or powdered, had been given mingled with meat or drink. Thus on one occasion Grillando was concerned in the prosecution of a cleric, a member of a religious Order, who, after certain black impieties, himself consumed a part of the Host, reducing the moiety to powder, which he sent to a courtesan with whom he was madly infatuated, that she might swallow it sprinkled over her food or in a draught of wine. A not dissimilar case occurred in Rome, where, hidden away in the secret coffers of a witch, were found two Hosts, both scrawled over with mysterious characters in blood. These, she confessed, she kept to send on to a loose woman, with whom a certain lordling was in love. The man had paid a considerable sum for this to be done, as he was persuaded the spell so wrought would keep his mistress faithful to him. In the *Malleus Maleficarum* it is clearly proved that "witches can infect the minds of men with an inordinate love of strange women" (Part I, Question 7; English translation, p. 51). Again, in Part II, Question I, Chapter 5 (English translation, pp. 114-17), it is shown how "Witches commonly perform their spells through the Sacraments of the Church", and why. Witches nearly always make their instruments of witchcraft by means of the Sacraments or sacramental things of the Church. A case came to light of a sorceress who, it was noticed, each time she received Holy Communion, suddenly lowered her head. She played this trick that she might the more easily and without being seen take the Body of the Lord out of her mouth by putting up her handkerchief. She then carried It home and placed It in a pot in which there was a toad, and hid It thus in the ground near her house. In the pot were also discovered a number of other things by means of which she worked her spells. A Jesuit father, C. G. Rosignoli, whose *The Wonders of God Wrought in the Blessed Sacrament* was published at Venice in 1717, mentions a Portuguese lady who used the Host as an aphrodisiac.

There were many other terrible profanations. A piece of the Host was even employed to obtain victory in a cock-fight (*The Reliquary and Illustrated Archaeologist*, II, 158, 1890). Certain lewd women at Rome were wont to smear their lips with the Baptismal Chrism in order to make their kisses the sweeter. It is on record that in the year 1460 a French priest was so maddened and devil-rid by hate of a man from whom he had received some injury that, following the advice of a witch, he solemnly baptized a toad, nourished it daily with the Host from the altar, and allowed the woman to employ it in some terribly mysterious way to destroy his personal enemy.

A bitter blasphemy is the "Reversed Journey", which is thus explained by Dr. Hyde, the Irish scholar: "This is the way in which the 'Reversed Journey' is carried out. A person is to go to Chapel, and then to make the 'Journey', i.e. the Stations of the Cross, backwards: that is, to begin the 'Journey' at the last picture, xiv, and to finish at the first— all the time invoking the Devil, and asking him to send misfortunes and bad luck upon the hated enemy." This ban is, of course, sheer witchcraft.

Grillando mentions the sprinkling of holy water to baptize the wax images so essential in certain deadly forms of black magic, and early in the thirteenth century Richard, Bishop of Durham, issued orders that all fonts in churches should be kept fastened securely and locked down on account of the sacred lymph of baptism being so constantly stolen to mix and mingle with poisonous potions brewed in midnight cauldrons. All these evil practices persist today.

By a strange abuse the Sacraments and Sacramentals (observances and things analogous to a Sacrament, such as holy water, chrism, blessed salt and tapers, and the like) are superstitiously regarded as healing charms, an abuse, however, which has a very solid foundation in fact and experience. Extremes meet indeed, for none will deny that the Blessed Sacrament is truly a Medicine. So also—in a lesser degree, of course—is the Oil of Holy Unction. The rubrics themselves emphasize this aspect: "The Sacrament of Extreme Unction was instituted by Christ as a Heavenly Medicine, not a ghostly healing alone, but also to be a physical cure."

The ancient lore of leechdom prescribes many a traditional remedy which prevails in our villages and among country folk today. Who is to say that there is not timeless knowledge and deep wisdom embodied in this pharmacy? This healing art is still known in some rural districts as tying or casting "the aaba knot" or "the wrestin teed". Thus, "wrestin" toothache or ringworm is spoken of, and in parts of Wales and Gloucestershire the water of baptism is regarded as an unfailing cure for toothache. For general debility and anaemia the eucharistic wine after consecration (but how can it be had?) is considered a certain specific. Mr. Albert Way, writing in *Notes and Queries* (First Series, Vol. III, p. 179, 1851), says: "In a remote hamlet of Surrey I recently heard the following superstition. In a very sickly family, of which the children were troubled with bad fits, and the poor mother herself is almost half-witted, an infant newly born seemed to be in a very weakly and unnatural state. One of the gossips from the neighbouring cottages coming in, with a mysterious look said, 'Sure, the babby wanted *something*—a drop of the sacrament wine would do it good.' On surprise being expressed at such a notion, she added, 'Oh! they often gives it.' " A correspondent, living in Kerry, further added: "In Ireland a weakly child is frequently brought to the altar rails, and the priest celebrating Mass is requested to allow it to drink from the chalice the ablution, that is, the wine and water with which the chalice is purified after the priest has made his communion, and which ablution ordinarily is taken by the priest. *Here* the efficacy is ascribed to the chalice having just before contained the Blood of Our Lord. I have heard it recommended in a case of hooping-cough." I have given the exact tenor of this communication, but surely the child was not permitted to consume the actual ablutions. I think wine and water were probably poured into the chalice after Mass, and the invalid then given to drink, but not of the actual ablution. This is borne out by a Yorkshire custom of which we have a record from a local antiquarian scholar writing in 1851. He tells us: "In one of the principal towns of Yorkshire, half a century ago, it was the practice for persons in a respectable class of life to take their children, when afflicted with the hooping cough, to a neighbouring convent, where the priest allowed them to drink a small quantity of holy water out of a silver chalice, which the little sufferers were strictly forbidden to touch. By Protestant, as well as Roman Catholic parents, this was regarded as a remedy." In Henry VIII's time, in 1538, there was an inquiry and a good deal of upset at Rye because "the curate, as a witch, gave Hamper's child drink three times of the chalice for the chyne cough". Chincough is still the name for hooping-cough in some rural parts. Truculent old John Bale denounced "their sipping cups for the hiccough".

In Devonshire scrapings of lead from a church window are a valuable amulet, but, as some say, the slivers of plumb-foil must be stolen unobserved during service time. On 2 February, 1835, a resident at Tavistock wrote as follows to the vicar: "Rev. Sir, I should take it as a great favour if your Honour would be good enough to let me have the key of the churchyard to-night, to go in at twelve o'clock, to cut off three bits of lead about the size of a half farthing; each from three different shuts [spouts], for the cure of fits. Sir, I remain your humbled obedient servant. J. M." A correspondent, H. G. T., in *Notes and Queries* (First Series, Vol. III, pp. 258–9, 1851), said that a Launceston man related how his father went into Lydford Church, at twelve o'clock at night, and cut off some lead from every diamond pane in the windows; with which he made a heart-shaped ornament to be worn by his wife afflicted with breastills, which is the country name for sore breasts. In the neighbourhood of Whitby the rain which ran off the roof of a church during a heavy shower was eagerly collected in pails and pipkins and drunk as an excellent physic. In Shropshire, grease from the church bells cured ringworm and other complaints. In some parts moss and lichen from a churchyard cross are wrought into a plaster of the greatest healing power.

A Devonshire charm to cure fits was "Go into a church at midnight and walk three times round the communion table." "This was done in this parish a few years since," notes a Launceston resident, writing in 1851. In *The Tamar and the Tavy*, 1836, Vol. II, p. 291, Mrs. Bray remarks that "the very old custom of going into the church at night whilst the chimes are playing twelve o'clock, in order to creep three times under the communion table to be cured of fits, is still held in repute. The present sexton, Mr. James Cole, has been applied to in such cases to unlock the church door." Chime-hours have a mystical significance, and in Somerset we say: "A child born in chime-hours will have the power to see spirits." This is referred to in Harris' *East-ho!* (1902): "I wor born in the chime-hours and can see what other folks can't see, leastways, so they tell me." Mr. G. E. Dartnell, of Salisbury, in a letter, 1905, wrote: "Some thirty years ago I remember remarking to a Somersetshire person how beautifully the church bells were being chimed, and getting an indignant reply to the effect that the ringers ought to be ashamed of themselves, as it wasn't one of the proper chiming hours!"

In Anglo-Saxon days women in some villages were wont to pass their children through the earth at the cross-roads, a supersitition justly stigmatized as "devil's craft" and on a par with healing "by any sorcery". Whether it is lawful to remove sickness cast by a spell through the means of a counter-spell is much debated. Some authorities, including Albertus Magnus, say that it is never lawful to remove even witchcraft by having recourse to further witchcraft or any other forbidden means. Other authorities, including Duns Scotus, say that it is lawful always to destroy the works of the devil, since he who does so cannot be an accessary to such works. Perhaps it is better to distinguish, and to say that it is in itself lawful to remove sickness and seek for health, which is manifestly a good thing, yet not by means which are essentially unlawful and evil, as, for example, would be any kind of consenting to or co-operation with a demon or familiar spirit, yet by means of observances or ceremonies which are, it may be, superstitious and vain, but which are not demonstrably unlawful, and in which no open or tacit invocation of evil spirits is used. The whole question is argued at length in the *Malleus Maleficarum*, Part II, Question 2 (English translation, pp. 155–64). With regard to the ancient rites of creeping through the cleft ash tree, or under the tolmen, the Cornish "hole of stone", in order to be cured of various disorders, these observances may be allowable if they are not inquinated by some accident or circumstances, as may prove the case. The ash, "for nothing ill", as Spenser describes it, and the rowan tree are lucky. The old rhyme runs:

> Rowan, ash, and red thread
> Keep the devils frae their speed.

"The reason for giving ash sap to new-born children in the Highlands of Scotland is, first, because it acts as a powerful astringent, and, secondly, because the ash, in common with the rowan, is supposed to possess the property of resisting the attacks of witches, fairies, and other imps of darkness." In Cornwall until recent years, and perhaps the practice is not unknown today, children affected with a rupture were passed through a slit in an ash before sunrise fasting; after which the slit portions were bound together, and as they unite the malady heals. Countrymen carry a splinter of ash to protect themselves against ill-wish, or as a grand specific for rheumatism. About five miles from Penryn, in Cornwall, formerly stood the Tolmen, resting upon two stones deeply sunk into the ground, and so placed that a man could crawl under it. The local belief was that anyone who did this upon certain holy days would obtain immediate relief from any malady or pain. The Tolmen was blown up about forty years ago. There is a Tolmen, a holed stone, in the Vale of

Lamorna, near St. Paul, Mounts Bay; but legend has it that this accursed spot was defiled by human sacrifice, and it would indeed be unfortunate to essay any healing spell in so bloodstained and horribly haunted a place. It is usual when passing under the archway of the Grande Porte at Saint-Malo to salute La Vierge Miraculeuse de la Grande Porte, and here prayers are often made for health. The same courtesy is observed at Vannes, where one of the gates is guarded by a seventeenth-century statue, in painted stone, of St. Vincent Ferrer. At Locronan, in Finistère, the granite tomb of St. Ronan is supported by six angels, and, the mensa or flat slab being raised some little way from the pavement, it is customary for sufferers to creep through the intervening space, since it is traditionally believed that cures will be effected by this devotion. An even more famous shrine in Brittany is the fifteenth-century tomb of Saint Yves at Minihy Tréguier. There is a narrow passage or interstice penetrating the tomb, and pilgrims crawl through this on their knees. In the Church of San Eustorgio at Milan is the elaborately decorated tomb-shrine of St. Peter the Dominican, who was martyred in 1252, and the list of whose miracles, wrought after death, fills twenty-two pages in the huge folio volume of the Bollandist *Acts of the Saints*, which calendars his name. The "ark", as it is technically called, which contains the body of the Saint, is exquisitely sculptured with appropriate scenes from St. Peter's life, and is supported by eight tall marble figures of great majesty. It is a pious and time-old custom for worshippers to pass between these statue-pillars, and on the Feast Day, 29 April, the church is thronged for this touching ceremony, in which I have been privileged to take part. It is very plain then that under certain conditions, and rightly done, the creeping through or passing under some hallowed shrine is not merely legitimate, but meritorious, and there is no reason why in its far lesser degree the observance connected with the ash tree, or even the holed stone, should not be tolerated.

It must be emphasized, however, that these simple ceremonies are altogether different from midnight visits to a church, although a communion table replace an altar, and these strange stealthy rituals are equivocal, to say the least. Even so, they may have no connexion with magic, and are very far removed indeed from such horrid practices as the abuse of Sacramentals, or, more hideous still, the profanation of the Host.

This particular blasphemy was most strictly inquired into during the witch trials at Neuchâtel in 1481. Jehanneret Regnal-le-Boiteux, a warlock of thirty years' continuance, when questioned whether he had ever abused the Sacrament, confessed how at Easter, two years previously, when receiving Communion in his parish church, he had not swallowed the Host, but secretly spat It out, and kept It until the following night, when he took It to a rendezvous of witches. Here the Host was cast into a blazing fire. Among those present on this occasion was one Pierre Croschard, who, upon being interrogated, said that he had never carried the Host to any meeting of the coven, but that nine years before, on a Holy Saturday, when feigning to make his Easter Communion, he had kept the Host in his mouth, and after ejecting It he had given It to Margot Tofle, a fearful beldame living at Couvet. When he asked her why she wanted It—for she had repeatedly plagued him to bring her the Host—she replied that she was going to knead It into the witches' flying ointment. Rollet Croschet, who had made a pact with the demon more than forty years before, had pretended to make his Easter Communion four years previously, but he had removed the Host from his mouth and concealed It until he took It to a Sabbat which was held in the Jewish cemetery. The Host was thrown to a dog—no ordinary animal, but a black ravening hound of hell. Precisely the same horrors were enacted at the Sabbats presided over by Louis Gaufridi, executed in 1611, who was known as Prince of Sorcerers. During the most infamous conjurations the stolen Host was often thrown to a hungry dog, whilst the abandoned wretches who were members of his witch society vied in bawdy and blasphemy.

Not many years ago in parts of Lincolnshire young maids were warned that if, when they make their first communion, they allowed themselves to be persuaded to keep half of the Bread in their mouths, they will become witches, and indeed there is some truth in the belief. There have been recent instances where old hags, learned in Satan's lore, have approached girls and endeavoured to bribe them to retain at least a part of the Bread they receive at the altar-rails. In the same county it is firmly believed that if a woman keeps the Communion Bread in her mouth and feeds with it the toad which she will find squatting in the churchyard, the man she desires for a husband will marry her. But at what a peril, what a cost! In Berkshire they hold that this desecration enables the woman to become a witch, since the toad is a demon. Leland writes: "Many gypsies have a superstitious belief in the efficacy of the sacramental bread and wine and there are many instances of their stealing them for magical purposes." A Manx "Obbery"—that is to say, a piece of witchcraft—is "Bringing home some of the Sacramental Bread and crumbling it, when a huge black stag-beetle will come and eat it".

The history of witchcraft amply bears out, and indeed proves beyond question, how right are these old traditions, the wisdom of generations. For example, we find that in 1582, a Sussex woman, the wife of one Edward Jones, was summoned before the Ecclesiastical Courts to prove to the satisfaction of the Archdeacon of Lewes "that she did eat the Communion Bread and put it not in her glove".

During the trial of the famous Lancashire witches, the first case in August, 1612, James Device confessed that "upon Sheare Thursday was two years" (Maundy Thursday, 1610) "his grandmother, Elizabeth Sothernes, alias Dembdike"—old Mother Demdike—"a general agent for the Devil" throughout the whole district—bade him go to the church to receive the Communion (the next day after being Good Friday) and then not to eat the Bread the Minister gave him, but to bring it and deliver it to such a thing as should meet him in his way homewards. Notwithstanding her persuasions, he did eat the Bread, and so as he was going back home and was about a couple of hundred yards away from the church door, there met him "a thing in the shape of a Hare", who accosted him and asked if he had brought the Bread as his grandmother had told him to do. When he answered that he certainly had not, the thing threatened to tear him to pieces. Trembling from head to foot, he "thereupon marked himself to God"—made the sign of the Cross— and the thing in a fury vanished out of his sight.

J. Ceredig Davies in his *Welsh Folklore* relates how "sometime in the beginning of the last century (about 1810), two old dames attended the morning service at Llanddewi Brefi Church, and partook of the Holy Communion; but instead of eating the sacred bread like other communicants, they kept it in their mouths and went out. Then they walked round the church outside nine times, and at the ninth time the Evil One came out from the church wall in the form of a frog, to whom they gave the bread from their mouths, and by doing this wicked thing they were supposed to be selling themselves to Satan and become witches. . . . There was an old man in North Pembrokeshire, who used to say that he obtained the power of bewitching in the following manner: The bread of his first Communion he pocketed. He made pretence at eating it first of all, and then put it in his pocket. When he went out from the service there was, meeting him by the gate, a dog, to which he gave the bread, thus selling his soul to the Devil. Ever after, he possessed the power to bewitch."

When the well-known spiritualistic medium, David Dunglas Home (1833–1886) was visiting Florence, a rumour spread that "he was a necromancer who administered the Sacraments of the Church to toads in order to raise the dead by spells and incantations". It is said that his life was attempted in consequence.

Mr. W. H. Gamlen, of Bramford Spoke, Exeter, in July, 1873, read at Sidmouth a paper, which, on account of its exceptional interest, was afterwards printed in the *Transactions of the Devonshire Association*. Mr. Gamlen exhibited and discussed a talisman of mickle might, the toadstone. This name is generally taken to denote any one of various stones from several origins likened in colour or in shape to a toad. The most-sought-for kind was that supposed actually to be found in the head of a toad, to which the Banished Duke makes reference in a very familiar passage from *As You Like It*, II, i, 13–14:

> the Toad, ugly and venomous,
> Wears yet a precious Jewel in his Head.

Toadstones were often worn as charms or ornaments, or set in rings. The specimen exhibited by Mr. Gamlen had belonged to a Mr. Blagdon, of Puddington, a village not a great way from Tiverton. To Puddington there resorted a constant stream of visitors from far and near, from every quarter of Devon, and even from Somerset and Dorset. The object was to borrow from Mr. Blagdon, paying him no inconsiderable fee for the loan of his property, the toadstone, since it was held to be an infallible remedy in the case of maladies which presumably baffled the doctors' skill, and which accordingly must (it was argued) have been caused by overlooking or the malice of witchcraft. In order to afflict poor folk with these illnesses the witch must have obtained power from the devil to do mischief. "The person to obtain the power must be a communicant of the Church of England or Rome", and the latter could be far more injurious than the former. "The power was said to be obtained by keeping such a portion of the elements on receiving the Sacrament, and, after carrying them round the church and using certain incantations, giving them to a toad met with in the churchyard."

Sir Walter Scott, in a letter, 4 April, 1812, to Joanna Baillie, says that among the family's most curious possessions was "a toadstone—a celebrated amulet. . . . It was sovereign for protecting new-born children and their mothers from the power of the fairies, and has been repeatedly borrowed from my mother, on account of this virtue."

The famous statute of 1604, I Jas. I, which remained in force until 1736, Stat. 9, Geo. II. c.v., whilst in the main following that of Elizabeth, passed by the House of Lords on 13 March, and by the Commons on 19 March, 1563, inserts a new clause making it felony to "consult, covenant with, entertain, employ, feed, or reward" any spirit for any purpose whatsoever. Incidentally, it should be observed that the new act did no more than the former in decreeing death on the gallows as the punishment for any invocation or conjuration of evil spirits, regardless of the outcome of such enchantery, which is to say even if the intent were alleged to be for healing or countercharming under the specious nomenclature of "white magic".

The jurists and legal writers naturally have much to say in explanation of and commentary upon this new clause. To sum it up briefly, we can hardly do better than follow a high authority, Michael Dalton, whose *The Country Justice*, first published in 1618, ran into edition after edition until the middle of the eighteenth century, and was long accepted as the ultimate and indispensable manual of nomography. Dalton thus presents and lends the weight of his learning, experience, and judgement to the articles set out in the Rev. Richard Bernard's *Guide to Grand Jurymen*, 1627, touching the means of discovery of witches, and the official procedure to be followed in the trials of such offenders. Dalton sets out how—"Firstly: Witches have ordinarily a familiar or spirit, who appeareth to them; sometimes in one shape, sometimes in another, such as in the likeness of a man, woman, boy, dog, cat, foal, fowl, hare, rat, toad, and many more curious guises. And to these spirits the witches give names, and they all meet together to christen them . . . if the good word may thus be reverently used. Secondly: Their said familiar hath some big, as it were, or little teat upon their body, and in some secret place, where he sucketh them. And besides their sucking, the Devil leaveth other marks upon their body, sometimes like a blue spot or red spot, like a flea-biting; sometimes the flesh sunk in and hollow (all which for a time may be covered, yea taken away, but will come again to their old form). And these the Devil's marks be insensible, and being pricked will not bleed, and be often in their secretest parts, and therefore require diligent and careful search."

These first two are capital points to discover and convict witches; for they prove beyond all question that these witches have a familiar whom they entertain, feed, and reward, contrary to the statute, and these witches have, moreover, made a league, covenant, and compact with the Devil.

The big—more correctly, perhaps, written "bigge" (an old word, now obsolete except in dialect, Lancashire and Essex)—or little teat upon the witch's body was generally found to secrete milk, which nourished the familiar, and this was quite justly regarded as an unmistakable, and indeed infallible, sign of the practice of witchcraft. Allusions to this phenomenon are extremely frequent in the records of English trials, and it must be carefully distinguished from the Devil's mark, "those imprest Marks", insensible spots, to be considered separately in the following chapter. There seems to be this confusion in W. Carew Hazlitt's *Faiths and Folklore*, 1905, Vol. II, p. 657, when without comment he takes the following from Bell, a MS. "History of Witchcraft", 1705: "This mark is sometimes like a little teat, sometimes like a blueish spot; and I myself have seen it in the body of a confessing witch, like a little powder-mark of a blue colour, somewhat hard, and withal insensible, so as it did not bleed when I pricked it." It may be noticed how Bishop Francis Hutchinson is nonplussed and foundered when he tries to find a natural explanation for these "*Teats* and *Magical Signs*, as they call them; and insensible Parts that are found upon" witches—*An Historical Essay concerning Witchcraft*, Second Edition, 1720, Chapter xi, pp. 171–81.

In 1596, when, by order of the magistrates, Elizabeth Wright, of Stapenhill, Burton-on-Trent, was searched, following upon an accusation of witchcraft, there was found "beneath her right shoulder a thing much like the udder of a ewe that giveth suck with two teats". Old Mother Wright, a fearful beldame of more than eighty, had long been defamed for her foul sorceries, and had more than once been before Justice Graysley upon strong suspicion of entertaining a familiar and other devilish malpractices. She was, indeed, known throughout the whole countryside as the "old Witch of Stapenhill'. At the trial of the Lancashire witches in 1634 (the second case) many of the accused, upon being searched, were discovered to have supernumerary paps or nipples, generally in the most private parts of their bodies. Such, for example were traced upon the bodies of Jennet Hargrave; Jennet Loynd; Harsley's wife; Jennet Device, old Mother Demdike's granddaughter; Mary Spencer, a witch's daughter; Jennet Wilkinson; Mary Ainsworth; Isabel Hargrave; whilst Margaret Johnson, a widow woman, confessed that she suckled a familiar. At the Essex Summer Sessions in 1645 precisely similar and detailed evidence was given as regards no less than twenty out of the thirty-six witches who were arraigned, and of whom nineteen were hanged, whilst four died in gaol. In January, 1655, a Yorkshire witch, Katherine Earle, of Rhodes, in Rothwell parish, West Riding, a labourer's wife, was examined on charges of having killed by a spell Mr. Frank; of killing a mare belonging to Henry Hatfield, striking the man himself with sharp pains, and so wasting him that he "dwindled, peaked and pined" for six good months. "And the said Katherine hath been searched, and a mark found upon her in the likeness of a pap." Nine years later, another Yorkshire witch, Alice Huson, a widow of Burton Agnes, a village near Great Driffield, a sorceress of most evil repute, upon her trial at York in

July confessed that she had "a witch-pap, which was sucked by the Unclean Spirit, the sucking lasting from supper-time till after cock-crowing". Bishop Hutchinson notes in his *Historical Essay*, as quoted above, pp. 60-1, that in 1694 "*Margaret Elnore* was tried at *Ipswich* before the Lord Chief Justice Holt. . . . Witnesses gave Account that her Grandmother, and her Aunt had formerly been hanged for Witches, and that her Grandmother had said, she had eight or nine Imps, and that she had given two or three Imps a-piece to her children. Others gave an Account of a Tet in her secret Parts. A Midwife who had search'd her Grandmother who had hanged, said, this Woman had plainer Marks than she." A very great many more examples might be cited from the English trials. No doubt a number of these are to be explained by the cases of polymastia and polythelia (supernumerary nipples), of which there occur continual records in recent medical works. It is freely admitted that these anatomical divagations are commoner than is generally supposed; doubtless, too, there is exaggeration in many of the inexactly observed seventeenth-century narratives. However, it must be emphasized that when every fullest allowance is made in respect of error and careless or ignorant examinations, the undoubted facts which remain—and the details are very ample—cannot be accounted for by physical peculiarities and malformations.

In Thomas Middleton's tragi-comedy, *The Witch*, when a Spirit like a cat descends to Hecate, a voice from above chants:

> There's one comes down to fetch his dues,
> A kiss, a coll, a sip of blood.

A coll is a fond embrace, a clinging round the neck of anyone. Blood is the vital stream. "The life of the flesh is in the blood", we are told in *Leviticus* xvii, 11, and in blood is some psychic personality, some spiritual copula or link. It is this truth which underlies the solemn sanctity of the blood covenant, most ancient and most inviolable of all human pledges between man and man.

Evil spirits are powerfully attracted by the smell of freshly spilled blood. It is popularly believed that, as so elaborately prescribed in the ritual laws of *Exodus* and the *Levitical* code, incense was burned by Aaron and his line to cleanse the air from the fetid stench of sacrificial blood. But there is a deeper meaning, a reason more mystical and profound. The new-shed blood would haply attract demons who greedily snuff up and batten upon the reek of gore. The pervading perfume of incense would drive them afar, and the sweet smoke would be a barrier and a ward. When, after the rebellion of Korah, a fierce plague broke out among the people, Aaron took a censer and put on incense and ran in the midst of the congregation, and the plague was stayed, since the demons who were spreading the disease had been put to flight by the fume of frankincense. So we burn incense today, a fragrance beloved of bright angels. It was at the hour of the burning of incense that old Zachary saw "on the right side of the altar of incense" the glorious vision who proclaimed: "I am Gabriel, that stand in the presence of God."

Henry Hallywell, who had been a Fellow of Christ's, Cambridge,

THE TRANSVECTION OF WITCHES

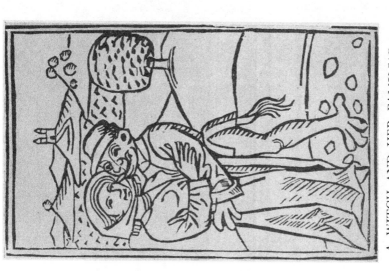

A WITCH AND HER FAMILIAR

THE DEPARTURE FOR THE SABBAT

in his *Melampronoea: or A Discourse of the Polity and Kingdom of Darkness: Together with a Solution of the Chiefest Objections brought against the Being of Witches*, 1681, p. 100, suggests that demons may enter into animals because they are eager for bodily warmth, and furthermore to acquire some species of corporeity, and since they are ever athirst for and delight in the smell of blood, they are the readier, in return for this kind of sensual gratification, to render service to the person who is willing to nourish them with blood. We know (*St. Luke* viii, 26–40) how a legion of devils, when the man of Gadara whom they possessed was freed from their thrall, begged to be allowed to enter into a herd of swine rather than to be cast out into the deep, and in view of this what Hallywell says seems very probable; at the same time it must be remembered that when familiars assume the tangible form of or enter into an actual animal they are by this very process no longer "perfectly *abstract* from all *body* and *matter*", wherefore the natural needs of the animal would persist, and hence it would require to be fed in the ordinary way as well as pampered with the sips of human blood which it drew from the body of the witch by whom it was employed. Frequently this gift of blood was granted to it as a sort of incitement or encouragement before the commission of some exceptionally atrocious piece of mischief upon which it was bound, or else as a reward for a wicked piece of work thoroughly done. George Giffard, the well-known minister of Maldon, Essex, says: "The witches have their spirits, some have one, some have more, as two, three, four, or five, some in one likeness, and some in another, as like cats, weasels, toads, or mice, whom they nourish with milk or with a chicken, or by letting them suck now and then a drop of blood." An ex-schoolmaster, John Steward, who in 1510 was living at Knaresborough, Yorkshire, and who had long been pretty well known as a diviner and a figure-caster, got mixed up in a case of treasure-trove which caused great scandal, and which certainly seems to have been a slippery enough business from first to last. The event proved that, with certain of his clientèle, he found himself haled before the Archbishop's Court on multiplied charges of sorcery, and prosecuted with some vigour by the Vicar-General. He at once shamelessly avowed that he was a mere impostor and charlatan, but none the less Sir Thomas Spurret, who appears to have consulted him on occasion, declared "that he saw Steward have 3 humble bees, or like humble bees, and kept them under a stone in the earth, and called them out by one and one, and gave each one of them a drop of blood of his finger". Nor was Steward's mock confession of jugglery and sham quite so easily believed as he would have liked it to be. The assessors were too shrewd for that; they knew him to be a witch, and although he could congratulate himself, perhaps, that he escaped a severer sentence, on 11 June, 1510, his judges formally excommunicated him as a notoriously defamed person, and he was publicly penanced into the bargain. Susanna Smith, of Rushmere, a Suffolk witch, at her trial in 1645, confessed that she entertained an evil spirit in the form of a black bee. A true bill was found. In 1617 Barbely Morel, a witch of Neuchâtel, was attended by a familiar who appeared as a large buzzing wasp with a deadly sting.

When Elizabeth, wife of Christopher Frauncis, a yeoman, was arraigned at the Essex Summer Sessions, held at Chelmsford, July, 1566, the very ample confession which she had made before Doctor Cole and Master Foscue was put in and allowed by the Judges. She avowed that at twelve years old she was trained in the art of witchcraft by her grandmother, Mother Eve, of Hatfield Peverel. This horrible hag made the child renounce God, and counselled her to feed with her blood Satan, as she called the familiar which she delivered to her in the likeness of a white-spotted cat. This demon cat she bade her feed with bread and milk, and to keep it in a basket, always being careful to use its proper name, Satan. Every time Elizabeth Frauncis employed the cat to do anything for her he required a drop of blood, which she gave him by pricking herself now in one place, now in another. After fifteen or sixteen years she gave the cat to a sister witch, Mother Waterhouse, her neighbour, telling her how she too must call him Satan, feed him with milk, and reward him with a drop of blood when required.

At the same Sessions was tried for sorcery Agnes Waterhouse, of Hatfield Peverel, a widow, aged sixty-three years. Mother Waterhouse confessed to having received the cat Satan from Elizabeth Frauncis. By his diabolical aid she had wrought terrible mischief among the villagers, injuring them both in body and property. She had bewitched to death William Fynee, and also her own husband. For his labour she gave the familiar a chicken, "which he first required of her and a drop of her blood. And this she gave him at all times when he did anything for her, by pricking her hand or face and putting the blood to his mouth, which he sucked, and forthwith would lie down in his pot again where she kept him." Mother Waterhouse was hanged on the following day. Elizabeth Frauncis escaped with a year's imprisonment, but, after her release continuing her evil career of sorcery, she was at the Chelmsford Lent Sessions, April, 1579, found guilty of killing by her foul arts Mistress Alice Poole, condemned, and hanged.

At the trial of 1566, when the depositions had been read, the Attorney-General, Sir Gilbert Gerard, asked Mother Waterhouse: "When did thy cat suck of thy blood?" "Never," she replied. "No? Let me see," he answered her very doubtingly. Thereupon the gaoler lifted the coif-kerchief on her head, and there were plainly visible several small wounds on her face and one upon her nose. "Then," asked Sir Gilbert very gravely, "in good faith, Agnes, when did he suck of thy blood last?" "By my faith, my lord," stammered the wretched woman, knowing all was discovered, "not this fortnight."

The famous Lancashire witch "of so long continuance", old Mother Demdike, described to Justice Roger Nowell how "a Spirit or Devil in the shape of a Boy" asked if she would give him her soul, and she was well content to let him have it. About six years later, one Sunday morning, when she was in her bedchamber, nursing a little child on her knee, and dozing off, the same Spirit appeared to her in the likeness of a brown dog, forcing himself on her lap to get blood under her left arm, and "the said Devil did get blood under her left arm".

In 1647 a Cambridgeshire witch confessed that she had joined this horrid society more than thirty years before, when the Devil manifested himself to her "in the likeness of a great cat, and demanded of her her blood, which she gave him", the demon sucking it from her body. Nearly twenty years later, Aubrey Grinset, alias Thrower, of Dunwich, a Suffolk witch, "did confess that the Devil . . . Appeareth to her in the form of a blackish Gray Cat or Kitling, that it sucketh of a Tett and hath drawn Blood". This was in 1665.

It does not require much perspicacity, nor is it a strained interpretation, to apply here the words we read in the Book of *Job* : "Her young ones also shall suck up blood."

When Odysseus, under the wrath of the gods, was wandering to and fro, the witch-woman Circe bade him seek counsel from the shade of Tiresias, the master of the seers of old. Needs must he then make his way to the shadowy bourne of the earth, where the realm of Hades lies, the intermediate region of ghosts. To summon these he digs a deep pit into which shall flow the warm blood of sheep he offers to Dis and to the Goddess of Ghosts, Persephone. For sacrifice to the deities of the world below must be directed downwards, as the sacrifices to the deities above are offered upon an altar built high and aspirant, raised upon a foot-pace with mounting steps, and furnished about with gradines. Evoked by his prayers, and scenting the hot reek and fume of new-spilled gore, a crowd of pale silent shadows throng the brink of the trench he has made, but with flashing steel he wards them off, as Circe warned him, until the ghost of Tiresias shall appear. At length the undefined vapoury figure of the prophet hovers near, and Odysseus draws back in order that the phantom may drink. And as it quaffs the sanguine stream the mists disperse and the denser shadows in some mysterious fashion concrete to form a material body clad in the priestly mantle, the head crowned with vervain and bay. So Tiresias gives the hero wise counsel, and further tells him that until they have tasted blood the shades are but simulacra, thin empty air, voiceless save for a low gibbering squeak as of the flinder-mouse or the shrill cicada's cheep. The blood it is which gives them form and voice, some flickering of faint transitory life.

There is an ancient truth, a primitive tradition, underlying Homer's poetic fancy. In the same way as he describes, the witch's familiar, the spirit, is tonicked and refreshed and endowed with a more vigorous corporeity by sips of human blood. This is admirably summed up by Joseph Glanvil when he gives it as his opinion that the sucking of blood "may be onely a *diabolical Sacrament* and *Ceremony* to confirm the *hellish Covenant*" whereby the witches become "*mischievously influential*". Which is indeed, briefly put, the end and aim of all witchcraft—Power and Evil, the cruel tyranny of Evil.

CHAPTER III

Witchcraft at Cambridge and Oxford—The Manichee Sorcerers—Revolutionary Witchcraft—The Witchcraft of the Templars—Witchcraft and Politics.

"Rebellion is as the sin of witchcraft."—*I Samuel* xv, 23.

THROUGHOUT the reign of Elizabeth, the University of Cambridge, which boasted not a few of the most famous scholars of the day, was in high honour and maintained close contact with the leading politicians and great public men. None the less a sense of uneasiness was stirring in those academic halls. It was felt that learning, philosophy, theology, even, and orthodoxism—in spite of the royal rules and regulations—were in the melting-pot. The younger generation was knocking at the door. There burned the fiery spirit of Kit Marlowe, student of dialectic, who had matriculated at Corpus Christi in 1581; a year later, biting bitter Thomas Nashe was at St. John's; that reckless Bohemian, Robert Greene, fresh from his tour in Italy, came up to the same college to proceed M.A. in 1584. In 1589 Francis Ket, a fellow of Marlowe's College, Corpus, was burned at Norwich for holding fantastical opinions which could not be entertained within the pale of the Established Church Elizabeth had so recently founded. In 1593 the Privy Council became unwontedly perturbed at reports of unbridled licence, "headship given to light and wanton companions, fencing and dancing schools crowded, taverns filled with scholars, statutes of founders contemned and broken"—as a particularly shrewd observer remarks—wherefore they directed an official letter to the Vice-Chancellors of the two Universities, bidding them reform the manners and morals of their subjects. Cambridge came in for special animadversion. Common players, it was understood, ordinarily resort to the University of Cambridge to recite interludes and plays, some of these entertainments being full of lewd example, and most of vanity, besides the gathering together of multitudes of people. The Vice-Chancellor was required immediately to put a stop to this by issuing orders that no stage plays were to be performed under any pretext within a radius of five miles of the University. A drastic enforcement of the statutes was counselled.

In spite of all the loose living, the free thought and rationalistic speculations, which were so rife, there stoutly held ground a very strong conservative element. Undergraduates, it must be remembered, were actually bound under all sorts of ordinances and decrees, whilst the breaking of the University laws was pretty severely dealt with by the authorities. Corporal punishment could be administered with unsparing rigour, as many a sizar knew to his cost, and an irksome, shameful imprisonment was by no means a thing of the past.

There were few weightier and soberer influences in Cambridge than William Perkins, Fellow of Christ's College from 1584 to 1594, an uncompromising Puritan minister who had won a universal reputation as a solid theologian. Born in 1558, his life was very nearly coincident with the years of Queen Elizabeth's reign, since he died in 1602. He "was buried with great solemnity at the sole charges of *Christs Colledge*, the University and Town striving which should express more sorrow at his Funeral; Doctor *Montague* Preached his Funeral Sermon upon that Text, *Moses my Servant is dead*". Dr. James Montagu was the first Master of Sidney Sussex College, and afterwards became Bishop of Bath and Wells (1608), whence he was translated to Winchester (1616). Perkins had delivered a series of sermons upon witchcraft to crowded congregations from the pulpit of his own church of St. Andrew, and when he died it was found these were arranged by him to be published under the title *A Discourse of the Damned Art of Witchcraft*. With a stately Dedication to my Lord Coke, this book was issued in 1608, *Printed by Cantrell Legge, Printer to the Universitie of Cambridge*. In the folio Collected Works of William Perkins "A Discourse of the Damned Art of Witchcraft; so far forth as is revealed in the Scriptures, and manifest by True Experience, framed and delivered . . . in his Ordinary Course of Preaching" occupies 54 pages, and is equipped with a separate title-page.

It has not untruly been said that "Perkins was a vital force in forming English opinion whilst he was alive". There can, I think, be little doubt that this special course of Sermons was preached—inspired in the first place by some vivid rumours of witchcraft and meddling with magic among the Cambridge men, dons and undergraduates, which had come to his ears. The whole thing was kept very secret, and details have not yet been traced. That Cambridge was the headquarters of a witch society hardly admits of question. Half a century later it was discovered that the witchcult was highly developed in Cambridgeshire and the Isle of Ely, and this did not grow up in a year or two. It has persisted throughout the centuries, and in Cambridge today bands of Satanists meet for their worship of hell. In 1605 a letter of Sir Thomas Lake tells us that two Cambridgeshire magistrates are examining some prophets and witches. It seems that a minister was extremely suspect. That certain physicians thought the diseases with which this coven had afflicted some young girls to be natural carries no weight. It is possible that these very doctors were leagued with the witches, or at least sceptical. The famous Dr. Barrow, of Cambridge, was not slow to recognize the bewitchment of the Throckmorton children. Dr. Henry More, of Christ's College, interrogated many witches, and especially notes that he examined at Castle Hill, Cambridge, several members of a notorious company, of whom at least one was afterwards hanged. In the British Museum is preserved (Add. MS. 36674) a grimoire which formerly belonged to the celebrated Dr. John Caius (1510–73).

Of the sister University the same can be said as of Cambridge. A tradition of a very damnable witchcraft, of black magic, has lingered through the centuries, and although lurking in secret, the evil thing is far from unknown and unpractised even today, when a certain fraternity of Satanists meet in modern Oxford "in Hellish Randezvouzes", to use a phrase of Cotton Mather. How true it is, "The *Evening Wolves* will be much abroad, when we are near the *Evening* of the World".

There is evidence that in Henry VIII's reign, during the ferment of the anti-papal measures and the Dissolution of the Monasteries, a knot of sorcerers at Oxford were skilled in image magic, which is sheer demonianism. Under Charles I an Oxford witch was hanged for attempting to kill her sister's child by means of the black art. She had, it seems, been long bound to the devil by a pact, and had attended countless Sabbats at Headington and on Boar's Hill. In 1659 John Bennett, living at Oxford, was a notorious witch, a common diviner, and a finder of stolen goods by unlawful scrying and conjurations. There was much resort to his house. For the end of the sixteenth and the beginning of the seventeenth centuries we have the witness of Thomas Cooper, of Christ Church, a figure of some importance. Although his treatise *The Mystery of Witchcraft* was not published until 1617, he drew largely upon his own experiences. Cooper had proceeded B.A. in 1590; Master three years later; and B.D. in 1600. In 1601 his College presented him to a living in Cheshire, which he resigned in 1604. This later year he was appointed vicar of Holy Trinity, Coventry, where he remained until 1610. Whilst an undergraduate his interest in magic was awakened, and he "admired some in the University famozed in that skill". He found that his chamber-fellow also was fascinated by these studies, and had somehow procured various cabbalistic manuals. But after a very few weeks "the snare was graciously espied"; they burned their abracadabra books, and were duly filled with a horror of such slippery studies. This episode of the Christ Church undergraduates setting out to investigate the darker shades of occultism is very striking, and we may be sure that Cooper and his friend were by no means exceptional save in one thing—namely, that they halted on the brink of their researches. Others, no doubt, pursued their inquiry to the bitter end, and were admitted to the Oxford witch societies.

It is evident, then, that the witches were by no means all the ragged beggarwomen; the doting hags and crazy crones who dragged out a weary old age in some tumble-down hovel or lonely haunted hut at the outskirts of the village or on the ill-famed wolds; they were not just the itinerant penny quack; the cow-doctor; the rustic midwife; the toothless gaffer with some half-memory of the use of healing herbs his mother taught him in the long ago; the impostor, himself uncertain whether he were a cheat all through or whether he had not some flashes of skill, and in either case eager and ready to fleece his too-confiding clients. There were high-placed witches, even witches of the reigning line; there were wealthy witches; diplomatists; would-be dictators; noblemen, not a few; stout burghers; warriors; scholars; philosophers; men of seeming godly life and conversation; rakes and lewd libertines; men about town; ladies of rank and fortune; kings' mistresses; the duchess and the maréchale; Court beauties; learned women; dainty courtesans. The worship of evil infected all classes of society, young and old, of every nation, every clime. They were and are a mighty host, the armies of Satan.

The witch, then, who took the first fatal step found himself no isolated unit, but the member of a vast and methodically regulated organization with cells and centres all over the world, with local masters and directors and managers; an international fifth column, which is all activity and energy today.

So has it been throughout all history. There are, of course, in the records instances of isolated witches, some perhaps who did not desire to be in touch with their fellows and who lived separate and apart; but mostly the members of the black band linked up with one another in knots and covens. Their numbers were enormous.

It is often superficially supposed that witchcraft was a disease of the Dark Ages, a term actually far more applicable to the present day than to any other known period of history. True, now and again in the centuries when witches seemed to abound and increase more fearfully, when witchcraft boldly blazed forth—as has proved the case—with extraordinary virulence and ferocity, it became necessary for kingdoms and nations to preserve their integrity—nay to secure their continued existence—by enforcing with an unusual yet wholesome strictness their laws which forbade and suppressed the evil thing, that secret commerce and foul conspiracy of the devils with wicked men, who join to bring about the destruction of all social order and harmony and who strive to hurl man to perdition, death, and doom.

Certain ignorant writers, ignorant of history, ignorant of politics, ignorant all round, have blamed the Church for witchcraft, and we have been treated to a good many diatribes and ranting dithyrambs in consequence.

It may not be amiss, then, to emphasize how, even under pagan emperors—the twelve Caesars, for example—when Christianity was *exitiabilis superstitio* "a baneful and noisome superstition", and earlier yet, both in Greece and Rome, before the Birth at Bethlehem, witchcraft was feared and banned and its professors punished with death. When the Athenian orator Aristogeiton was being tried, Demosthenes in his first speech for the prosecution reminded the judges how recently they had condemned to death on account of her foul drugs and enchantments that detestable poisoning witch Theodoris of Lemnos. This was a little after the year 338 B.C. Herodotus the historian, who was born 484 B.C., has a reference to "evil Lemnian deeds", a proverbial phrase practically equivalent to sorceries. Under the Roman Law of the Twelve Tables, originally drafted in the fifth century B.C., malevolent spells were punished with death. Particular penalties were directed against those who blasted corn or infested vines with phylloxera by their hellish incantations. In the year 139 B.C. Cornelius Scipio Hispalus the Praetor—that is, chief acting magistrate—issued an edict ordering all necromancers, charmers, and common fortune-tellers to leave Rome and even the coasts of Italy within ten days. This sentence of outlawry was made necessary on account of the mischief the soothsayers and Chaldeans were almost openly contriving by stirring up intense political excitement, by sowing discontent among the people, and fomenting one crisis after another, so that, as the event proved, there broke out not many years later civil war. It was beyond dispute that the machinations of the black occultists were in no small measure responsible for all this misery and disaster. Under the Triumvirate of Octavius, Antony, and Lepidus, the most influential politician of the day, Marcus Vipsanius Agrippa, drove from the city the horde of star-gazing wizards, all mages chanting uncouth runes, and diviners entertaining familiar spirits. They were banished in perpetuity. Yet not long after Octavius had assumed supreme power as Augustus Caesar he was urgently called upon by his close friend and prime minister, C. Cilnius Maecenas, the cultured and enlightened patron of Horace and Vergil, to cleanse his imperial city of the magians and necro-maunts with whom Rome was literally swarming. At once a new edict was published, and as the result of an official inquisition considerably more than two thousand witch-manuals, grimoires, books of spells and death, were discovered and publicly burned. In the reign of Tiberius, the successor of Augustus, a decree of the Senate exiled all traffickers in base occult arts. Lucius Pituanius, a notorious warlock, was thrown headlong from the Tarpeian Rock on the Capitoline Hill, the mode of execution reserved for the worst and vilest criminals. Another master sorcerer, Publius Martius, had his head struck off by the common hangman without the Esquiline Gate, so that his shameful death should not defile the city. The brief four-year reign A.D. 37-41 of the crazed Caligula followed that of Tiberius, and the next Caesar was Claudius, at whose command the Senate re-enacted with severer penalties the laws exiling the whole crew of magicians from Italy. "A ruthless and unpitying decree" the famous annalist Tacitus calls it. The Emperor Vitellius was ad-mittedly a gross voluptuary and lewd, but none the less he had in some things a shrewd native insight. He had known the secrets of the Caesars from Tiberius to Nero, and this training at Court, whilst debauching his character, sharpened his wits. During the few months of his reign in the year A.D. 69 there were no offenders he prosecuted with more implacable severity than the astrologers and soothsayers, many of whom, when formally accused, he ordered to instant execution, not even allowing them the empty show of a trial. Immediately upon his triumphal entry into Rome as emperor he issued a proclamation commanding all those who used these curious arts to leave not merely the capital but Italy as well, before the first of October. The whole sodality of black occultists was furious with rage. A few mornings later Rome was found to be placarded with mysterious bills: "Know all men by these presents: The Necromancers decree that Vitellius Germanicus shall be dead by the first of October". Who was actually responsible for the placards could never be discovered. Curiously enough, those very soldiers with whom the Emperor had been so popular, and who had enthusiastically hailed him Caesar, suddenly revolted. Disaffection also broke out in the provinces, particularly in Palestine and Syria. Before the first of October Vitellius had been cruelly murdered, and Vespasian was Caesar. Such was the vengeance of the witch-folk. They had their agents in camp and Court, as they have today. None the less they gained little by their plots and conspiracies. Vespasian, a strong ruler, was fully aware of every circum-stance of their malice and mischief, and consternation filled the whole crew when the existing statutes, so far from being disregarded or allowed to lapse into desuetude, were enforced once more with new prohibitions and penalties, for during his reign Vespasian would not permit astrologer, enchanter, or mage so much as to set foot in Italy. A hundred and thirty years later Septimus Severus (A.D. 193–211) ordered the summary execution of not only all astrologers, diviners, warlocks, figure-casters, but also of those who consulted them. This seeming harshness was, in fact, entirely justifiable, for the Emperor was very well aware how the secret predictions of the Chaldeans would put heart into his enemies and encourage complots and dangerous cabals to undermine his power. Julius Paulus, one of the greatest of Roman legal writers, whose period is A.D. 200, and who was regarded as an ultimate authority, lays down that capital punishment is due to all and any who consult with and inquire of warlocks, charmers, fortune-tellers, seers, concerning the life of the prince or changes which may occur in the government of the State, and that the wizards who erect schemes and seek to familiars to satisfy such questionings are also worthy of death. It is plain how the gravest and wisest thinkers recognized that witches were an ever imminent political danger, that they were ever planning and restlessly scheming for the overthrow of the common weal and the disruption of any stable social order; their aim, revolt; their end, red-hot anarchy and confusion. There have been few more active or more cruel foes to Christianity than Diocletian, A.D. 284–305, who unleashed the Tenth Great Persecution. Yet Diocletian proclaimed: "We absolutely and entirely prohibit and forbid the damnable science and foul practice of Black Magic."

It is very significant—when we learn who those emperors were—that certain emperors encouraged by favour and example demonianism and the horrid rites of witchcraft. The blood-maniac Commodus (A.D. 180–192), the hag-ridden Caracalla (A.D. 211–217), apostate Julian (A.D. 361–363), all offered human sacrifice to devils, sought oracles from familiar spirits, and companioned with the fraternity of sorcerers and the past-masters of goety.

We may well echo the words of a French scholar, De Cauzons, who writes: "It is nothing more than a sour bad joke or crass ignorance to pretend that Witchcraft was born in the Middle Ages, and begotten of the teaching and influence of the Church."

Witches, satanists, and the whole unhallowed crew were meddling with and mixing in politics from the first, and as their liege lord, the Devil, rebelled against God in heaven, so do they rebel against any ordered and legitimate form of government on earth.

To enter into any history or discussion of the heresies which vexed the Church almost from her very foundation is unnecessary. Many, false enough in themselves, seemed to be purely intellectual errors (so to speak), obstinate, perverse, corrupt and a source of corruption; but even more dangerous and deadly were those cabbalistic philosophies which presented dualism and hylotheism, so glozed over and glamoured in a web of ambiguous chameleon words and fevered fantasy that men were hoodwinked by some elysian angelology into the belief that through ascending aeons and the Gorgoneion and Abraxas they were approaching nearer and nearer the Divine, whereas they were in fact falling lower and lower, sucked down by the cruel deceit of the sophist and the thaumaturge into the darkest cult of hell. The very father of the Gnostics was that Simon Magus who would have purchased the Holy Ghost of the Apostles for money, and in his mysterious teachings gave himself out to be none other than "the great power of God". Black magic lies at the core of many a heresy, and old Thomas Stapleton hit the mark when he said, "Witchcraft is a weed that grows intertwining with heresy; heresy is a weed that grows intertwining with witchcraft."

Thus the doctrine of the Manichees, first taught by the Persian Mani, who was executed in A.D. 277, with its worship of the "younger brother" Satanaki, is sheer diabolism, and so infamous and subversive were these irreligionists, his disciples, as to be loathed and abhorred throughout the ages by the faithful Christian, the Islamite, and the pagan alike. A bare three years after he had assumed the Caesarship, in A.D. 287, Diocletian sent to the stake the leaders of the Manichees; many of their followers were beheaded; a few, considered less culpable, were exiled to perpetual forced labour in the Government mines. In A.D. 296 the same Emperor commanded the absolute extermination of these firebrands of anarchy, whom he characterizes as a most foul, impure, and reckless knot of revolutionaries. The name is changed—indeed, when it grew too vile it was changed more than once—but the spirit of the Subversives persists and is hideously active today. It is they who are responsible for the wreck and ruin of the world. The Manichean system from the first was no other than a simultaneous attack upon both Church and State, a well-planned and directed organization whose object was and is to destroy the whole fabric of society, to reduce civilization to chaos.

There have been many subsections and divisions and offshoots of the early Gnostic societies. The Ophites worshipped the Serpent, the emblem of evil; the Cainites preached evil as their gospel and reverenced Cain, the first murderer, as their founder; Carpocrates carried these doctrines to their furthermost limit, and made the performance of all and any species of crime a solemn duty; whilst the Messalians or Euchites taught that divine honours must be paid to the Devil, who is to be propitiated by means of every possible outrage done to Christ. These are the beliefs and practices today of the Satanists, the Sinistri, who go by many popular and familiar names.

From time to time throughout the centuries bands of Manichee sorcerers were unearthed and duly punished. Thus in 556, at Ravenna, almost by accident, as it appeared, a centre or "cell" of Manichees was tracked down, and the members, being found guilty after a long and most equitable trial, were executed as the safety of the city required. In 1022, during the reign of Robert the Good of France, there was discovered at Orleans the existence of a company of Manichees, who were wont to assemble on certain fixed nights in a lonely and deserted house without the city walls, a terribly haunted spot where once (tradition had it) stood a temple dedicate to the Lords of the Underworld. Each member of the coven bore a lantern wherewith a curious signal known only to the initiate could be given, and at the door there was a password of revolting blasphemy. After the performance of a gross and ribald ritual, during which, to the sound of rebecks and the shrill cornemuse, they psalmodized under grotesque and evil names Satan and his demon hosts, all lights were extinguished and both men and women abandoned themselves to the most promiscuous debauchery. Three or four times a year, upon the great days in the calendar of hell, at these gatherings a child was sacrificed, and of the fresh-spilt blood and portions of the warm flesh a paste was made to be moulded into wafers and kneaded with stolen Hosts to serve in their hideous parodies of Holy Mass. The wine of their chalice was mingled with satyrion, with betony and bhang. It was all in vain that, with infinite patience, learned priests and religious strove to convert them as they lay in prison, and finally these wretches, one and all, were sent to the stake. In 1028 Count Alduin burned a coven of Manichees, men and women, at Angoulême. Between 1030 and 1040 it came to light that the Castle of Monteforte, near Asti, in Piedmont, was the rallying-point of an important Manichee community, whose poisonous propaganda was infecting the whole countryside. The Bishop of Asti, acting in concert with some great noblemen of the neighbourhood, arrested a large number of these wretches, who upon their obstinate refusal to retract and amend were at last handed over to the civil authorities. Under judgement of the law they were burned at the stake. Ariberto, Archbishop of Milan, then ordered that certain of these Manichees should be brought to his city, where they were lodged under nominal surveillance, since he hoped he might convert them. They showed their appreciation of the good prelate's kindliness by disseminating their vile doctrines and endeavouring to make proselytes. Thereupon Count Lanzano, a nobleman held in high honour by his peers, and leader of the popular party, represented to the Archbishop that their effrontery was likely to cause something like a riot. He asked that they should be handed over to the senior magistrates. Three aged senators came in person to entreat His Grace to allow the civil authorities to deal with men who had so flagrantly outraged every law, human and divine. With some difficulty Ariberto consented, and the Manichees, having been formally attached by the sbirri, were very summarily tried by a High Court and executed without further respite.

In the year 1159 a gang of thirty foreign Manichees, disguising their aim and their beliefs, privily settled in England, and were soon busy at work sowing dissension, evil, and unrest. They were tracked down in 1166, and after they had been examined by the Council of Oxford the Bishops remanded them, as criminals of no ordinary guilt, to the civil authorities. In an access of fury Henry II ordered them to be soundly scourged, to be branded in their foreheads, and cast adrift outside the city walls, straightly forbidding any to succour such vile and unnatural offenders, and so all perished from cold and exposure.

Drastic measures were necessary, since now the south of France and Northern Italy were especially plagued by these satanists and revolutionaries. From very early days a degraded Gnosticism commixed with Oriental sorceries and the practice of black magic had been steadily, if secretly, filtering through to the West, and in some cases poisoning the very founts of philosophy and learning. A famous French scholar, M. E. Aroux, traces two routes by which the West was thus invaded, the one a sea route by means of the trading relations and intercommunications between Provence and Syria, with its coasts, whence France and Sicily and Spain would be reached. The other route, overland, was through Bulgaria, the infernal missionaries and incendiaries penetrating Moldavia, Pannonia, Moravia, Bohemia, and Dalmatia, the gateway to Italy. These two confluent streams of poison would converge somewhere about the plains of Lombardy, and here, and in adjacent Provence, we might expect to find the strongholds and central cells of the organization.

Incidentally, it may be remarked that the diffusion of Sorcery and Satanism in the Iberian Peninsula was given a terrific impetus and power at the fall of the Gothic kingdom, when, after King Roderic was slain, the victorious Arabs overran Andalusia, and occupied Toledo, the Gothic capital, whilst the Jews, who were numerous in the cities, facilitated their advance. With the capture of Saragossa in 714 by Musa, Governor of Barbary, the Mussulman domination had begun, and this town remained a Moorish centre for more than four centuries. In Saragossa and Toledo were soon established schools of medicine and philosophy, under which latter term were cloaked judicial astrology, divination by the stars, and every kind of magical science. Saragossa, Toledo, and the University of Salamanca (founded in the twelfth century) gained throughout all Europe an evil notoriety as hotbeds of necromancy, nurseries and thriving-grounds of sorcerers. Toledo, in particular, was so ill-famed that we find it incidentally spoken of in popular poem and story as a seminary of magic. It is said that at one period a Chair of Black Magic was openly established there, and certainly Guazzo (English translation, p. 195) speaks of a seven years' course of the Black Arts and Magic at Toledo. In the earlier part of the thirteenth century a Toledo Master of Arts was practising theurgy at Maestricht, and was resorted to by a large number of clients, acquiring by his unholy spiritism considerable wealth. In the *Roman of Eustace*, which is of the same period, Eustace is supposed to have passed six months in the schools of Toledo studying necromancy; and in another famous fiction, the old French Roman of Maugis, son of the Count of Aigremont, the hero in the course of his adventures gains admittance to the secret societies of Toledo, where he completes his researches into wizard sciences, and eventually obtains the professorial chair of goety in that University. These horrible and ill-famed schools were gradually driven underground, and finally rooted out by Queen Isabella the Catholic (1451–1504), who thoroughly purged Toledo and Salamanca of these abominations. There is an interesting contemporary reference to Toledo in the *Morgante Maggiore* of the Italian poet Pulci (1432–1474):

> The city of Toledo erst
> Fostered the lore of necromancy,
> Professors there, in magic versed,
> From public chair taught pyromancy,
> Or geomancy; or rehearsed
> Experiments in hydromancy.

Pyromancy is divination by fire or signs arising from and connected with flames. Geomancy is divination by lines and figures, which originally were formed by scattering earth upon some plane surface, and in later use by jotting down on paper various dots at random and reading the pattern thus drawn. Some geomancers considered the most sure way was to divine from the manner in which dust or churchyard mould fell when thrown upon the coffin lid.

Hydromancy is divination by means of water, or through spirits who appear in or near water, which element, says Thales, is the beginning of all things. This form of sorcery, almost universal in antiquity, is common enough at the present day. The seer, or it may be the inquirer himself, by gazing fixedly into a pool or basin of still unruffled water, will see therein reflected as in a mirror an exact picture of that which it is sought to know. Strabo, in his *Geography*, speaking of the Persians, says that among them are held in great reverence the Magi, who are in fact necromancers, and skilled in every sort of divination, especially reading the future by gazing at clear water which has been poured out ceremonially into pots and pans of curious shape, and this art is called lecanomancy, the Greek work *lekane* meaning a dish, as also by gazing into standing lakes and ponds, and this art is called hydromancy, the Greek word *hudor* meaning water. The Latin historian Livy tells us that during the early period of the kings of Rome, Etruscan divination was much practised throughout the newly-founded city. He goes on to relate how Numa, the second king of Rome, was wont to retire into the heart of a deep grove, where he would recline by the banks of a crystal brook, and so commune with the nymph Egeria, and she taught him many things. Now Numa, according to one very ancient tradition, divined by seeing gods in this spirit-haunted stream. Varro, a later author, says plainly that Numa was devoted to hydromancy, a charm of Persian origin, since Egeria was an undine, and dwelt in these waters. This agrees with the doctrines of Paracelsus, and would be fully admitted by the learned Sinistrari, who relates the strange history of the young maiden long importuned by an Incubus, and since they suspected this spirit lover might be an aqueous demon, they put him to flight by hot suffumigations, and by the warm perfume of musk, amber, and civet. Guazzo, too, speaks of the demons of the water, that dwell under water in rivers and meres. "When such demons appear they are more often women than men, for they live in humid places and lead a softer manner of life." Upon Varro's statement St. Augustine in *The City of God* comments: "Now Numa himself, not being instructed by any true prophet or Angel of God, was fain to fall to hydromancy, making his gods (or rather his devils) to appear in water, and thus to instruct him on what lines he should form his cults and religious institutions. This particular kind of divination, Varro says, originally came from Persia, and was practised by Numa and afterwards by Pythagoras, and so that their incantations should be more effective they spilled blood also, and so they evoked demons and familiar spirits to advise them. Necromancy the Greeks more plainly term it, but call it necromancy or hydromancy, whichever name pleases you best, here it is that the dead seem to speak and deliver oracles." So the Saint considered King Numa to have been no more or less than an old warlock.

A very similar form of divination is crystal-gazing, so widely practised at the present time; as well as scrying by jewels, consecrated beryls, shew-stones and the like. Mirrors and burnished steel are employed to see reflected therein passing events or to glimpse the shadow of futurity. "For Occult Students, 'Memphis' Magnetic Mirrors, 4/6. A handy little instrument for inducing clairvoyance. Booklet of full and plain instructions included. 'Memphis' Crystals, 10/6. New coloured variety, perfectly ground and polished. Rapidly develop clairvoyance. With booklet." I quote an advertisement of May, 1919. The most renowned of all crystallomancers was Dr. John Dee, several of whose shew-stones seem to have been preserved. The results which he obtained at his séances with Edward Kelley as his medium are in greater part to be found in a printed volume, *A True and Faithful Relation Of What passed for many Years Between Dr. John Dee (A Mathematician of Great Fame in Q. Eliz. and King James their Reigns) and Some Spirits: Tending (had it Succeeded) To a General Alteration of most States and Kingdoms in the World. . . . With a Preface Confirming the Reality (as to the Point of Siprits) of This Relation.* By Meric Casaubon, D.D. London, folio, 1659. Some matter concerning these Relations, which it will be noted are to some extent, at any rate, concerned with politics, yet remains in manuscript. The Oriental use of black ink as a charmed mirror is very well known, and has been admirably employed by Wilkie Collins in that masterpiece of fiction *The Moonstone* (1868), when the three Indians, in order to trace the whereabouts of the jewel, pour a fluid like ink into the palm of the boy's hand. "The little chap unwillingly held out his hand", and passing into trance he gazes at the ink in the hollow of his hand, answering such questions as are put to him. What Peter Quivil, a thirteenth-century Bishop of Exeter, thought of this kind of divination very clearly appears from his charge to a local Synod: "Let the penitent confess if he has broken the First Commandment by rendering unto demons or other creatures the worship due to God alone . . . by having recourse to conjurations . . . in a sword or a basin." These ceremonies were generally preceded by unholy invocations to aid the vision, and the Parson in *The Canterbury Tales* sums the matter up very justly: "Let us now consider this horribly profane practice of adjurations and conjurations, as is the common use, of these vile enchanters or necromancers scrying in basins full of water, or in a bright sword, in a circle, or in a fire, or in the shoulder-bone of a sheep. I can but say that they act most wickedly and damnably in despite of Christ and the teaching of Holy Church."

In a brief of 27 February, 1318, Pope John XXII, ordering the prosecution of nine witches, particularly specifies that among other magical practices they made inquiry of and consulted familiar spirits and controls in polished mirrors.

The fifth column of the witches carried on their evil work with infinite cunning, so that amid the welter of political events, kingdoms rising and kingdoms falling, confusion largely engineered and always turned to full account by the witches themselves, the inroads of satanism could only be, as it were, spasmodically checked, and although the laws of every Christian code doom the sorcerer and the necromancer to death, the forces of evil in their myriad ramifications made terrific headway.

Various sects, all of debased Manichean origin—Bogomiles, Cathari, Paterini, Vaudois, Waldenses, Albigenses, Pauvres de Lyon, and half a score beside, differing perhaps in some negligible and insignificant details, but all devoted to Satan, their lord and god, all zealots in the cause of anarchy and revolution, subversives, fanatics whose aims and end were sorcery, destruction, and red terrorism—swarmed over the face of Europe. In 1051 a gang of Cathari were hanged at Goslar, in Hanover, by order of and in the presence of the Emperor Henry III. About the same year, a monk of Angoulême, Adhémar de Chabannes, writes in a letter how "even in Italy many adherents of this pestilential creed were found, and these wretches either perished by the sword or at the stake".

Some fifty years later Flanders was sorely troubled by "the black angel of Satan", Tanchelin, who journeyed up and down the country-side proclaiming the most monstrous doctrines. In Arras, Cambrai, and many other cities he preached in foulest terms an incoherent mixture of anarchy and blazing blasphemy—in a word, diabolism. Accompanied by an apostate priest, Everwacher, and a Jew, Manasses, a lusty villain who had formerly been a blacksmith, Tanchelin managed to collect around him the riff-raff of the district, and was soon at the head of an organiza-tion of no less than three thousand gangsters—brigands, murderers, thieves, outlaws and the like—whose ranks were daily swelled by the scum of the prisons, which at his command were broken open in each place they visited, and the prisoners set free on condition of joining his followers. His ultimate object was to overturn the existing state of things and to evolve a communistic chaos with himself as dictator and overlord. In order to achieve this he must needs first destroy the Church, the supreme representative of authority, order, and justice throughout the world. Accordingly the priesthood must be exterminated; the churches were closed or turned into public brothels and filthy taverns; the Sacrifice of the Mass assailed with the most ribald abuse; the worst infamies encouraged—nay, commanded and enjoined—so that incest, fornication, adultery, were declared to be works of spiritual efficacy, and virtue became an offence. The city of Antwerp, where he established himself, was given over to bloodshed, vice, and crime, and it seemed as though hell itself had broken loose upon earth. Amid orgies of lust and murder Tanchelin reigned as king. But that was not enough for his ambition. He caused himself to be hailed as the Son of God, the Perfect Man, the Perfect God, the sum of divinity. A temple was built in his honour, where the frantic ruffian, clad in a robe of brocaded gold sewn with starry gems, and set high upon an altar-throne, was proclaimed divine and solemnly worshipped with sacrifice, with incense, and with chanted litanies. The end of Tanchelin was swift, sudden, and bloody as his life. One afternoon, in pompous state, he was sailing down the River Schelde, when a bystander, appalled at some more than ordinarily hideous blasphemy which fell from him in horrid jest, and unregarding his sabred janizaries around, with one blow from a pike scattered the wretch's brains upon the deck of his royal barge. Unhappily, his pernicious errors did not perish with their fiendish author. Antwerp was plunged in riot and wickedness, whilst Everwacher and Manasses established a duumvirate, reigning as coequal kings. It was not, indeed, until after seven long years, and then by the efforts of St. Norbert of Premontré, that rule and order were restored and public safety secured. It seems that with the visit of the saint to Antwerp a mass conversion took place. Crowds of men and women in deepest penitence delivered up quantities of conse-crated Hosts, which they had purloined from the tabernacles and kept hidden away in boxes and cupboards to employ for charms and con-jurations, to profane in the devil-worship of the Sabbat. The famous artist Cornelius de Vos has painted the scene of the restitution. Elie Maire in one brief word terms Tanchelin "witch."

Forty years after these events the anarchists and similar firebrands of revolution were so openly advocating the most subversive measures and so sedulously setting aflame the whole of the south of France that Pope Alexander III, one of the most glorious and far-seeing of the Roman pontiffs, then in residence at Sens, summoned a council of the Bishops of Gascony at Tours in 1163 and impressed upon them the urgent need for co-operation in the enforcement of most drastic measures to check this menace. Whether it was that the bishops did not appreciate the gravity of the moment, or whether their orders were unfaithfully and negli-gently carried out, when the situation was reviewed in 1179 at the Third General Council of the Lateran, convoked at Rome, Pope Alexander was horrified at the monstrous growth of the evil, and by letters couched in the most pressing terms the Holy See made a strong appeal to the civil authorities throughout Languedoc. By now the bailies and prefects of many towns were in fact already seriously alarmed, nor were their well-founded apprehensions allayed upon the publication of a bull of Alexander's successor, Lucius III of Lucca, who anathematized Cathari, Patarini, Humiliati, Pauvres de Lyon, Pasagians, Josephins, and the rest, whilst in complete concert with ecclesiastical authority, Frederick Barbarossa put them under the imperial ban, which was equivalent to outlawry. All these sectaries, in fact, formed one great secret society, a society with officials and spies and hidden agents in all lands intent upon their particular propaganda. They held that God, the Creator of Heaven and Earth, was a demon and a liar. He was a murderer, because he had slain the Egyptians in the Red Sea. He was Satan, Lucifer, who gave the law to Moses. Others held that the Supreme Being had two sons, but that the Younger Brother had usurped the place of the Elder Brother, the fallen angel, whom they worshipped. The doctrine of the Trinity was wholly rejected by the Albigenses, many of whom denied the existence of the soul. A visible Church with all its rites and sacraments must be abolished; the Cross must be spurned with contumely; all abominations and lusts must be practised in honour of their god, who is the Evil Prin-ciple. In politics they advocated the extremist communism and chaos. Elias the Prophet and St. John Baptist were possessed with demons. Amongst themselves the members of the various organizations were known as "brother", "sister", or "comrade", and they were carefully taught a regular freemasonry of gestures and phrases used in a special manner or with a curious intonation by which the initiates could recognize

WITCHES TRAMPLE ON THE CROSS

WITCHES SWEAR FEALTY TO THE DEMON

THE EVIL EYE

one another without betraying themselves to outsiders who did not belong to their section or centre. Thus Ivan de Narbonne, who was once an active worker in the ranks of these satanic revolutionaries, but who was fortunate enough to escape out of their toils, told the Archbishop of Bordeaux how in every city he visited when he was travelling he was able to make himself known to the clubs there by a code of signs and passwords. These societies had, as we should suppose, their ogpu, and a reign of terror spread throughout half Europe. "In the twelfth century," writes Dean Milman, "Manicheism is rampant, bold, undisguised. Everywhere are Puritans, Paterines, Populars, suspected or convicted or confessed Manicheans. . . . Innocent III, on his accession (1198), found not only these daring insurgents scattered in the cities of Italy, even, as it were, at his own gates (among his first acts was to subdue the Paterines of Viterbo), he found a whole province, a realm, in some respects the richest and noblest of his spiritual domain, absolutely dissevered from his Empire, in almost universal revolt from Latin Christianity."

The very names of these Manichean organizations were often taken in hideous mockery. Thus the Cathari, or Catharans, were the "Pure Ones", the Greek word for "pure" being *katharos*. Among their tenets was the idea that the soul was so distinct from the body that it could not be affected or contaminated by anything pertaining to the then fleshly envelope, and hence it was permissible for man to give himself up to any licentiousness and pollute himself by the grossest beastliness and yet remain virginal and innocent and pure. The Humiliati dubbed themselves "humble" and enjoyed the gibe. The Paterini, Paterines, or Patarines, were so called from Pattaria, the lowest quarter of Milan, the brothels and the slums. The name is identical with an old dialect word, *patarino*, a low, dirty fellow. Many other curious nomenclatures are either too obscure or too obscene for it to be worth while to trace them.

Assassination was the most frequent weapon of these apostles of anarchy. Among the vilest and bloodiest of the sections were the Paterini, whose two local leaders, Ermanno of Parma and Gottardo of Marsi, terrible and wolf-like men, caused Peter Paranzo, the governor of Orvieto, a magistrate of most honourable and indeed holy life, to be foully murdered by their followers in the year 1199. At the Council of Albi, convened by Gerard, Bishop of that diocese, in 1176, the Albigenses were condemned, upon which they broke out into open rebellion and the whole district was soon in a turmoil. Peter of Castelnau, a Cistercian monk, was dispatched as Papal Legate to confer with the leaders of the Albigenses at Carcassone. He soon saw that the meeting had merely been designed as a studied insult, but none the less thereupon he redoubled his efforts, himself visiting the villages and lowliest hamlets. His success alarmed the rebels, and a new conference was called for by Raymond, Count of Toulouse, to be held at St. Gilles on the banks of the Rhone. On the morning of 15 January, 1209, Peter was preparing to cross the river when there hastily ran up two men, one of whom brutally pierced him through the side with a lance. He fell, exclaiming, "Lord, pardon him even as I forgive!" In a few moments he was no more.

On 6 April, 1252, Peter of Verona, than whom none had been more active in opposition to the Manichees .and other revolutionaries, was returning on foot from Como to Milan. There was with him a certain Brother Dominic. Not far from the city their way lay through a lonely and darkling wood. Suddenly from behind the trees leaped out two bravoes armed to the teeth. The former of these, Carino by name, aimed a couple of fearful blows at Peter with a heavy curtal-axe, almost severing his crown. They then pursued his companion, who was fleeing in terror, and slashed him down with their swords. Retracing their steps, they found that Peter, half-risen to his knees, had traced the word *Credo* (I believe) on the ground with the blood streaming from his head. A swift rapier-thrust finished the business. Peter of Verona was canonized the following year, and his shrine by Balduccio of Pisa in the Church of San Eustorgio at Milan is one of the loveliest sculptures of the fourteenth century. Mrs. Jamieson has eloquently written: "Among the most celebrated pictures in the world is the 'San Pietro Martire' of Titian. . . . The dramatic effect of this piece is beyond all praise; the death-like pallor in the face of San Pietro, the extremity of cowardice and fear in that of his flying companion, the ferocity of the murderers, the gloomy forest, the trees bending and waving in the tempest, and the break of calm blue sky above, from which the two cherubim issue with their palms, render this the most perfect *scenic* picture in the world." It was by assassinations such as this that the Manichees sought to intimidate whole provinces, and to compel men's allegiance with violence and blood.

In Spain the underground subversive societies were largely recruited from and assisted by the Moslems, both of Granada and Morocco, and the Jews, who, in spite of repeated legislation which permitted them to lend money at enormous interest, were never contented, not even when the usurers were authorized to charge as much as forty per cent. A number of apostates known as *Muladiés* covered the southern part of the peninsula like locusts, and in some cities they seized and long held all civic posts, exercising a fearful tyranny. Thus as early as 853 they became dominant in Toledo, where they lorded it for well-nigh a century. Through the years the menace grew, and so insidiously that it was but fully realized by such keen intellects and truly great souls as a Ferran Martinez or Vicente Ferrer, to both of whom not only Spain but (it is no exaggeration to say) Europe itself owes no small debt of gratitude for such liberty and prosperity as she has once enjoyed. Among the *Marranos*, or *Conversos* as they were called, were to be found the fifth-column anarchists, a desperate and terrible junto. The cunning with which they concealed their real aims and played their parts as faithful and loyal supporters of the Church and the King almost evaded detection. That their poison filtered deep is amply proved by the political upheavals of our own time.

As was discovered by the prior of the Dominican house of San Pablo at Seville, Fray Alonso de Hojeda, the night of Good Friday was the great annual occasion when the members of these foul fraternities —all one in their aim and ends, call them by what name you will—met in unholy revel to celebrate their Satanic rites. It was necessary then, for the preservation of social integrity and civil order, that the monarchy should speedily organize throughout the kingdom and amply empower some body or bodies to deal with so serious a menace. The local authorities seemed intimidated or supine, and accordingly there was constituted a central tribunal, the Suprema, whose function it was to delegate officials in the various principalities, provinces, counties, and dependencies, with jurisdiction sufficient to enable them to combat everywhere this fearful menace of sedition and insurgency. The task was a delicate one, since there existed in many places ancient rights which must not be infringed, and chambers whose jurats would jealously maintain their traditional privileges. There must be no clash. The new tribunals must be very carefully chosen and composed of judges who were not merely learned but practical and experienced administrators, not swayed by fear or favour, mild but resolute, men of standing and unblemished probity, and so far as possible with some knowledge of local conditions and tendencies. The kingdom of Aragon presented a particularly difficult problem, since it was known to be little other than a nourishing-ground of these subversive societies, in whose ranks, it was shrewdly suspected, not a few of the wealthiest and most exalted grandees, not to mention alcaldes and burghers, were already enrolled. On 4 May, 1484, there were appointed for Aragon ten commissioners, which number included an assessor, two notaries, an advocate, and an alquazil. Among these was nominated, as one of the principal justiciars, Peter Arbués, a canon of the Cathedral Church of Saragossa. There could, indeed, have been no fitter person for the task, for he was much beloved on account of his charities to the poor, and he never wearied of relieving those who had been brought to destitution by the Marranos, who, in their aim at exclusive political power, had with truly satanic cunning established members of their society as money-lenders throughout the district. Once these extortioners had been able to get either peer or peasant in their toils the unfortunate victim was threatened with ruin unless he agreed to join their brotherhood. Again and again Arbués had baffled their devices and rescued the dupes upon whom they preyed. Already he was a marked man, and when these freemasonries of evil heard of his appointment they determined upon his destruction. The train was laid with great caution, and the plot was long in hatching. A fund was opened to hire assassins, and so vast were their resources that this was administered by no less than three treasurers, who collected about ten thousand réals, which in spending value today would be something between two and three thousand pounds. A leather-merchant, notorious for his brutal and cruel manners, undertook to find assassins, and before long he had hired nearly a dozen gangsters, all of whom were charged to shadow the good Canon and attack him at the moment likeliest to effect their purpose. It was known, for example, how in the cool of the day he enjoyed a walk along the river-banks, and had it not been that upon a certain evening two gentlemen, his friends, joined him as he strolled to and fro, a couple of thugs were ready to throttle him and throw his body into the Ebro. Relays of ruffians kept a watch on his house for months together. At last, late on the night of 15 September, 1485, the currier, who had been given the hint by servants he bribed heavily, sent a hasty message round to collect as many of his toughs as could be found in the taverns and brothels within half an hour or so, and in all, including himself and Durange, his French valet, eight quickly assembled. Covering their faces with black masks and being well wrapped up in cloaks, they all made their way to the Cathedral, entering by the Chapter door, which was open, since the office of Matins was being sung in choir. Canon Arbués was kneeling in prayer not far from the high altar, or, according to another account, in the Lady Chapel. They crept up behind him in the shadows, when the leader of the ruffians whispered to the valet: "There he is, give it to him." Durange, with a back-stroke of his sword, dealt the Canon a fearful wound in the neck, and as the bleeding man in his agony rose staggering mechanically towards the choir a second blow nearly severed his arm, whilst another of the murderers passed his sword through the body. He fell, and the assassins hurried away as the canons, alarmed at the clash of steel and the unwonted noise, came hurrying from their stalls. They instantly raised the dying man and bore him gently to his house hard by, where the surgeons who had been summoned declared the injuries to be mortal. From time to time his voice was heard praying in broken murmurs, but these gradually ceased, and he died between one and two o'clock on the morning of 17 September. This midnight assassination is the subject of one of Murillo's masterpieces.

Some writers have been pleased to draw a picture of the witch as a poor, harmless old woman, her broomstick behind the door, her black puss at her side, sitting over her little bit of fire, spinning maybe, or sorting out simples and country herbs good for cleansing a sore or healing a bruise. She may be a little sharp-tongued at times, a trifle peevish and eccentric in her loneliness, age, and poverty. But she is perfectly harmless and innocent, wishing ill to none, always ready, indeed, to do a good turn to a sick neighbour, only asking for a kind word or two and to be let alone. Then for no known reason save the stupid gossip of ignorant rustics—the sickly dreams and longings of a servant-wench ill with the hip or some confounded thing, the chlorotic repressions of a great lady, the frantic superstition of a half-starved priest—bedlam is let loose, countries are turned topsy-turvy, popes launch thundering bulls against her, kings ponder weighty tomes, panic-stricken parliaments legislate fast and furiously, butcher bishops hound on hordes of torturing inquisitors, and for centuries murderous judges are drenching Europe in blood. As for the art and practice of witchcraft, how much saner to agree with good Dr. Samuel Harsnett, sometime Archbishop of York: "these things are raked together out of old doting Heathen Historiographers, Wizarding Augurs, Imposturizing Soothsayers, Dreaming Poets, Chimerical Conceiters, and Coiners of Fables". Nay, more, any who believe in Satanism can, at once, he sensibly says, be assigned to "one of these five ranks: Children, Fools, Women, Cowards, sick or black melancholic discomposed Wits". A pretty sweeping statement.

A statement, indeed, to which history has given and still gives the lie. The hideous mischief done in all countries, in all parts of the world, by devilish secret societies; the subversive movements which have thrown, first in this land and then in that, all social order and well-being into strife and confusion—the French Revolution, the troubles and risings in Mexico and in Spain—these are not mere "Imaginations and Apprehensions". The murders of Peter of Verona, Peter Arbués, and many another assassination—were these myths and illusions?

With reason enough did clear-sighted and shrewd men dread and defend themselves against the activities of the satanists and the subversives. With reason did governments make laws, and magistrates punish.

The Stedingers—a word meaning "dwellers by the seashore"—were a large tribe of Frisian peasants, generally recognized as a particularly brutal and backward race. For many years satanists had secretly been training them in every evil and anarchy until in 1204 they broke out in open rebellion to put in actual practice the fruits of their teaching. Multitudes of the most ferocious half-savage brigands swarmed over the whole land, seizing cities and castle and putting man, woman, and child to the sword. With these ruffians went a band of sorcerers and sibyls, who prophesied that ultimately they should possess the whole world, and spurred them on by their vaticinations to every outrage and abomination. Troops which were sent against these revolutionaries were defeated, and it was not until Pope Gregory IX had preached a crusade against them that the coalition of several great princes and suzerains, under the leadership of the Duke of Brabant, who brought into the field an army of forty thousand men, crushed the revolutionaries in a pitched battle on 27 May, 1234, when more than eight thousand of the Stedingers were killed, and the rest scattered in flight. "The Stedingers," says Pope Gregory, "seduced by Satan, have abjured all laws, human and divine; they have derided the Church, insulted and horribly profaned the Sacraments; consulted with witches to raise evil spirits; shed innocent blood like water; burned and plundered and destroyed; they are in fine enemies to all good, having concocted an infernal scheme to propagate the cult of the Devil, whom they adore at their secret sabbats."

A very similar society were the Luciferians, who actually saw and worshipped demons at their midnight assemblies, and sacrificed to them with the foulest ceremonies. These wretches seemed particularly zealous in the cause of evil and revolt, stopping at nothing to inculcate their hellish beliefs. When Conrad of Marburg and a Franciscan friar named Gerard were commissioned to preach against and check so far as possible the inroads of this sect, both were brutally assassinated. This was in 1233. To come forward boldly as an opponent of the Satanists was a step fraught with no small danger, and today those who denounce and expose the self-same secret societies, masquerading under a score of names, run equal risks.

At the beginning of the fourteenth century all Christendom from Great Britain to Cyprus was convulsed by the fearful catastrophe of the Templars. This Order was directly founded in consequence of the Crusades, since immediately after the deliverance of Jerusalem, when Godefroi de Bouillon became King of the Holy City at the end of the

First Crusade, the Warriors of the Cross, considering their vows fulfilled, returned to their several homes. Pilgrims from the West now began to visit the Holy Places in ever-increasing numbers. But it was a journey undertaken at imminent hazard. At every point the Moslems lay in wait for the pious travellers, to rob and murder them, sometimes almost within sight of the walls of Jerusalem itself. Accordingly, in 1118 two French knights bound themselves by a most solemn promise to God that they would defend the pilgrims from the infidel, and keep guard over the public roads. These were immediately joined by other companions, and religious vows were formally taken "between the hands of the Patriarch" whilst Baldwin II, who had succeeded as King of Jerusalem, not only accepted their services but bestowed upon them as their mother-house a portion of his palace, buildings long held as peculiarly sacred, being the site of Solomon's Temple, from which circumstance the Order derived its name. In an incredibly short space of time a vast number of novices had joined the Order, which has a long and, in many respects, a glorious history. In a few years the Templars established commanderies in well-nigh every country. Popes and kings heaped favours, spiritual and temporal, upon so noble and magnificent a chivalry. The Knights were largely drawn from the ranks of the higher nobility, many of whom brought vast possessions to the general coffers, so that very soon this Order, which began in a lowly and simple manner enough, was wealthy beyond imagination. Treasures untold were hoarded up in the Temples (as their houses were called) of London and Paris. Recognizing no superior save the authority of the Pope, richer than any reigning monarch, it can hardly be wondered at that the Templars made their influence felt throughout Europe. With boundless prosperity came boundless pride. "As proud as a Templar" was a proverbial simile of the day. The old word *Tempelhaus* signified a brothel.

It has been said by a facile and rather fanciful author that the Templars were "sacrificed by a poltroon pope to appease a rapacious king", and "guilty or innocent, the Order would have escaped suppression had Philip the Fair been less ambitious or Clement V more resolute". If delivered with sufficient assurance and aplomb, this sort of thing is apt to go down with certain people, but the problems of history are not to be disposed of so easily. Philip IV of France, surnamed Le Bel (1268–1314), succeeded to the throne in October, 1285. His proceedings against the Templars have been denounced as hypocrisy and avarice, two very specious charges easy enough to make and effective, but difficult to substantiate, especially in the present instance, since it is a fact beyond dispute that Philip, who could without much difficulty personally have impropriated the larger part of the immense wealth of the Templars, only allowed the royal treasury to be reimbursed to the extent of the costs of the trials. These were, of course, very great. In November, 1309, Pope Clement V paid a noble tribute to the disinterested policy of the King, who was "not prompted by any spirit of covetousness, since he did not desire to retain to his own use and spending any part of the property and estates of the Templars, but on the other hand he liberally and in a spirit of true devotion left them to Us, and to the Church by Us to be administered and expended". "From the outset," wrote M. Funck-Brentano, "people have been cruelly unjust to Philip the Fair. This young prince was one of the greatest kings and finest characters who have played their part in history." Without expressing an appreciation of Philip in quite such enthusiastic terms, it can at any rate be agreed that the one serious blot on Philip's character was his insubordination to Boniface VIII.

Thirty years before Philip was born, as early as 1238, Gregory IX was voicing his suspicions that all was not well within the Order of the Templars. A quarter of a century later Clement IV contemplated a searching examination into the tenets and practices of the brethren. The same rumours had reached the Cardinal Archbishop of Bordeaux, and when he ascended the throne as Clement V in 1305 he called before him the Grand Master of the Temple, Jacques du Molay, who arrived in France with a royal retinue and bringing 150,000 gold florins as well as huge ingots of silver and jewels of incalculable value. The Pope was making searching inquiry concerning the crimes of "unspeakable apostasy against Almighty God, detestable idolatry, enormous vices and horrid heresies" which had been alleged "by no light or trivial witnesses". Yet he was very reluctant to believe that such could possibly be the case, and so the proceedings were unhurried, deliberate, impartial. Irrefragable proof must be forthcoming. King Philip, on the other hand, was shocked and alarmed—as indeed he very well might be—and he kept urging immediate and decisive action.

At any rate there already existed strong grounds for believing that the Templars were, to say the least, far from orthodox and monstrously impure, whilst many did not hesitate to give it as their opinion that the Order was rotted with Satanism and strange idolatries. In the face of overwhelming evidence it seems idle to deny that these and other grave charges proved in the main well founded, but it must be borne in mind that the degrees of culpability differed in different countries, even in different preceptories and commanderies (individual houses), and the majority even of members in a given preceptory may have been to a large extent ignorant of the interior occult worship and all its abominations. It is possible that comparatively few were found secret, bold, and bad enough to be initiated into the ultimate mysteries. Says Éliphas Lévi, "The Chiefs alone knew whither they were going," and that was to anarchy and diabolism. Every new member, however, was compelled to swear to a blind obedience, whatever might be ordered him or required of him; he was for ever the bondslave and vassal of the Temple.

To recapitulate, even were it as shortly as may be, the various accusations brought against the Templars would be no brief task, and it must suffice to say that the real initiates, who formed the backbone of the Order, the chosen Knights and Masters who filled the posts of highest responsibility and trust, were both in act and creed Gnostic Manichees, Satanists devoted to every licentiousness and blasphemy. That this poison began to infiltrate very subtly but very evilly soon after the founding of the Temple seems certain. From the outset there was necessarily some intercourse and intermingling in the East with their neighbours, not only with Mohammedans, but with the quasi-Christian sects and frenzied philosophies that abounded in Palestine, where flourished the Assassins and the Ishmaelites, and above all the Mandaeans, who taught that the Christ of the Christians was an impostor, a false Messiah, whose Crucifixion was brought about by the true Messiah, the great younger brother. They were plainly devil-worshippers. There is something more than a tradition that the Grand Pontiff of the Mandaeans invested with his powers the Master of the Temple, whom he recognized as his successor. This is fully borne out by the ceremony in which each new member had to bear his part. He was compelled to trample and spit upon the Crucifix, and at the same time he must thrice deny Christ. Accumulated evidence from every country shows that this initiation ritual was common to the whole Order, and although many of the accused attempted the most far-fetched explanations—some protesting that they spat only beside the Cross, others that they spat merely to show their implicit obedience to their Superiors—so horrid an act admits of no palliation. "Alas! alas! that ever I was born, for I have denied God and become the devil's man." These were the words in which a good Franciscan, Brother John Wedderal, heard a young Templar, a novice, lamenting with sobs that seemed to be bursting his heart. Upon Good Friday the Rood was subjected to the foulest sacrilege, and one can hardly be surprised that in the round letter dispatched by Philip Le Bel in September, 1307, to his seneschals and royal officials, the King should have expressed himself as shaken by a great horror and shame at the bestial blasphemies which were reported by most sober and weighty witness.

The main feature of the idolatry of the Templars was the worship of a fearful Head, which it was generally believed in the Order was the source of all their wealth and prosperity. This Head was powerful to save. In fact to the Templars it represented Deity, the Gnostic Deity, and was known by the mysterious name *Baphomet*, which may imply "Absorption into primal Wisdom". Some said it was the Head of the first Grand Master, "who made us and has not left us". According to many accounts the Head was bearded, and a servitor of the Temple confessed that he had seen the idol and the Knights adoring it. "I believe," he said, "it was the head of a devil, *un mauffé*, for it was terrible to look upon with huge staring eyes, two faces, and a great silver beard." It was carried in solemn procession under a canopy with lights and incense. Sometimes it was veiled in silk, and unswathed with many genuflexions and lowly obeisance. The highest grades of the Templars wore magic girdles which had encircled the Head, and with which they were ceremoniously invested. There were, of course, many of these Heads. The English province possessed at least four specimens: one concealed in the sacristy of the London Temple; one at Bottisham, near Cambridge; one at Brewer, near Lincoln; and one beyond the Humber. In some provinces the Head was a stuffed human head, so it is described in the Chronicle of St. Denys —"a very old mummified Head of a man, the skin of which seemed varnished with some strange embalming". It will be remembered in the Biblical narrative, *Genesis* xxxi, 19, when Jacob departed from

Laban, Rachel stole the teraphim that were her father's, and when, pursuing after them, Laban overtakes his son-in-law, he asks: "Wherefore hast thou stolen my gods?" In the Jerus-Targum to this passage (v, 19) these gods are stated to be mummified Heads, who gave Laban knowledge of the future. "They used to slay the first-born of a man and cut off his head, salted it and embalmed it, and wrote incantations on a plate of gold, which they put under its tongue, and stood it up in the walls and it spake with them, and unto such Laban bowed himself." Elias Levita, quoted in Selden *De Diis Syris*, Syntagma I, cap. 2, says the Teraphim consisted of a human head, that of Adam, cut off and preserved in spices, which spake of things to come. This is all exceedingly significant, and in fact throws a flood of light upon the origins of the cult and practices of the Templars.

The trials of the Templars in various European countries extended over a period of more than five years, and in March, 1312, by a bull Clement V officially announced that the Order was found to be so corrupt beyond hope of remedy or reform that it must be dissolved, and accordingly it was declared to be absolutely and entirely suppressed.

It is hardly necessary—and indeed the repetition would be wearisome—to record instance after instance of the mischiefs, the outbreaks and turmoils caused by these freemasonries of evil, great and small. The Franciscan missionary preacher Berthold von Regensburg (*c.* 1220–1272) again and again deplores in his sermons that the villages are full of witches. A certain Ramon de Tarrega (*c.* 1370) was openly proclaiming the doctrine that as their right and by the law of nature worship and sacrifice should be offered to demons. John Nider (died 1438), prior of the great Dominican house at Bâle and Rector of the University of Vienna, who was also a member of the Councils of Constance and Bâle, in his vast work *Formicarius* laments the fearful increase of sorcery, whilst the authors of the encyclopaedic *Malleus Maleficarum* at the end of the fifteenth century, Part I, Question 5, discuss: "Whence comes it that the Practice of Witchcraft hath so notably increased?" When William Wycherley, tailor and witch, was examined in 1549, he confessed that "there be within England above five hundred conjurers, as he thinketh; and specially in Norfolk, Hertfordshire, and Worcestershire, and Gloucestershire a great number". So we see that this terrible society had already firmly established itself on English soil. Some have expressed incredulity at the avowals of a French sorcerer, Troisechelles du Mayne, when in 1571 Charles IX himself out of curiosity interrogated the accused. This wretch boasted that there were more than thirty thousand satanists at that time in France, and the numbers do not appear to be at all exaggerated. During fifteen years, from 1576 to 1591, Nicolas Remy, Provost of Nancy, in Lorraine—that is to say the judge in all criminal cases throughout that particular district—condemned nine hundred sorcerers to death. "There are witches by the thousand everywhere, multiplying upon the earth like worms in a garden," wrote Henry Boguet in 1590. "What figure can we estimate the number of those which could be found in all the different countries of the world?" he asks. Lambert Daneau, writing in

1574, tells us that in many districts "the witches are so defiant and audacious that they say openly, if only they had an eminent and renowned man for their captain, they would become so strong and numerous that they could march against a powerful king in pitched battle, and easily vanquish him with the help of their art and their strategies". Well might the learned Pierre Nodé, a Minim friar, entitle his valuable work, published at Paris in 1578, *A Protest against the Execrable Errors of Witches, Sorcerers, Enchanters, Magicians, Diviners and the like Observers of foul Superstitions, all of whom at the present Time are secretly swarming throughout the length and breadth of France.*

Had, indeed, their leaders been ready and united at the end of the sixteenth century it was planned that in practically every European country these satanic revolutionaries should rise at a given signal, when universal chaos and confusion would have ensued. It happened, humanly speaking, by a mere accident that the crisis was averted. In one kingdom, at least, their conspiracies almost succeeded. Under the direction of Francis Stewart, Earl of Bothwell, who was aiming at the throne, the whole body of witches combined to attempt by any possible means they could the life of King James VI (of Scotland, I of England). On All Hallows Eve, 31 October, 1590, a full assembly of more than two hundred witches was convened at midnight at the old haunted church of North Berwick, where the Grand Master, Bothwell himself, harangued them from the pulpit. After they had performed their devilish ceremonies they debated how to kill the King. Some of the gang had already brewed strong poisons and corrosive ointments with which they proposed to smear a shirt or any linen worn by James, and they had, indeed, endeavoured, but with no success, to bribe one of the valets of the royal chamber to procure them some article of apparel which would be next the skin. Others urged different methods, and they wrangled and jarred for a good while together.

Barbara Napier, one of the chief witches, openly acknowledged that their designs on the King's life had as their object "that another might have ruled in his Majesty's place, and the government might have gone to the Devil". On one occasion Bothwell and certain of his followers forced their way almost to the royal bedchamber in a ferocious attempt to murder him. There was no man whom the King hated and feared so much as his unruly cousin, and this not only because he knew him to be aspiring to the crown, but also because he knew he was the leader of the Satanists and anarchists. The trial of the witches in 1590 caused a terrific scandal. There is no more thrilling piece of journalism than the contemporary pamphlet which describes the whole affair in most graphic detail. This rejoices in the title, *News from Scotland, Declaring the Damnable life and death of Doctor Fian, a notable Sorcerer, who was burned at Edenbrough in January last,* 1591. *Which Doctor was register to the Devil that sundry times preached at North Berwick Kirk, to a number of notorious Witches.* John Fian, alias Cunningham, who was quite a young man, was Bothwell's secretary, and a moving spirit in the conspiracy. The most recent reprint of *News from Scotland* is that in the Bodley Head Quartos, No. 9, with an Introduction by Dr. G. B. Harrison. Bothwell's claims to be considered heir to King James were finally quashed upon the King's marriage with Anne of Denmark and the birth of children. He was perforce driven into exile, where in after-years we catch a curious glimpse of him living at Naples, for old George Sandys, the traveller, tells how, when he was in the south of Italy, "a certain Calabrian, hearing that I was an Englishman, came to me, and would needs persuade me that I had insight in magic, for that Earl Bothwell was my countryman, who lives at Naples, and is in these parts famous for suspected nigromancy".

Well might the grave Richard Baxter, in his weighty and carefully considered treatise, the summing up of more than fifty years' experience, *An Historical Discourse of Apparitions and Witches* (1691), speak of "Satan's great and dangerous Army", and point out that Revenge is "the most ordinary Business of Witches and of Devilized Souls", who may be known by three marks, Lying, Malignity, and Hurtfulness. Where, indeed, do these three appear more clearly than in the members of Secret and Subversive Societies, and is not the whole business of revolutionaries Revenge, revenge upon all orderly and peaceful life, upon religion, upon culture, upon beauty? Revenge is always itching to destroy. Baxter certainly hit the mark when he wrote "that Devils make no small number of the Laws and Rulers that are made in the World, and have no small number of honoured Servants, and are the Authors of most of the Wars in the World".

It can be proved that the French Revolution was carefully planned and mapped out in detail many years before it happened. The whole upheaval was manipulated and designed by Satanists from first to last, and that not merely in its broad outlines and events, but even in detail. This has been shown beyond all dispute by the testimony of Professor Robison, Abbé Barruel, and many other solid historians.

Since then the same evil forces have planned and carried out other revolutions, until at last they have involved the whole world in chaos and strife. Definite instructions have been handed down to successive officials: figurehead governments are set up, and "secret advisers" reduce monarchies to a mere legal fiction.

One hundred years ago Disraeli published his political novel *Coningsby; or, The New Generation*, in which (Book IV, Chapter xv) Sidonia makes the following very ominous and pregnant remark: "So you see, my dear Coningsby, that the world is governed by very different personages to what is imagined by those who are not behind the scenes."

Origin

CHAPTER IV

The Origins of Witchcraft—The Sons of God and the Daughters of Men—Who was the First Witch?—Assyrian and Egyptian Witchcraft—The Mummies—The "Dianic Cult".

"And the magicians of Egypt did so with their enchantments."—*Exodus* vii, 23.

FROM the very first moment that he was conscious of and could correlate his own experiences, primitive man realized that he possessed a spirit separable from his body, and capable of an independent incorporeal existence. With unpremeditated, yet none the less strictly accurate logical, deduction, he could not see that this spirit ceased to be with the death of the body; in other words, to him the dead were not dead in the sense that they had for ever left the scenes of their earthly life. They were still interested in the places they had known, in the persons with whom they had companioned, in the pursuits they had followed and preferred. Naturally their individual affections and dislikes were conceived of as enduring. They would yet lend their aid to their families and friends, and bear their part against personal enemies or the tribal foe. Frazer points out (*The Fear of the Dead in Primitive Religion*, 1933, Lecture II, pp. 38-9—quoting from C. G. Seligman, *The Melanesians of British New Guinea*, 1910; and F. E. Williams, *Orokaiva Society*, 1930) how the Roro-speaking tribes of British New Guinea believe that the ghosts of the departed still linger in the villages of their people, and should they desert the village, the inhabitants would have no luck at all. The favour of these ghosts, however, has to be sought and secured. It is not an unconditional goodwill, since if they are offended they will send bad luck in hunting and fishing. Again, with regard to the Orokaiva people in the east of British New Guinea, every Orokaiva gardener and hunter thinks that the spirits of the dead can send him success in tilling and the chase. Since, then, these spirits can take a very definite part in man's affairs, and prosper, or it may be hinder and balk, the ordinary businesses of daily life, it is advisable to be on good terms with the departed, to propitiate and placate them. Mr. E. Baxter Riley, in his study *Among Papuan Headhunters*, 1925, tells us that the Kiwai of British New Guinea "are all firm believers in the existence of their ancestors' spirits, that these take an interest in their daily lives, and thᵃᵗ they are able to help or mar their undertakings. In …" … ies—for fighting, hunting, fishing, gardening— … d toasts drunk to their ancestors, who are earnestly … d to come to their aid on the projected enterprise. … n site chosen, a garden fence built, a yam planted, … on undertaken without these spirits being called … sper the enterprise." These spirits are obviously … greater powers than any living man, and it is a … nportance to stand well with them, so that they … ers beneficially. If their good pleasure may be … rections carried out, man has won them as very potent allies and guardians. There can, then, be no person more influential and esteemed than the individual who by some means is able to get in touch with these spirits, to converse with them, to learn and interpret their wishes to his fellows who are less favoured in this respect than he. Thus the primitives of Mortlock Island in the Caroline Group believe that they are surrounded by the spirits of their forefathers, who walk unseen with them wherever they go, who protect them from all kinds of dangers, who guide them right, and who have a clear vision of what the future holds. In which belief, of course, the islanders are perfectly correct, save only that the spirits are not those of their ancestors, and with regard to the future they know no more than is permitted. But the Mortlock folk recognize that only certain gifted persons can communicate with and talk to the spirits, so when a man wishes to consult and hold intercourse with them he must do so through the proper channel, that is to say by the help of a professional seer. The medium seats himself upon the ground and invokes the spirits, emptying so far as possible his mind and brain of any thought, and leaving, as it were, a blank for the spirits to take possession. This they do, at a shorter or a longer interval, and their presence is shown by convulsive movements all over the medium's body. His breast heaves, his fingers twitch, his hands quiver and beat the air, his head wags, his whole frame teeters and wambles to and fro. Then the spirits in hoarse hollow voices speak through his mouth. Mr. W. G. Ivens, in *The Melanesians of the South-East Solomon Islands*, 1927, says that in the Solomon Islands there is a large professional class of mediums, who can be consulted concerning various circumstances of everyday life, especially on behalf of the sick, when they pass into trance and the spirit who has taken possession of the medium answers the querent. Dr. R. H. Codrington (*The Melanesians*, 1891) tells us that among the Melanesians a forecast of the future, counsel and advice, will often be imparted by one of the "gifted", who not only appears to be quite unconscious whilst the spirit speaks through him, but who does nothing to invite such a visitation. In the island of Florida, if any course of action is being debated the man known to have the prophetic spirit will sometimes begin to tremble and then sneeze violently two or three times. His eyes stare into vacancy, his limbs writhe, and strong shudders rack his whole frame. His lips are flecked with foam: he utters curious guttural noises. Then suddenly he breaks forth into a flood of speech, but the voice is not his own. He has passed under control, and the spirit dictates the best way of dealing with the matter under discussion; it may be the chances of success in a foray, or some similar expedition. When he returns to himself the man is quite exhausted and spent, and has no knowledge of what the spirit, using his organs of speech, has said. More often, indeed, the man makes some effort to summon the spirit, and he informs the rest what the spirit conveys to him. These practices and possessions, these epilepsies and trances, and controls giving messages and advice, can in every detail be paralleled in hundreds of séance-rooms in London and New York, in Paris and Vienna, in every large town the whole world over.

Charles Godfrey Leland, in his *Gypsy Sorcery and Fortune Telling*, 1891, gives his views at length on "The Origin of Witchcraft, Shamanism, and

Sorcery". He pictures how "out of the earliest time, in the very two o'clock of a misty morning in history, man came forth believing in terrors and evils as soon as he could talk, and talking about them as fast as he formed them. . . . We all know how difficult it is for many people when someone dies out of a household to get over the involuntary feeling that we shall unexpectedly meet the departed in the usual haunts. In almost every family there is a record how someone has heard a voice the others cannot hear, or the dead speaking in the familiar tones. Hence the belief in ghosts, as soon as men began to care for death at all, or to miss those who had gone. So first of all came terrors and spectres, or *revenants*, and from setting out food for the latter, which was the most obvious and childlike manner to please them, grew sacrifices to evil spirits. . . . Then there sprung up at once—quite as early—the *Magus*, or the *cleverer* man, who had the wit to do the sacrificing. . . . This was the Shaman. He seems to have had a Tartar-Mongol-mongrel-Turanian origin, some-where in Central Asia, and to have spread with his magic drum, and songs, and stinking smoke, exorcising his fiends all over the face of the earth. But the earliest authentic records of Shamanism are to be found in the Accadian, proto-Chaldaean and Babylon records. According to these all diseases whatever, as well as disasters, were directly the work of evil spirits, which were to be driven away by songs of exorcism, burning of perfumes or evil-smelling drugs, and performing ceremonies, many of which, with scraps of the exorcisms, are found in familiar use here and there at the present day. . . . It would seem, at least among the Lap-landers, Finns, Eskimoes, and Red Indians, that the *first* stage of Shaman-ism was a very horrible witchcraft, practised chiefly by women, in which attempts were made to *conciliate* the evil spirits; . . . fragments of dead bodies and poison, and unheard-of terrors and crimes formed its basis. An immense amount of it in its vilest conceivable forms still exists among the negroes as *Voodoo*." It has, indeed, persisted throughout the ages, for black magic is, as its master, unchanging and unchanged. The Erichtho of Lucan prowls among the tombs to collect fragments of dead bodies, and gathers from the gallows-tree the rotting limbs of long-executed criminals. Francesco Guazzo, in his famous *Compendium Maleficarum*, Book II, Chapter i, discusses how witches use several parts of corpses to confect their soporific spells, and the following chapter has as caption, "Witches use Human Corpses for the Murder of Men". Remy, again, in his *Demonolatry*, has a chapter, Book II, iii, "That Witches make Evil Use of Human Corpses; especially of Abortive Births, Criminals put to Death by the Law, or any that have died some Shameful or Dishonourable Death". Witches have always been adepts in poisoning, and have had an extraordinary knowledge of baneful herbs and mortal drugs. There is not a single writer upon the subject who has not remarked on this. The terrors inspired by this "cursed vermin", as Boguet well terms them, and their crimes are the theme of every book in the whole vast library of witch-craft.

I have thought it useful to quote *in extenso* from Leland because, although his views are obviously coloured, it is easy enough to discount his bias, and if, instead of his rather unfortunate and misleading phrase "the *cleverer* man", we substitute "the *psychic* man", what he says is in the main well worth serious attention. The reason why man "came forth believing in terrors and evils" is simply because the terrors and evils were there and very real, and the simplicity of primitive man was sensibly conscious of their activities and of their presence all about him. He had, we must never forget, his guardians, the good Angels, concerning whom Noel Taillepied has written so eloquently, an authority who justly sums up: "It is quite certain that there are Spirits, both good and bad, who appear to men. There is also a third kind of Spirits, which we call Ghosts, that is to say after the soul is separated from the body."

In antediluvian times it is recorded "that the sons of God saw the daughters of men that they were fair; and they took them wives of all which they chose. There were giants in the earth in those days; and also after that, when the sons of God came in unto the daughters of men, and they bore children to them, the same became mighty men which were of old, men of renown. And God saw that the wickedness of man was great in the earth" *Genesis* vi, 2, 4, 5 (A.V.). Philo in his Platonic treatise *On the Giants*, for all his vein of transcendental allegory, warns us: "Let no one suppose that what is here said is a myth."

In his tragedy *Heaven and Earth*, a much finer poem than is generally allowed, Byron has some very striking lines. The patriarch Noah, coming upon the Angels Samiasa and Azâzêl in the company of the two sisters Anah and Aholibamah, exclaims:

> These are they, then,
> Who leave the throne of God, to take them wives
> From out the race of Cain; the sons of heaven,
> Who seek earth's daughters for their beauty? . . .
> Woe, woe, woe to such communion!
> Has not God made a barrier between earth
> And heaven, and limited each, kind to kind?

Samiasa, with great sophistry, replies to excuse this sexual love between spiritual and material creatures:

> Was not man made in high Jehovah's image?
> Did God not love what He had made? And what
> Do we but imitate and emulate
> His love unto created love?

Byron poetically regards these Angels as bright spirits, who have come down from the empyrean to conjoin with the daughters of Cain, but on his title-page he sounds a note of warning that all is not as it seems by quoting Coleridge's line, "And woman wailing for her demon lover", *Kubla Khan* (I, 16. 'And' should be 'By'). We may now inquire who exactly are meant by the expression "sons of God" in this passage of *Genesis* vi, 2? The understanding of this must to some extent depend on the description of the offspring of the unions between the "sons of God" and the daughters of men.

It may be remarked, however, that Dr. Driver, in his excursuses on the *Book of Genesis*, fifth edition, 1906, pp. 82-3, a commentary which has as its aim "to interpret the meaning of each book of the Bible in the light of modern knowledge to English readers", explicitly states: "The 'sons of God' (or 'of the gods') denotes elsewhere semi-divine, supra-mundane beings, such as, when regarded, as is more usually the case, as agents executing a Divine commission, are called Angels (i.e. 'messengers'). And this, which is the oldest interpretation of *Genesis* vi, 2, is the only sense in which the expression can be legitimately understood here." If we read "sons of God", it is figurative, and signifies spiritual beings created by God. If we are to take it as "sons of gods," it implies members of that class of divine beings to which Yahweh Himself in one sense belongs, although immeasurably inferior to Him. This is hardly admissible, and we are far safer if we prefer "sons of God". Dr. N. P. Williams, in his Bampton Lectures, *The Ideas of the Fall and of Original Sin*, 1927, writes of the first eight verses of the sixth chapter of *Genesis:* "As these verses stand, the only construction to be put upon them appears to be as follows: The 'sons of the gods' are divine beings, of an order inferior to Yahweh—or, to employ a later and more familiar term, 'angels'—who gave way to lust, and committed sin by deserting their heavenly abode and mingling the divine essence with the seed of man. This unnatural action introduces the principle of evil into humanity." In the Ethiopic *Book of Enoch* these "sons of God" are termed "watchers", the wakeful ones, because they were of the Angels who rest neither day nor night, but in lowly reverence watch Almighty God so as to be ready on the instant to obey His commands; Angels who, as the Psalmist says, are "mighty in strength, and execute His word, hearkening to the voice of His orders". In the *Book of Daniel* (iv, 13, 17, 23) the Angel is called "a watcher and an holy one coming down from heaven". The *Book of Enoch* relates that these Angels who desired the daughters of men were in number two hundred, that they descended from Heaven and lay with the women whose beauty ensnared them. The leaders of these sinning Angels were Azâzêl and Semjâzâ. Far back, before Time was, Angels fell through Pride, and there seems to have been a second fall of the Angels through Lust. The "watchers" corrupted the world with hideous wickedness, and in the course of the years, when God looked upon man, He saw "that all the thought of their heart was bent upon evil at all times".

The women who had mated with these Angels bore "mighty men", that is to say, according to the Revised Version, the *Nephilim*, or giants—the Vulgate has "gigantes" and "potentes", "the mighty men of old", Douay. In the *Book of Wisdom* they are spoken of as the "proud giants", and the prophet Amos further says that their height was like the height of cedar trees, and they were as strong as an oak. An admirable commentary on the Douay Version explains that though these men were truly of an immense stature and most formidable strength, "these here spoken of are called *giants*, as being not only tall in stature, but violent and savage in their dispositions, and mere monsters of cruelty and lust". "Not only," says Sinistrari, "were they distinguished by their huge size, but also by their physical powers, their rapine and their tyranny. Through their abominable misdeeds the Giants, according to Cornelius à Lapide, in his *Commentary upon Genesis*, were the primary and principal cause of the

Flood." Since, then, the intercourse of the daughters of men with these "sons of God" gave birth to beings of vast bulk and unexampled ferocity and wickedness, it is very plain that these "sons of God" became upon their apostasy Incubi demons, who, Sinistrari points out, may in one sense be called "sons of God". This is unquestionable, since it is recorded in the *Book of Job*, ii, 1, "on a certain day the sons of God came, and stood before the Lord, and Satan came *among them*, and stood in His sight". That the "sons of God" spoken of in *Genesis* were, or at any rate became, Incubi demons is maintained by a very large number of learned men, as, for example, Archbishop Paul de Santa Maria of Burgos, Lord Chancellor of Spain (died 1435), and Francisco Valesio, a famous Spanish physician whose translations of and excursuses upon the old medical writers are highly esteemed. Hugh of St. Victor says that Incubi are spiritual beings who assume corporeity and thus commit lewdness with women. Michael Psellus, the famous Byzantine scholar of the tenth century, in his treatise *On the Activities of Demons*, makes it quite clear that demons are capable of sensual passions, and he explains how they are able to perform the venereal act. "Almost all Theologians and learned Philosophers are agreed, and it has been the experience of all times and all nations, that witches practise coition with demons, the men with Succubus devils, and the women with Incubus devils." Thus writes the judicious Guazzo. St. Augustine says quite positively that the fact of such uncleanness being practised is so well known and so well assured that it were brazen impudence to deny it. The physiological and psychological bearings of these unions are treated of in detail by all demonologists, who are further unanimous in believing that children can be generated by Incubi. The *Malleus Maleficarum* discusses this question at great length and is entirely convincing. Guazzo lays down that a human child can be born of a witch and an Incubus devil. This is also the studied opinion of the learned Martin Delrio, who cites a very large number of authorities to that effect. There is an account of such a union in *Annales Médico-Psychologiques*, for the year 1843, Vol. II, p. 304, and in *Folk-Lore*, 1911, Vol. XXII, pp. 330–1; there is the more recent history of a Perthshire woman who was wooed by a demon, but who fortunately escaped the snare. Peter Thyraeus, S.J., in his treatise upon Apparitions, sums up in these weighty words: "It is so rash and inept to pretend to deny the fact of these unions that in order to maintain this attitude of doubt and scepticism you must needs reject and spurn the whole catena of solid arguments and carefully considered conclusions of the most holy and authoritative doctors, nay, you must wage war against man's sense and human consciousness and experience whilst at the same time you are shamefully exposing your ignorance of the power of the Devil and the empery evil spirits may obtain over man." Dom Dominic Schram, a famous Benedictine writer, in his *Institutes of Mystical Theology*, published at Paris in 1848, gives it as his opinion: "It is positively certain and proven that—whatever the incredulous may say—there actually exist such demons, incubi or succubi. The men and women who suffer these impudicities are either so abandoned that they invite and allure demons, or else they freely consent to the prompting of demons tempting them to indulge in so dark abominations. That these and other filthy wretches may be assaulted and overcome by the demon we cannot doubt, and I myself have known several persons who, although they were greatly troubled on account of their crimes and utterly loathed this foul inter-course with the demon, were nevertheless compelled by violence and sorely against their will to endure these horrible assaults of Satan." I remember Monsieur Aubalt de la Haulte Chambre relating how once, when he was accidentally benighted, he was given hospitality and slept in a very ancient bedroom, where he passed a most unhappy and dis-turbed night. There appeared in the darkness strange lascivious shapes which seemed absolutely corporeal and human. He was in misery until the dawn. The result, after he had reached home, was an indisposition of several days due to fatigue and excessive nervous strain. This caused him to miss an engagement with J.-K. Huysmans, to whom, when they next met, he disclosed the reason of his recent illness. "My poor boy!" exclaimed the great man. "Did you not know that, explain it as we may, the house you were staying at, at least the room you actually occupied, is infested by these fleshmongering spirits, these bawdy incubi?" So it would appear that some places are particularly obnoxious to these lewd hauntings, and indeed Sinistrari tells us as much.

In literature references to these unions are a poetical commonplace. Thus in Coleridge's Sonnet "To Mrs. Siddons" we have

> hags, who at the witching time
> Of murky midnight ride the air sublime,
> And mingle foul embrace with fiends of Hell.

The curious question has been asked—Who was the first witch? The Abbé Simonnet, in his work *The Reality of Magic*, summarizes St. Augustine to the following effect: The whole race of Cain proved in-herently evil, bloody and murderous, turning almost instinctively, as it were, to wickedness. Accordingly, whilst God declared His will to Seth by the mediation of good Angels, Cain, who had gone out from the presence of the Lord, sought the aid of the demon and his angels. Satan deceived and deluded the children of Cain by the glamour of false and lying wonders, so that they worshipped him, and this was the beginning of diabolism. St. Clement, St. Augustine, Eusebius, Lactantius, and other writers are of opinion that sorcery and the worship of the devil were the chief reasons for the Deluge. Of the three sons of Noah, two, Shem and Japheth, followed the example and precepts of their father, the third, Cham (Ham), who fell under his father's curse, revived the forbidden science and initiated his son Mizraim into these horrid mysteries.

Bovet, in his *Pandæmonium*, writes of "the Idolatry of the first Ages after the Flood, and the defection to Devil-worship, a great step to Infernal Confederacies". Cham was the father of Canaan, from whom descended Sidon, the father of the Sidonians, who worshipped "the Devils themselves for Deities". "It cannot be supposed difficult that the Destroyer (having brought the Nations to bow to his altars and worship him for their god) should work them into those diabolical practices and instruct them in those Hellish Arts such as were Divinations, Charms, Enchantments, converse with Spirits, with the dependent Arts and black mysteries concomitant thereto." Jacob Boehme, the mystic, says: "Cham's progeny became unspiritual man, materialists, on whom was the curse, who were blind to the light of nature, blind to the interior light." In the *Book of Enoch* we are told that the "sons of God", the Watchers, after their fall, corrupted the whole human race, by imparting to man mysterious knowledge which it was not good for him to know. In some sense they may be said to have betrayed the secrets of God, and their sin was very great. Azâzêl taught his sons metallurgy, the manner of welding armour and making sharp blades, so to him are due strife and murders. He also revealed to his concubines the cosmetical arts, how to prepare fard and maquillage, how to adorn and perfume their bodies, whence arose strange jealousies and much wantonness. Other of these angels unfolded to men the sciences of magic and astrology, and instructed them in the darker crafts of power, in necromancy, in the rituals and incantations of sorcery. Cham learned these arcana and studied them deeply, whence after the Flood he was able to hand on the ancient knowledge which, save for him, had been so well lost and forgotten. The satanism of Cain and his race was primitive, uncouth, and barbarous; the goety inculcated by the fallen Watchers and transmitted by Cham was an exactly systematized science, and if possible even more dark and dangerous.

The family of Cham separated into various tribes, and one group, of which he was the leader, found their way to Persia. The native Bactrians were so wrought upon and amazed by the glamour of his enchantments that they named him Zoroaster, which being interpreted means "Living Star", or "Bright Star of Life". Cham-Zoroaster, inspired by the devil, was the first to teach that the stars are gods and to be worshipped. (Philo held that the stars were souls divine, and this was also the doctrine of the Stoics.) Hence men began to sacrifice to the stars, and they adored all the planetary host of heaven. Anne Catherine Emmerich spoke of "planetary spirits". There was Aku the moon-god, who in some places was worshipped as Sin. In the *Book of Joshua* xv, 7, mention is made of a very ancient brook or rivulet "the waters of En-Shemesh", on the borders of Judah. This name means "fountain of the sun", and the spring had from time immemorial been connected with sun-worship. In *Numbers* xxxii, 3, we find a reference to Nebo, a word equivalent to Speaker, the planet Mercury worshipped by the Babylonians. When St. Stephen was before the Council (*Acts* vii) in his speech he quoted from the prophet Amos:

> O house of Israel,
> Ye took up the tabernacle of Moloch,
> And the Star of the god Rephan,
> The figures which ye made to worship them.

Moloch, king of heaven, was the god of the Phoenicians and Ammonites. Rephan, or Rempham, as the word is variously written, is the Egyptian name for the planet Saturn, and occurs in the book of Amos in the Septuagint version. The Douay translates: "You carried a tabernacle for your Moloch, and the star of your god Rempham, figures which you made to adore them."

In later days the Ophites, a fearful secret society, were accused of paying divine honours to a demon whom they identified with the constellation Ophiuchus, the Serpent-holder. Pliny, in his *Natural History*, writes that Zoroaster was the first to teach and practise systematized magic, and hence may be considered the first magician. The evil tradition was handed on by his pupil Azonaces. Apuleius, in his famous *Apologia*, says that Zoroaster and Oromazus were the inventors of magic; but then he is using "magic" in a very different sense. The fact is that, as the celebrated Dominican Sisto of Siena emphasizes, there were at least two persons named Zoroaster, and a good deal of confusion has been caused. There was Cham-Zoroaster, traditionally believed to have been the first magician, and there was a second and much later Zoroaster, the prophet of Iran, who lived (as modern scholars have computed) about 1000 B.C., and was a great doctrinal reformer. Francis Barrett, in his biography of Zoroaster, writes: "We find no less than five Zoroasters mentioned in history: to these five may be added a sixth, mentioned by Apuleius." This latter Zoroaster, called by Suidas, Zares, and by Plutarch, Zaratus, was according to some authors the master of Pythagoras. Another Zoroaster, whom they name Zardhust, came from China and was an adept in ancient magic.

Pliny relates that magic penetrated into Greece by means of Osthanes, a soothsayer who accompanied Xerxes on his expedition against the West, 480 B.C., and this may be the case, but this Osthanes must be another and later necromancer than the Osthanes or Hostanes, who is regarded by some as Nimrod, the son of Cush, eldest son of Cham-Zoroaster, and who lived 2300 B.C. Others, again, have it that Hostanes is Balaam, the prophet of Pethor, a city of Mesopotamia, who lived about 1452 B.C. Be that as it may, there was a Hostanes of blackest infamy among the patriarchs of evil.

According to the *Annals of Clonmacnoise*, the Tuathy De Danan, princes ruling Ireland, 2000 B.C., were master-magicians whose sorceries enabled them to wield immense powers. The ancient chronicles declare that these despots were the most skilful of all reim-kennars, which is to say wizards versed in runes and spells, in the known world, the world (of course) known to the old scribes.

When the Spaniards discovered Mexico they found that for dateless centuries among this and all previous civilizations was practised a system of sorcery which could be exactly paralleled in almost every detail by the witchcrafts of Europe. Again and again the first explorers and the earlier Spanish authors express their horror at the pantheon of foul demons whom the native peoples placated with the most hideous abominations of lust and cruelty. It was indeed a devil-ridden land. One of the most powerful of the Mexican devil-deities was Tezcatlipoca, of whom Bernal Diaz del Castillo writes in his *True History of the Conquest of Mexico*, "He was the god of hell and had charge of the souls of the

Mexicans, and his body was girt with figures like little devils with snakes' heads." He was also known as *Yaotzin*, "The Enemy", and during the dark hours he roamed the forest depths ever seeking new votaries whom he could terrify into serving him. The Mexican witches held their Sabbat at the cross-roads, where they adored Tezcatlipoca, who would appear to them under some hideous phantom form, and it is not in the least surprising to learn that the business of these hellish rendezvous was precisely the same as the foul horrors enacted at the *Aquelarre* of the Navarre witches in the sixteenth and seventeenth centuries. Aquelarre was the local Sabbat, and the term is derived from a Biscayan word signifying "field of the goat". Tezcatlipoca was none other than Satan, the old serpent, the adversary, the Enemy of God and man. As early as 1531, the first Bishop of Mexico, the saintly Juan de Zumarraga, who had had great experience in witch-trials at home during the prosecution of the witches of Biscay, writing to the Chapter of Tolosa, sends news that "five hundred and more great temples dedicate to demons have been utterly destroyed, and above twenty thousand graven images and statues of devils, which were worshipped therein, have been broken to pieces and burned with fire to completest calcination". And yet even in the seventeenth century the priests of the Province of Oaxaca were appalled to learn that numbers of Indians who professed to be zealous in the true faith were meeting secretly at night in certain terribly haunted spots to hold their Sabbats and worship the demon.

When we find that at the very dawn of history countries so distant and far removed as Ireland and Mexico were thus deeply imbued with magic, it is plain that, although strictly the East was the original and fount of all occult arts, we must allow for very early and wide ramifications. Regarding Cham-Zoroaster as the first wizard after the Flood, and the depositary of antediluvian sorceries, then his sons, Cush, father of the Ethiopians; Mizraim, father of the two Egypts, Upper and Lower; Phut, father of the wandering Bedouin tribes; and Canaan, father of the Phoenicians, were four missionaries of diabolism. From Cush are derived all African witchcraft, all secret cults of the black tribes—whether we class them as Bantus or as Negroes in the stricter sense of the words—all leopard, hyena, and jaguar societies, African ophiolatry, voodoo, and obeah. Cush was himself the father of Nimrod (or Nembroth, Nebroth), a giant wizard of mickle might, the beginning of whose kingdom was Babylon, and Uruk (modern Warka), on the Euphrates, the capital of Babylonia as early as 4000 B.C. According to the *Malleus Maleficarum*, Nimrod was the first who compelled men to worship fire, and he is said to have been "a mighty hunter", "not of beasts", writes an old commentator, "but of men, whom by violence and tyranny he brought under his dominion, although in later days the proverb ran as if Nimrod were a stout follower of the chase and venery, as indeed was also no doubt the case". Mizraim, who was, tradition tells us, even more deeply versed in occult arts than his brethren, and who had been initiated by his father into the ultimate secrets of his dark science, left a legacy of magic to the Egyptians, his descendants. We know that the various peoples inhabiting the land of Canaan—the Hivites, Perizzites, Jebusites,

Amorites, and the rest—used divination, observed times, were charmers, enchanters, consulters with familiar spirits, wizards, and necromancers, which practices were denounced as "the abomination of these nations", and it was said "because of these abominations the Lord thy God doth drive them out from before thee". Among the sons of Cush were Sebah, whose children travelled far and wide over the face of the earth, and Sabtah, whose sons built a city which had in later days sixty temples of demons to whom they offered much frankincense, and the mysterious Sabatacha, and it may well have been that from these the mysteries of magic and the Satanic cult penetrated to Mexico and Ireland. Among the sons of Mizraim was Caphtorium. Caphtor is usually identified with Crete, so we are beginning to be linked up with the Minoan civilization, with the traditions of Pasiphae and the Minotaur, which may have some close connexion with a demoniac society. Crete also was the home of many mysterious cults, and the Cretans were reputed to be fascinators, able to cast the evil eye, the modern Neapolitan *jettatori*. These are the "eye-biting" witches, or "basilisk" witches, and, as Boguet says, they cause injury by their very glances. In fine, the descendants of Cham-Zoroaster were scattered abroad here and there, in the course of centuries, over the whole earth, and they carried with them and sowed diligently their dark secrets and sorceries. For, as Kramer and Sprenger observe, "these evil arts did not suddenly burst upon the world, but rather were developed in process of time".

That the fallen Watchers, the Incubi, should have taught their concubines magic lore is not at all strange. The Devil and his angels, Guazzo explains, did not in sinning, lose the great gifts of knowledge and perception which are of the essence of the angelic nature, and in which they are infinitely superior to man. The intelligence of a demon is of a very high order, far greater than human intelligence. "In addition to this," says Remy, "the demon is endowed with extraordinary keenness and subtlety of apprehension; amazing agility and speed of motion." This enables us to understand why evil spirits raised by sorcerers, or evil spirits speaking through mediums, appear to be able to prophesy and foretell future events, and very often their prognostications prove correct. Not that they have, nor can they have, any knowledge of the future, for this belongs to God alone, and if they appear (as is indeed often the case) to be possessed of such knowledge, it is nothing more than presentiment and clever conjecture drawn by a shrewd induction from the past, or else it is a simulated prediction of events which they have already determined, so far as lies in them, to bring about, or it may be that it is an early announcement of something which has actually just happened, which they can make to seem as if it were prophesied before it happened by reason of their lightning speed from place to place, even from most remote and distant regions. Demons have the memory of all that has happened from the remotest antiquity, from the dawn of time and the very beginning of all things, and then they are immensely experienced, and, as St. Basil remarks, even we, by comparison and a probable induction from things past, can often conjecture with wonderful accuracy what is to come. Moreover, evil spirits delight to corrupt men by teaching them the foulest mysteries.

Bovet argues of spirits that "their essences being soft and subtil, and uncompounded, not manacled with textures of flesh, nor encumbered with solid Bones and Joints; they can dilate or condense themselves into what forms they please, and appear in semblances bright, or obscure, to effect their Airy purposes; they are in Capacity to collect distant Intelligences, and to make Observations from causes foreign and remote from Mortal apprehensions. Sometimes with an officious kind of Friendship, discovering such things as may seem to the advantage of those that consult them; when all the while such beguiled Inquirers are drawn into palpable and destructive delusions: At other times they are Ministers of Terrors unto such as their Confederates direct them to, and sometimes to the Sorcerers themselves. There is a manifest grant that Spirits have things known and revealed to them that are hidden from and above the ken of Man; or why should Men use means to ask and inquire of Spirits concerning contingencies and events, as hath been usual and customary in all Ages? Neither can we suppose that the Almighty would have forbidden such Inquiry as He doth expressly in the eighth chapter of the Prophecy of *Isaiah*, verse 19: And when they shall say unto you, Seek unto them that have familiar spirits, and unto wizards that peep and that mutter: should not a people seek unto their God? for the living to the dead?''

There are many recorded cases in which women have learned extraordinary things from their demon lovers, and by promulgating the same have come to be regarded with great veneration—nay, have even won disciples and been honoured as saints for their pseudo-revelations and prophecies.

This is extremely difficult and most debatable ground, complicated as the question is by the phenomena of telepathy and second sight, when all suspicion of deceit, quackery, or devilry must without the least scruple be entirely discarded. There are, also, the border-line happenings. No doubt even in the cases of most honourable, honest, and even pious, mediumistic individuals, the devil may, if permitted, occasionally interfere, although there be no thought of implicit, far less explicit, invocation. The fallen angel, however, invariably betrays himself, and that very soon.

A famous Parisian clairvoyante, Mlle C——, who attracted great attention about forty years ago, declared, and without question genuinely believed, that she was influenced and assisted by St. Gabriel, for the spirit who utilized her professed to be the great Archangel. Certain predictions were suggested to her, and in May, 1896, at a séance held at the house of Mme la Comtesse de Maillé, the seeress in halting rhymes foretold, with amazing exactitude of detail, the tragedy of the fire at the Bazar de la Charité, which took place on 4 May, 1897. This prophecy occasioned widespread comment in Paris, and after the fatal catastrophe it was quoted on all sides. Now, the fire was caused by a horrible crime, and the devil who inspired this arson, and who could calculate how far his wretched instruments were to be relied upon, did not go far astray in delivering through the clairvoyante a prophecy of this kind.

One of the most notorious historical instances of a woman tutored by her incubus was that of Magdalena de la Cruz, of the convent of Santa Isabel de los Angeles, of Cordova, which she entered when seventeen years old, in 1504. For thirty-nine years she successfully exhibited a series of phenomena, trances, visions, prophecies, which deluded well-nigh all Spain, and caused her to be regarded with the utmost veneration by the highest and the lowest in the land. Some, however, were not deceived. St. Ignatius Loyola entirely distrusted these exterior marvels, and rebuked one of her followers with great severity. Blessed Juan de Avila, one of the directors of St. Teresa, and a profound master of the mystical life, refused to believe in the heavenly origin of these ecstasies and soothsayings. In 1543 Magdalena fell dangerously ill, and was given over by the physicians. Believing that she lay on her death-bed, the sick woman, with floods of tears, made a full and ample confession of her imposture, and acknowledged that almost from the first she had acted under the influence and by the help of two evil spirits, Balban and Patorrio. These incubi not only were her paramours, but had taught her all kinds of juggling sleights and instructed her in seeming prophecies and visions of future events. The tale was a long and terrible one. Magdalena recovered, and the ecclesiastical authorities began an examination into these extraordinary happenings. A vast number of witnesses were heard, so that the process did not conclude until 3 May, 1546, when judgement was pronounced. This, in effect, was perpetual seclusion in the convent of Santa Clara, at Andujar, where she passed her days in the most exemplary penitence, and died, an old woman, in 1560, having given as much edification by her repentance as she had caused scandal by her impostures. The whole affair was extraordinarily talked of, and is continually referred to by writers during the following two hundred years. Thus Baxter, in his *Historical Discourse of Apparitions and Witches*, 1691, p. 224, speaks of "the Witch *Magdalen Crucia*, who got the Reputation of a Saint, . . . and confessed how from twelve years old the Devil had lain with her thirty years". Bodin says that Magdalena de la Cruz confessed that at twelve years old she had entertained an evil spirit who visited her in the shape of a tawny Moor, and who enjoyed her, and for more than thirty years she admitted him to lie with her. He taught her many curious arts, and so instructed her that she seemed an oracle of wisdom. Bodin is of opinion that she must have been born of a witch and dedicated to Satan from the first. He cites a parallel case, Jeanne Hervillier, who at the same age, twelve years, took an incubus as her lover. The account of Magdalena de la Cruz, says the *Demonomanie des Sorciers* (1580), is known and notorious throughout all Christendom.

Practically, then, we may regard those mighty empires, Assyria, Chaldea, Persia, as the cradle of sorcery. The Assyrians recognized three separate classes of evil discarnate entities, and any one of these was ready to attack and molest the man who by some chance had fallen into their power. It was especially dangerous, they believed, for any

person who was not safeguarded by occult runes and amulets to wander
alone, solitary, far from his fellows, as he might chance upon some
haunted spot and easily become a prey to the demons. The first class
or black choir of evil spirits was that of the ghosts who were unable to
rest, those who lay unburied in the desert, who had perished suddenly
or by some violent death and so became fearfully malignant spirits,
hating the human race. These were:

> The Night-wraith that hath no husband,
> The Night-fiend that hath no wife.

The second class were amorphous monstrous hobgoblins, half-demon,
half-human. The third class were the devils, fiends who raged in the
whirlwind and the sand-storm, who smote mankind with pestilence and
famine and every ill. There were many divisions and sub-divisions in
these hierarchies of hell, dark intelligences of whom the old rune says:
"In heaven they are unknown, On earth they are not understood."
There were rulers among them, rulers of fearful malevolence and power.

> Seven are they! Seven are they!
> In the womb of the deep seven they are!
> Nor male nor female are the seven.
> But as the swift blast of the roaming wind.
> No wife have they, no heir, no son.
> Knowing naught of mercy, of kind pity naught,
> Their ears are deaf to prayer or supplication.

Necromancy among the Babylonians and the Assyrians was extensively
practised. Certain priests are referred to as "exorcists of the spirits of the
dead", "questioners of the dead", "evokers of dead men". The ghost
might be a shadowy sapless phantom, or it might be completely visible
and audible. The *Ekimmu* was particularly unlucky. This "robber sprite"
would utter a torrent of hideous jargon, threatening, as it seemed, and
angry. It was of the nature of a vampire, and once lodged in a house
could only be banished with the utmost difficulty. Dire misfortunes
invariably followed such a visitation, and more often the place had to
be abandoned and allowed to fall in ruin, or else demolished. The
vampire nature was shown by its power to suck the life out of all the
household, so that they were drained dry as hay, and did indeed
"dwindle, peak, and pine".
    The Seven Spirits, "of giant strength, and giant tyranny", appear
both in Syriac and Palestinian magic. Demons, full of violence,

> They rage against mankind,
> They spill human blood like rain,
> Devouring the flesh of man, and emptying his veins of blood,
> Ceaselessly quaffing hot human gore.

They are, moreover, closely akin to the Babylonian night-demon Lilitu,
who is undoubtedly the Hebrew Lilith. Rabbinical lore is rich in legends
of Lilith, the first wife of Adam, and a mother of devils. She is a spirit

of uncleanness, and according to Johann Weyer the princess who presided over the Succubi. Jean Baar, in his monograph *Le Malin*, Liége, 1927, reproduces an illustration of a Magic Pentagram of evil whereon the names *Samael*—"the Lucifer Spirit Samael"—and *Lilith* are inscribed.

We have seen that Mizraim, father of the Egyptians, was skilled in magic beyond all his brethren, and it is hardly surprising to find that in the earliest days the Egyptians were regarded as a nation of sorcerers and magicians. Hebrew, Greek, and Latin writers invariably make reference to them as past-masters in the lore and practice of all wizardry and enchantment. These powers might, of course, be used for the benefit as well as for the bane of man. There was good reason for such a view. Certainly, every man, woman, and child in ancient Egypt habitually wore some periapt or charm, whilst communication with the dead and apparitions of the dead were regarded as familiar, if not normal, experiences. The elaborateness of their funeral rites and solemn buryings, the vastness and mystery of their tombs, the awe with which the Egyptians regarded their cemeteries, all these deeply impressed strangers in the land of the Nile, and travellers were not slow to make wondering report of so startling and unfathomable esoteries.

In the prehistoric or pre-dynastic graves at various places in Egypt have been discovered large numbers of amulets and talismans, of many curious shapes, made from green schist inscribed with *hekau* ("words of power") or magical formulae. M. J. de Morgan, in his *Prehistoric Ethnography* (*Ethnographie Préhistorique*, p. 144), says that they undoubtedly belong to the cult, and that their use was almost universal until the end of the Neolithic Age. The green schist amulet survived in the green stone scarab of dynastic times.

Joseph, whom Pharaoh Nub appointed ruler of Egypt, used a silver cup of rare power for his divinations (*Genesis* xliv), and he was also, we know, a heavenly-inspired oneiroscopist, an interpreter of dreams. Dreams and visions wherein future events might be revealed and foreshown were greatly craved by the Egyptians, and the wise men of Egypt by art magic were able to induce such dreams for those who consulted them. In a Papyrus (No. 122) preserved in the British Museum are contained spells and incantations for inducing fateful dreams from the god Bes, from the Aeon Chthetho, and the "lords of the gods", Seth, Chreps.

St. Stephen, before the Council (*Acts* vii, 22), proclaimed how "Moses was learned in all the wisdom of the Egyptians, and was mighty in words and in deeds". The history of the prophet and legislator shows that he had been trained by the priests in every branch of magic and occult lore, and, like Aba-aner and King Nectanebus, and indeed all other Egyptian magicians, he and Aaron possessed a rod which was the instrument they employed for working their wonders. To give only one instance in Egypt, when Moses stretched out his rod over the land, locusts went up from the east and rested in all the coasts of Egypt, very grievous were they; before them there were no such locusts as they, neither after them shall be such. Again, in the desert, when the people thirsted for water, Moses smote with the same rod the rock in Horeb and· water gushed out abundantly so that the people drank. At Rephidim, when Amalek came up against Israel, Moses said: "I will stand on the top of the hill with the rod of God in mine hand." So Moses, Aaron, and Hur went up to the top of the hill, and Moses stretched forth the rod, and Israel prevailed. But when in weariness he let down his hand, Amalek prevailed. So he sat upon a stone, whilst Aaron and Hur, the one on the one side, and the other on the other side, stayed up his hands. And he held the rod outstretched, and his hands were steady until the going down of the sun. And Amalek was. discomfited utterly. The rod, then, was an instrument of magical power, of divine magic, that is to say, because the miracles of Moses were wrought by the command of God. And the Lord said unto Moses, "Thou shalt take this rod in thine hand, wherewith thou shalt do signs" (*Exodus* iv, 17). Francis Barrett, in *The Magus*, describes as one of the instruments of the adept a wand of black ebony with golden characters, and he explains what characters are to be engraved and how they must be written. Some writers direct that the wand should be cut from a hazel tree. That Moses was an Egyptian, the son of the Princess Thermutis, is unquestioned today. It follows almost as a matter of course that he was versed in all the wisdom of the Egyptians.

"Mighty in words" means not only that Moses knew the words of power but also that he was able to utter them with the correct intonation, which was a supremely important detail, in fact an essential of the spoken spells and evocations. When he was first sent upon his mission he endeavoured to excuse himself, and said, "I am slow of speech, and of a slow tongue". It would almost appear from the narrative (*Exodus* iv)· that he half feared he was not able to utter the mystic mantras in the right tone, and he was chidden for his diffidence. "And the anger of the Lord was kindled against Moses, and he said, Is not Aaron the Levite thy brother? I know that he can speak well . . . And I will be with thy mouth, and with his mouth . . . and he shall be thy spokesman unto the people." The exact rhythm of the occult intonation has seldom, if ever, been committed to paper, and is taught verbally.

There are holy invocations and vocal aspirations, the celestial music of masses and litanies, echoes caught from the choristers of Paradise, having the harps of God, such music as Milton heard when he wrote:

> There let the pealing Organ blow,
> To the full-voic'd Quire below,
> In Service high, and Anthems clear,
> As may with sweetness, through mine ear,
> Dissolve me into ecstasies,
> And bring all Heaven before mine eyes.

As there are evil incantations for the evoking of demons, so there are combinations of sound and music which are definitely and essentially evil. I must not for a moment be supposed to be speaking of anything merely light, frivolous, and frothy, which is of no account. But there is evil, very evil, music. There are the horrid cacophanies of the negro "swamp-stuff", and "jazz", which is so nearly related to the sound of the Ashanti talking drums, the antiphonal chanting of Obeah revelries, the restless tom-tomming of the Voodoo Bamboula and the screech of the four-stringed Banza.

One of the most famous of all Egyptian magicians was King Nectanebus, the last native monarch, whose skill in astrology, in divination of all kinds, in prophecy, in brewing philtres of love and hate, in confecting charms and casting the runes, was reputed to be unsurpassed in the ancient world. He ruled about 358 B.C. Tradition has it that when Egypt was threatened with invasion he sent out no soldiers to repel the foe, but retiring to a certain secret chamber or sanctuary, he filled with Nile water a great bowl which was placed there. He then fashioned with wood and wax mimic figurines of the ships and men of the enemy, and also of his own fleet and sailors. These he set afloat in the water, his host on the one side, the enemy on the other. Next he donned his mystic mantle and took his ebony wand. Intoning the words of power, he summoned with many a sign and sigil the elemental forces to his aid. The wax poppets sprang into life; the galleons moved to and fro and fought a mimic battle in the water. The figures of his own men vanquished their opponents, whose little navy and crews plunged foundering to the bottom of the bowl. In the same instant of time were the real armadas of the invading hosts wrecked and scattered, and sank to the bed of the ocean. It chanced one day that news was brought to Nectanebus that all the nations of the East had leagued against him, and were mustering a multitude great as the sands of the sea upon his frontiers. With a scornful jest and mocking laughter, in no great haste he repaired to his privy chapel, poured water in the bowl, and proceeded with the charm, chanting the ritual invocations. To his dismay, as he watched the wizard fantoccini, he saw that his own ships and men were being destroyed and all dopped down to the depths. By this he understood that the end of the kingdom of Egypt had come, and leaving the chamber with all speed, he shaved off his beard and close clipped his hair. Taking with him an immense sum in gold and jewels, and putting on mean attire, he fled, crossing by ship to Pella, in Macedonia, where he purchased a house, and under another name won great renown as an Egyptian physician and a figure-caster of rare skill. The story goes that by his magical sleights and the conjuring of a dream he persuaded Queen Olympias that the god Amen (or Ammon) was enamoured of her beauty and would visit her that night. Under the guise of this deity he cuckolded King Philip, and so was the father of Alexander the Great.

Apart from these histories we can form a very good idea of the terrific force and persistent potencies of ancient Egyptian magic by its manifestations even today. The Curse of the Pharaohs which descended upon the excavators who were concerned in the opening of the tomb of King Tut-Ankh-Amen in the Valley of the Kings at Luxor and its terrible workings are matters of common knowledge and cannot reasonably be denied in spite of all the scoffers and the sceptics may pretend.

From time to time prominence has been given in the newspapers to the death of some victim of this fearful malison.

In the First Egyptian Room in the British Museum is (or was) the very fine inner cover of a coffin, painted in bright colours. According to a catalogue this is No. 22542, the mummy being supposed to have been that of a princess of the royal house and a priestess of the great College of Amen-Ra. She lived in Thebes some sixteen hundred years before the birth of Christ. One writer has definitely claimed to have traced the long story of accidents and misfortunes which have beset all who have had anything to do with this mummy case. There is no reason to question his word when he says: "I have now in my possession proofs of the identity of all those who suffered from the anger of the priestess of Amen-Ra." Whilst an undergraduate at Oxford, the late Mr. Douglas Murray bought the mummy case from an Arab in Egypt, and immediately after lost his right arm in a gun accident, and nearly lost his life on the sands at Thebes before his arm could be amputated. It may be remarked that the gun exploded from no known cause. Others of the party were similarly unlucky. Thus one gentleman was killed, and upon their return to Cairo the most distressing news was awaiting another member of the expedition. Two servants who had handled the mummy case, perhaps without sufficient respect, both died within a twelvemonth, whilst a far swifter fate overtook a third who had made some jesting sally. The cause of these mishaps being altogether unsuspected, the case was presented by Mr. Douglas Murray to a friend, Mr. Wheeler, who very shortly experienced several sad reverses, and died not long afterwards broken-hearted. He had given the case to a married sister living near London, and from the day it entered her house this lady was pursued by troubles and sorrows which it is hardly necessary to detail. A well-known clairvoyante, who was lunching at the house, abruptly told her hostess that the place was infested by a most malignant influence, and in a few moments pointed to the mummy case as a source of fearful danger. The lady was perplexed, but not altogether convinced. She dispatched the case to a leading photographer in Baker Street, and when the plate was developed, although the negative had not been touched in any way, it was seen that there looked out the face of a living Egyptian woman whose eyes stared furiously with an expression of singular malevolence. In the course of a few weeks the photographer died suddenly and in most mysterious circumstances.

The lady was now seriously alarmed. Just then she happened to meet Mr. Murray, and naturally poured out to him her pitiful story. He urged her to get rid of the case immediately, whereupon it was offered to and accepted by the British Museum. A carrier conveyed it to the Museum. Within a week he died. The man who assisted in removing the case from the van into the Museum buildings a few days after met with a serious accident, fracturing a limb. "Every one of these facts is absolutely authentic." There have been official denials and vague prevarications, but this blague carries not the slightest weight. Indeed, certain gentlemen went so far in their efforts to evade the truth that the late Mr. Douglas Murray's brother, Colonel Sir Wyndham Murray,

K.C.B., was obliged to send a letter to the public press stating that their remarks were "Wholly inappropriate and misleading". He further added: "There is no doubt that many tragic events had an apparent connexion with this mummy case, as all those who owned it before it came to the British Museum, and many of those who only came in contact with it, met with great trouble." He strongly and very rightly went on to deprecate the jarring flippancy of these denials, which, to put it in the mildest terms, were not in accordance with the facts.

A scholar, who was interested in Egyptology, very much desiring a photograph of the mummy case, commissioned a firm of photographers in Oxford Street, Messrs. W. A. Mansell, to photograph it for him. A junior member of the firm accordingly visited the Museum to arrange for this to be done. Upon the way home, in the train, he injured by some unaccountable accident his thumb, and hurt it so badly that he was unable to use the right hand for a long time. When he reached his house he found that one of his children had fallen through a glass frame and was suffering from severe shock and serious cuts and bruises. Not in any way connecting these mishaps with the business he had undertaken, he returned to the Museum on the following day and photographed the figure on the lid. Lifting his head rather suddenly, he struck himself against a glass case and gashed his nose to the bone, whilst at the same time he upset a valuable screen, which was smashed to pieces in the fall.

Many other untoward and luckless happenings might be cited, but this is the true and authentic history of the mummy case.

To abstract a mummy from the coffin is an act of fearful desecration, and when we remember the awful and solemn ceremonies with which the ancient Egyptians entombed their dead, when we consider the sacred and mystical liturgy under whose safeguarding the departed were laid to rest, the embalmings, the burial psalms, the evocations, the ritual of power, there can be no surprise felt that those who are bold enough to disturb the holy sleep of the departed should be visited with swift and relentless retribution. It is natural that the spirits in the other state are incensed at such sacrilege, and no doubt (as experience has shown again and again) God in His inscrutable wisdom allows them to punish offenders in this kind. It is a grievous and a very terrible thing that an exhibition of mummies and mummy cases is permitted. No plea of archaeology or of scholarship can avail to excuse or warrant such sad profanations. It is to be hoped, and happily it is to be believed, that those of us who are filled with horror at and lament these impieties may ourselves be held scatheless and clear of the great offence.

It cannot escape particular remark that the mummy case with which the foregoing terrible accidents were connected is that of a Priestess, so the malison is wrought and launched forth with sacerdotal knowledge and sacerdotal power. It is worthy of observation and is significant that the most famous writers upon witchcraft have generally been priests and priestly trained. Such, for example, were Jean Nider, the Dominicans Kramer and Sprenger, Bishop Binsfeld, Martin Delrio, S.J., Guazzo, Père Michaelis, the Capuchin Jacques d'Autun, Sinistrari, l'abbé Simonnet, and of the present day the late Cardinal Lépicier, Father Blackmore, and Father Joseph J. Williams, the great authority upon voodoos and obeahs. Lambert Daneau, Glanvill, the two Mathers, Richard Baxter, Dr. Frederick George Lee, were learned and grave divines of no small standing. Bodin, Boguet, Remy, Pierre Le Loyer, De Lancre, were jurisconsults who had presided at the trials of witches and were ripe in legal experience. This is not, of course, to say that there are not other and weighty names, men of vast erudition, Johann Weyer, Jean-Jacques Boissard, Dr. Richard Boulton, of Brasenose College, Oxford; the astrologer, Ebenezer Sibly; Éliphas Lévi (Alphonse Louis Constant); Stanislas de Guaita, who died in 1897; and, indeed, several authors happily yet with us. (It should, perhaps, be repeated that only those writers who have dealt mainly with black magic and the demonologists are being considered, not those who have treated more generally of the supernatural, since in the latter wider field such a study as Mr. Sacheverell Sitwell's *Poltergeists* must be mentioned as of no little importance. And here it may be remarked that, as often as not, poltergeist disturbances are more or less connected with ancient sorceries. Satan counts for much in these saturnalia.)

It is apparent that the priest and the psychologist stand out as those best qualified to investigate the subject of witchcraft, that Satanism which as a political and social factor permeates all history, and is the undercurrent influencing and polarizing events today in its hell-born eternal impulse to precipitate the world into the abyss of utter perdition, to ruin the human race here and hereafter.

Magic as more broadly understood, the genesis of magical cults and ceremonies, the worship and crude ritual of primitive folk, ancient fetishisms and traditional superstitions with their ancillary lore and legend, all these have been made the matter of vast and erudite volumes often conceived purely in a spirit of antiquarian research or written from an ethnological point of view. That such studies, the patient fruit of most faithful and painstaking exploration from the pen of well-approved and solid scholarship, even if a little opinionative, a trifle narrow, maybe, take their recognized place as standard works of permanent value, and indeed of essential importance, no one, I suppose, would seek to question, but it is hardly to be doubted that the gravamen of the whole black business lies something deeper, and in order to appreciate with full understanding the malice of witchcraft and the foul activities—disguised under many a fanciful ism—of the witch today we must probe even more profoundly, until we find ourselves scrutinizing that black mystery which lies outside the province of the most cultured historian, the most travelled anthropologist.

There is a very shrewd and significant observation by Mrs. Nesta H. Webster in her *Secret Societies and Subversive Movements*, 1924 (p. 79, n. 1): "It is curious to notice that Sir James Frazer, in his vast compendium on magic, *The Golden Bough*, never once refers to any of the higher adepts—Jews, Rosicrucians, Satanists, etc.—or to the Cabbala as a source of inspiration. The whole subject is treated as if the cult of magic were the spontaneous outcome of primitive or peasant mentality."

Witchcraft is a religion, the religion of the lord of evil, that tremendous power and personality who is the prince of this world, the adversary of God and man.

Herein is the one and only explanation of the cult of the witch. If this great fundamental fact is not recognized, or if it is attempted to be denied, it is hardly to be surprised at that we should meet theorizing of vainest fantasy, fables, and chimeras of wonderland.

Dr. G. B. Harrison has said that, roughly speaking, students of witchcraft "in the main belong to one of three groups: believers who admit the evidence and, in part at least, its diabolical explanation; sceptics who deny both and regard the whole business of witchcraft as the product of hysteria and gross credulity; rationalists who accept the evidence but deny the supernatural explanation".

The way of the sceptic—and at least three recent writers of scholarship and authority are largely sceptical—is comparatively easy, but the rationalists (I use the word according to Dr. Harrison's classification) have been hard put to it to excogitate their several explanations, and in their endeavours they have advanced and argued the most far-fetched and tortured theories. Nor do they agree amongst themselves. In fact, theirs is a truly perplexed position.

From the very novelty and strangeness of the ideas some of these vagaries have attracted amused and bemused attention for the moment, only to dissipate and be quickly forgotten. Not the least unballasted and bizarre of these "rationalistic" "Dreams, Conjectures, fancies, built on nothing firm" was that put forward by Girolamo Tartarotti (1702–1761), one of the many facile journalists and hangers-on to literature who swarmed throughout Italy during the eighteenth century. These *abbatini* were for the most part elegant triflers, masters of clinches and mild anagram, whose *chef d'œuvre* was a tinkling sonnet daintily printed in silver lettering on rose-coloured silk to be thrown from the boxes to the stage by some perfumed beau at the gala triumph of a favourite cantatrice.

Tartarotti, a "member of the Republic of Humanities", as he blazons himself, was rather more brainy than the ruck. He had found the time to dip into a good many books, and proved an adept in the art of persuading people that he had plumbed the depths of his subject, whereas he had barely skimmed the surface, a hoodwinkery which for success requires a certain native coolness and poker-face skill. Thus he wrote *The History and Antiquities of Rovereto*, the town of his birth, a study which, from his familiarity with every street and corner of the place, is not without interest. His *Origins of the Church of Aquileia*, too, is sufficiently learned, or at any rate it appears to be so. In his excursions into *belles-lettres* he will be found to be saying once again and quite pleasingly a good deal which has often been said before, and which no one would trouble to deny. Thus an essay *On Criticism* and an essay *On Style* are certainly agreeable, and as certainly quite unoriginal and second-hand. As is often the way with such easy pens, he was fond of a pseudonym, but everybody knew perfectly well that Giusto Fontanini and Selvaggio Dodoneo were Girolamo Tartarotti.

THE BLOCKSBERG SABBAT

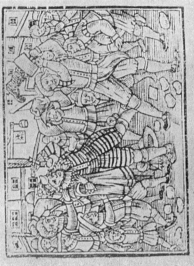

THE MURDER OF DR. LAMBE

MATTHEW HOPKINS' EXAMINING TWO WITCHES

In 1749 Tartarotti published at Rovereto a large quarto volume to which he gave a very selling title, *A Study of the Midnight Sabbats of Witches* (*Del Congresso Notturno delle Lamie*). This was bound to catch the public eye, for just then there could have been no more topical theme. The echoes of the Cadière-Girard scandals at Toulon, not twenty years before, had by no means died away, whilst it was an open secret that the profligate duc de Richelieu was a devotee of black magic and unblushingly courted professors of the darker occult sciences. Gossip was still busy with the curious experiments of the late Regent of France, who —Saint-Simon vouches for it—was extremely addicted to sorceries of blackest infamy. In June, 1749, Maria Renata Sænger, a Satanist of fifty years' continuance, was executed at Würzburg, a prosecution which awakened vivid memories of the witch-trials of the Val Camonica a century before. In Paris necromancers, figure-casters, alchemists, wizards who brewed philtres of love and death, spiritists, traffickers in goety, abounded, and Paris was the capital of fashion and pleasure. Such works as the *Traité de la magie* (A Treatise on Magic, Divination, Possession, Obsession, and Sorcery), 1732, by Antoine-Louis Daugis; the *Critical History of Superstitious Practices*, 3 vols., 1732, by the Oratorian Pierre Le Brun; Nicolas Lenglet-Dufresnoy's *Hermetic Philosophy*, 1744, were in everyone's hands. A French translation of the *Magical Works* of Cornelius Agrippa, published in 1744 with the fudge imprint "Rome", had an enormous circulation under the rose. When Saint-André, a physician of Coutances, issued his *Letters on the Subject of Magic addressed to a friend* in 1725, and argued that the operations of witchcraft were— with the exception of events narrated in Scripture or upon the highest ecclesiastical authority—one and all capable of a natural explanation, he was answered by Boissier in a formidable treatise which ran through three editions in 1731. A critical study of the Manichees by Isaac Beausobre, the first volume of which appeared at Amsterdam in 1734, was very widely read. In his second volume, published in 1739, the year following his death, this author discusses the most curious tenets of the Gnostic societies, such as the Manichean sabbats with their abominable communions, the materialization of evil spirits, the loves of the demons, the sovereignty of the Prince of this world, the hatred dark entities bear to all that is good, the foul teachings and practices of the Luciferians, the orgies of the Adamites, the sorceries of Basilides and his followers, who worshipped a god under the name Abracax, from which is said to be derived the mysterious vocable "Abracadabra", first found in the writings of Quintus Severus Sammondicus, a physician who died about A.D. 230, and who left an extraordinary poem *On Medical Prescriptions*, in the course of which he recommends as a remedy a paper inscribed with this cabbalistic word. Beausobre also investigates the cult of Ischas, and other fiend-religions which are by turn horrible and obscene.

It is plain from these and many other notable and notorious works of the first half of the eighteenth century that the interest in magical lore and supernaturalism was very wide and real. Many of the books, as was almost inevitable, fell into the wrong hands and were misused,

nor is it difficult to see in this perverted occultism the foundations of
Illuminism, itself purely Gnostic, and the inspiration of the Order (yet
active and persisting) founded in 1776 by the abominable Adam
Weishaupt, who can fittingly be described as one of the greatest
criminals and most evil minds known in the history of the human
race.

Daugis, who is an author of great learning and authority, gives
it as his considered opinion that the possibility of Witchcraft is "an
article of faith which cannot be denied without falling into heresy".
He found it necessary to emphasize this, for a little polite and very
ignorant scepticism had already begun to be fashionable. Society toyed
with the notion that there was something rather piquant, something
rather audacious, in half betraying an inclination towards free-thinking.
It showed an open mind, a "spirit of philosophy". Coxcombs and
coquettes liked to be considered just a trifle agnostic when they murmured their vapid incredulities with a pungent pinch from the enamelled
tabatière or a pretty shrug of the shoulders. Tartarotti knew exactly
how to tickle the palates of the younger fry, and he was equally adroit
in his appeal to older and graver heads, who demanded a guise of
scholarship and cogitabundity. Accordingly we find that, whilst for the
sake of the latter he stuffs his *Study of the Midnight Sabbats of Witches*
with references and quotations—he cites nearly four hundred authors—
he is careful to let his more modish readers see all the while that things
are really not too bad, since a vein of elegant unbelief, sugary and suave,
permeates his every page.

Although to be found in the larger libraries, *A Study of the Midnight
Sabbats of Witches* is an uncommon book for the simple reason that
nobody has ever thought it worth remembering. In the course of his
chapters, which assure us that the sabbat was purely imaginary, that
Satanists never met in hellish rendezvous because there were in fact no
Satanists to meet, Tartarotti speaks of certain women who are persuaded that by demoniacal aid "they ride forth upon strange beasts
in a chase with Diana, a goddess of the old pagans" when they join
with her liege train, multitudes of women flying through the air, attending
upon her and doing her service. These heathenish legends of long ago
have been exploded times out of number. John of Salisbury (1120–1180)
knew all about them and rejected them as idle and mischievous night-
mares. Among later English writers, Henry Holland, in *A Treatise Against
Witchcraft*, 1590, discusses the possibility of this meeting "with Herodias,
Diana, and Minerva", and decides that "to ride on the moon to meet
Herodias, etc., all such things are indeed but mere delusions". William
Perkins, again, notes how some witches believe "that they are brought
into far countries, to meet with Herodias, Diana, and the Devil, and
such like; all which are mere fables and things impossible". Holland
holds that the transvection of witches is not only credible but proven,
and in the supreme authority, the *Malleus Maleficarum*, considerable
space is devoted to a consideration of the actual experience of aerial
transportation, instances of which were known to at least one of the
authors, sabbat fleetings which must be carefully distinguished from

these phantasmatical journeyings to companion with Herodias or Diana.

Yet Tartarotti, fastening upon the myth, evolves from so shadowy premises the notion of what he is pleased to call a "Dianic cult", and he proceeds to assert that witchcraft is nothing else save this fabulous cult. His ninth chapter carries as its caption: *The identity of the Dianic cult with modern witchcraft is demonstrated and proven.* His romancing, which, considered as extravaganza even, is not ingenious, convinced and could convince nobody, and after a little idle chatter in the salons of Bergamo and the coffee-houses of Venice the whole thing vanished in smoke.

Now and again some later writer, chancing upon so whimsical an idea, out of curiosity would give a few lines to these oddities. Ennemoser, for example, in his *History of Magic*, translated by William Howitt for Bohn's Scientific Library, 1854 (Vol. II, p. 143), refers to "the stories of old heathenish origin concerning women who profess to ride about at night on all kinds of beasts with Diana and Herodias".

Tartarotti, who is nothing if not finicky, distinguishes between witchcraft and sorcery. At best, it resolves itself into a quibbling question of words. This theory, and indeed his whole book, was admirably answered and confuted by a Franciscan, Fra Benedetto Bonelli (1704–1783), in his *Some Critical Remarks upon the Midnight Sabbats of Witches*, Venice, 1751.

Tartarotti has collapsed, just as the agnostic Balthasar Bekker and the academic Thomasius collapsed before him.

In 1899 Charles Godfrey Leland published *Aradia, or, the Gospel of the Witches*, an interesting but rather jumbled-together collection of country rhymes, snippets of folk-lore, and nursery tales obtained from oral tradition. In his Preface he speaks of "the old r ligion, of which Diana is the Goddess, her daughter *Aradia* (or Herodias) the female Messiah", who "came down to earth, established witches and witchcraft, and then returned to heaven". We are at once in the realms of pure fantasy. Aradia-Herodias, it may be remarked, a mere mythical lamia, cannot be even remotely connected with or derived from the historical Herodias, whose daughter danced before the tetrarch Antipas on his birthday-feast (*St. Matthew* xiv, 3–12; *St. Mark* vi, 14–29). She is rather to be regarded as a replica of a legendary Lilith. Although Leland has a good deal to say about the worship of Diana, and those who "adopted witchcraft or sorcery for a religion, and wizards as their priests", his folk-lore has nothing at all to do with the Dianic cult invented by Tartarotti, and elaborated in other writers. In Leland's opinion witchcraft was "introduced by the Church since 1500" (op. cit. p. 98), and "*diabolical* witchcraft did not find general acceptance till the end of the fifteenth century, when it was, one may almost say, invented in Rome"! (p. 104). This makes it difficult to see how witchcraft, then, can be regarded as an "old religion, earlier than the lore which may be found in Cato and Theocritus, going far back to Etruscan rituals, and before".

However valuable and deeply interesting the study of folk-lore may be, the attempt to elucidate thereby the hideous mysteries of Satanism is foredoomed to failure.

Witchcraft is not merely an historical fact, it is a present menace.

As Charles Sainte-Foi finely says, the phenomena of mysticism, both divine and diabolical, have never ceased in the world. At certain junctures they are more numerous, more obvious, than at other periods. So there are times when, by the permission of God, the very abyss of hell seems to gape open, and. the myriad activities of the demon betray themselves and are recognizable by signs so manifest and clear that there can be no mistaking their nature and their end.

The cult of Satan is formally established and methodically practised in Europe, especially in those unhappy countries and cities where impiety and rank atheism are flourishing foully like rank poisonous weeds.

It is nearly one hundred years ago since these wise words were set on paper, and today they are as vital and as true as when first they were written.

CHAPTER V

The Library of the Witches—The Sibylline Books—The Grimoires—le Grand Albert—The Witches' Bible—Zekerboni—Printed and Manuscript Books of Spells—The Scene of Conjuration described by Restif de la Bretonne.

"Many of them also which used curious arts brought their books together, and burned them before all men: and they counted the price of them, and found it fifty thousand pieces of silver."—*Acts* xix, 19.

It is recorded in ancient chronicles that when King Tarquin the Proud, who reigned 534–510 B.C., was ruling Rome, there came to the palace an old wife of very venerable and grave aspect who demanded audience. So dignified was her port, so commanding her voice, that without demur she was admitted to the royal presence. Here she drew from under the folds of her ample cloak nine books, which she offered to Tarquin at a price. When he asked what price, she named so large a sum that the King burst into a fit of laughter, and with a derisive gesture of his hand dismissed the stranger, whom he thought crazed and doting. She stood, however, in no way moved, and her countenance was unchanged. She merely bowed her head solemnly, and a little sadly, as it seemed. Now, it was winter-time, and there was a brazier of fire set near the chair of the King. Without a word the woman took three of the books and cast them upon the live charcoal, and they were consumed. She then turned again to Tarquin, and asked him whether he would buy the six books. A little startled, he inquired at what price. The price was the same. Whereupon he laughed yet more loudly, and said, "Go to! Dost thou think I am a fool to purchase six books for the price of nine?" To which the woman made no answer, but again cast three books upon the fire. "O King, wilt thou then buy these three at the price of nine?" she asked. Not a little perturbed, and wondering greatly, Tarquin bought the three books, paying her much gold. The woman turned and left the palace with slow, majestic step, nor did any man dare to bid her halt or question her who she was or whence she came. But never thereafter was she seen of any.

When examined by the priests and wise men it was found that the books were full of magic lore and counsel and prophecies concerning the welfare of Rome. Since some said that the woman was assuredly the Sibyl of Cumae, she who prophesied "God shall descend from heaven and as man be born of a pure Virgin, and walk and talk with men on earth," the three mystic scrolls were known as the "Sibylline Books", and deposited in a shrine in the great temple of Jupiter on the Capitol. When Augustus, in the year 14 B.C., assumed the dignity of Pontifex Maximus, an office of the highest importance both because of the sanctity attached to the person of the Pontifex and the influence it gave him over the whole system of religion, he ordered that all pseudo-prophetical writings, all books of conjuring and grimoires, should be searched out and collected. More than two thousand volumes of this sort were burned. The three Sibylline Books, however, were with great reverence removed from the Capitoline temple and preserved in two golden caskets of magnificent workmanship, which were placed in a specially constructed shrine in the base of the statue of Apollo, whose temple was on the Palatine Hill. In his *Lives of the Caesars* the historian Suetonius terms the Sibylline Books *libri fatales*, "the Books of Destiny". Porphyrius, the Neo-platonist philosopher, mentions "the ancient books of the seer Marcius, the Sibylline Books, and others of the same kind". There is a reference to Marcius in Cicero's work *On Divination* (I, 50, cv), when, speaking of Phrygian magical songs and oracles delivered in rhythmic chant, he says: "Likewise Marcius and Publicius according to the old tradition uttered their prophecies in verse, and so they were written down, and the oracles of cryptic Apollo were expressed in poetical form." Professor Teuffel, in his great work on Latin Literature, is of opinion that the Sibylline Books as well as other ancient sentences and prophecies were in the Saturnian metre, the oldest Italian metre, lines of loose structure, each being divided into two halves of different rhythmical movement, the first half ascending in the scale and the second half gently falling. This metre more or less survived until about 200 B.C. Apparently the name is derived from Saturn, and comes from the chant of the litanies sung in the worship of that very primitive deity, who is (it may be remembered) by some even identified with Chronos, or Old Father Time. The Arvalian Brotherhood and the Salii, an occult college, had hymns and psalmody which descended from the immemorial years, and which were in fact magical incantations. Many of these songs were recited in choric tone to solemn ritual movements, often varied by a lively dance-like step to the clashing of metal and the shriller note of timbrels. Popular tradition, and perhaps rightly, assigned these to King Faunus, who instituted tillage and brought grazing into Latium, and who is said to have introduced the cult of Pan. There was a famous oracle at his tomb-shrine, much frequented by shepherds. Others of these ancient litanies were said to have been taught by Carmentis, a Latin goddess of prophecy, and the mother of Evander, whom she accompanied from Arcadia to Latium. In historic times she had her temple on the Capitoline Hill, where she was adored as "Postverta" and "Prorsa", the lady who can look backwards into the dimmest past and who can gaze forward into the farthest future, reading the riddling secrets of all time.

King Tarquin the Proud appointed two priests to be custodians and expounders of the Sibylline Books, which were with much ceremonial observance and purifications to be consulted at any crisis in the national history. In 367 B.C. the two priests were augmented to ten, and in the days of Cicero there were fifteen priests in charge of these mysterious volumes. This mystical society continued until the reign of the Emperor Honorius, who ruled the West from A.D. 395–423. The great general, Stilicho, ordered the three Books to be burned, and something very like a revolution followed. With the barbarians on the very borders of Italy and the menace of the Goth Alaric the land was full of dismay. The people, more than half pagan, says Dean Milman, hated Stilicho "as the enemy, the despoiler of their religion; as having robbed the temples of their treasures, burned the Sibylline Books, stripped from the doors of the Capitol the plates of gold". When the wife of Stilicho, Serena, "stripped a costly necklace from the statue of Rhea, the most ancient and venerated of Rome's goddesses, and herself ostentatiously wore the precious spoil", their fury knew no bounds, and perhaps this was the last straw which led to the disgrace, the betrayal, and death of Stilicho. Whilst Alaric was advancing from the Alps upon Rome the senate were obliged to order the judicial execution of the widowed Serena, who certainly was at fault in herself wearing the necklace. Had it been given to adorn a statue of the Madonna, Rome might yet have been saved. As it was, the distracted and enfeebled government proposed to deliver the city by the sorceries of certain Etruscan diviners who claimed the power to wield and direct the lightnings of heaven, whereby they promised to annihilate the hosts of the Goths. Their efforts proved utterly bootless and in vain, not because they had not commerced with demons and could work extraordinary feats by means of their familiars, but because Almighty God had otherwise ordained the outcome.

There were preserved in Rome in addition to the Sibylline Books other ancient volumes of spells and evocations of which we know little more than the bare names. Such was the book *The Commentaries of the Augurs*, from which Cicero quotes a brief sentence in his *On Divination* (II, 18, xlii), to wit: "When it thunders, or lightning flashes in the heavens, it is impious to hold an election." There were also *The Books of the Salii*, and the *Commentaries of the Fifteen*, to which Censorinus makes reference in his treatise *On Reading Nativities*.

Pliny, in his *Natural History*, mentions the Tuscan rituals, books containing the liturgy of Summanus, Monarch of Night and the terror that walketh in darkness. The cult of this deity is surrounded with mystery and fear. His temple stood near the Circus Maximus, and St. Augustine says that his worshippers were few, the fact being that this horrid cult was conducted with such secrecy that even the most curious antiquarian inquirer could ascertain no particulars. This was the case with Ovid, who frankly confesses he was unable to discover any details of this dark god, and in his *Fasti*, or *Annals*, he speaks of a temple dedicated to Summanus—whatever power he may be. Ovid died A.D. 17. A later writer, Festus, whose date is uncertain, but who is possibly to be placed towards the end of the second century, notes that cakes were superstitiously offered to Summanus, "round cakes of wheaten bread, made in the shape of a wheel". In his great encyclopaedia, written during the fifth century, Martianus Capella, a native of North Africa, explicitly says that Summanus is lord of hell. Assuredly then in the worship of Summanus we have sheer demonolatry.

A certain rich man, Terentius, the owner of several fields on Mount Janiculum, decided to have his land ploughed up, and one day when they were turning over a part of the ground not far from the ancient tomb of Numa Pompilius, second King of Rome, the husbandmen discovered just underneath the soil a number of parchments and scrolls carefully wrapped up in linen and silk coverings. When these were deciphered they proved to be written by that monarch, and Terentius carried them to the Praetor Urbanus, the chief magistrate. By him they were laid before the Senate, who after due examination commanded them to be immediately destroyed. And little wonder, for these mysterious writings, says St. Augustine, proved to be "filled with the Devil's bestial desires", the liturgies and evocations of devils who delight in obscenest ministries, they were stuffed full of dark wonders and how to cause the glamour of lying miracles and amaze.

Under Tiberius, Nero, and their successors, vast numbers of grimoires were being circulated in Rome, some very much under the rose, and some almost openly. The greater numbers of these clandestine books went under the name of Berosus, the astrologer of Cos, or were attributed to the Chaldeans, Astrampsychos, Gobryas, and Pazalas, just as in England chap-books of popular prophecies and cheap magic were hawked as by Merlin, Mother Shipton, the mythical monk of Dee, and in France every little *Dragon rouge* or *Poule noire* or *Secrets merveilleux* might be indifferently ascribed to Pope Honorius or le Petit Albert or Alexis the Piedmontese. These pseudo-Chaldean manuals were imported in large quantities from Syria and Egypt, whilst there was a regular traffic in this kind of merchandise between Rome and various towns in Asia Minor. Ephesus in particular became the headquarters of "vagabond Jews, exorcists", such as "Sceva, a Jew, and chief of the priests", and his seven sons. In fact the city was a hotbed of necromancy and the foulest sorceries, so that in A.D. 59, when St. Paul was preaching there, many "came, and confessed, and showed their deeds. Many of them also which used curious arts brought their books together, and burned them before all men: and they counted the price of them, and found it fifty thousand pieces of silver", which at the lowest calculation in modern money represents an enormous sum (*Acts* xix).

The Emperor Salvius Julianus, who literally bought the Roman Empire, but whose reign, closed by assassination, lasted only two months of the year A.D. 193, was excessively given to the study of magical lore, to expound and experiment with him in which he summoned sorcerers from all parts. It would seem that his chief aim was to acquire some sort of popularity by means of foreign spells and wizardries, for he was (as he knew) much disliked by the people. Although Alexander Severus, who reigned A.D. 222–235, secretly consulted and even regularly salaried astrologers and magicians, his two great ministers, the celebrated jurists Ulpian and Julius Paulus, obtained his approval of acts which they had drawn up forbidding and condemning under heavy penalties the use of grimoires and books of spells. The very possession of such books was in itself illegal, and the man in whose house such were found was either sent into exile or fined in a large sum. If he were unable to pay, or if he were a slave, he suffered capital punishment. The books themselves were to be publicly burned by the common executioner.

Gordian the Elder (A.D. 238) advised with astrologers concerning the nativity of his son, and when they had drawn a horoscope they appealed to "certain old secret books" to prove the truth of their prognostics. Aurelian (A.D. 270), who at the time of his election was campaigning on the banks of the Danube, at once resorted to certain very ill-famed Gaulish sibyls, Druidesses, to discover the events of his reign, and later, whilst he was at Rome, learning that a savage northern tribe, the Marcomanni, had debouched upon Italy, he immediately ordered that the Sibylline Books should be ritually consulted to learn how the danger might best be met.

Under Constantine, Firmicus Maternus, in Sicily, commenced his work, divided into eight books, named *Matheseos*. This was finished in A.D. 370. Mainly a treatise upon astrology, to which science he gives almost a sacerdotal character, it is largely mixed up with magic, and Teuffel does not hesitate to say, "The sources whence he derives his learning are as superstitious as the pages in which he sets it forth." What seems curious is that here we meet the first mention of alchemy, unless, indeed, as a few scholars suppose, the passage be a slightly later interpolation. From this magic literature was derived the application of astrological symbols to parts of the human body, the moon being in some mystic sense the mother of all. This especially commended itself to the Priscillianists, a Gnostic sect which arose in Spain towards the end of the fourth century and whose doctrines are saturated with oriental corruption and theosophies. Firmicus Maternus inculcates and is a firm believer in judicial astrology, which, says St. Gregory, entered so largely into the tenets of the Priscillianists, some of whom, it is believed, worshipped with divine honours the Star which appeared at the Epiphany, adoring rather the Star in the heavens than the Child on His Mother's knee.

Firmicus Maternus highly regards the subtile arts of the Egyptians and the Babylonians, and advocates the use of the *Petosiris*. This instrument, in later times known as the "Wheel of Beda", was a superstitious device by which the motions of luna, the moon, were observed in place of the multitudinous and highly complicated details of the stars and planets. It came to be so much employed in connexion with magic and reading the future that its use was prohibited. The consulting of the *Petosiris* with regard to the deaths of individuals was productive of much mischief, and even of crime, since it was frequently shown that the querent relying upon the predictions of Beda's Wheel would bring about the desired result, and consequently the vending of poisons notably increased. Many times, of course, the *Petosiris* may have been more or less innocently employed to solve difficulties and pierce the clouds of the future, but even so there are great and manifest dangers, and the whole business can hardly be excused from divination. As late as 1796 we find the Holy Office proceeding against a lay-brother of the Alcantarines, Fray Miguel Alberola, of Valencia, who was alleged to have much skill in turning Beda's Wheel, and to whom there was continual resort of impatient sons and over-anxious heirs, which gave the whole thing a very ugly complexion.

It should be noted that there lived at the same time as Firmicus Maternus another author of the same name who dedicated his works to the two sons of Constantine, Constantius and Constans. His book is entitled *On the Dark Errors of Heathen Cults*, and although from the similarity of name it is probable that the two writers were cousins or even brothers, the very different outlook of the books makes it impossible for one individual to have published both, as was sometimes thought to be the case.

Amongst other peoples, even more ancient perhaps than the Romans, there have survived references, scattered and brief, it is true, to grimoires and magical books which were used by their priesthood. Old Mexico, for example, held that each one of the dark night hours was presided over by a particular deity, or rather demon, a grim and grisly company, to whom the Spaniards gave the name "Señores de la Noche", "the Lords of the Night". Their powers were full of fate and doom, and there existed certain rituals or exorcisms by means of which the soothsayers and wizard priests could placate these evil spirits and so avert or at least mitigate their balefulness. These runes were written in the *Tonalamatl*, or Book of Fate.

Other Gnostic sects besides the Priscillianists had their grimoire-gospels. Many taught a doctrine of salvation by knowledge, wherefore man may, or rather must, pass through every experience and can indulge his vilest passions, wholly devoting himself to evil. The Cainites regarded those characters held up to reprobation in the Old Testament as worthy of all reverence. They especially honoured the dark angel of the pit and their father Cain. They possessed a "Gospel of Judas", and a secret book "full of wickedness". The dogma of the Antinomians was that they *must* break the law. Their gospel was "full of monstrous evil", a tome of Tophet.

One of the vilest and most terrible of the older magic books is the

Sepher Toldos Jeschu, a Syro-chaldaic work, so intricate and so riddling as happily only to be understood by the very few. In bitter mockery these volumes of evil enchantments were often fathered upon some famous scholar or some saint. In Latin the word *notaria* means a cipher or a secret communication in shorthand. There was printed a volume entitled *Ars notaria*, which might roughly be taken to mean "*Stenography*", and this purported to be by St. Jerome. Actually it is nothing else than a grimoire, and has, of course, nothing to do with the great Biblical Commentator and Saint. Popularly, St. Cyprian, Bishop of Carthage and martyr, A.D. 258, the famous ecclesiastical writer, was confused with his namesake St. Cyprian of Antioch, the converted magician, who was put to death during the persecution of Diocletian, A.D. 304. Cyprian of Antioch was, says Alban Butler, devoted by his parents "from his infancy to the devil, and he was brought up in all the impious mysteries of idolatry, judicial astrology, and the black arts". He collected a large library of magical books which, upon declaring himself a Christian, and before baptism, he burned in the presence of the Bishop of Antioch. In the course of time and error a number of mediaeval spells were attributed to St. Cyprian, supposedly the Bishop of Carthage, and even today in Denmark and Scandinavia *Liber Cyprianus*, *The Book of Cyprian*, is a name given to almost any grimoire. St. Ubald, Bishop of Gubbio, in Umbria, who died in 1160, was honoured for his powers of exorcism and casting out devils. A theurgical treatise which cannot have been written earlier than towards the end of the sixteenth century brazenly bears his name as author on the title-page. In France, during the days of the later Valois, all sorts of alchemical and goetic opuscules were being sold as from the pen of St. Thomas Aquinas, and were eagerly bought by peer and peasant alike. The most famous, and perhaps the most infamous, of all printed grimoires, which has as running title *Les secrets admirables du grand Albert* (*The Marvellous Secrets of Albert the Great*), was actually attributed to the learned Dominican Bishop of Cologne, St. Albert the Great, who died 1280. A very similar book of necromancies is *Le Petit Albert*, *Rare and Cabbalistic Secrets of Albert the Less*, said to be compiled by Alberto Lucio Minore. These two books are among the most extensively employed, and hence the most mischievous, grimoires today. Each has run through a very large number of editions. Over thirty reprints of *Le Grand Albert*, as the work is conveniently known, have been recorded by bibliographers, and there are many more which are uncatalogued. R. Yve-Plessis enumerates twenty-seven reprints of *Le Petit Albert* and says that this list is very incomplete. The whole question is immensely complicated by title-pages carrying fudge names of printers, publishers, and place, by dates of issue deliberately falsified and intended to mislead, by surreptitious issues, and by a number of cheap chap-books in bad type on poor paper which are only abridgements and extracts made (it would seem) haphazard to charm the halfpence out of the rustic pocket. It must always be remembered, too, that the many editions and clandestine texts, both of *Le Grand Albert* and *Le Petit Albert*, vary so widely that a reprint of the present century may prove to be an entirely different book from the sextodecimos and little octodecimos of a hundred years ago, and these, again, are quite another thing from the duodecimos of the eighteenth century. There is, for example, an edition, 18mo, with imprint "Lyons, At the Sign of Agrippa, 6516". This is said to be a translation from the Latin of Alberto Lucio Minore. It is magic rampant and undisguised. Herein are contained erotic charms, charms to prevent the consummation of marriage, to render a man impotent and a woman sterile, directions how to brew poisonous philtres, to mingle aphrodisiac drinks, the art by which one may see in a dream the future partner of wedded life, the means whereby cabbalistic talismans may be made and darkly graven with horrid runic signs, the foul mysteries and use of the Hand of Glory, how to weave the magic garters and carve the magic staff for a traveller, the magic ring, the powder of sympathy, and numberless charms for preserving cattle, and remedies in case of sickness in the house, all of which are mixed with the grossest superstition, and most of which are just bedevilment.

Amatory philtres, exciting lust, not love, and erotic charms—charms for wakening both the passions of desire and of hate—are among the oldest items in the witches' pharmacopoeia. The Chaldean warlocks brewed them in Babylon. The Scandinavian ballad of "Ridder Stig" bears witness to the power of runes in "lovemagic". At the Synod of Exeter in 1287 Bishop Peter Quivil banned any form of "love sorcery" as a sacrifice to demons, which, indeed, it is. The besotting of Edward III, infatuated with Alice Perrers, was commonly ascribed to spells of this nature. A mysterious Dominican, who "in outward show professed physic" and as a doctor was attached to the lady's household, in secret practised art magic and was an occultist of mickle might. This friar, by fashioning certain wax poppets and rings, and baptizing these with the juice of herbs, had enslaved the King's heart to his mistress.

Some sixty years later Dame Eleanor Cobham was alleged to have enforced good Duke Humphrey to woo and wed her through "medicines and drinks" prepared by Margery Jourdemain, the witch of Eye-next-Westminster, that is the manor of Eia or Eye (see W. L. Rutter, *Archaeologia*, 1910, pp. 31–58).

"Public voice and fame" persistently accused the Duchess of Bedford of having entrapped King Edward IV "by Sorcery and Witchcraft", and so lured him to marry her daughter, Lady Elizabeth Grey. When the time was ripe for his usurpation in 1484 Richard III very well knew how to take fullest advantage of these rumours.

It was commonly believed, and it seems certainly proved, that Anne Boleyn was a witch, who by her glamoury caused Henry VIII to dote upon her, so that he put away his Queen and well-nigh wracked England for this wanton's sake. It is significant that witches delight in wholesale destruction. Wolsey spoke of Anne Boleyn as "the night-crow". St. John Fisher, Cardinal Bishop of Rochester, knew the woman for what she was, and declared as much. Naturally she resented being unmasked, and in revenge pursued the holy prelate with the most inveterate malignancy. When, on 22 June, 1535, he was martyred on Tower Hill, she had the severed head brought to her, and in hideous mockery, with a coarse bitter gibe, thrust a silver bodkin through the

dead tongue. Anne went through a form of marriage with Henry VIII
on or about 25 January, 1533. The whole affair is more than obscure,
and the learned historian Brewer says that even the date of these pseudo-
nuptials is a mystery. Like the witch she was, Anne Boleyn had great
skill in poisons. She attempted the life of St. John Fisher by poison.
At his London house the broth for supper one evening was mixed with
a strange white powder. Several persons who ate freely of the dish died,
and the Bishop himself, who had but tasted it sparingly, was so weakened
and shaken that he was ill for a month after. Eustace Chapuys, the
Imperial ambassador, than whom no man was better acquainted with
the darkest secrets of the Tudor Court, says that Anne Boleyn was formally charged with poisoning Queen Catherine, and in the same way
attempting the life of the Princess Mary. In a burst of unusual candour
Henry VIII on one occasion exclaimed that his sister and his natural
son, the Duke of Richmond, "might thank God for having escaped
from the hands of that damned poisonous witch who had conspired
their death" (*Anne Boleyn*, by Paul Friedmann, 1884, Vol. II, p. 177).
In a passion of fury Henry VIII to her face called Anne Boleyn, "You
old devil, you witch" (*Henry VIII*, Hackett, p. 349). Chapuys, in a letter,
24 April, 1536, speaks of her as a "diablesse", a witch devoted to Satan.
It may be remarked that the ambassador always alludes to her as the
"concubine". The Latin poet Joannes Secundus (Jan Everaerts, 1511–
1536), in an elegy refers to Anne Boleyn as a "cheap and common concubine", which shows how Europe generally regarded her. In a letter
to the Emperor Charles V, dispatched on 29 January, 1536, Chapuys
says that a close confidant of the King told the Marquis and Marchioness
of Exeter how Henry swore he had been subtly and diabolically snared
into a union with Anne Boleyn. "I was seduced into this marriage,"
he cried, "and forced into it by sorcery. I was wrought upon by witchcraft. Yea, that is why God will not suffer me to have male children."
It is known that the wretched woman was marked with the devil's
mark in a secret place upon her back. Even so cautious a writer as
Friedmann (*Anne Boleyn*, Vol. II, p. 265), when reviewing the evidence
at her trial, during which something was obviously being kept in the
background, gives it as his opinion that she was "guilty of crimes which
it did not suit the convenience of the government to divulge".

"The revulsion of feeling which Henry VIII manifested with regard
to Anne seems to have been far more vehement than a man might be
expected to show who had simply got tired of one mistress and taken
up with another," says Gairdner. Froude declared that the "tragedy"
of Anne Boleyn "is one of the most mysterious in English history".
The riddle, however, has been read. Brutal, bestial, and impious as he
was, one thing Henry VIII justly feared—black magic.

Some few editions of the Albert grimoires, as, for example, that
published at Lyons (Paris), Les Héritiers de Beringos, 18mo, no date,
have coloured illustrations. These are excessively rare. A duodecimo
edition of 1729, published at Lyons (Paris), by Beringos fratres, has
five very choice copperplates of considerable artistic merit and is highly
esteemed, being an uncommon book. An edition, said to be printed at

Lyons (probably Paris), carrying the date 1668, has schemes of necro-
mantic figures, sigils, engraved talismans and pentacles, which are
found in no other issue. A facsimile in very small numbers was made
early in the present century. A well-known French occultist, Mons.
Marius Descrepe, edited in one volume, no date, but actually Paris,
1885, the Grand Albert and Petit Albert, printing the most integral
texts which could be established, and furnishing a valuable preface and
many annotations. This is the edition most prized by modern adepts.
Mons. Descrepe proves that neither of these two works has anything
at all to do with St. Albert the Great, nor have they been transcribed
by some scholar of the fifteenth century from an unedited manuscript
of the learned Dominican doctor. It is certain that the two books were
compiled from the writings of several hermetic philosophers and commingled with a number of spells and evocations of dark tradition.
Stanislas de Guaita (1861–1897), a great authority upon the literature of
witchcraft, and a great collector of magical volumes, drew attention
to the fact that in spite of the numerous editions and reprints both
Le Grand Albert and *Le Petit Albert* are (one is happy to say) extremely
scarce books.

It may be worth while to give some further account (with due
reservations) of the reprint *Les Secrets Merveilleux du Grand et du Petit
Albert*, edited in 1904 by Dr. Jean Fauconney, to whom reference has
previously been made. The text is perhaps not entirely that of the two
grimoires, as they were originally printed, but it has been considerably
augmented by extracts from a manuscript grimoire which was in the
library of Antoine René Voyer, Marquis de Paulmy d'Argenson (1722–
1787), at whose death it passed into the hands of the Comte d'Artois, and
afterwards it was acquired by the Bibliothèque de l'Arsenal (No. 92,
Sciences et Arts Français, a quarto MS.). In 1868 Jules Cousin printed
certain extracts from this manuscript.

This edition (1904) of *Le Grand Albert* commences with a number
of charms under the title "A Treasury of Marvellous Secrets", of which
some concern health, some teach how to fashion various amulets, some
are frankly erotic, and some pretend to ensure good luck at cards and
dice. Of these last the following may be taken as a specimen: "On the
first Thursday of the new moon, at the hour of Jupiter, before sunrise,
write upon a virgin parchment these words: *non licet ponare in egoborna
quia pretium sanguinis*. Then take the head of a viper, and set it full in
the midst of the parchment, folding the four corners thereof over the
serpent's head, and when you are going to gamble tie it around with a
red silk ribbon, attaching it to your left arm. You alone will win at the
tables." A foolishly superstitious periapt and spell. Virgin parchment,
says Barrett, is the fairest, cleanest vellum which may conveniently be
had, but actually it should be made from the skin of a young kid un-
defiled or an eanling, an animal which has never covered nor tupped.
The Latin words are (perhaps designedly) incorrect. The text, *St.
Matthew* xxvii, 6, reads: *Non licet eos mittere in corbonam: quia pretium
sanguinis est.* "It is not lawful for to put them [the thirty pieces of silver]
into the treasury, because it is the price of blood."

The curious properties of plants and herbs are detailed. Thus stinging-nettles and yarrow* give courage; lesser celandine cures certain complaints, which is, of course, common knowledge; blue periwinkle is an aphrodisiac; and so on. There are also various charms connected with animals, and a long list of the virtues of precious stones. Red chalcedony will bring prosperous fortune, especially if it be engraved with the figure of a man grasping a sceptre; the emerald and the sapphire are good for the eyes; garnets are febrifugal and healing; pink coral is very fortunate. The luck of coral is a very ancient belief, and Pliny, in his *Natural History* (xxxii, 11; Bohn's translation, Vol. VI, p. 12), has the following reference: "Branches of coral hung at the necks of infants are thought to act as a preservative against danger."

We next have "The Cabbalistic Secrets of le Petit Albert". These are mostly concerned with sexual matters, and many of them are extremely lewd. Black magic enters undisguisedly into several of the charms, as, for example, that which instructs a young girl how to obtain a vision or dream of her future husband. After certain ceremonies the maiden is instructed to recite a prayer, or rather incantation, which, although addressed in seemingly devout and orthodox manner, concludes by an appeal to the ministry of evil spirits. We are the less surprised to find a recipe for the Hand of Glory, a particularly ghoulish piece of witchcraft. The hand of a murderer swinging from the gallows is severed at the wrist, and after being mummified in a brine of salt, black pepper, brimstone, and other ingredients, a kind of wick is plaited from the dead man's hair steeped in fat and sesame, so that a horrible candle may be formed. When these wicks are lighted it is believed that a deep stupor or sleep falls upon all who are in the house, whence the Hand of Glory was largely employed by burglars. There were various methods, and sometimes one tall taper was used, kneaded after a certain fashion, the dead hand being clasped round it as a candlestick. This charm is known the whole world over, and is of the greatest antiquity.

In the next section we return to love charms, which seem to grow fouler and fouler and more frankly diabolical as they are presumably more potent. Yet to my knowledge some of the worst of these are employed today. There are diagrams of mysterious tables and figures and geomantic characters to be engraved upon silver or copper discs. Many of these signs are said to be derived from "*The Book of Sacred Magic*", which is blasphemously supposed to have been delivered to Moses on Mount Sinai. There are also directions to lard collyries and unctions, to brew love philtres and potions from eryngoes and mandragore. All these hellish businesses must be accompanied with ceremonial cantrips and cantations, mainly derived from the Greater Grimoire, which is further drawn upon to instruct the neophyte how to make a formal pact with the demon, and in order that he may not miss to learn the darkest secrets of this infernal knowledge an elaborate diagram is furnished for the exact guidance of the besotted witch.

Sympathetic magic, ill-wishing, overlooking, the moulding of

---

* In Devonshire, country maids pluck yarrow from a man's grave, place it under their pillows, and repeat a certain rhyme, and so their true loves appear to them in their dreams.

wax figures to be wasted before a fire or stuck with pins, the solemn ritual of blood, conjurations stronger than before, and other horrible sorceries to blast with disease and death, culminute in the black mass and the unhallowed feats of necromancy. With the exception of the celebration of the black mass, all these are described in detail, and in brief these pages are neither more nor less than a text-book of goety.

There follows a long tractate on divination and astrology, regarded from the worst possible aspect. Planetary influences, horoscopes, anthroposcopy, cheiromancy, are discussed; some pages are given to the sorcerer's instruments and secret cabinet, the composition of perfumes and kinds of wax. A short chapter on the sabbat, taken and badly put together from De Lancre and Soldan, must be a late addition. The book concludes with a few paragraphs, not unimportant in themselves, on the art of healing and out-of-the-way remedies, which are legitimate enough. Yet these belong to the witches' pharmacopoeia.

That it is an evil book admits of no question. The learned Vasquez has profoundly remarked that the existence of grimoires is a necessary evil, since God suffers witches to be and to exercise their evil arts in order that so-called freethinkers may at any rate be turned from their atheism and materialism by means of these servants of the devil, who are a living witness to a spiritual world, since they àre able to give idle curiosity and the sceptic proof of intelligences not always to be discerned by mere touch and sight.

In the Channel Islands the *Grand Albert*, which is locally known as *Le Grand Mêlé*, is dubbed "the Witches' Bible". The *Petit Albert* is *Le Petit Mêlé*, the word *Mêlé* itself meaning nothing more than a book. The two *Alberts* are often called *les Albins*, and everyone knows that only a sorcerer would keep such "bad books". Indeed, if it is discovered by any accident that somebody has either of these two grimoires in his house he is incontinently set down as a warlock. The old gossips say that once a man has possessed himself of the *Grand Albert* he will have a hard task to disburden himself of it, do what he will. The book invariably returns in some mysterious manner to its place on his shelves. He may throw it into the sea, he may tear it to pieces and scatter them to the four winds of heaven, he may burn it and stamp the ashes to dust; for all that the book, I ween, will reappear on the shelves, an ill-omened, fateful thing. There is only one sure way of getting rid of it: Let the owner bury the book deep in a newly-made grave in consecrated earth where lies some good and blameless body, now with God, and let him read in solemn measured tones the Burial Service over it. Or let him hand the book to the priest, who will sprinkle the leaves with holy water and sign it with the redeeming sign before burning it in the fire with litany and prayer, and so shall it perish and its power.

In Jamaica, upon the arrest of Monteul Edmond for the murder of a twelve-year-old boy, Rupert Mapp, there were found upon the prisoner a number of magical formulas "copied from a work entitled *Petit Albert*, the pretended author of which is claimed to be a monkish occultist of the Middle Ages". The boy's body had been obscenely mutilated for the purposes of Obeah.

Among the Police News in *The Daily Gleaner*, 30 January, 1934, the Kingston, Jamaica, paper, is reported that at the Sandy Bay Court, Leonard Weakley, of Cold Spring, was sentenced to six months' imprisonment for practising witchcraft. In his house the following books were found: *The Sixth and Seventh Books of Moses*; *Albertus Magnus, or the White and Black Arts for Men and Beasts*; *The Great Book of Black Magic*; *The Book of Magical Art*; *Hindoo Magic and Indian Occultism*.

The following extract is from a Manchester paper of 1865:

"At the Salford Town Hall, yesterday, John Rhodes, apparently a respectable man, living at 226, Regent Road, was charged, under the Vagrancy Act, with telling fortunes. A girl, named Ellen Cooper, stated that she saw the prisoner at his house, on Tuesday. After she had told him the date of her nativity, the prisoner cast her horoscope, and told her what she might expect would be her future fortune. For this she paid a shilling. . . . From information given by the girl, Cooper, two detective officers called at the prisoner's house on Thursday, where they found him with a female standing beside him, whose future destiny he was busy calculating, aided by an astrological work. . . . In the prisoner's house the officers found a large number of books, including 'An Introduction to Astrology' by William Lilly [the famous astrologer, 1602–81]; 'Raphael's Prophetic Alphabet'; 'Occult Philosophy' by Cornelius Agrippa (*in manuscript*); a work on horary astrology, etc. . . . In addition to these were manuscripts with forms of invocations to spirits to do the will and bidding of the invoker; also lovespells, and forms for invoking evil destinies. The text of one of these was as follows: 'I adjure and command you, ye strong, mighty, and most powerful spirits, who are rulers of this day and hour, that ye obey me in this my cause by placing my husband in his former situation under the Trent Brewery Company, and I adjure you to banish all his enemies out of his way, and to make them crouch in humiliation unto him and acknowledge all the wrongs they have done unto him, and I bind you by the Name of Almighty God, and by our Lord Jesus Christ, and by His Precious Blood, and on pain of everlasting damnation, that you labour for him and complete and accomplish the whole of this my will and desire, and not depart until the whole of this my will and desire be fulfilled, and when you have accomplished the whole of these my commands you shall be released from all these bonds and demands, and this I guarantee through the Blood of the Redeemer and on pain of my future happiness. Let all Angels praise the Lord. Amen.' [The Magistrate] Mr. Trafford said the practice was so mischievous that he could not let the prisoner off without some punishment; he must therefore send him to prison for seven days." These invocations and impious adjurations are plain witchcraft. This prosecution was under the Vagrancy Act of 1824, which includes "Every person pretending or professing to tell fortunes, or using any subtle craft, means, or device, by palmistry or otherwise, to deceive and impose on any of His Majesty's subjects". It is urged that from the very precise wording of the Act it cannot apply to anyone who has no intention to deceive. None the less, it has been held by the divisional

A - A Witch B - A Spirit rais'd by the Witch
C - A Feast engsing his Imperious Revels D - A Fairy Revels
E - A Witch raising up the Devill thorough the fire
F - An Inchanted Castle

BOVET'S "PANDÆMONIUM" (1684)

A CHINESE SORCERER

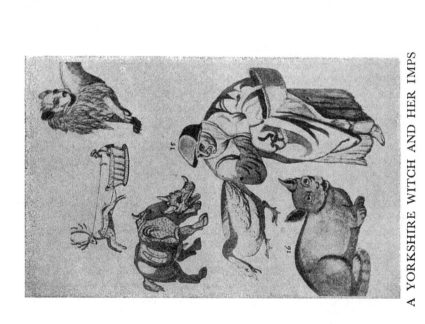

A YORKSHIRE WITCH AND HER IMPS   CHINESE WIZARDS AT WORK

court that a person "telling fortunes", however firmly and honestly such an individual may believe in his (or her) occult powers, commits an offence under the said Act.

A leader, headed "Hullo Gemini", in *The Times* of 24 January, 1939, observes: "The Air Ministry's weather forecasts can still be denounced in law as witchcraft."

The *Daily Mail*, 12 August, 1938, remarked that "at a dozen South Coast resorts and at many places in London, discreet notices are to be seen in teashop windows that 'Clairvoyant Teas' are to be had there. . . . One prophetess who describes herself as a Rumanian gypsy said: 'If you desire me to go into a trance it will cost two guineas.' A 'Gypsy Princess' declared: 'However often people in my profession are prosecuted, the authorities will never be able to stamp out fortune-telling'."

A typical case is that reported in the *Daily Mirror*, 6 January, 1939, when a Mrs. Finnegan, of Portsmouth, was told by a gypsy, "That ring you are wearing belonged to a dead woman. It is through that you are suffering from ill-health and bad luck." The gypsy was reading her fortune by the cards. Mrs. Cotgrove said that the same gypsy advised her to put a human hair in a pound of the best steak, to bury it, and to sleep with a small crystal under the mattress. She also burned a glove containing a needle and a pin. This dissolved an ill-wished charm. Bessie Birch, the gypsy, was bound over for two years at Portsmouth Quarter Sessions, on a charge of undertaking to tell fortunes and obtaining rings and money by a trick.

On Wednesday, 9 January, 1929, at York, York County, Pennsylvania, U.S.A., John H. Blymyer was sentenced to imprisonment for life for the murder of Nelson Rehmeyer, who had long locally been notorious as a practitioner of black magic. Rehmeyer, a farmer, was killed in a struggle to secure a lock of hair from his head, which lock was to be buried with certain ceremonies, in order to remove a "hex", or spell, that he had cast on the Hess family. Wilbert Hess, a boy of eighteen, and John Curry, Blymyer's assistant, who was aged fourteen, were concerned in the killing of Rehmeyer. A powwow doctor had told them that the only way to dissolve the spell Rehmeyer had cast upon the Hess household was to obtain a lock of the sorcerer's hair and use it as a counter-charm. That the Hess family were overlooked and afflicted in this way there can be no doubt. The question arises how far were the victims and their friends justified in the means they employed to free themselves from the spell? Scotus admirably argues that such methods are quite legitimate, and Sylvester Mozzolino (Prierias) warmly upholds the views of the great Franciscan doctor. The *Malleus Maleficarum*, Part II, Question 11, Chapter v, instructs us concerning the "Prescribed Remedies for those who are Obsessed owing to some spell". Remy certainly holds "That there is nothing which can so quickly and effectively induce Witches to remove an Evil Spell as Threats and Blows and Violence", and I should not venture to differ from him. Moreover, Guazzo says, "Threatening or Beating Witches is the Best Method of Removing the Spells cast by Them", which is conclusive. That the warlock Rehmeyer should have been so obstinate in evil and resisted until he was accidentally killed by a blow from a piece of wood is unfortunate, but his blood was upon his own head, and every good man's hand should be against sorcerers. It would have been more equitable, truly, had the warlock been brought before a competent tribunal, but as this course was not open to the afflicted they took the best means they could.

Jacob von Hoogstraeten, who acted as inquisitor at Cologne from 1508 to 1527, published in 1510 a tractate, which he dedicated to the Archbishop of Cologne, with the title *The Fearful Sin of those who seek to Witches for Help*. Silvester Mozzolino, O.P., Master of the Sacred Palace from 1512 until his death in 1523, who has been just quoted as following Scotus, treats of the whole question in his great work *On the Horrid Marvels wrought by Witches and Demons*, edition Rome, 1575 (first edition, Rome, 1521), Book II, Chapter ix, pp. 189–98. He agrees that the witch may be asked to destroy the spell and undo the evil, and Hubertinus says that an evil may be cured either through the prayers of the Saints or even through those means whereby it was caused. But St. Thomas, St. Bonaventura, St. Albert the Great, the Dominican Peter of Palude, and all authorities lay down that it is never permissible to do evil that good may come. Yet if it is not certain that the method by which the sorceress removes the spell is essentially witchcraft, that is to say unquestionably a consequence of and dependent upon her pact with the demon, but possibly merely superstitious and ethnic, then she may be required thus to break the spell. For it cannot be a bad thing to do good.

Thomas Tamburini, the famous Jesuit theologian (1591–1675), in his *Commentary upon the Commandments*, 1651 (*Opera*, Venice, 1719, pp. 71–3), discusses in ample detail "Evil Spells, and how they may be broken". The much-debated question, he says, inevitably arises as to whether a spell may be removed by a counter-spell. To have recourse to a sorcerer and to ask him to remove a spell by some exercise of the black art, even if this may mean a recovery from sickness, is not permissible. On the other hand, it is allowable to ask that a spell may be broken if it is probable that only lawful and wholesome methods will be adopted. If the querent is uncertain whether the means employed will be lawful or unlawful, it is allowable to request that a spell be removed, for there is at any rate a presumption that the right and licit method will be employed. Even if there is a definite possibility (but not a certainty) that unlawful means may be resorted to, yet if there are lawful means and the sorcerer to whom application is made knows both, it is probable that he may be quite legitimately consulted. The querent seeks a good end by good means, and the responsibility rests with the operator. It is certainly legitimate to consult a wise man, since although he may know the mysterious secrets of magic, he will also have a knowledge of the properties and healing qualities of herbs and medicines, of the science of the stars, and of those antidotes and protective acts and counter-charms which dissolve and destroy evil influences, and which therefore must be themselves inherently good. This is the opinion of the great

Sanchez; of Suarez; of Vincenzo Filliucci; of Lessius; of the Roman Inquisitor Giovanni Alberghini; and of many more doctors.

The poet Dryden, it is true, speaks of "white witches mischievously good", but this has reference to the black art being exercised for an end proximately good yet ultimately and *in esse* evil. Which is altogether forbidden.

Girolamo Menghi, the great Capuchin exorcist (1577), says that it is far safer not to advise with occultists who are even remotely suspect of dark and crooked practice. On the other hand, he warmly approves of a close search for and, when found, the destruction of the "instrumenta maleficialia", those objects used in casting and confecting a spell.

It was very generally and anciently believed that a spell could be broken by scratching and drawing blood from the witch who had overlooked the sufferer. William Perkins, in his *Discourse of the Damned Art of Witchcraft*, published posthumously in 1608, rejects such a test or remedy, but his line of argument is unconvincing. In the English trials there are constant references to this scratching. Thus in 1596 a boy, Thomas Darling, of Burton-on-Trent, who had been overlooked by the witch Alice Gooderidge, scratched the woman until blood "came out apace". When young Booth drew blood with a pin from the Yorkshire witch, Margaret Morton, the lad amended (1651). In his *Daimonomageia* (1665) W. Drage records that Margaret Bell, a witch who lived near Lutterworth, having ensorcelled a child, was scratched. There are many examples in the nineteenth century. In 1802, at Poughkeepsie, Nicholas Toncroy was charged with assault on an old woman, whom he had caught and scratched, upon suspicion of the black art. Much more recently a Welsh farmer was summoned for assault. He had drawn blood from a witch who had laid a spell on his churns (*Bye-Gones for 1893-94*, p. 481).

At the Warwick Winter Assizes in 1867 John Davis, a maltster, of Sheep Street, Stratford-upon-Avon, was charged with assault upon and wounding Jane Ward, his next-door neighbour. There were mysterious happenings in the house which filled him with terror. Headless shadowy phantoms were seen in dark corners. In every room furniture was thrown about and smashed, glass and china broken, the sheets and counterpanes whisked off the beds and torn to flinders. Obviously it was a case of poltergeist hauntings, and Davis may very likely have been quite correct in suspecting that old Mother Ward was responsible. At any rate he was convinced that she had ill-wished his family, and that the only remedy was to draw blood from her. He accordingly made his way into her house, and inflicted a gash on her cheek. When he saw the blood flowing, he exclaimed: "There, you old witch, I can do anything with you now!"

A contemporary newspaper, giving an account of the Blymyer trial, says: "York's trust in 'medical' treatment by charms and incantations based on mysterious rites culled from mediaeval books on witchcraft, seems unbreakable."

It was stated during the trial that the principal grimoires used by witches are: *The Sixth and Seventh Books of the Magical Spirit*; *The Art of*

Moses, popularly known as *The Black Art Bible; Heaven's Letter (Himmels-brief);* and *The Long-lost Friend,* a horrible volume containing necro-mantic rituals and evocations together with the dark creed of pow-wowism. *The Art of Moses* is a translation, or rather perhaps an adaptation, of the notorious sixteenth-century *Magia divino-mosaica . . . cum nigroromantia, The Art of Magic as revealed by God to Moses with the manner of Raising the Dead.* Jewel, the Elizabethan Bishop of Salisbury, remarks how "commonly conjurers and sorcerers make their vaunts, that they have all their books and their cunning from Athanasius, from Moses, from Abel, from Raphael the Archangel". In another place he notes: "The conjurers and sorcerers say that their books of conjuration and sorcery came from Moses, from Enoch, and from Abel".

That a tradition, unwritten and not divulged save to initiates, has descended from Moses is by no means impossible. If such be the case, it was handed down by the Essenes, a society of mystics under obligation, says Dr. Christian Ginsburg (*The Kabbalah,* 1920), "not to divulge the secret doctrines to anyone", and "carefully to preserve the books belonging to their sect and the Names of the Angels or the Mys-teries connected with the Tetragrammaton and the other Names of God and the Angels, comprised in the theosophy as well with the cos-mogony which also played so important a part among the Jewish mystics and the Kabbalists". Antoine Fabre d'Olivet (1768–1825), a profound and absolutely impartial scholar, in his great work *La langue hébraïque* ("The Hebrew Tongue"), which Caillet says is a classic of occultism that must be studied deeply by all who have any intelligent interest in the arcane sciences, writes: "If it be true, as there is amplest witness to prove, that Moses left an oral law, it was among the Essenes that it was preserved. The Pharisees, who prided themselves so greatly upon possessing it, only practised the empty outward observances, and it is for this sterile formality that Jesus so frequently rebukes them. It is from these that the teaching and philosophy of the Jews today are descended, with the exception of a few really learned men whose esoteric knowledge is derived from the tradition of the Essenes."

In bitter mockery the names of certain Popes were proclaimed as the authors of grimoires. The *Enchiridion* of St. Leo III, fabled to have been presented by that great and noble Pontiff on Christmas Day, 800, to Charlemagne, whom he crowned Emperor of the Romans, is wholly apochryphal. An early edition printed at Lyons, 1584, calls itself "The Manual or Enchiridion of Prayers containing the Seven Psalms, together with certain Secret Orisons made by Pope Leo against the dan-gers of the world, being also a sure and certain way to learn various mysterious secrets". The text is in Latin. A French translation, Rome, 1740—both place and date are false—is embellished with a number of coloured illustrations which are very curious. Yet another edition, Paris, 1840, but purporting to be printed at Rome, has a vignette of a triangle enclosed in a double circle, and in the midst are engraved the words *Tsabaoth Alchim.* Mr. A. E. Waite justly says of the *Enchiridion* that "it is in all respects worthless, whilst its ascription to Leo III is an insult to that pontiff".

The Grimoire of Pope Honorius is pretended to be found in manuscript as early as the thirteenth century, but the first printed copy which has been traced has the imprint Rome, and the date 1629. Another edition, Rome, 1760, has eleven coloured plates, and there should be nine additional pages, which are unnumbered. It is even disputed whether the work is that of Pope Honorius II (Lambert Scannabecchi, of Fagnano, near Imola), who reigned 1124–1130, or whether it is by Pope Honorius III (Cencio Savelli), who reigned 1216–1227. Actually, of course, it belongs to neither pontiff. Mr. Waite finds its source in *The Sworn Book of Honorius*, which belongs to the fourteenth century. This Honorius is the mythical Grand Master of a coven of magicians who assemble at some mythical place. He is described as the Master of the Thebans, and the son of Euclid! The book is impious and vile, being nothing more or less than a Ritual for the summoning of demons and familiars. At the midnight of this evocation the operator, having prepared with horrid spells and blasphemy a candle of yellow wax, must betake him all alone and very privily to an empty church where no human eye can see him at his work, and there by this dim light he must intone in a low voice the Office of the Dead, substituting, however, for the Ninth Lesson of Matins (*Job* x, 18–22) a vehement adjuration of evil spirits. Presently the warlock retires to some ill-omened haunted spot, the grave of a suicide or a place where murder has been done, and here kindles a fire from the wood of a mutilated cross, tracing a circle upon the ground with the grey ashes of a crucifix he has basely and with contumely burned. Meantime in set cadence he chants the words of power, a strain mingled with versicles from the holy Psalms, and so he proceeds to the conjuration of the Four Kings ruling the quarters of heaven, and a horrid evocation of the Seven Black Angels who are regents of the several days of the week.

The *Grand Grimoire* and the *Grimorium Verum* are in their main features both excerpted from the abominable *Clavicula Salomonis*, which is *The Key of Solomon the King*, also known as *The Book of the Pentacles*. Very similar manuals are *The Keys of Rabbi Solomon*, *The Black Book of Agrippa*, and *The Elements of Magic of Pietro d'Abano*, which latter has been characterized as "the vilest of vile books".

In 1510, when a young man, the famous Heinrich Cornelius Agrippa von Nettesheim (1486–1536) wrote *Three Books of Occult Philosophy*, a treatise which was not printed until more than twenty years after. Actually the work is a commixture of Neoplatonic ideas and the cabbala. The last section, however, has a lengthy chapter on demons, and Agrippa in his angelology trenches upon some very ticklish matters, whence it is hardly surprising that these *Three Books of Occult Philosophy* "alone constitute him a conjurer", as his biographer has it.

It was indeed unfortunate then that not so many years after his death there appeared, clandestinely it is true, but none the less under his name, a Fourth Book of the Occult Philosophy, a most damning tractate, since it is just a manual of darkest goety. In print it is generally, and very aptly, companioned by *The Elements of Magic* and *The Treatise of Art Magick of Arbatel*.

Pietro d'Abano was a most notorious warlock. Born about 1246, in the village from which he derived his name—a small Venetian fief, Abano Bagni, with extensive quarries of trachyte, some seven miles from Padua—Pietro at a very early age seems to have fallen in with a certain Moslem physician, a sorcerer, who instructed him not only in the secrets of medicine but also in the secrets of magic. The wretched pupil acquired extraordinary skill as a leech, and yet more extraordinary skill as a necromancer at a fearful price. So bold and braggart were his sorceries, so confidently did he vaunt his unhallowed traffic with Satan, that the Holy Office was compelled to take note of the scandals, and he was at length laid by the heels. Before he could be brought to trial, during the course of his arraignment, he died in prison.

The Elements of Magic is sometimes known under the title *Heptameron*, by which name it was adjoined to the Fourth Book of Occult Philosophy when this treatise was printed for the first time in 1565 and reissued two years later, in both cases without any indication of publisher or place. In the edition usually known as the "fudge and bowdlerized" edition of the Works of Cornelius Agrippa—although how bowdlerized it is a little difficult to see—this Fourth Book not only has as a kind of ancillary treatise the *Heptameron* of Pietro d'Abano, but is also accompanied by the *Art Magick* of Arbatel, the *Ars Notaria* (*The Secret Cipher-Key*), a book of conjurations sometimes profanely ascribed to St. Jerome, the *Goety* and *Demonomania* of Pictorius Villinganus, and other opuscules of the same character. The Bibliothèque de l'Arsenal at Paris has an old manuscript of Pietro d'Abano entitled "The Elements of All Magical Sciences", a treatise which sets forth the whole art of drawing the goetic circles and explains the Conjuration of Angels, clearly showing the days and the set hours when these Intelligences may most meetly be invoked. There is a Latin edition, Marpurg, 8vo, 1559, of the "Magical Ceremonies of Henry Cornelius Agrippa, to which are added the Elements of Magic of Pietro d'Abano" which is perhaps the amplest and most abominable of these reprints. It is happily an exceedingly scarce volume. There is a French translation of these two works, Liége, 1788, which has an appendix of "Rare Secrets", detailing erotic charms, and a conjuration of the Angel Uriel by means of a bowl of fair water, which is hydromancy, divination through spirits whose shapes appear in water, the ancient wizardry of Numa.

One of the most notorious and most often named of all grimoires is the *Key of Solomon*, *Clavicula Salomonis*, to which reference has already been made. No Hebrew manuscript of this grimoire, which legend says was written by Solomon for Rehoboam his son, has ever come to light, although there is a strong presumption that such actually exist. A Greek manuscript was in the library of Charles VII of Bavaria (1697–1745). There are several Latin manuscripts, and a manuscript which is dated 1634, and said to have been copied out by F. F. Fyot, is preserved in the Bibliothèque Nationale.

"*The Keys of Solomon*. Translated from the Hebrew into Latin by the Rabbi Abognazar, and from Latin translated into the vulgar tongue", i.e. French, by Monsignor Barault, Archbishop of Arles.

There was, of course, no such prelate. This particular manuscript has been reproduced in photographic facsimile, only a very few copies being done, by the firm of Chamuel, Paris, in 1892. This talbotype consists of 141 pages of conjurations and unholy prayers, and there are many cabbalistic drawings and intricate designs of necromantic circles and pentangles.

The *Key of Solomon*, often in Latin with a facing translation in various languages, has several times been printed, but the authentic book is rare and the contents of the older editions differ very materially. One of the earliest of these is *The Keys of Solomon*, a quarto of 125 pages, bearing the date 1655 but without any place of printing. It is in small close lettering, which may be described as ruby-nonpareil. In the middle of the eighteenth century there were known to be three works, printed in France, bearing the title *The Key* (or *Keys*) *of Solomon*, one of which was certainly of the early sixteenth century, and none was later than 1650. All copies seem to have disappeared of that exemplar which was divided into twelve sections, the ninth being a hideously profane Exorcism and Commanding of the Prince of the Power of the Air, "the spirit that now worketh in the children of disobedience".

Casanova mentions that *The Key of Solomon* was deeply studied by Venetian occultists, amongst whom were many senators and members of the most aristocratic houses. He is referring particularly to the years 1746–1750, when he had obtained an introduction to certain alchemistical and cabbalistic circles at Venice.

An even more abominable grimoire, and fortunately an extremely uncommon book, is "*The True and Only Key of King Solomon*, translated from the Hebrew, being a Complete Treasury of all Occult Sciences, to which is adjoined a large number of rare and curious secrets, and in particular the Famous Secret of the Great Cabbala, known under the symbol of the Green Butterfly; the whole carefully revised by Agaliarept. Printed at Memphis, at the house of Alibeck the Egyptian". This is an octodecimo, and carries no date but was printed about 1830. For Memphis read Paris. The translation is said to have been made by an occultist named de Plaingière. There are a great many coloured talismanic figures of most evil import, and certain ill-looking signatures said to be those of demons as affixed to compacts of diabolism. The full rites and conjurations for evoking Lucifer are given. This tractate, which is indeed a manual of sheer demonolatry, numbers ninety-nine pages, and is marked on the title-page with the Sign of the Butterfly. A most unsafe and dangerous compilation.

In a private English collection there exists a manuscript translation of the *Clavicula Salomonis*, by Frederick Hockley, an astrologer and adept who died about the middle of the nineteenth century. It is entitled "*Solomon's Key*, by Frederick Hockley, 1828". The manuscript has been superbly bound, and pasted inside the front cover is a label with the following inscription: "Magia de Profundis, seu Clavicula Salomonis Regis, the Key of Solomon the King, or a Complete System of Profound Magical Science with a great number of coloured drawings of the Characters of the Spirits, Seals, Pentacles, etc., elegant in brown calf gilt leaves." At the beginning we have: "Key of Solomon in Four Books. These books were found in the Chaldee and Hebrew tongue by a Jewish Rabbi at Jerusalem and by him translated into Greek and from thence into Latin and transcribed by Fredk. Hockley the first day of Marche 1828."

Magia de Profundis! The Magic of the depths of darkness! Several of the world's greater libraries possess even more perilous manuscript grimoires, which naturally are only allowed to be examined under the most stringent conditions and by approved scholars. To particularize and describe these would be far from profitable, dangerous even, and a brief mention of one for example's sake will serve to give a sufficient idea of the whole class.

The manuscript *Zekerboni* was written by Pietro Mora, who styles himself "an occult philosopher". In the earlier part of the seventeenth century this mysterious and menacing personage dwelt at Milan, in one of the oldest houses of the most obscure and out-of-the-way quarter of the city. He was wealthy without question, but how he had acquired his money seemed altogether uncertain. True, he practised physic and had wrought some astonishing cures. It was popularly believed that by means of a certain red powder he could transmute base metals to gold. He was also a figure-caster of unerring skill. Further, it was whispered that for a price he would sell you a pomander, or a nosegay of exquisitely wrought artificial flowers, whose fragrance was an apoplexy; or, should you prefer it, a basket of blushing apricots, to bite one mouthful of which was to waste gradually away; or a flagon of rare Cyprus wine in whose ruby depths lurked death inevitable. Many a wealthy wanton widow, many a smiling heir whose old sire had gone gently to his rest, many a jealous cuckold whose wife, poor soul, was suddenly snatched away, at stealthy nightfall had knocked on Mora's door. There were even darker rumours yet. Some did not spare to say that the cunning man trafficked with the powers of darkness, and had bartered his immortal soul. During the Great Plague of 1630, a sickness which swept Milan like a raging fire, suspicion grew to open accusation, and one evening the pursuivants were ordered forthwith to surprise and search the ill-omened house. Here were laboratories well stocked with curious instruments and utensils, retorts, lembecs, cucurbits, aludels, spheres and charts celestial and terrestial, astrolabes, all vessels of chemical experiment and astronomical furniture, unusual but legitimate enough. The books on the shelves were almagests, with Cardan, the Planetary Tables of Regio-montanus, Porta, Bernard Trevisan, duly licensed authors. Mora himself was protesting completest innocence all the while. At last a magistrate, shrewder—or, it may be, better informed—than the rest, directed especial attention to a certain wall, which when sounded seemed hollow. A more thorough rummage unmasked a secret door, concealed by trick carpentry, which gave entry to a cellarage of unusual extent, a vast crypt wherein were discovered the High Altar of Satan at which the devil's mass had been celebrated times without number. In a padlocked chest were stored hideous vestments, magic ephods, cloaks and girdles, together with wands tipped with silver, cups, wax for moulding images, small tripods, crystals and polished obsidian for scrying, talismans graven with the names and sigils of fiends—in fine, the whole paraphernalia of sorcery. There were also grimoires not a few and magical manuscripts. Apart, in a cupboard carefully secured, were, ranged in rows and ticketed, phials of strange shape containing liquids, some coloured, some crystal clear, and gallipots full of a noisome black unguent which stank extremely. When these cosmeticals, these Hungary waters and fucuses, as they purported themselves, were analysed by the physicians they proved to be essential poisons and virus of the deadliest kind.

Upon examination before the podesta Mora confessed that not only was he a Satanist, but the Grand Master and preceptor of a band of Satanists, who with infernal malice were leagued to spread the pestilence by all means they could devise, and who had sworn that in the end they would contaminate the whole city of Milan. With the corroding ointments they smeared the latches of house doors, the knockers, the handles of church doors, gates, bolts, and keys. They poisoned the springs of water at the source and defiled the courtyard wells and public fountains. They even poured acids and oil of vitriol into the cathedral holy-water stoups. The baker's flour they infected with ergot, and prepared from foul toadstools the gypsy venom dri, which induces all the symptoms and fatal result of enteric fever. In Roman days Claudius Caesar was killed by poisonous fungi mingled with a particularly savoury dish, and his successor Nero was wont to call this fungus "the food of the gods", since, as he added with a mocking laugh, "it certainly sent the old man to heaven". In his study *Fetichism* (New York, 1885) Schultze notes that "the Shamans of Siberia drink a decoction of toadstools at their orgies". According to Eusèbe Salverte (*Philosophy of Magic*, New York, 1862, Vol. II, pp. 19, 20), the use of this fungus must be referred to the category of Sacred Intoxicants, and a drink brewed from it was quaffed at the witches' sabbats.

Under the guise of charity Mora and his gang distributed among the very poor infected clothing and foul linen from the beds of those who had died of the plague, thus fearfully increasing the ravages of the disease in the most crowded and wretched slums, until the rookeries of Milan were nothing else than rotting and gangrened lazar-houses and stews of contagion. Thirty years later in Paris the Marquise de Brinvilliers was visiting the hospitals, and as a corporal work of mercy brought the sick all kinds of meats, confections, and wine, which she had previously doctored with poisons, so that she might watch the effects and be able to gauge the process of the operation of the toxic she had administered. Sainte-Croix, the paramour of the Marquise, was taught the whole art and science of poisoning by the Italian Exili, or Eggidi (in French, Gilles), who, gossip said, had been employed by every dukedom and petty court in Italy quietly to remove political rivals and inconvenient friends. Exili remains a mysterious figure, but there can be little doubt that he was a Grand Master of the witches and one of the highest figures among the Satanists of the day. He had lived in Rome, and once on some unknown dark business had made a journey to Paris which resulted in five months' imprisonment in the Bastille, from

February to June, 1663, for the authorities were very watchful, and even when nothing could actually be proved Monsieur Desgrez, an important official, escorted him to Calais, whence he crossed to England. The last mention of this extraordinary man is at Rome in 1681, when he wedded most brilliantly, his bride being the Contessa Ludovica Fanta-guzzi, cousin of the reigning Duke of Modena. It is certain that Exili had been an intimate of the notorious poisoner and witch Hieronyma Spara, and there are good grounds for believing that one of his pupils was Toffania, who began her career of crime at Palermo in 1650, when she was little more than a girl, and later, having established herself at Naples, from 1659 onwards, distributed her Acqua Toffana all over Italy, sending it out in bottles painted with a representation of St. Nicholas of Bari, the phial being called "Manna of St. Nicholas". Toffania was a witch, and a society of witches used to forgather at her house. By the aid of many disguises, and by renting under various names several houses in entirely different quarters of the city of Naples and its suburbs, this abominable hag escaped conviction for many years, and her nefarious trade flourished amazingly meanwhile. Before her capture and execution, in 1709, she caused the death of nearly a thousand persons. Garcelli, physician to Charles VI of Austria, analysed a number of bottles of this Acqua, and states that the main ingredient proved to be a solution of arsenic, colourless and tasteless, but with some poisonous combinations of such strength that from four to six drops in a goblet of wine would be fatal to the strongest.

At a rather earlier date than Mora and Exili the wizards Maître Réné and Cosmo Ruggieri, who both lived in Paris under the Valois, were resorted to by large numbers, who purchased at a high rate charms, and at a higher rate subtle poisons. A little later than Exili's detention in the Bastille and subsequent banishment from France, broke out the resounding scandal of La Voisin and her company of sorcerers and poisoners, who celebrated black masses for Madame de Montespan and trafficked in arsenic and aphrodisiacs with persons of the highest quality. It will be seen that the tradition of evil persists with the Satanists, and is handed on from one generation to the succeeding, whilst, as there will be occasion to note again, their pharmaceutical lore was deep and dangerous indeed.

Mora and his whole coven of witches having been thus apprehended and convicted of foulest blasphemies, of sorceries, murders, and mischiefs innumerable, upon proofs as plain as the open day, one and all paid the penalty of their atrocious crimes. The very house where Mora dwelt, the theatre of unutterable abominations, was razed to the ground, and upon the spot they built a tall pillar whereon was set a bronze tablet engraved with the full story of his wickedness and all the evil he had wrought.

It cannot be definitely stated that the manuscript *Zekerboni* which still exists is Mora's own holograph, indeed experts incline to think that it is in a rather later hand. That Pietro Mora was the original author or compiler of this grimoire admits of no question, and a circumstance which serves to bear this out lies in the fact that *Zekerboni* interweaves into many of the spells and incantations obscure words and technical phraseology derived from alchemy, and we know that Mora diligently sought after the Grand Elixir and with many an experiment quested the Philosopher's Stone. It is probable, then, that *Zekerboni* as now preserved is a copy made by a member of Mora's coven from the original volume. Such copies, it should be remarked, were always transscribed with minutest care.

Zekerboni has many mysterious and cabbalistic designs, especially a drawing of the "Great Pentacle", where four intersecting circles enclose a reticulation of curious patterning, scattered and starred with Hebrew and Greek letters and punctuated by paraph and points in endless entanglement. It was not intended that the manual should easily be understood. Considerable stress throughout is laid upon the dignity and office of the Master (i.e Mora himself), and the major conjuration is performed by the Master, attended by several disciples, of whom one holds the lanthorn by the light of which the Master reads from his parchment; another has paper, quill, and inkhorn, so that the answers given by the demon may be noted down; and a third carries the naked sword, whose blade is engraven with unlawful names and rune-staves not a few. It is the Master who kindles the charcoal for the suffumigations, who with lighted taper in one hand and mystic rod of might raised high in the other, when all have taken their places securely within the circle, begins to intone the conjurations of devils, for such, in spite of every disguise and deceit, the spirits truly are. To mask the horrid blasphemy of this business, nay, to add to their impieties, the warlocks call upon the Thrice Holy Name of God, and further the fiend is bidden manifest himself "in a pleasing form and appearance, without any horror of shape or monstrous size, without any dinning and discordant noise or loud alarm, without attempting to harm him who is evoking thee, without hurting any who are of his company".

A significant condition is that the archimage must impose certain commands upon the spirit or familiar, and at the end give him very definite licence to depart. Should he seem to linger or tarry, he must be urged to go and hastened on his way. If necessary, he must be even rebuked and chidden in sternest terms for loitering. This shows that these familiars were essentially of the most evil and malignant, since once evoked and permitted to manifest they were loath to disappear and would fain have attached themselves to some one of the assistants, becoming his "control", as modern witchcraft jargon has it. So at Gergesa, the devils who were bidden "Come out of the man, thou unclean spirit", and who were Legion, "besought Him that He would not command them to go out into the deep". At the foot of Tabor, when the foul spirit possessed the boy and was driven forth, it went with a rending, as it were, and a wallowing upon the ground, for in the access it was said of the lad that the control "teareth him that he foameth again, and bruising him, hardly departeth from him". These phenomena may be almost exactly paralleled in séance-rooms today, where the mediums often experience similar assaults from the evil spirits.

A very striking and significant example, which is not generally known, came within the experience of the late Cardinal Vaughan, and may be briefly related here, as showing the horrible obstinacy and persistence of these demon entities.

It was about the year 1901 that an Australian visitor to London found himself obliged to enter a nursing home for an immediate, although not very serious, surgical operation. Three or four ladies, interested in the work, used to call periodically at the home, to cheer the patients, especially strangers, by reading to them and chatting pleasantly. The Australian, being lonely, much appreciated these kindly attentions, and showed himself so friendly and grateful that one of the ladies ventured to remark upon a curious thing she had noticed in his behaviour, which struck her as distinctly uncanny and unusual. She could not help observing that he seldom answered any save the most trivial questions without a pause and addressing some unseen person who appeared to be instructing him what to say. The patient replied quite candidly that he was in communion with a spirit, whom he had been consulting for years. This being had attached itself to him at a séance in Melbourne, and had become a complete "control" without whose advice he did nothing, and from whom he found it impossible to break free. In all other respects the invalid was perfectly normal, and would sometimes lament the fact that he was hampered and tied in this way. One of the ladies, anxious to help, asked him if he would see a gentleman who had deep experience in psychical phenomena, to which he gladly consented. The late Mr. J. Godfrey Raupert—there can be no breach of confidence in writing the name, as it has already been mentioned in a public lecture when this incident was told—called upon the patient and found him in excellent dispositions, and most wishful to be freed from this tyranny. Mr. Raupert consulted several priests, who all agreed that the evidence of demoniacal possession was not to be gainsaid, but at the same time they declared the matter was too high for them. At last a Benedictine monk of great learning, who was unfortunately himself at a distance and unable to come to London, sent a letter advising that the case should be laid before Cardinal Vaughan. His Eminence heard the story with keen interest and understanding, and an appointment was made for an audience. The Australian consented to the interview, although not without difficulty, as the control protested and grew angry, saying it would be a vain and fruitless waste of time. Mr. Raupert and the afflicted man were received by the Cardinal, as prearranged, in private in his study. His Eminence then inquired more fully into the particulars of the phenomena. I now take leave to quote Mr. Raupert's own words. "While my narrative was in progress the man was suddenly lifted out of his chair and thrown violently to the floor, his body twisting and shaking, a villainous expression distorting his face, and froth foaming from his lips. A harsh rasping voice, wholly unlike his own, poured from his mouth, uttering the most unheard-of blasphemies, and declaring that no damned invocation of ours would be successful in dislodging him (the spirit control). He had, exclaimed the voice, had possession of the damned carcass for years and he meant to retain possession at all costs. We sat spellbound, feeling quite unable to do anything that could terminate this extraordinary and hideously repulsive manifestation."

After a while the man, haggard and pale, sat up and opened his eyes, looking about him in wonderment, sick and ill, but knowing nothing of what had occurred. When he was informed of the demoniacal crisis, he begged to be freed from this horrible thraldom of evil. He was enjoined certain devotions by the Cardinal to prepare himself for the solemn rite of exorcism in a week's time. On the morning of the very day, early, he was to pay his second visit to the Cardinal the spirit returned and told him that his financial affairs in Australia were in a most disastrous condition, and to save himself from ruin he must return by the next boat. He rushed off, bag and baggage, to the docks, caught a boat about to sail, and thus did not again interview Cardinal Vaughan. The evil thing, "a murderer from the beginning, a liar and the father of it", had, of course, cheated and deceived his victim, who upon his arrival home found his business flourishing and all in perfect order. There had been no sort or shadow of a collapse.

Such a history serves to show very vividly the fearful jeopardy in which the sorcerers stand who conjure up demons not lightly to be dismissed, or who invite and hold communion with familiars by way of the "New Black Magic", as these practices have been very exactly termed. That these intelligences conceal their identity is, of course, only to be expected. Later, when the medium has become merely an automaton through which the spirit speaks and by which he acts, he no longer takes the trouble to mask his evil nature, which has never been human. Sir William Barrett wrote: "It seems not improbable that the bulk, if not the whole, of the physical manifestations witnessed in a Spiritistic séance are the product of human-like, but not really human, intelligences . . . inhabiting the air around us, and able injuriously to affect mankind."

From time to time a manuscript grimoire appears in the sale-rooms. In April, 1934, when a part of the collection of M. Lionel Hauser was put up to auction at Sotheby's, "A Treatise of Ceremonial Magic", written on vellum in cypher in French, *circa* 1750, which had belonged to and been used by the Comte de St. Germain, fetched forty guineas, whilst a nineteenth-century manuscript collection of spells, conjurations, and the like, realized ten pounds.

Although it may seem a little irrelevant, it cannot be without interest to mention the golden disc of Dr. Dee, dated 1589, which was sold at Sotheby's on 4 May, 1942. This Golden Disc of the Vision of the Four Castles seen at Mortlake by Edward Kelley, the scryer, on the morning of 12 June, 1584, has been aptly called "a vivid reminder of the adventures, spiritual and physical, that Dee and his Medium shared between March, 1582, when they first met, and the final rupture in January, 1588". The disc, which is made of alchemical gold, is engraven at equidistances with the four watch-towers. The design, which is extremely elaborate and shows processions of Kings, Princes, and Seniors with "Angels of the Aires", was sketched out by Kelley, an excellent draughtsman, and it is believed that Dee himself did the engraving on metal. "Its explication was made with the help of Ave, one of the demons or presences with whom Kelley was at that time in communication." It is impossible not to be suspicious when we remember that Kelley was a notorious and most ill-famed necromancer, and in the lonely churchyard of Walton-in-le-Dale, assisted by a fellow warlock, Paul Waring, he put in practice the "diabolical questioning of the dead for the knowledge of future accidents". The disc was bought by the British Museum.

In their great Catalogue of Medicine, Alchemy, Astrology, No. 520, 1929, Messrs. Maggs, the well-known London house óf booksellers, listed "A Manuscript Book of Black Magic written in Shakespeare's England", which was very concisely and accurately described as "An Elizabethan Devil-Worshipper's Prayer-Book". The date suggested is *circa* 1600. There is no clue whatsoever to the identity of the transcriber of this grimoire, which is very clearly written on twenty-three leaves of fair vellum, and illustrated with thirteen extraordinary drawings, some of which are coloured, of King Vercan, who is named as the most powerful of the demon hosts and invoked in thirteen prayers, or rather conjurations. Vercan Rex is shown under various forms, semi-human, wholly bestial with a man's face, triheaded, and once mounted upon a huge bear, the emblem of cruel ferocity. It is significant that when summoning this fiend the operator is warned to be careful to keep within the magic circle which no manifestation has power to cross, and he must be well on his guard not to be enticed out of his ward, for the demons are cunning and full of persuasion and deceit.

In addition to Vercan there are six other drawings of spirits, all of whom have their particular invocations, which are written out in Latin, on the page facing the pictured familiar. The six names are Maymon Rex, Suth Rex, Samax Rex, Sarabotres Rex, Mediac or Modiac Rex, and Arcan Rex. These grotesque figures are linked with corresponding planetary influences. Thus Maymon, a hideous black figure with clawed hands and feet, two human heads at his knees, and, Janus-like, two bird-heads not dissimilar to monstrously deformed crows with evil hanging beaks, is under Saturn; King Suth is brown and under Jupiter; King Samax, who is antlered like Herne the Hunter, is under Mars; King Sarabotres, a leering great green goblin, is under Venus; King Mediac has huge tusks and animal horns, is clad in a blood-red corselet, and strides a savage bear under Mercury; King Arcan is a coal-black fiend with fiery eyes and sharp-whetted fangs, who shoots with bow and arrows under Luna, the moon. There is something indescribably horrible in these portraits of fiends, for it has been said by one who saw the grimoire, "They were drawn from the life."

A Magic Book which formerly belonged to Dr. John Caius (1510–1573), the famous Cambridge scholar, co-founder of Caius and Gonville, is preserved by the British Museum, Additional MSS. 36674.

In a seventeenth-century manuscript black ritual with evocations of the demons Sathan, Barentur, and Barbason in order to obtain wealth the blood of a black cock is prescribed as necessary to confect the charm. (British Museum, Sloane MS. 3846, 27–29.) In Ireland in 1879 a black cock was cut into quarters and offered at the four corners of a farmer's field to bring ill-luck upon the owner of the land and blast his tilth.

A curious incident was published in the *Daily Mirror*, 12 July, 1944. It happened in the autumn of 1916. A captain, the writer of the letter, and a friend walked to the top of Malenny Camp, near Edinburgh. On the summit of the hill, a small plateau, they discovered that a round pond, about a foot deep and twelve feet across, had been dug. On a little tussock in the middle, above the surface water, lay a white cock, trussed as for the table, but not plucked. Voodoo magic had obviously been at work. It is highly probable that an African, a soldier or a seaman, was stationed in the vicinity.

On 7 May, 1432, King Henry VI sent two high officers to take the person of Thomas Northfield, a learned Dominican of Blackfriars, Worcester, and especially were they to seize his books of sorcery and other curious instruments of magic, and so to hale him before the Council to answer charges of necromancy and figure-casting. In the same year, an old chronicler tells us, there was a regular drive all over the country against witches, seven of whom (from various districts) were committed to the Fleet prison for plotting the King's death by enchantments. On the other hand there were released—the accusations of black magic being unproven—from their confinement in Windsor Castle, Friar John Ashwell, of London, and John Virley, a cleric, together with the notorious Margery Jourdemain, the "Witch of the Manor of Eye-next-Westminster". The Privy Council required securities for all these three persons. The reason why they had been imprisoned in Windsor Castle is that they had been prosecuted "pro sorcerye" by Walter Hungerford, the Constable of Windsor, the alleged offence having been committed within his jurisdiction. Nine years afterwards, in 1441, Mother Jourdemain was intimately concerned in the case of Eleanor Cobham, Duchess of Gloucester, who had consulted with wizards and conspired to put a term to the King's life by evil spells. The accusations and trials are well known to us all from Shakespeare, 2 *Henry VI*. "The Witch in Smithfield" was "burned to Ashes"; not, be it noted, for sorcery, but for high treason—endeavouring to compass the death of the sovereign. The other accomplices of the Duchess were duly sentenced; one was hanged, another died in prison, whilst she herself "after three Days open Penance done" was banished to the Isle of Man, and incarcerated in Peel Castle, which is yet said to be haunted by her restless guilty ghost. John Foxe includes both the Duchess and the warlock Roger Bolingbroke, her chief assistant in these necromancies, as Martyrs in his Kalendar, which perhaps is not altogether a surprising view to have been held by the author of the *Book of Martyrs*.

It should not escape remark how closely witchcraft is here mixed up with politics.

In 1466, the reign of Edward IV, Robert Barker, of Babraham, a small Cambridgeshire village, was brought before the Bishop of Ely. Barker confessed how he had obtained a number of magical books and instruments from one John Hope, to wit "a great book, and a roll of black art containing characters, circles, exorcisms and conjurations;

a hexagonal sheet with strange figures; six metal plates with divers characters engraved; a chart with hexagonal and pentagonal characters and figures, and a gilded wand". Since he had intended to raise spirits to "direct him to gold and silver in abundance" the accused was made to abjure these profanities, and then suitably penanced by the Bishop to make amends both publicly and privately, whilst the books and implements of sorcery were burned in the Market Place of Cambridge by the common hangman.

When Elena Dalok, a professed witch, was arraigned before the Commissary of London in 1493 she exhibited a most impudent and brazen effrontery. All her neighbours went in terror of her ribald scolding tongue, and evidence was given that she claimed the horrid power of being able to blast and wither by a curse. Moreover, she had boasted often and before much company that she had a Secret Book wherein she could learn all things that were to come. "With my books of hell," quoth this rampant hag, "I have forby rid me of John Gybbys and am avenged." It appears that this Master John Gybbys, with whom she had fallen out, was suddenly taken with a most strange wasting disease, and died in so short a space of time as amazed the physicians.

It may be remarked that in *Folk-Lore*, Vol. LV (p. 162), December, 1944, Miss Marian F. McNeill gives a most interesting account of a witch's cursing-bone, recently presented to the Scottish National Museum of Antiquities. The object, of which a photograph is reproduced, is the bone of a deer, enclosed in a ring of bog oak, roughly oval in shape. It certainly has some phallic association. Miss McNeill tells us that it belonged to a witch who lived near the head of Glen Shira, Argyllshire. When this woman died, about forty years ago, none of the Glen folk would so much as touch any of her possessions. The minister, the late Rev. J. Finlay Dawson, found the bone on the window-ledge of her cottage, and, taking it away, presented it to a lady who has now given it to the Museum. When the witch intended to "ill-wish" a man she resorted to his croft between sunset and cockcrow, and visiting the poultry-house seized the hen which was perched beside the chief rooster. Having wrung the bird's neck, she poured the blood through the bone, muttering her ritual curses as the warm stream flowed.

During the episcopal visitation of Bishop Redman, of Northampton-shire, in 1500, Canon Thomas Wright, of the Premonstratensian Abbey of Sulby, which is six miles south-west of Market Harborough, was presented for using "Books of Experiments". These were impounded, but the Canon himself escaped with little more than a reprimand, since it was evident he had only studied them out of curiosity and not to practise any conjuration or spell. None the less, thoroughly to understand them he had pretty liberally rewarded a certain mysterious "vagabond" who instructed him in the secrets of this art.

Great scandal was caused throughout the Knaresborough district in 1510 by Canon Wilkinson, of Drax, who, with a number of other experimenters, tried to raise the spirit Belphares. This familiar was to be conjured to reveal a vast treasure believed to be buried at Mixindale Head, near Halifax. The Canon possessed a very old Book of Magic, which he lent to Sir James Richardson, in order that this priest might prepare a leaden tablet inscribed with the image of a certain demon, Oberion, and four other foul entities.

Richard Jones, a warlock of Oxford, in 1532 was approached by Sir William Neville, who required him to make a magic ring of sympathy. The seer declared that he only knew of these rings by hearsay, and had never attempted to forge one, although he "had read many books, and especially the works of Solomon [the grimoire, *The Key of Solomon*], and how his ring should be made and of what metal; and what virtues such rings had according to the canon of Solomon". None the less Jones raised four "king devils" at Neville's behest.

In 1535, when Abbot Thomas, of Abingdon, apprehended a priest living in the town and sorely defamed for magic, it was found that he had very secretly hidden away in his chamber a book of conjuring which gave full directions for consecrating rings with stones in them. These were largely employed for the art of dactyliomancy, that is to say divination by means of a finger-ring. They were also worn to ensure luck in gambling. In 1544 old Doctor Wisdom, a sorcerer who had acquired considerable wealth by his malpractices, made such a ring for Harry, Lord Nevell, son and heir of Ralph, Earl of Westmorland. This young profligate—he was barely one-and-twenty—wore it to bring him fortune at the tables. He had already lost huge sums by dicing. Wisdom declared that he "could work the ring by two ways, by good or evil spirits", and since my Lord had some scruples he would only invoke the holy angels. Similar pretexts are not uncommon today in the mouths of those who hold communion with spirits, who (they argue) can only be good spirits. In this they are, if genuinely deceived, much imperilled, since they are trafficking with demons. It was by the aid of demons that Wisdom (as he was very well aware) wrought his ring.

In 1552, under Edward VI, the Duke of Norfolk's secretary, Clerke, was accused of sorcery. He lodged in the house of one Richard Hartlepoole, and when his room was searched there were discovered, hidden away, many "Books of Nigromancy and Conjuration". Hartlepoole's wife acted as a medium, and the Countess of Sussex had frequently consulted with them. All three were sent to the Tower, but set at liberty after some six months, no doubt on account of influence at Court, which was a hotbed of dissension and intrigue. The young King had scarcely recovered from measles and smallpox, and was plainly consumptive. He died on 6 July, 1553, his end hastened (it is believed) through a noxious draught administered by a witch, who had been introduced into the palace under the guise of a skilled nurse. Again politics and witchcraft intermingle.

James Walsh, of Netherbury, Dorset, who was examined on 20 August, 1566, by the Commissary of the Bishop of Exeter, touching certain suspicion of divination and sorcery, very naïvely acknowledged that he had a Book which had come to him from his late master, and "which had great circles in it, wherein he would set two wax candles and a cross of virgin wax to raise the familiar spirit, of whom he would then ask for anything stolen". The spirit appeared, he said, in various shapes, as "a gray blackish" bird; or a dog; or as a man. On each occasion he rewarded the goblin by a gift of some living thing, a chicken maybe, or a cat. Walsh declared he had never harmed, and never wished to harm, anybody, but it is clear that he had dipped pretty deeply into the science and practice of evil, although perhaps he did not fully realize the heinousness of his crimes. He kept a familiar at his beck and bidding until his Book was taken from him, after which the spirit would not come again, and he could do nothing at all. In this he differed from Pole, a scrivener of Crooked Lane, London, a warlock who was steeped in the black art, and who proudly declared that although my lord Privy Seal had deprived him of his Books, he could yet do many things without them. Moreover, this sorcerer had friends in the country who had books enough for all purposes. We see how the witch organization was linked up throughout the greater part of the land. This transpired in January, 1538, when Pole was questioned by the authorities.

That witches even in a very humble walk of life, and living in small country villages and towns, possessed grimoires which they conned diligently is plain from the evidence given at the trial of Elizabeth Clarke, of Manningtree, Essex, who was hanged for witchcraft in 1645. On one occasion when several members of the coven forgathered one evening at her cottage there was read aloud a book wherein was no goodness. Since Elizabeth Clarke came of a witch family—her mother and others of her kin had suffered for witchcraft and murder—this grimoire was no doubt handed down from mother to daughter, possibly for several generations, and the older sibyls would instruct the younger women in the use of it.

Anne, the wife of Edward Bodenham, of Fisherton Anger, near Salisbury, was eighty years of age and more when justice overtook her in 1653. She had formerly been a servant to the notorious Dr. John Lambe, of Westminster, a warlock who perished miserably at the hands of the mob during a City riot on Friday, 13 June, 1628. Lambe was a wizard of the vilest description, an invoker of evil spirits, a poisoner, a murderer, a common bawd, a practiser of "certain evil, diabolical, and execrable arts, called Witchcrafts, Enchantments, Charmers, and Sorcerers". Anne Bodenham he trained in all his evil knowledge, and she proved an apt and ready pupil. At Fisherton Anger she held the post of village schoolmistress, but actually she throve upon the money she made by vending poison, casting spells, furnishing wicked men and abandoned women with charms, raising spirits to satisfy the caprice of folk more curious than cautious. Mother Bodenham having taken a maid, Anne Styles, to live with her, the girl, herself not a very reputable character, was so alarmed by the strange noises she heard and the stranger sights she saw in the cottage that one fine morning early she stole away and set out for London. Since, however, she was shrewdly suspected of an attempt at poisoning she was followed and apprehended, and after an examination before a Justice of the Peace, Sir Edward Tucker, committed to Salisbury Gaol. In the course of this preliminary inquiry the wench had made such astounding revelations that it was only a matter of a few hours before the witch also found herself in custody. It is true that Mother Bodenham had taken the precaution of making Anne Styles seal a covenant not to discover, but the wretched girl, in great agony, unburdened her soul. She told how the witch had "made a circle, and looking in her Book, called, 'Beelzebub, Tormentor, Lucifer, and Satan appear!' " when were materialized two familiars in the form of ugly loutish boys with hideously malignant countenances shadowed by long shagged black hair. The witch then pricked the girl's finger with a sharp pin, squeezing out the blood, "and put it in a pen, and put the pen in the maid's hand, and held her hand to write in a great book, and one of the spirits laid his hand or claw upon the witch's, whilst the maid wrote . . . the Witch said Amen, and made the Maid say Amen, and the Spirits said Amen, Amen". Now the spirit's hand was clayey cold, the hand of a long-dead thing.

It is clear from the narrative that Anne Styles was a powerful medium, and it was precisely on account of this quality, which Mother Bodenham would at once have recognized, that the old sorceress showed herself so anxious to persuade the girl to live with her. Anne Styles, unconsciously perhaps, would have been an invaluable assistant at the séances. It is possible, then, that the materializing spirit built up the form in which he manifested ectoplasmically from the medium, and ectoplasm, the emanation from a medium at an occult sitting, is described as a clammy viscid extravasation, most unpleasant to the touch. Anne Styles was frequently observed to pass into trance-state, suffering great agony in violent fits, which "drew pity and admiration from all beholders". The notorious Eusapia Palladino is reported by Baron von Schrenck Notzing, in his *Phenomena of Materialisation* (English translation, E. E. Fournier d'Albe, 1923, p. 10), to have "had hallucinations, delirium, fits of laughter, weeping, or deep sleep" and "other typical hysterical convulsions". The cases are precisely parallel, and very many instances of other mediums who suffer in the same way could be cited.

The "great book" in which Anne Styles was compelled to inscribe herself was a red one "written half over with blood, being the names of witches that had listed themselves under the Devil's command", and at the first suspicion of danger it had been sent away to Hampshire to be secreted by a wizard living in that county. This was the roll of the coven, and unfortunately it could not be traced. Naturally these registers were kept and guarded with the utmost care, most often being in the charge of the Grand Master of the district. Guazzo speaks of a big black book in which newly-admitted warlocks are inscribed by the Demon himself.

Mother Bodenham, however, also had her book of charms, a grimoire which there is reason to suppose was written by Dr. Lambe, and whilst in durance she made a great outcry about the Book, and pleaded to be set at liberty for the space of only half an hour that she might secure it. She refused, of course, to divulge where it was concealed. At the Salisbury Lenten Assizes, before John Wilde, Chief Baron of the Exchequer, Anne Bodenham was found guilty on each of three separate indictments, and executed—"a wicked life, a woeful death".

In *The Confessions of Madeleine Bavent*, upon whom sentence was pronounced on 12 March, 1643, that unhappy demoniac relates how Father Pierre David, the chaplain of the convent at Louviers, who so long concealed his sorceries under a guise of extraordinary piety, had a register of the sabbat, and also a grimoire written out by his own hand.

From the various examples which have been given it is plain that many, if indeed not most, witches possessed a grimoire, and more often these manuals of goetry were in manuscript. The reason for this is obvious. Few printers indeed would care to set up in type the blasphemies and horrid conjurations of a grimoire; in fact only Satanists themselves would dare to do such an evil thing. Moreover, there were the legal penalties which would be incurred. Actually, the printed conjuring-books and collections of spells which were given to the Press are abridgements, and (although bad enough) pale reflections of the manuscript grimoires, whose diabolism is rampant and undisguised.

Reginald Scot's *Discoverie of Witchcraft*, a blatantly sceptical work, first appeared in 1584. It may incidentally be remarked that, rationalizing as he shows himself, it is a mistake none the less to regard Scot as a complete disbeliever and an atheist. He fully accepts and is convinced of the existence of evil spirits, but he will hardly allow that they can have any commerce with mankind, save indeed in the most exceptional circumstances. Such a position is utterly unreasonable, and King James was perfectly justified in denouncing these "damnable opinions". Indeed, Scot's arguments, for what they are, sail so near the wind that we feel he alone is to blame if he has been pilloried as an agnostic. Much of what he advances is as repugnant to sober piety as it is to the world's experience and the findings of plain common sense. As for the rest, he trifles away his pages in describing juggler's tricks and feats of legerdemain, which are all beside the point.

When a new edition—the third—of the *Discoverie* was issued in 1665 the publisher inserted nine chapters at the beginning of Book XV, and further added a Second Book to the "Treatise on Divels and Spirits". This "Second Book", which reprobates in very honest terms "the villany of Necromancers, and wicked Magicians, in dealing with the spirits of men departed", is entirely opposed to Scot's own view and contradicts the whole tenor of his writings. It is certainly a very wholesome corrective, but singularly misplaced. The nine chapters prefatory, as it were, to Book XV are even more anomalous in their context, since they furnish instructions for drawing magical circles, for calling up a suicide, "the ghost of one that hath hanged himself", and for conjuring various demons and familiar spirits. It has very justly been said: "They appear to be, and are, practical directions for magic and necromancy." It is all very well to speak of these additions as a mere trick of the bookseller. More goes to it than that. Of course these chapters are babydom to the contents of a real grimoire.

Among the most widely famed of English grimoires was the Red Book of Appin, all trace of which seems to be lost, although it is known to have been actually in existence a hundred years ago, and was last heard of as in the possession of the now extinct Stewarts of Invernhayle.

This mysterious volume, a manuscript and unique, conferred dark powers upon its owner, who knew what inquiry would be made before the question was poised. The runes and spells, which also included some healing charms, were of the most horrible, and only the lawful owner of the book dare turn its pages and read therein.

The celebrated Welsh physician and diviner of Cwrt-y-Cadno, a lonely hamlet in the heart of Carmarthenshire, Dr. John Harries (1785–1839), to whom there was constant resort from near and far and who was accounted a wizard of unusual adeption, possessed a great Book of Magic, which he allowed no one to handle save himself. The stout old leather cover was even secured by a brass lock and clasps. Often visitors out of curiosity offered quite considerable sums to be allowed to examine the mysterious Book, but he always refused, because, as he warned them, a few words idly read or a formula spoken from its pages might let loose wrathful influences of power, which could not easily be controlled and were dismissed with difficulty. Folk were continually consulting Harries concerning the issue of a sickness, their own fortunes, or the good estate of friends and relations. If anyone inquired about such-a-one who was ill, Harries would pass into trance for a few minutes, and on coming to himself was wont to reply, "He will surely recover," or else, "I am sorry for you, but so-and-so will die," as the case might be, and it is said he was never known to be wrong.

The Book of Magic passed to his son Henry, who was a warlock openly confessed. At any rate he boasted of his traffic with familiar spirits, and he is supposed to have served an apprenticeship with a professor of the black art in London. Henry Harries died in 1849. Different accounts are given of the fate of the Book. We are told that it was purchased together with the wizard's shewstone and some cabbalistic parchments from the descendants of the Harries. These good simple farmers had inherited as the nearest, if very distant, relatives, but they regarded the occult paraphernalia with a not unreasoning fear, and kept them locked up in a cupboard. A London barrister, who had heard of the fame of Harries, visited Cwrt-y-Cadno on a walking tour, and eagerly bought the grimoire and the magical instruments. Another account is that all these telesmatical papers and rattletraps passed under a pledge of profoundest secrecy into a private collection.

Less than ten tears ago a wise man, to seek whose help and advice people came from all parts of Wales, was living near Llangwrig, Montgomeryshire. He countercharmed the evil spells of "the wicked who have power", that is to say witches. In a rosewood box he kept two books, an astrological almanack and another. An old man, who lived at Trawscoed, in Cardiganshire, and who died in 1910, enjoyed a great reputation as a diviner and a healer. He worked cures with the spell of the scarlet yarn, commonly known as "measuring the yarn".

Mr. Charles Godfrey Leland used to relate how in the year 1886 he became intimately acquainted with a peasant woman named Maddalena, who led a vagabond gypsy life in Tuscany, and from her he learned that not only was she an adherent of the secret cult, *la vecchia religione*, but that there was in existence a manuscript setting forth the doctrines of the Italian witches. This he persuaded her to obtain for him, and on 1 January, 1897, he received a manuscript entitled *Aradia, or the Gospel of the Witches*, which two years later he published with a Preface and certain annotations. The Gospel (*Vangelo*) of the Witches proves to be nothing more than a miscellaneous collection of folk-lore, and although there are so-called conjurations and charms, and even a chapter on the Sabbat, *Treguenda*, or Witch-meeting, it all has very little to do with witchcraft at all, and if frankly superstitious is of no importance and without power. It is true the cloven hoof may be glimpsed now and again, but even to call the book a grimoire were a gross exaggeration. It is an entirely different thing, for example, from Voodoo, which Mr. Leland apparently regarded as a fairly close parallel. I can only suggest that if Maddalena was a witch she choused the inquirer. If she were not a witch she would, of course, know nothing of the secrets of that infernal synagogue. In any case *Aradia*, save to the folk-lorist, is of little interest. Moreover, when Mr. Leland speaks of "*diabolism*, introduced by the Church since 1500", he shows himself so hopelessly misapprehensive that it is difficult to follow his train of thought or to attach any meaning to his phrase.

It is true enough that even today Italian sorcerers, especially in the South and in Sicily, possess very terrible manuscript grimoires and cabbalistic charts, which are (it is said) similar to those used by the Arab magicians in Cairo, and of great antiquity.

It is not surprising that manuscript grimoires should be more plentiful than the printed manuals. In making his own copies for his own use, even if such were largely based upon the *Alberts* or *The Key of Solomon* or *Zekerboni*, each sorcerer would be able to add with his own pen those charms and conjurations he had learned from oral tradition, and he could, moreover, amplify or abridge the rubrics at will. It must not be supposed that the ceremonies of necromancy can be lightly essayed or undertaken in any jesting spirit. Inevitable failure and foolishness will be the result, as has more than once proved the case with ignorant experimenters. A strict training, a discipline even, are necessary to obtain the impious ends. Again and again the wizards themselves warn neophytes not to meddle with these mysteries until they have been schooled by masters of the art and practice of magic. It is no mere maygame, but a very horrible and serious business.

Before the secrets of the grimoire can be fully understood, before these infernal businesses can achieve success, Satan demands that the terrible barter shall be made, the compact with hell must be struck, the price paid.

Éliphas Levi enumerates five *Conditions of Success in Infernal Evocations* which are: (1) Invincible obstinacy; (2) a conscience hardened to crime and untouched by the least shadow of remorse or fear; (3) ignorance, affected or natural, of all good things, and a rooted hate of all goodness; (4) blind faith in all that is incredible, which is to say complete trust in the devil; (5) an entirely false idea of God—that is, putting Satan in the place of God, falling down and worshipping him when he promises his deluded servant and slave "all the kingdoms of the world, and the glory of them", which are not his to bestow, for the only gifts he has are evil and filthy foolishness, and the satiety of lust, empty glamour, cruelty, and hate, the tyrant power of a moment, delusion all, and in the end eternal death. Yet it is for these things men risk their immortal souls.

Most of the manuscript grimoires are written in calligraphy of exceptional neatness and precision, and elaborately adorned, the Greek and Hebrew lettering, the cabbalistic designs, the circles, trigons, and pentacles being draughted with an extreme of nicety and care. Wealthy occultists treading the forbidden path would pay immense sums to the best scriveners and most learned clerks to make these transcripts of the books of blasphemy. The amanuensis who let it quietly be understood in certain coteries that he was willing to engross a grimoire, and no questions asked, could be sure of a large and steady income.

Gilles de Rais, who in the days of his pride was perhaps the richest subject in all Europe, had a large collection of magical books, manuscripts written by the first hands in France and Italy, the pages bordered and illuminated with leaf of gold and minium, bound in richest velvets parsemés with jewels. Truly they might be said to "appear beautiful outward, but are within full of dead men's bones and of all uncleanness". Éliphas Levi says that Gilles de Rais "sought the Philosophical Stone in the blood of murdered children, and it was covetousness which drove him to this hideous debauchery, for he relied on the faith of the necromancers. He had doubtless derived his recipe from some of those old Hebrew Grimoires which, had their origin been known at that period, would have been sufficient to call down on Jewry at large the execration of the whole world."

The making of many of these monstrous books was superintended by the young Florentine priest, Francesco Prelati, who also at midnight consecrated them with the ritual of hell upon the dark altar in the secret chapel of the castle. The "consecration" of a grimoire was a ceremony of particular horror and impiety, and was supposed to lend the spells written in the book a more efficacious and swifter power. In 1549, when seven sorcerers were burned at Nantes, one of the chief articles against them was that they had composed a grimoire which they intended to take to the witches of Norcia for consecration in this kind. Norcia was long infamous as a centre of witchcraft. Cellini, in his *Memoirs*, tells us of the wizard priest who had with great pains written out a book of spells, and was minded to consecrate it among the Norcian hills.

The name of the first victim of Gilles de Rais does not appear to be known. He is described as a very comely lad about fourteen years old or rather more. When he had been outraged and murdered in the most horrible manner, Prelati wrapped the body in a linen sheet and under cover of darkness buried it in the cemetery of St. Vincent hard by, but the blood was collected in phials and with it on virgin parchment (that is of the first calf that a cow has) they wrote out a grimoire and the liturgy of Satan.

Because of their knowledge of Hebrew and cabbalistic lore Rabbis were greatly in request to transcribe books of conjuration. M. Gaster, in his article on Jewish magic, Hastings' *Encyclopaedia of Religion and Ethics*, says that the *Zohar* "from the fourteenth century held almost unbroken sway over the minds of the majority of the Jews. In it the Talmudic legends concerning the existence and activity of the *shedhim* (demons) are repeated and amplified, and a hierarchy of demons was established corresponding to the heavenly hierarchy . . . Manasses Ben Israel's *Nishmat Hayim* is full of information concerning belief in demons. . . . Even the scholarly and learned Rabbis of the seventeenth century clung to the belief." According to Voltaire, Catherine de Medici, the Maréchal d'Ancre, and many other persons of the highest rank always employed Rabbis to transcribe the books of conjuration they required.

In 1642 Mons. Olier founded the Seminary and Community of St. Sulpice in Paris. The life of that saintly man, written by Abbé Faillon, shows us how magic was systematically practised at that time, and that the Blessed Sacrament of the Altar was the object of the vilest profanations. "Books on the diabolic art were publicly sold at the very doors of the Church of St. Sulpice, and shortly after Mons. Olier entered on the duties of the parish, the baillie of the suburb, being in pursuit of three persons accused of sorcery, and mistaking one house for another, found an altar dedicated to the evil spirit, with these words inscribed upon it: Gratias tibi, Lucifer; gratias tibi, Beelzebub; gratias tibi, Azareel. The altar was a foul travesty of that consecrated to Catholic worship; the candles were black, the ornaments about it were all in keeping with its infernal object, and a great book of prayers, as if in mockery of the Missal, consisted of diabolical incantations. The baillie took possession of the book, but the affair was not prosecuted any further on account of the numbers and high position of those who were implicated."

This "great book of prayers" was not exactly a grimoire, but the book which is known as "Satan's Black Missal", which had its origin far back in the centuries and was used in the obscurer Gnostic rites, as, for example, when Marcos, the disciple of Valentinus, said Mass—or rather parodied Mass—with two chalices, into the smaller of which he poured wine, whilst upon his pronouncing certain magical formulas the larger cup was filled with a liquor like new-spilled blood, which boiled and bubbled up, running down over the brim on to the linen corporal and altar-cloths. St. Irenaeus says that at his wonder-working Eucharist Marcos filled two goblets with thick heady wine and a little water; he then breathed over them certain uncouth words and made strange signs, upon which the liquids seethed and incarnadined, the one blushing to fiery red, the other empurpling with an exotic fragrance. It was, of course, hypnotic glamour. The effect upon those present was the madness of Convulsionaries. Women screamed and tore their hair, passing into trance-states and uttering with incredible rapidity a jargon of ugly sounds which were declared to be the oracles of deity. The ceremony, whatever its secret purport was, evoked a nymphomaniac delirium.

The coven of sorcerers at Paris, whose iniquities, poisonings, murders, treasons, and witchcraft were investigated by La Reynie and the

Chambre Ardente from 1679 to 1682, employed a schoolmaster, named Protain, to write the Satanic pacts in a very fair hand. The transcribing of grimoires was the business of a professional calligrapher, Duprat, who charged enormous fees for a complete manuscript with the diagrams of circles and pentacles and rubricated conjurations. Some short-sighted folk thought that with the execution of La Voisin, in February, 1680, the imprisonment of the Abbé Guibourg, and the closing down of the Chambre in 1682, witchcraft had practically been stamped out in the capital. There could not have been a greater mistake. The Princess Palatine, the second wife of the King's brother, Monsieur, writes in a letter of 1701: "Everyone seems simply crazy to become an expert in the art of conjuring up familiar spirits and other bedevilments." Another generation of sorcerers had succeeded La Voisin and her gang. Black masses were again being said, and it was fairly generally known that if a sufficient sum were forthcoming nobody need apply in vain to Guignard, the curé of Notre Dame de Bourges. Three notorious witches, la Créancier, la Ducatel, la Loysel, and a warlock Picault, who hardly disguised his practice of black magic, were sent to the Salpêtrière. Before long, Protain, whose pen had been kept exceedingly busy all the while, joined them in durance. The Duc d'Olonne paid no less than 113 livres for a goatskin inscribed with cabbalistic signs, devilish futhorks, and a grim Satanic invocation.

A very interesting episode of French peasant sorcery is related by Restif de la Bretonne in his "Mémoires intimes", *Monsieur Nicolas*. Restif was born on 23 October, 1734, and was therefore twelve years old when the incidents he describes took place. His family had long been resident at Sacy, a village of farmers and vine-dressers, some twenty miles from Auxerre. In the employ of Restif's father was a young shepherd lad, aged about sixteen, François Courtcou, who bore anything but a good reputation. His usual conversation was grossly obscene, and Restif, who frankly confesses he had an itch that way, when accompanying him to the fields used to listen eagerly to all his dirty stories. François when he was alone with Restif persisted in talking about witchcraft, concerning which he had a hundred tales. His particular delight was to describe the lubricities of the sabbat, no detail of which did he spare to picture so graphically that it seems very certain he himself had assisted at these blasphemous orgies. He also related how a certain warlock, who had been excommunicated for his foul life and profanities, possessed a mysterious magic skin, written over with charms and spells, a kind of grimoire. From the description this must have been almost precisely similar to the pelt which the Duc d'Olonne purchased at so considerable a price. François also knew of highway robbers and brigands who resorted to black magic to ensure success in their nefarious undertakings. No question the sabbat was held in the half-ruined castles and caves where these wretches made their lair. The very first day he came to work at the farm Restif asked: "Do you know any stories, François?" "Do I know any stories, Master Nicolas!" was the reply. "I should rather think so. I can spin you many a good yarn, and true ones beside. I can tell you all about witches, and ghosts, and men who have made a pact with the devil, men who have been cursed by the Church and who change themselves into animals, or at any rate seem to change themselves. Then there are the shepherd-sorcerers, witches too who can take the shape of hares, and a score beside. As many as you like."

These traditions of evil practices, this shape-shifting and the foulest forms of magic, all of which there can be no doubt were being extensively practised throughout the countryside at that very time, are extremely significant. Werewolfism is a sorcery which has persisted from dateless centuries. In Brittany it is still credibly believed that certain warlocks at night either dress themselves in wolf-skins or assume the form of wolves in order to repair to those assemblies over which the demon presides. This craft of the men-wolves comes down from the earliest days of ancient Armorica. That women-witches in this part shared the power is mentioned as far back as the old Latin geographer Pomponius Mela, who wrote in the days of Caligula and Claudius, A.D. 41.

In the Middle Ages it was widely believed that upon the rebel against God who had been denounced from the altar, and showed himself stubbornly impenitent, fell the curse of lycanthropy. In Normandy the excommunicate became a werewolf for a period of three or seven years; in Basse-Bretagne he who had not been shriven nor sprinkled himself with holy water for ten years could learn the secrets of werewolfery; in La Vendée the outcast who was banned of the priest became a werewolf for seven years; and very similar traditions prevailed throughout the departments of Loiret, Yonne, Côte-D'Or, and the districts of Franche-Comté. Nor was so widespread a persuasion without support. In 1521, at Poligny (Jura, Franche-Comté), three werewolf sorcerers were executed, and their atrocities commemorated by pictures hung in the Dominican church to serve as a lesson and a solemn warning. Fifty years later the Parliament of Franche-Comté, appalled at the horrid increase of lycanthropy, issued special edicts regarding the punishment of witches who practised this inhuman foulness. Pierre de Lancre has left us a very full account of the werewolf of Bordeaux, Jean Grenier, a lad about fourteen years old, the cowherd of a well-to-do farmer who lived near St. Sever (Landes). This wretched youth had bound himself to a demon, whom he worshipped as the Lord of the Forest. In 1858, two gentlemen, benighted after a long day's hunting in the Forest of Châteauroux (Indre), had perforce taken refuge in a woodcutter's little shelter. In the light of the full moon they saw coming down one of the glades an aged verderer, who bore a very evil reputation throughout the whole countryside. He halted by an old ruined cross, and with certain mysterious signs threw back his head, uttering a kind of curious long-drawn howl. Through the thicket there came padding swiftly thirteen wolves, one of which was apparently larger and fiercer than the rest. The animal seemed to fawn upon the man, who caressed it and stroked its head as if it were a favourite dog. Then with a sharp shrill whistle he turned and plunged into the thicket, the whole pack following at his heels. The hidden witnesses of this extraordinary incident, who were men of standing, education, and sound common sense, swore that, be the explanation what it might, they could not have been mistaken.

The Rev. Sabine Baring-Gould, having lingered rather late whilst sketching the venerable cromlech at La Rondelle, a hamlet ten miles from Champigni (Vienne), on seeking some sort of conveyance, or at least a guide to show him the shortest way back, found it impossible to persuade anyone to cross the marais after dark, although the sky was unclouded and lit by a clear new moon. The fen was horribly dangerous, since there roved all over it a man-wolf fiend. He had been seen only a week before, prowling along the edge of a buckwheat field just beyond the end cottage of the little street. Both the good curé and the maire affirmed as much, nor could they have been mistaken. This was in 1863.

In 1879, at the frontier village of Ste-Croix, Vaud, there occurred an indisputable case of shape-shifting and the etheric double, the result of sorcery.

In 1925 there was a case of werewolfery at Uttenheim, near Strassburg. The lycanthrope was a youth in his teens, and in some respects the history is not dissimilar to that of Jean Grenier, to whom reference has been made.

It is more than probable that François Courtcou had been initiated into these horrid mysteries of animal glamour and bestial phantasmagory. This young reprobate also spoke of witches appearing in the guise of hares. This metamorphosis is so frequently recorded and so widely recognized that comment can hardly be necessary. I have in my own experience known instances of a witch who seemingly transformed herself into a hare (Somersetshire and Devonshire); as also the case of an Oxfordshire witch who was seen under the form of a cat. In all these examples there was, of course, glamour induced by the black art; in modern parlance (perhaps) crowd hypnotism. In 1934 Mr. Walter Cooper, of Wallop, Hampshire, related how, when he was a boy, about 1870, there lived in the village a witch named Lydia Skeers. "She used," he said, "to turn herself into a hare. One day when she was abroad Mr. Pothecary shot a hare, but it vanished. He knew he'd hit un in the shoulder. Next day he saw Lydia Skeers in her cottage. She was picking shots out of her shoulder." In Scotland the transformation to a hare, or more precisely the vizoring as a hare, of witches, male and female, is a notorious fact which cannot be gainsaid. I know those who have themselves witnessed these subtle manifestations. In his *Witchcraft and Second Sight in the Highlands and Islands of Scotland*, the Rev. J. G. Campbell, mentioning the various forms under which the warlock may be disguised, emphatically says "very frequently cats and hares". Again, he remarks: "The stories of witches assuming the shape of hares are numberless." Mrs. Leather, in *The Folk-Lore of Herefordshire*, notes: "At Much Marle (near Lebdury) it was believed that witches became hares." At the Taunton Summer Assizes in 1663 Julian Cox, aged about seventy, was indicted on a charge of witchcraft. Several witnesses positively swore that she had assumed the form of a hare, and Glanvil, who gives a full account of the proceedings, has a very philosophical explanation of this phenomenon, showing how, although a *"Hare-like Spectre"* which was Julian Cox was verily and indeed seen, there was no real and substantial *"Metamorphosis of her body"*.

François Courtcou proved so abominably lazy and negligent of his flock—his watch and care consisting of sleeping under a hedge in the sun—that at the end of the month he was sent about his business, and his brother, Pierre, who was a year younger and known to be far smarter and more active, was given the post. This would be at the beginning of September. In a very short time he stood high in the favour of his master and mistress, who were never tired of praising his readiness and good humour. Actually he was, if possible, more lascivious and more foul-mouthed than even his brother, although he had the wit to cover it up and pose as being a simple good fellow. Restif, of course, eagerly asked him if he knew any stories. To the boy's intense delight Pierre rejoiced in a much larger and much lewder repertory than François, and he could tell his tales far more cleverly, and with such drama that he delighted his little auditor. This went on for some time, and when he had won the boy's heart, which had indeed been his aim all along, after a good deal of beating about the bush, vague hints, and interrogations, he one day asked: "Do you know how to write a letter?" Restif proudly enough boasted of his penmanship. "Ah! If I could only write I could have everything I want," was the shepherd's comment. "How? What do you mean?" "Well, I should make a compact." "A compact? What's that?" "A promise made in writing." "A promise? To whom?" "To the devil, little simpleton." "The devil!" "Yes, of course. No need to upset yourself. Haven't I told you a hundred times that he's not as black as he's painted? The Prince of Darkness is a Gentleman. Now listen; if we make a pact with him he will give us all we want, yes, we can have any girl we like." Restif began to get alarmed, but he was more inquisitive than afraid. "I tell you," continued the young rascal, "that there is no occasion to be frightened. You must not let him see that you are the least bit in awe of him, they say, and then you can command him, and make him do what you jolly well please. I knew a chap who used to tell us that there was a sort of conjuration in the *Shepherds' Almanack*. If we could only get hold of it! And I have a very shrewd idea that it is on the shelf at home. Your brother was looking at it the other day, and I recognized the pictures. There's a pretty kind of drawing for each month in the year. See if you can manage to hook it. Then you can read it through to me, and I shall know the conjuration right enough when we come to it." Restif, all agog, rushed off, and by a little wheedling persuaded his sister Margot to lend him the *Almanack*.

He ran back to Courtcou, and the precious pair sat down to con the *Almanack*. There was an account of the raising of Lazarus, and an old legend of what he had seen beyond the grave. Then came *How a Shepherd may call up the Devil, and talk to him face to face*. "We've got it!" cried Courtcou, highly excited. "That's the spell all our shepherd-boys use." "The Evocation: Kill a large black cat, a black hen, a black eanling, a crow, a pie, a blackbird, and mingle their blood together in order to confect the charm. This commixture must be made in some remote and solitary spot. Burn the entrails, the feet and claws, the heads, the skin or the feathers, except only the skin of the black cat; and then scatter a little of the ashes to the four quarters of heaven, crying aloud these words: '*Spirit whose breath is in the four winds, breathe, breathe on me.*' What is left of the ashes carefully collect to infuse them in a quart of white wine. In some out-of-the-way barn, or better still in an empty and deserted house or hut, roast over a slow fire or on charcoal embers the remains of the animals, with the exception of the carcass of the black lamb. This must be let lie just where it fell, since it is the Devil's share. Whilst the flesh is cooking the air will be full of smoke. Then set down on the floor, in the midst, a large open vessel full of water, which water must be crystal clear so that you can plainly see the bottom of the vessel. Gaze fixedly into the water, and meanwhile drink one half of the measure of white wine wherein the ashes have been dissolved. The operator must be fasting. From the beam or from that part of the ceiling which is directly above your vessel of water a lamp shall have been suspended in such a way that a shadow is thrown on the surface of the water although the rest of the room may be light. Holding the skin of the black cat, or wrapping it round you, finish drinking the white wine to the very last drop. The Devil will suddenly stand behind you and look over your shoulder into the water, wherein you will see his face quite plainly reflected among the shadows. You may speak to him, making terms, asking questions, and he will answer. If there are two of you, only one will actually be able to see the Devil, but the other will hear him speaking and understand all that he says."

Pierre did not wait twenty-four hours to perform these beastly ceremonies, half black magic, half tomfool cruelty that they are. He forthwith stole the lamb from his master's flock, swearing lustily that a wolf had rushed out of the thicket and carried it off, as indeed might very well have happened in that lonely part of the country, on the borders of Nitry Wood. One is not surprised to learn that François was called upon to help the would-be sorcerers. Restif managed to filch the wine from his father's cellar, and late that night, under a harvest moon, they forgathered in an old unused bothy at some distance from the main farm buildings. Pierre greedily gulped down the two pints of white wine with which he had mixed the ashes as prescribed, and being a very strong vintage it excited him fearfully. Of the cat-skin, which he cleaned and carefully dried, he had made a rough kind of loo mask or blinkers to enable him to concentrate his gaze more steadily on the water in the great bowl.

Restif confesses that by the time the conjuration was well on its way he stood, trembling from head to foot like an aspen leaf, half in and half out of the door, ready to take to his heels if the Devil appeared in some monstrous or fearsome shape. Courtcou, who was leaning over the water, exclaimed that he saw the Devil's face staring at him from the bowl, and he at once began a string of questions, to which Restif declares he heard a hoarse deep voice reply. This terrified him to such an extent that in spite of the fact that he had paper, an ink-horn, and a quill all ready, he was far too nervous to write anything, although Pierre kept shouting to him, "Write the pact! Look sharp! Write the pact! The Devil is willing to give us all we want on condition that for each good turn he does us we pledge ourselves to commit a mortal sin, and that we lead somebody else, man, woman, or child, into mortal sin. That's his rate of payment." Courtcou was now half-seas over. In the end Restif did manage somehow to scrawl a kind of pact, which, stammering and halting, he read out to Courtcou, who bawled it loudly at the very top of his voice. By this time Restif was worked up into a regular panic.

Courtcou afterwards told his young companion that although he had never experimented before he was not altogether a novice at that kind of thing, since he had been taught how to patter the conjuration by the abram-cove of a pack of thieving beggars with whom he had tramped the countryside when he was quite a little boy.

Restif could never forget the horrible husky voice which he heard answering, although he saw nothing, and writing in 1791, forty-five years later—*Monsieur Nicolas* was printed in 1794—in order to find some rationalizing explanation he suggests that Pierre Courtcou may have been a skilful ventriloquist, which, to say the least, sounds extremely unlikely and far-fetched. It would need a very practised ventriloquist and require a very clever brain to carry out such a deception. It hardly seems possible that an ignorant country shepherd-boy should be so perfectly qualified, and in any case what had he to gain by this sort of jiggery-pokery? Nothing at all. On the other hand, he was running a pretty considerable risk.

No such explanation is necessary. The whole beastly business seems to have been fantastic and grotesque, in one sense child's play even and fee-faw-fum, yet it is not at all impossible that, muddled and uncertain as the rites obviously were, the carrion cruelty and the rank offensiveness of the whole thing, energized by the will and determination of the operator, a lad of the vilest character and dispositions, may have powerfully attracted some of the very lowest order of spirits, not merely mischievous but malign entities, and probably it was one of these who manifested in the water and gave replies, which is nothing other than the old bedevilment we have met before, yclept hydromantia.

The proceedings which Restif describes are, on the surface, not a whit more ridiculous than those reported as taking place in many séance-rooms today and accepted as veridical and evidential in perfectly good faith by hundreds of educated and normally intelligent persons. Once he had pronounced the pact Pierre Courtcou, on his own showing, had been promised by the spirit all kinds of luck and good fortune, and that he should at will enjoy a sultan's seraglio of beauty. Actually what happened was that very soon after the midnight diablerie in the hut complaints were made to Goodwife Barbe, Restif's mother, of Courtcou's incorrigible lewdness and bawdy talk, whilst almost at the same time he was overheard discussing with young Restif the details of the conjuration and urging the boy to write him out another compact. To top all, the lecherous lad seduced one of Restif's half-sisters. Excellent labourer and shepherd as he was, this sort of thing could not be tolerated, and one fine Saturday morning Master Pierre, to his great surprise, was sent packing with his wages in his pocket. So much for the splendid promises the spirit had made!

In precisely the same way "invisible and oftentimes masquerading spirits", as Sir William Barrett calls them, are continually attempting to delude circles of sitters today, and often with the unhappiest results, and tragic disappointments for those who are induced to place any reliance on their predictions and assurances. The lower in order these communicating intelligences who "come through" may be, the clumsier is their simulation, and, generally speaking, the swifter, the more extravagant, and highly-coloured their psychic phenakistoscope. Yet they are—even the basest—possessed of infinite cunning, and they invariably prove as treacherous as they are crafty. One can hardly be surprised that an ignorant ill-conditioned peasant boy living in a remote French hamlet in the mid-eighteenth century should be drawn in and choused and cheated, when even now in our largest cities scores of keen-witted clear-headed gentlefolk have been fascinated and decoyed, until indeed many reach such a point that they seem to modulate their conduct, to adopt their ideas, to stake the most material issues of the present life and —what is more important yet—implicitly to accept their beliefs concerning the life to come from the dictates and at the suggestion of some control or familiar, whose identity it is impossible to establish, but whose very nature and whose veracity are (to say the least) in the highest degree suspect, deliberately shrouded and kept obscure. It has been shrewdly observed that "to refuse to entertain even the hypothesis that certain psychic phenomena are mostly due to evil spirits is simply to shut our eyes to one possible explanation of the whole business; and an explanation that does really explain".

Witchcraft may adopt many names and wear many robes, but throughout all ages and from all ages it is essentially the same unchanging cult, communion with the Devil and the hosts of evil. As yesterday, so today, are men everywhere obeying the command of Satan—"Fall down and worship me."

CHAPTER VI

The Magus (1801) *of Francis Barrett—Ceremonial Magic—The Evil Eye—Ranks of Demons —Necromancy—Evocations—Ebenezer Sibly—Satanism Today—Obeah—Witchcraft in Mauritius.*

"There shall not be found among you . . . an enchanter, or a witch, or a charmer, or a consulter with familiar spirits, or a wizard, or a necromancer. For all that do these things are an abomination unto the Lord."—*Deuteronomy* xviii, 10-12.

AMONG the most interesting and most valuable books of English occult lore *The Magus, or, Celestial Intelligencer,* of Francis Barrett, "Student in Chemistry, Metaphysicks, Natural and Occult Philosophy, etc., etc.," holds a prominent place. The full title of this encyclopaedic manual is as follows: "The Magus, or, Celestial Intelligencer; Being a Complete System of Occult Philosophy. In Three Books: Containing the Ancient and Modern Practice of the Cabbalistic Art, Natural and Celestial Magic, etc.; shewing the wonderful Effects that may be performed by a Knowledge of the Celestial Influences, the occult Properties of Metals, Herbs, and Stones, and the Application of Active to Passive Principles, Exhibiting the Sciences of Natural Magic; Alchymy, or Hermetic Philosophy; Also the Nature, Creation, and Fall of Man; His natural and supernatural Gifts; the magical Power inherent in the Soul, etc.; with a great Variety of rare Experiments in Natural Magic: The Constellatory Practice or Talismanic Magic; The Nature of the Elements, Stars, Planets, Signs, etc.; the Construction and Composition of all sorts of Magic Seals, Images, Rings, Glasses, etc.; The Virtue and Efficacy of Numbers, Characters, and Figures, of good and evil Spirits. Magnetism, and Cabbalistic or Ceremonial Magic; In which the secret Mysteries of the Cabbala are explained; the Operations of good and evil Spirits; all Kinds of Cabbalistic Figures, Tables, Seals, and Names, with their Use, etc. The Times, Bonds, Offices, and Conjuration of Spirits. To which is added *Biographia Antiqua, or the Lives of the most eminent Philosophers, Magi,* etc. The whole illustrated with a great Variety of Curious Engravings, Magical and Cabbalistical Figures, etc. By Francis Barrett, F.R.C., Professor of Chemistry, natural and occult Philosophy, the Cabbala, etc., etc. London: Printed for Lackington, Allen, and Co., Temple of the Muses, Finsbury Square. 1801."

The title-page to the alchemical section of this book runs: "The True Secret of the Philosopher's Stone; or, Jewel of Alchemy. Wherein the Process of Making the Great Elixir *is discovered*; By which Base Metals may be Turned into Pure Gold; Containing the Most Excellent and Profitable Instructions in the Hermetic Art; Discovering that Valuable and Secret Medicine of the Philosophers, *To make· Men Healthy, Wise, and Happy.*"

Another section contains: "The Constellatory Practice, or Talismanic Magic. Shewing The true Properties of the Elements, Meteors, Stars, Planets, etc., etc.; likewise the Nature of Intelligences, Spirits,

FALLEN ANGELS

HEADS OF EVIL DEMONS

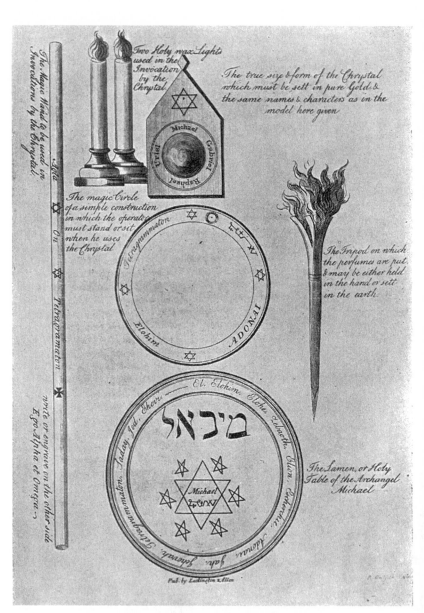

THE MAGICIAN'S ARMOURY

Daemons, and Devils; the Construction and Composition of all Sorts of Magic Seals, Images, Rings, Glasses, Pictures, etc., etc.; the Power and Composition of Numbers, Mathematical Figures, and Characters of Spirits both good and evil. The Whole of the Above illustrated by a Great Variety of Beautiful Figures, Types, Letters, Seals, Images, Magic Characters, etc., forming a Complete System of Delightful Knowledge and Abstruse Science; Such as is warranted never before to have been published in the English Language."

This introduces us to: "The Cabbala; or, the Secret Mysteries of Ceremonial Magic Illustrated. Shewing the Art of Calculating by Divine Names; The Rule, Order, and Government of Angels, Intelligences, and Blessed Spirits; Holy Seals, Pentacles, Tables of the Cabbala, Divine Numbers, Characters and Letters; Of Miracles, Prophecy, Dreams, etc., etc., etc. Embellished and beautified with a vast Number of Rare Figures, Pentacles, Characters, etc., etc., etc. Used in the Cabbalistic Art."

In addition to the explanations and directions contained in *The Magus* it appears from the following "Advertisement" that Barrett gave oral instructions and conducted practical occult experiments, in fact that he trained serious inquirers into these esoteric arts and seekers after mystical knowledge. "The Author of this Work respectfully informs those who are curious in the studies of Art and Nature, especially of Natural and Occult Philosophy, Chemistry, Astrology, etc., etc., that, having been indefatigable in his researches in those sublime Sciences, of which he has treated at large in this Book, that he gives private instructions and lectures upon any of the above-mentioned Sciences; in the course of which he will discover many curious and rare experiments. Those who become Students will be initiated into the choicest operations of Natural Philosophy, Natural Magic, the Cabbala, Chemistry, the Talismanic Arts, Hermetic Philosophy, Astrology, Physiognomy, etc., etc. Likewise they will acquire the knowledge of the Rites, Mysteries, Ceremonies, and Principles of the ancient Philosophers, Magi, Cabbalists, Adepts, etc.—The Purpose of this School (which will consist of no greater number than Twelve Students) being to investigate the hidden treasures of Nature; to bring the Mind to a contemplation of the Eternal Wisdom; to promote the discovery of whatever may conduce to the perfection of Man; the alleviating the miseries and calamities of this life, both in respect of ourselves and others; the study of morality and religion here, in order to secure to ourselves felicity hereafter; and, finally, the promulgation of whatever may conduce to the general happiness and welfare of mankind.—Those who feel themselves thoroughly disposed to enter upon such a course of studies, as is above recited, with the same principles of philanthropy with which the Author invites the lovers of philosophy and wisdom, to incorporate themselves in so select, permanent, and desirable a society, may speak with the Author upon the subject, at any time between the hours of Eleven and Two o'clock, at 99 Norton Street, Mary-le-Bonne. Letters (post paid) upon any subject treated of in this Book, will be duly answered, with the necessary information."

I have been told that Francis Barrett actually founded a small sodality of students of these dark and deep mysteries, and that under his tuition—for he was profoundly learned in these things—some advanced far upon the path of transcendental wisdom. One at least was a Cambridge man, of what status—whether an undergraduate or the Fellow of a College—I do not know, but there is reason to believe that he initiated others, and until quite recent years—it perhaps persists even today—the Barrett tradition was maintained at Cambridge, but very privately, and his teaching has been handed on to promising subjects. At any rate, I have myself been shown and examined cabbalistic manuscripts written by Francis Barrett, and certain secret matters which he did not think proper to entrust to the publicity of print.

The first section of *The Magus* treats of Natural Magic, so termed, and it is well to state that as a preliminary Barrett insists that from the very outset these studies must be entered upon gravely, reverently, and with decorum, not in any spirit of mere curiosity or frivolousness, which things are bound to lead only to disappointment, to nugatory results and vain endeavour, if not indeed to actual mischief and harm.

Our author commences with a dissertation on "The Influences of the Stars" as second causes, and is justly severe on those who imagine that the celestial bodies take cognizance of, and give in their configurations and aspects, continual information of the lowest and vilest transactions of dotards, the most trivial and fribbling questions, that are *pretended* to be resolved. If an odd silver spoon is but lost, the innocent stars, forsooth, are obliged to give an account of it!

The wonders of Natural Magic are displayed in a variety of sympathetic and occult operations throughout the families of animals, plants, metals, and stones. Upon this factor depends the use of amulets, periapts, and charms, which have a certain magnetic alligation whereby the accidents of mind and body may be in some measure influenced. Thus the loadstone is an example both of sympathy and antipathy in connexion with divers objects.

These considerations introduce "The Art of Fascination, or Binding by the Look or Sight". Barrett observes that witches through their evil powers are able to afflict by a look or a glance; they have "the evil eye". The word *Fascination*, which in modern use we generally associate with some kind of magnetism, more often perhaps with animal magnetism, has not completely lost its original technical meaning as an alternative for "evil eye". The belief in a blighting influence darted from the eyes is universal, and its origin is lost in dateless time. Who, indeed, can venture to suggest when this truth was first observed and recorded? For true it assuredly is. All ancient nations knew it. From the *Malleus Maleficarum* we learn that there are witches who can bewitch by a mere look or glance from their eyes (Part II, Question 1, Chapter xii). The learned and judicious Boguet has a chapter discussing how witches cause injury both to man and beast by their evil glances. In Ireland, formerly, "eye-biting" witches were executed for harming and even killing cattle. Throughout Italy nobody is so feared as he who has this baleful influence, *mal d'occhio*. In the South *jettatura* is the common term. At the appearance of a person having this reputation the most crowded street of Naples will

WITCHCRAFT AND BLACK MAGIC 163

empty in a moment. The cry *Jettatore!* is heard. Everyone vanishes, rushing into shops, into churches, up entries, down side-alleys, helter-skelter, anywhere. In Corsica the influence is known as *innochiatura.* Throughout the West Country and in most other parts of England it is believed that sick animals may have been "overlooked". Some years ago in the West an old lady, speaking of a girl who was always ailing and ill, remarked to me that she had probably been "owl-blinked". When I asked exactly what "owl-blinked" meant I was told it amounted to "ill-wished" or "begrudged". The wench was suffering from the spite or vengeance of some witch who had cast a maleficent glance upon her with a curse. The idea probably is that the witch has great staring yellow eyes like an owl. Many country folk hold the "evil eye" in such terror that they prefer not even to speak of it. Dr. Jessop, in his *Arcady, for Better or Worse* (1887), says: "The firm belief in being 'over-looked' is very much more common, and very much more deep-seated than is generally supposed." One old remedy was a certain powder which the village wise-woman knew how to triturate with words of weal, and this scattered over the afflicted person or animal would snap the spell. William Bottrell, *Traditions and Hearth-side Stories of West Cornwall* (Third Series, Penzance, 1880), speaks of "witch powders to be cast over such children or cattle as may be ill-wished, begrudged, or over-looked".

In the Scottish Highlands, should a stranger praise a fine cow too admiringly, and keep gazing at her, it is thought the animal will waste away from the evil eye, and the spell must be broken at once by offering the visitor some of her milk to drink, after which no ill result can ensue.

In January, 1934, the *Daily Express* gave an account of a man, living in a remote Dorset hamlet, who had been overlooked. He was slowly wasting away, and there could be but one end. Doctors had thoroughly examined him in every limb, and tested every organ. Medically he was pronounced perfectly sound. Yet he was doomed. Science was powerless to save him. There he was just waiting for the fatal outcome "in his tiny cottage in the heart of the mysterious Dorset hills—hills that are honey-combed with strange superstitions, with belief in witchcraft, in black fairies, and the transformation of humans into animals". "I knocked on his door," said the Special Representative of the paper. "It was opened by a tall, gaunt man in middle age. His cheeks were sunken, his face was a pasty colour. It was the man himself, so weak that he could scarcely stand." Two and a half years before he had been "passed by", and there remained nothing for him but death. A gypsy who had casually come to his cottage could suggest no remedy. She was only able to see that someone—a woman—had "looked over" him. And for one case which finds its way into a paper there are scores that remain unknown save perhaps to a few neighbours of the victim. The witch has been at work. "Consumption", "pernicious anaemia", "tabes" are some of the names the perplexed and baffled doctor gives the disease, which can only be cured—as it was well cured in former days—by the execution of the wicked witch, who smiles evilly to think that an "enlightened" age no longer believes in the power of sorcery and black magic.

A writer in the *Graphic*, December, 1882, remarked that witches are much more common in the West of England than they were in the realms of Cetewayo. Savage as he was, the Zulu king had, at any rate, the sense to recognize and stamp out the pest of sorcery.

In Italy, and particularly in the south, all sorts of charms are worn to avert the evil eye. Many are phallic and of great antiquity. Perhaps the best known are the *mano fica* and the coral horn. In England, to baffle an evil spell one doubles the thumb in the right hand and protudes the first and fourth fingers to make horns. In some districts the first and second fingers are crossed. Dean Ramsay, who was at a school in Yorkshire from about 1800 to 1810, recalled how he and his class-mates "used to put one thumb between the first and second finger, pointing it downwards as the infallible protection against the evil influences of one particularly malevolent and powerful witch".

In Latin there is an encyclopaedic study, *On Fascination* (*De Fascinatione*), by John Christian Frommann, published at Nuremberg in 1674. The learned Delrio also has many valuable observations on the subject. In English, F. T. Elworthy's *The Evil Eye*, 1895, is a standard work of great interest and erudition.

The second section of Francis Barrett's *Magus* is a little treatise, "truly spiritual", on the "Jewel of Alchymy".

In Part II is laid the ground-work "of our studies in the Talismanic, or Magical Art". The Four Elements as well as compound or mixed bodies are considered, and there is a chapter on the mystery of the First Cause, God, working through second causes. Seals and characters are impressed by Celestials upon Natural Things. Suffumigations and perfumes are considered, especially those appropriated to the Seven Planets, such as saffron, ambergris, musk, and others for the sun; for the moon, frankincense, camphor, in which is great virtue of chastity, and others; for Mercury, mastic, frankincense, cloves, and the herb cinquefoil; for Venus, musk, ambergris, lignum aloes, red roses, and red coral, commingled with sparrow's brain and pigeon's blood. "Know that, according to the opinion of all magicians, in every good matter (as love, goodwill, etc.), there must be a good perfume, odoriferous and precious;—and in evil matters (as hatred, anger, misery, and the like), there must be made a stinking fume that is of no worth." At the sabbat the devil's incense is the fume of heavy and noxious weeds, which stink extremely.

In the patois of the Pyrénées wizards were commonly known as *poudoués* and witches *poudouéros*, both words being derived from *putere*, which means to have a very bad smell. Many demonologists say that witches could often be detected by their foul and noisome odour. St. Philip Neri, the father of the Oratorians, could distinguish great sinners by a very evil stench, and when meeting them in the street he was often obliged to turn away and hold his nose. St Catherine of Siena experienced the same sensations, whilst St. Bridget of Sweden was almost suffocated by the fetor proceeding from a notoriously wicked man who conversed with her. On the other hand the "odour of sanctity" is no mere symbolical phrase. It is spoken of as a recognized physical phenomenon as early as the second century, and innumerable instances might be cited. St.

Catherine de Ricci, the Dominican nun, smelt of sweetest violets. Even in the depth of winter her habit seemed fragrant, and the odour of violets was noticed by strangers to be clinging round her tomb for more than a year, although her body had been enclosed in a lead coffin. The stigmata of St. Veronica Giuliani, a Capuchin nun, emitted so delicious a fragrance throughout the cloister that it could not be disguised. In the case of Sister Marie de Jésus Crucifié, a Carmelite nun of Pau, who died at Bethlehem in 1878, a most penetrating perfume clung for many months about the places she had once frequented. The room in which she died smelt of exquisite flowers, and the odour clung to the dresses of all who entered it.

After speaking of the magic virtue of rings prepared in a certain way, which Barrett hints he will communicate orally to those who follow a course of mystical studies under his direction, our author proceeds to treat at great length of numerology, and of "the Great Power and Efficacy of Numbers". Commencing with the scale of unity, he describes in very considerable detail, with intricate tables and calculations, the numbers up to and including twelve. These are set forth with corresponsive diagrams: "The Magick Tables, Seals and Characters of the Planets, their Intelligences and Spirits." Thus we have a drawing of "The Table of Mercury in his Compass", "The same in Hebrew", "The Seal or Character of Mercury", The Character of the Intelligence of Mercury", "The Character of the Spirit of Mercury". The seventh and last table is of the Moon. The Moon, being fortunate, engraven on silver, makes the bearer amiable, pleasant, cheerful, and honoured, removing all malice and ill-will; it causes security in a journey, increase of riches, and health of body; drives away enemies, and other evil things from what place soever thou shalt wish them to be expelled. But if the Moon be unfortunate, and it be engraved on a plate of lead, wherever it shall be buried it makes that place unfortunate, and the inhabitants thereabouts, as also ships, rivers, fountains, and mills; and it makes every man unfortunate against whom it shall be directly done, making him fly his place of abode (and even his country) where it shall be buried; and it hinders physicians and orators, and all men whatsoever in their office, against whom it shall be made. And seeing the moon measures the whole space of the Zodiac in the time of twenty-eight days, hence it is that the wise men of the Indians, and most of the ancient astrologers, have granted twenty-eight mansions to the Moon. They made, also, images for every Mansion of the Moon. The twenty-eight images are set out in detail by Barrett, but one or two examples will amply serve.

In the first mansion, for the destruction of some one, they made, in an iron ring, the image of a black man, in a garment of hair, and girdled round, casting a small lance with his right hand: they sealed this in black wax, and perfumed it with liquid storax, and wished some evil to come.

In the third, they made an image in a silver ring, whose table was square; the figure of which was a woman, well clothed, sitting in a chair, her right hand being lifted up on her head; they sealed it, and perfumed it with musk, camphor, and calamus aromaticus. They affirmed that this gives happy fortune, and every good thing.

In the fifteenth, to obtain friendship and goodwill, they made the image of a man sitting, and inditing letters, and perfumed it with frankincense and nutmegs.

Moreover, together with the aforesaid images, they wrote down also the names of the spirits, and their characters, and invocated and prayed for those things which they pretended to obtain.

The next section of Barrett's book consists of a treatise on Magnetism, that is to say the sympathies or antipathies between natural things, which are inherent throughout all nature. Upon this principle of sympathy and antipathy is founded that spiritual power commonly known as magnetic attraction. Here Barrett seems to be following the teaching of Jean Baptiste van Helmont, the famous Belgian alchemist and physician (1577–1644), who studied at Louvain under Martin Delrio, and by whom, it is said, he "was initiated into the mysteries of the cabbala". Van Helmont, justly considered the greatest chemical philosopher prior to the age of Lavoisier, was the first to deal with the concept of and to use the words *elective affinity*. Commenting upon the passage "the life of all flesh is the blood thereof", *Leviticus* xvii, 14, Barrett has the following very striking and mystical phrase: "There are in the blood certain vital powers, the which are soulified or enlivened." Incidentally he discusses bilocation.

In Chapter vi, "Of Witchcraft", he holds it a sure thing that a witch "can strongly torment an absent man by an image of wax, by imprecation or cursing, or also by a foregoing touch alone". Satan is the sworn and irreconcilable enemy of man, and therefore he most readily procures whatsoever mischief he is able to cause or wish unto us. And then, although he be an enemy to witches themselves, for as much as he is also a most malicious enemy to all mankind in general, yet, in regard they are his bond-slaves, and those of his kingdom, he never, unless against his will, betrays them, or discovers them to judges, etc. If Satan were able of himself to kill a man who is guilty of deadly sin, he would never delay it; but he doth not kill him, therefore he cannot. Notwithstanding the witch doth oftentimes kill, no otherwise than as a privy murderer at the liberty of his own will slays any one with a sword. There is therefore a certain power of the witch in this action, which belongs not to Satan, and consequently Satan is not the principal efficient and executor of that murder; for otherwise, if he were the executioner thereof, he would in nowise stand in need of the witch as his assistant. How much greater then is the guilt of the witch lending himself to be an efficient instrument in the hands of Satan, who instigates and inspires all evil, and, "he that committeth sin is of the devil; for the devil sinneth from the beginning", *I John* iii, 8. Spiritual power or magical power is in the inward man, which is the soul or the vital spirit.

The last treatise, "The Cabbala; or the Secret Mysteries of Ceremonial Magic", in one sense gathers up all Barrett's teaching, although he warns his readers that there are some occult matters and businesses which must be passed over in silence, "because we are not permitted to divulge certain things". Moreover, close reading and clear understanding are required to perceive the secret within the secret, and those who do grasp the esoteric meaning are strictly charged not to "expose or babble them to the unworthy. And we would caution you in this beginning, that every magical experiment flies from the public, seeking to be hid, is strengthened and confirmed by silence, but is destroyed by publication; never does any complete effect follow after."

Much is to be learned of the Most Holy Name of God, and "of the Power and Virtue of the Divine Names". We then pass to the consideration "of Intelligences and Spirits, and of the three-fold Kind of them, and of their Different Names, and of Infernal and Subterraneal Spirits".

There are some theologians who distribute the evil spirits into nine degrees, contrariwise to the nine choirs of Angels. The first of these are called the false gods, who demand worship from besotted and wretched men, and among these is Beelzebub of whom King Ahaziah, when sick, sent to inquire, saying: "Go, inquire of Baal-zebub the god of Ekron whether I shall recover of this disease." And Elias the prophet met the royal messengers and said: "Is it not because there is not a God in Israel, that ye go to inquire of Baal-zebub the god of Ekron? Now therefore thus saith the Lord, Thou shalt not come down from that bed on which thou art gone up, but shalt surely die," *II Kings* i, 2–16.

The second degree are the spirits of lies, and to this degree belonged the spirit who with the permission of God went forth and was a lying spirit in the mouths of all the prophets of King Ahab before Ramoth-gilead, *I Kings* xxii, 5–40. The prince of these is named Pytho, and to this degree belonged the familiar of the Witch of En-dor, and the spirit of divination which possessed the damsel, who brought her masters much gain by soothsaying, *Acts xvi*, 16–19, and séance-spirits and lying controls.

The third order are the vessels of iniquity, which are also called vessels of wrath; these are the inventors of evil things, and all wicked arts. From these proceeds all manner of monstrous wickedness, malice, and deformity. They are mentioned when the patriarch Jacob prophesied of his two sons Simeon and Levi, whose fury he cursed, comparing them to "vessels of iniquity", *Genesis* xlix, 5 (Douay); the Psalmist calls them "vessels of death"; Isaiah, "vessels of fury", and Jeremiah, "vessels of wrath"; Ezekiel, "vessels of destroying and slaying", and their prince is Belial, which signifies without a yoke, and disobedient, a prevaricator, and an apostate. Belial originally means worthlessness, wickedness in the abstract.

The fourth order are the revengers of evil, whose prince is Asmodeus, a fearful fiend. He was the devil who slew the seven husbands of Sara, the daughter of Raguel, and when Tobias wedded Sara "the angel Raphael took the devil, and bound him in the desert of upper Egypt". "Some spirits there be that are created for vengeance, and in their fury they lay on sore strokes."

The fifth order are the deluders, who imitate miracles and serve conjurers and witches. They are the cunning ones, who inspire those false Christs and false prophets, who show and have shown great signs and great wonders, "insomuch that if it were possible, they shall deceive the very elect". They delight in "deceitful divinations and lying omens and the dreams of evil doers", all of which "are vanity", that is to say empty cozenage and treachery. Of this order was the familiar Balban who possessed Sor Magdalena de la Cruz, and by whose aid she seemed to work extraordinary miracles, healing the sick and foretelling future events.

The sixth order are the aerial powers, those demons to whom it is given to hurt the earth and the sea, and who serve witches destroying harvests, blighting the orchards, raising storms. The *Malleus Maleficarum* says: "That devils and their disciples can by witchcraft cause lightnings and hailstorms and tempests, and that the devils have power from God to do this, and their disciples to do so with God's permission, is proved by Holy Scripture in *Job* i and ii." St. Thomas, in his *Commentary upon Job*, writes: "It must be confessed, that with God's permission, the devils can disturb the air, raise up winds, and cause fire to fall as from the skies."

Remy explains how demons are able to send upon the fruits of the earth and the crops great numbers of caterpillars, locusts, green fly and pests of all kinds to ruin the harvest, since there is deathless hatred between the Devil and nature. Many witches have confessed how they blighted corn-fields and gardens. The hailstorms which destroyed the flax and the barley of Egypt, and the plague of locusts which ate every herb the hail had left, were brought about by the ministry of evil spirits, obeying the command of God, as the Psalmist says. Guazzo gives several examples "of Incendiary Witchcraft", the devilish work of witches who by the aid of demons seem to call down fire and mysteriously cause conflagrations in houses, endangering streets and whole villages and towns. Schiltach, a small town in Switzerland, was burned to the ground on 13 April, 1533, by the machinations of certain witches. St. Paul tells us that the disobedient spirit is "the prince of the power of the air", *Ephesians* ii, 2. And Satan has his ministers, the aerial powers. Some theologians name the prince of this sixth order, Meririm, "the destruction that wasteth at noon-day".

The seventh order are those fiends whom occultists term the Furies, and these are perhaps the worst of all the hierarchy of hell. They are the "powers of evil, discords, war, and devastation", and the world is under their dominion today. As we are told in the Apocalypse, they have "a king over them, which is the angel of the bottomless pit whose name in the Hebrew tongue is Abaddon, but in the Greek tongue hath his name Appollyon", that is to say *A Destroyer*. They arise from the smoke of the bottomless pit, and they have swarmed over the earth like locusts in number, and "their torment was as the torment of a scorpion, when he striketh a man".

In the eighth order are the Accusers, that is to say the accusers of the brethren, evil spirits "which accused them before our God day and night", *Revelation* xii, 10, those who, as Shakespeare puts it,

> abound
> In the division of each several crime,
> Acting it many ways . . .
> Uproar the universal peace, confound
> All unity on earth.

It is they who fill men's hearts with jealousies and bitter envy, inspiring them to ascribe bad motives to every action. It was they who reigned in the hearts and minds of the Pharisees, who, when Christ cast out devils from the possessed, murmured: "He casteth out devils through the prince of the devils."

The tempters and ensnarers, says Barrett, have the last place, one of which is present with every man, which we call the evil genius, and their prince is Mammon. That some of these orders or grades are very exactly to be defined and true we can hardly doubt, but this last division seems a little vague and uncertain. Nor are we able without considerable reservation to accept the theory of the "evil genius". That every man has his Angel-Guardian we know. It is true that Origen (A.D. 185–254), in his Homily on *St. Luke*, xii, voiced the opinion that every man is attended by two angels, the one good, the other evil. However, he was certainly very unorthodox, and his most learned and profound editor, Dom Charles Vincent de la Rue, whilst warning us against the several errors to be met with in this great scholar's works, lays particular emphasis on those false ideas relating to the human soul and to angels. Bandinus, in the twelfth century, when speaking of the Guardian Angel, adds that every man also has a bad angel who may tempt (or try) him. J. S. Fairfax, in his *Demonologia*, 1827; 1831; and 1833 (edition 1831, pp. 324–5), tells how a spectre hailed a man, crying out: "Ho! I am thy evil genius", and he speaks of the "notion of every man being attended by an evil genius" as abandoned quite early. He may be referring to Origen. In any case Fairfax is an unreliable and unsatisfactory writer. St. Thomas says nothing about bad angels being assigned to every man. In fact, he will have none of it, for he teaches us that the Guardian Angel drives away demons and all harmful things, both spiritual and corporeal enemies. Which is conclusive.

It were, perhaps, too curious to inquire into the mystery of particular devils. At any rate such an investigation would necessarily be extremely long and difficult, and it is not fitting to enter upon it here. In one—and a very real—sense the familiar of a witch is her particular devil. Alban Butler says of the hosts of the shadow: "The rage, malice, and envy of the devils against man, their enmity to all good are implacable; and their natural subtilty and strength are exceeding great, as appears from the perfection of their being, which is purely spiritual, and from examples where by Divine permission they were allowed more remarkably to exert their power. . . . The devils are sometimes permitted by God to exert their natural power and strength on natural agents by moving second causes, in producing distempers in human bodies, raising storms, and causing other physical evils in the world. . . . By clear proof it is manifest that God sometimes permits corporal possessions (in which the devil seizes on some of the corporeal organs or senses in a

Corporal possession

human body), and obsessions (in which he represents certain images as present to the eyes or imagination with an invincible obstinacy); and that these have been more or less frequent in different times and places. This is confirmed by the testimony and experience of all ages, and of all nations, even to the remotest India, as John Le Clerc observes."

Barrett writes that the fallen angels "being cast out into this valley of misery, some that are near to us wander up and down in this obscure air; others inhabit lakes, rivers, and seas; others the earth, and terrify earthly things, and invade those who dig wells and metals, causing the gaping of the earth, to strike together the foundations of the mountains, and vex not only men but also other creatures; some being content with laughter and delusion only, do contrive rather to weary men than to hurt them; some heightening themselves to the length of a giant's body and again shrinking themselves down to the smallness of pigmies, and changing themselves into different forms, to disturb men with vain fear; others study lies and blasphemies".

After a detailed consideration of cabbalistic calculations and the "seals of spirits" we have a chapter upon necromancy. "Necromancy has its name because it works on the bodies of the dead, and gives answers by the ghosts and apparitions of the dead, and subterraneous spirits, alluring them into the carcasses of the dead, by certain hellish charms, and infernal invocatons, and by deadly sacrifices and wicked oblations.

"There are two kinds of necromancy: raising the carcasses, which is not done without blood; the other sciomancy, in which the calling up of the shadow only suffices." Those who experiment in such matters "easily allure the flowing down of wicked spirits, by reason of the similitude and property of every familiar. . . . The witches easily abuse them for effecting witchcraft . . . compelling them by their devilish charms." These horrid businesses would seem to be precisely similar to a cult which has many devotees today. The intention of the experimenter may be only to attract good entities, but it is very certain that there are attracted evil intelligences, who, when questioned, masquerade as quite another kind of spirit, and who by being able to read the inquirer's mind can with the utmost readiness and a preternatural cunning return replies which seem to be evidential, but are not.

It is truly astonishing that Dr. H. C. Lea, in his posthumously published *Materials toward a History of Witchcraft*, 1939, Vol. I (p. 106), whilst rightly stressing how "the experts always include necromancy in their enumeration of the forbidden arts and properly describe it as divination by means of the dead", should have added: "It is apparently a lost art." I can only observe that there is no occult art which today is more openly exploited and sedulously missionized. Necromancy is an attempt to enter into communication with the souls of the departed. In 1856, when questions were asked of the Sacred Congregation of the Holy Office concerning certain popular practices, the reply came: "That to evoke the spirits of the dead, to receive answers from them, to seek knowledge of unknown facts or of events happening at a distance, and all superstitious traffic of this kind is a deceit absolutely unlawful and heretical, and a grave scandal against morality."

With regard to complete materializations, Gougenot des Mousseaux, in his study *Remarkable Phenomena of Magic* (1864), gives an account of a séance which took place on 17 July, 1844. The circle consisted of seventeen girls, and in the course of the proceedings there entered the room an extraordinarily handsome young man, who spent several hours in their company. When he had gone there was a good deal of discussion as to who it might be, what was his name, whence did he come? They hoped to see him again, and apparently sat several times without any result. Exactly a year after, to the very day, on 17 July, 1845, one of these girls was alone in her bedchamber, when the door opened and the same young man walked in, and passed the night with her. This happened eleven years in succession, until she found courage to interrogate her lover, who confessed that he was an incubus. "If you are a spirit," she asked, "how is it that you have a body and are in every point exactly a man?" "I enter a dead body," he replied, "and animate it, moulding it as I will." The unhappy woman, who averred that no husband could be more tender, more caressing and more affectionate than her inamorato, was happily able to free herself from this terrible spouse who had obliged her to pledge herself to him, and we are given to understand that under the direction of a holy and learned priest she entered a convent to expiate her offence by penitence and prayer, and so (as we trust) she found pardon and peace.

Astonishing as this re-animation may appear, and rarely as it may occur, that it is possible is not be be doubted. Many authors record such happenings. It will be sufficient to refer to three great scholars: Pierre Le Loyer (1550–1634), a Councillor of Angers; Heinrich Kornmann (*ob.* 1620), a famous jurisconsult of Frankfort; and the Franciscan Ludovico Maria Sinistrari (1622–1701), Roman Consultor to the Holy Office.

In Chaucer's *The Friar's Tale* the summoner asks the demon in what shapes devils appear:

> 'Yet tel me,' quod the Sumnour, 'feithfully,
> Make ye yow newe bodies thus alway
> Of elements?' The feend answerde, 'nay;
> Som-tyme we feyne, and som-tyme we aryse
> With dede bodies in ful sondry wyse.'

A somewhat similar, but not exactly parallel, re-animation was described by Mr. William Buchler Seabrook in his *The Magic Island* (1929) when he wrote of the Zombies, a Zombie being "a soulless human corpse, still dead, but taken from the grave and endowed by sorcery with a mechanical semblance of life—it is a dead body which is made to walk and act and move as if it were alive". That necromancy can seemingly endow a dead body with life, speech, and action is not to be disputed, but the spell is invariably of short continuance and the operation, from the confessions of sorcerers, is considered to be one of the most difficult and most dangerous in all witchcraft, a feat only to be accomplished by wizards who are foulest and deepest in infernal crime. This "diabolicall questioning of the dead" was essayed by Edward Kelley and his fellow warlock Paul Waring, and is recorded of other black magicians.

We cannot, however, accept Mr. Seabrook's *Zombie* fantasies, these stories of dead men toiling "day after day dumbly in the sun", of walking corpses being registered as field-labourers, of Croyance taking a party of *Zombies* on Corpus Christi day to see the procession, which by the way is very incorrectly depicted. Mr. Seabrook, further, confuses Corpus Christi with Shrove Tuesday, a pretty bad blunder which serves to shake our confidence in his narration. Indeed, not only are his pages more highly imaginative than veracious, but there is good reason to suspect that much of the information placed in the mouth of his "devoted yard-boy" and others is derived from fairly recent and quite well-known books on Haiti. The greatest living authority on Voodoo regards *The Magic Island* as "a weird conglomeration of fact and fancy worthy of little serious consideration and of even less credibility".

The history of Kelley's necromancy is related in the *Ancient Funerall Monuments* folio, 1631, of John Weaver, the full flavour of whose fine old English phrase is far too good to be lost. Chapter ix, "Of such male-factors . . . who violated Sepulchres." "Kelley (otherwise called Talbot) that famous English Alchymist of our times" is taken as a notorious example of these profaners. "This diabolicall questioning of the dead, for the knowledge of future accidents, was put in practice of the foresaid Kelley; who, upon a certaine night, in the Parke of Walton in le dale, in the county of Lancaster, with one Paul Waring (his fellow companion in such deeds of darknesse) invocated some of the infernall regiment, to know certaine passages in the life, as also what might bee knowne by the devils foresight, of the manner and time of the death of a noble young Gentleman, as then in his wardship." Kelley, who had previously inquired "what corse was the last buried in Low-churchyard, a Church thereunto adjoyning", was told that a poor man had been buried that very day. Kelley, Waring, together with a servant of the young Gentleman, an assistant who was well paid and who "did helpe them to digge up the carcass of this poor caitiffe", betook themselves to the lonely churchyard at dead of night, and after certain conjurations over the cadaver they had so profanely and beastly disinterred, "by their incantations, they made him (or rather some evill spirit through his Organs) to speake, who delivered strange predictions, concerning the said Gentleman. I was told thus much by the said Servingman, a secondarie actor in that dismall abhorrid businesse. And the Gentleman himselfe (whose memorie I am bound to honour) told me a little before his death, of this conjuration by Kelley; as he had it from his said Servant and Tenant; onely some circumstances excepted, which he thought not fitting to come to his Master's knowledge." "The blacke ceremonies of that night being ended", Kelley and Waring packed away, leaving their wretched accomplice a prey to great horror. Weever justly comments: "These injuries done against the dead who ought to sleepe in peace untill the last sound of the Trumpet, have ever beene, even amongst the very Pagans themselves, esteemed execrable."

In his last book, *The Perfection and Key of The Cabbala, or Ceremonial*

Magic, Barrett indicates that "in this Key you may behold, as in a mirror, the distinct functions of the spirits, and how they are to be drawn into communication in all places, seasons, and times". He writes at considerable length "Of Magic Pentacles and their Composition", and instructs us "if a deprecation would be made for the overthrow and destruction of one's enemies, we are to mind, and call to remembrance how God destroyed the face of the whole earth in the deluge of waters; likewise, how God overthrew Pharaoh and his host in the Red Sea . . . so likewise in deprecating and praying against perils and dangers of waters, we ought to call to remembrance the saving of Noah in the deluge of waters, and also we are to mind how Christ walked on the waters, and how He commanded the winds and the waves and they obeyed Him. And lastly, with these we invoke and call upon some certain holy Names of God, to wit, such as are significative to accomplish our desire."

"The Consecration of all magical Instruments and Materials which are used in this Art" is given in detail, and it is explained that "the virtue of consecrations chiefly consists of two things, viz., the power of the person consecrating, and the virtue of the prayer by which the consecration is made", all of which is perfectly orthodox if by "the virtue of the prayer" we understand the doctrine of intention. Water, fire, oil, are to be consecrated, and there follows "the Benediction of Lights, Lamps, Wax, etc." "When you would consecrate any place or circle, you should take the prayer of Solomon used in the dedication and consecration of the Temple."

The next section is sufficiently startling: "Of the Invocation of Evil Spirits, and the binding of, and constraining them to appear." Directions are given to prepare a certain book, "made of the most pure and clean paper, which is generally called virgin paper", and "this book is to be consecrated a book of Evil Spirits, ceremoniously to be composed in their name and order, whereunto they bind with a certain holy oath the ready and present obedience of the spirit". The book when completed is to be bound between two lamens, a lame or lamen being a thin plate of metal inscribed with "two holy pentacles of the Divine Majesty out of the Apocalypse". The illustration of "The Lamen, or Holy Table of the Archangel Michael" shows a round disc of metal engraved in the centre with the name Michael within a double pentacle, fortified all around with six double pentacles, certain sigils and Hebrew letters, and about the circumference are written the thrice Holy Names of God.

On the left side of the Book of Spirits is drawn the image of the spirit, the ruler of the hour and day, and on the right side thereof his character, with the oath above it, containing the name of the spirit, his dignity and place, with his office and power. A table gives the names of the Angels governing the seven days of the week with their Sigils, Planets, Signs, etc., and although Sunday is St. Michael; Monday, St. Gabriel; Wednesday, St. Raphael; he would surely be very temerarious who would dare to invoke the Archangels in this manner, and when we find that Saturday is Cassiel, invoked "through the power of the name of that star who is Saturnus", something more than suspicion is awakened. We at once remember, "Ye took up the tabernacle of Moloch, and the star of your god Remphan, figures which ye made to worship them." The prophet Amos, who is here quoted, has "the tabernacle of your Moloch and Chium your images, the star of your god". Remphan or Rephan is the Egyptian name for the planet Saturn, whilst Chiun is the Assyrian *Kaivanu*, the star of Saturn. He who invokes Cassiel has embarked upon very deep and dangerous waters. Moreover, the angel of the air ruling Saturday is "*Maymon*, king", and the demon Maymon, "Maymon Rex", was invoked in the Elizabethan Devil-Worshipper's Prayer Book, the manuscript of about 1600, which was fully described in the previous chapter. Moreover, Barrett names as an angel ruling the air on the Lord's day, Varcan, king; on Monday, Arcan, king; on Tuesday, Samax, king; on Wednesday, Mediat, king; on Thursday, Suth, king; and on Friday, Sarabotes, king. All these appear in the MS. grimoire of 1600 under the same planets. Barrett must have known that these "angels" were black angels, and we are the less surprised to find that he writes "Of the Method of raising Evil or Familiar Spirits by a Circle; likewise the Souls and Shadows of the Dead".

It is true that Barrett repeatedly warns his neophytes to use every caution, and at the very beginning of his book bids "the faithful and discreet Student of Wisdom: Take our instructions; in all things ask counsel of God, and He will give it; offer up the following prayer daily for the illumination of thy understanding; depend for all things on God, the First Cause, with whom, by whom, and in whom, are all things". The Prayer or Oration is very beautifully and very reverently expressed. He asks "power and strength of intellect to carry on this work, for the honour and glory of Thy Holy Name, and to the comfort of our neighbour; and without design of hurt or detriment to any". That he is thoroughly in earnest in thus expressing himself there seems no manner of reason to doubt, but it is not altogether easy to reconcile these aspirations with the later development of his art, and one can only suppose that his thirst for psychic knowledge and a certain learned curiosity led him further than was expedient, or indeed lawful. He probably argued that since his intention was single and clear he ran no risk, and was indeed the Master over the spirits.

He emphasizes in the most weighty and serious words the essential importance of the Circle, which is the barrier and protection against evil. Minutest directions with diagrams are given on how to make "the Magic Circle", how to write therein the Four Divine Names with four crosses interposed, and how the circle must be sakered and hallowed in the Name of the Holy, Blessed, and Glorious Trinity. In the ritual benediction of the Circle it is said: We "consecrate this piece of ground for our defence, so that no spirit whatsoever shall be able to break these boundaries, neither be able to cause injury nor detriment to any of us here assembled; but that they may be compelled to stand before this Circle, and answer truly our demands". The spirits will use every cunning, every trick, to try to tempt the operator and his assistants out of the Circle, but in no circumstances and for no reason whatsoever must anyone so much as put a foot beyond the magic line. First, the spirits must be licensed to depart, which, says Barrett, must never be omitted, whether a spirit appear or not. "They who neglect licensing the spirits are in very great danger, because instances have been known of the operator experiencing sudden death." The operator must be equipped with various instruments: the pentacle, the rod or wand, the lamens. He must wear a long garment of white linen, a kind of alb, girt about the loins with a girdle. Consecrated wax-lights must be burning, and it is convenient that there be suffumigations of frankincense. There are many other observances, and "these things being duly performed, there will appear infinite visions, apparitions, phantasms, etc., beating of drums, and the sound of all kinds of musical instruments, which is done by the spirits, that with the terror they might force some of the companions out of the circle, because they can effect nothing against the exorcist himself: after this you will see an infinite company of archers, with a great multitude of horrible beasts, nevertheless fear not". These are termed, and truly termed, iniquities. Barrett gives some of the shapes in which spirits may appear: a little boy; a creature with many feet; a she-goat; a red garment; a magpie; a green garment; an old man with a beard; an owl; an old woman leaning on a crutch; a hog; a black garment; a sickle. These figures "are generally terrible at the first coming on of the visions, but as they have only a limited power, beyond which they cannot pass, so the invocator need be under no apprehensions of danger provided he have a firm and constant faith in the mercy, wisdom, and goodness of God". But it is written, "Thou shalt not tempt the Lord thy God."

Surely the very grotesqueness and sullen horror of the forms the spirits so frequently assume, the half-animal, half-human phenomena, are in themselves sufficient indication of the nature of these hideously manifesting intelligences. Even if it were unblamable, it is useless to inquire of or question such entities. They only deceive, and mock and betray.

A scholar deeply read in occult lore suggested that by various abuses, especially that of alcohol and certain drugs, the veil is not so much lifted as rent, and there show themselves evil correspondences in their natural forms, direful and atrocious. Man's interior sight is opened by violence and crapulence, so that in truth the hideous shapes a sufferer from delirium tremens sees thronging about him are real and actual; they are the lowest and most bestial of spirit forces.

What folly, what worse than folly, to attempt to establish some communication, to traffic with beings such as these by conjurations and evokings, however self-protected a man may deem himself to be! The very essay is in itself an act of insensate wickedness.

That Barrett's mind misgave him is, I think, clear enough to understand. Before he ends his work he has a most emphatic "Caution to the inexperienced in this Art, and a Word of Advice to those who would be Adepts".

The Magus concludes with a "Biographia Antiqua" which comprises eighteen brief biographical sketches of such occultists as Apollonius of Tyana, Cornelius Agrippa, Raymond Lully, George Ripley, Paracelsus, John and Isaac Holland, Dr. Dee, and Edward Kelley, together with a note upon "the antiquity of occult learning among the Chaldeans of Babylon". There is an interesting account of "Zoroaster, the son of Oromasius, First Institutor of Philosophy by Fire, and Magic"; "the magic he taught," says Barrett, "was only the study of the divine nature, and of religious worship". Oromasius "is the name given by Zoroaster and his disciples to the good God", so the expression "son of Oromasius" is only allegorical or figurative. H. F. Talbot, "Contributions towards a Glossary of the Assyrian Language", *The Journal of the Royal Asiatic Society of Great Britain and Ireland*, New Series, Vol. III, Part I, 1867 (pp. 10–11), says: "The sun is sometimes called in Persian *Zartushti* or *tasht-i-zer*, the golden orb (zer, gold; tasht, a disk). And in honour of the sun, I conceive,. was named the celebrated philosopher *Zerdusht*, whom the Greeks have called *Zoroaster*, retaining the first part of his name, but altering the second into *Astron*, equivalent in their language to the Persian *tasht*, an orb or disk. It may be added that the first Zoroaster was evidently mythical (probably a mere name for the sun himself)." Barrett mentions that some would have Hermes Trismegistus to be Moses, but himself prefers to follow the "best authorities" who do not accept this identification.

Not the least remarkable thing about this remarkable book *The Magus* is that it clearly proves how at the beginning of the nineteenth century esoteric traditions were preserved, ceremonial magic was practised, and the secrets of cabbalistic lore were eagerly studied.

If any further evidence to this effect were needed it could be very amply supplied from the works of Ebenezer Sibly, the famous astrologer, from whom quotation has already been made (Chapter I), and whose *New and Complete Illustration of the Occult Sciences* had reached a tenth edition by 1807. Nor is Sibly forgotten today. In the "Book Catalogue Supplement" to *Foulsham's Original Old Moore's Almanack for the Year 1942* I note the following: "Wonderful Talismans on Parchment. Do you know the history of the famous Rothschild Talisman, which is an heirloom, and on the possession of which the fortune of the family is believed to depend? The secret of its power lies hidden in words inscribed. Everyone should have a Talisman. Those supplied are copies of Rabbi Solomon, Agrippa, Sibly, Éliphas Lévi."

Sibly has some very significant things to say about the Black Art, that is witchcraft. He first discusses spirits and spiritual entities. "To suppose a human spirit void of a human form and senses, is to annihilate the very idea of spirit; for as every essence has its proper form, and every form its own essence (they being necessarily correlative) so every spirit has its body suited to the world it belongs to, according to that distinction laid down by the Apostle: 'There is a natural body, and there is a spiritual body' (*I Corinthians* xv, 44).

"That the form of the spirit of a man is a human form, or, in other words, that the spirit is the true formed man, may be evinced from many articles, particularly from these, viz., that every angel is in a perfect human form, and also, that every man is a spirit as to his inner man. This also more evidently appears from man's being denominated Man from his spirit, and not from his body, and because the corporeal form is an

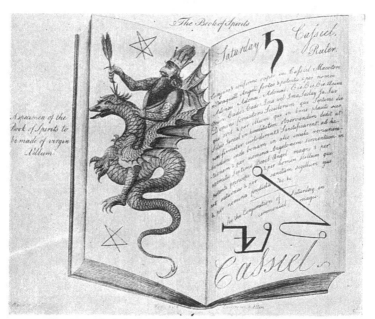

THE BOOK OF SPIRITS

MODERN NECROMANCERS

THE PHANTOM MONK OF THE HAUNTED POOL

adjunct to the spirit after its form, and not contrariwise, the former being but the clothing of the latter."

Good and evil, truth and falsehood, are of a spiritual nature.

Evil spirits are in "continual horror and despair". "That they are materially vexed and scorched in flames of fire, is only a figurative idea, adapted to our external senses, for their substance is spiritual, and their essence too subtle for any external torment. The endless source of all their misery is in themselves, and stands continually before them, so that they can never enjoy any rest, being absent from the presence of God: which torment is greater to them than all the tortures of this world combined together."

The origin of devils and infernal spirits proceeded from conspiracy and rebellion in heaven under the arch fiend, "king of the devils".

Sibly speaks of other spirits "being subject to a beginning and an ending", and it is these spirits, he holds, which can be brought into league with magicians and witches. There are Astral spirits, who haunt ancient buildings, ruins, places of the slain, deep woods and rocky mountains. Igneous spirits of a "middle vegetative nature" are monsters, rather than rational animals. They are often inspired and used by demons, and are "obsequious to the kingdom of darkness". These are "very apt for conjuring" and "much more inveterate and malicious in their agency than the rest". Terrene spirits belong to the earthy kingdom, and are especially dangerous. They haunt mines, caves, "hiatus or chasms of the earth", and are violently inimical to man. Thus Georgius Agricola (George Bauer, 1494–1555), the famous metallurgist, towards the conclusion of his treatise *De Animantibus Subterraneis* (*On Subterranean Hauntings*), 1549, relates how at Annaberg, in the mining district of Saxony, there appeared in a mine, locally known as Rosy Crown, "a Spirit in the similitude and likeness of a horse, snorting and snuffling most fiendishly with a pestilent blast" which killed twelve men, and at last, although there was a rich ore, the workings had to be abandoned through this demoniacal persecution. Moreover, in the mine of St. George at Schneeberg, Saxony, there was an evil spirit who wore a large black cowl, a most dangerous phantom to encounter, since with terrific force he seized one of the metal workers, and heaved the unfortunate man to a great height, hurting him badly and bruising his limbs as he fell. These elemental spirits seem actuated by a blind, aimlessly random hate.

It must be borne in mind that although the theories of elemental spirits may be true to a certain extent and as set forth in the learned Sinistrari, yet witches traffic directly with demons, and it is by the aid of devils that necromancers of whatever sort perform their foul businesses, their unresting of the dead.

"The manner and seasons wherein apparitions and ghosts appear are various as they are uncertain." This truth which Sibly emphasizes needs saying yet once again, and it has been proved a truth by all investigators of haunted houses and troubled localities. It is confirmed, moreover, by the learned Taillepied, who in his *Treatise of Ghosts* (1588) has a chapter, "To Whom, When, and in What Places Spirits are wont to Appear". Sibly continues, "Their appearance is often attended with great difficulty and delay, as well on account of the natural timidity of human beings, as for want of the proper organs of corporeal voice and touch in the spirit, which, being no part of their quality or essence, is procured with great difficulty, and at best but inarticulate, doleful, and in broken accents. That this is true, the usual manner of their appearance in a great measure proves." There are, of course, exceptions to this generalization.

Why apparitions are so seldom seen is that spiritual substances have their life, breath, and vital motion in another source; very different from the elements of this external world : and consequently their manifestations and continuance in this state, whenever they appear to us, must be both painful and irksome.

Sibly treats of conjurations in some detail. He who would raise a demon or spirit must seek some lone and deserted place, a subterraneous vault, the depths of a wood, some unfrequented moor where several roads meet, "or amidst the ruins of ancient castles, abbeys, monasteries, etc., or amongst the cruel rocks on the seashore, or in some private and detached churchyard, some solemn melancholy place, between midnight and one o'clock, either when the moon shines very bright and full, or else in a storm of thunder, lightning and rain". Spirits can at such times and in such places more easily appear.

Directions are given with regard to circles and pentacles, very similar to those we find in Barrett. Sibly is, however, rather more detailed and precise when speaking of the magician's robes, "or *de pontificalibus*", which comprise "an ephod made of fine white linen, over that a priestly robe of black bombazine", all girt with a consecrated girdle. The operator further dons a high-crowned cap of sable silk, and his sacerdotal shoes are written over with the name Tetragrammaton, that is the word of four letters, the Hebrew YHWH or JHVH (vocalized as *Yahweh Jahuah*, or *Jehovah*), often substituted for the ineffable word and treated as a mysterious symbol, but no more, of the Hidden Name of Deity.

The spirit is summoned "by the blood of Abel, by the righteousness of Seth, and the prayers of Noah; by the voice of Thunder, and by the dreadful day of Judgement". There are fumigations and odours, which Barrett terms perfumes. Certain spirits require sacrifices of blood. Above all, Sibly is careful to insist, the familiar must be discharged and bidden go at the finish of the rite. This dismissal is imperative, and the formula to be employed is exactly prescribed. We have seen how Barrett emphasized the same "license to depart". It is to be feared that these are very deep and muddy waters.

Sibly also gives the ritual to conjure back a suicide, a horribly profane ceremony. There must first be provided a consecrated torch, bound about with St. John's wort, a holy herb withal. "The Greeks call it *hypericon*, the English call it St. John's grass" is noted in the twelfth-century Life of St. Hugh, Bishop of Lincoln. Robert Holkot, in the thirteenth century, speaks of "the wort of holy John whose virtue is to put demons to flight". Many references to the efficacy of St. John's wort in expelling evil influences are to be found in a vast number of authorities. The old English rhyme, remembered today, runs:

> Trefoil, vervain, John's wort, dill,
> Hinder witches of their will.

John Aubrey (1626–1697), in his *Miscellanies*, first edition, 1696, tells us: "A house (or chamber) somewhere in London, was haunted; the curtains would be rashed at night, and awake the gentleman that lay there, who was musical, and a familiar acquaintance of Henry Lawes. Henry Lawes to be satisfied did lie with him; and the curtains were rashed so then. The gentleman grew lean and pale with the frights; one Dr. —— cured the house of this disturbance and Mr. Lawes said, that the principal ingredient was *Hypericon* put under his pillow."

Sibly was well advised to bid those engaged upon this unhallowed conjuration protect themselves with the blessed herb of might. Further, there were to be at hand a chafing-dish of fire fed with a little wine, mastic, and gum aromatic, with charcoal, and a vial full of sweetest oil to nourish the flame and make it burn bright at the instant of the rising of the carcass.

Sibly gives fumigations of different kinds for the spirits under several planets, and many of these are of an extremely unpleasant nature. One of the most powerful and most dangerous was confected with certain rare spicery, bdellium, euphorbium, loadstone, hellebore white and black, with sulphur to be made "into an amalgama with man's blood, and the blood of a black cat".

If Sibly experimented upon these lines he cannot be excused from the horrid practice of necromancies and black magic. Actually he has admitted as much when he writes that his "Display of the Mysteries of Witchcraft, Divination, Charms and Necromancy" was "Compiled from a Series of Intense Study and Application, and founded on *real Examples and Experience*".

It may seem a little startling that a man should thus candidly avow himself a warlock, but today in our midst the same witchcraft and necromancies are being openly practised, masqueraded under other terms, it is true, but yet without any pretence at concealment, and not merely practised but advertised, inculcated, and glorified as a veritable religion, which, of course, in one sense black magic undoubtedly is. At any rate, had we the witnesses of Ebenezer Sibly alone, necromancy is most certainly not a revelation ushered into the world about one hundred years ago, as some would seem to suppose.

There is no law against witchcraft *per se* in the British Isles. When, however, ritual murder and abominable profanations are mixed with witchcraft, of which in fact they are an integral part, these black businesses at once become the concern of the civil authorities. In October, 1931, a peasant drawing water from a well in a wood near Helsingfors, the capital of Finland, was horrified to find an arm which had quite recently been severed from a man's body. The police forthwith drained the well, and discovered a number of mutilated human remains—heads, arms, and legs. Upon investigation it proved that several graves in Malm cemetery had been disturbed, which led to the arrest of the caretaker, a man named Saarenheimo, in whose house was found a small library of works dealing with the black arts. One manual, which had been printed in England, described various charms which could be made and magic lotions to be brewed from parts of corpses. Hidden away was a membership card of an English occult society. "It is stated"—to quote the Press of October, 1931—"that the Helsingfors police have appealed to Scotland Yard to help them in tracing the origin of the book. The horrible practices explained in this volume are believed to form part of the activities of a society of devil-worshippers scattered all over Europe, with the 'high priest' in London." Reuter announced: "Scotland Yard, it is said, have been asked to trace a nationalized Englishman who is described as the head of the cult" (Monday, 12 October, 1931). Some years ago there existed in Finland a "Black Bible" recommending for conjurations the horrid mutilating of dead bodies, which were also employed in secret magical rites. In all, fifty or more bodies had been exhumed by the Satanists in Malm churchyard. On 11 October the Press stated that "The Finnish Legation has asked Scotland Yard to help round up a secret society with a naturalized Englishman, living in London, at the head, believed to be responsible for the murder of more than forty people in Helsingfors, Finland."

"London Search for Satanist." "It is believed that at Helsingfors a band of people are practising the grotesquely horrible rites of a form of Black Magic. Chief among these is the mutilation of dead bodies." It was found that Saarenheimo, who obstinately refused to give any information, possessed a number of works on black magic, which, it was thought, were printed in England.

In December, 1934, it was stated in the Press that four active "occult magic circles" were operating in London, each having a secretly initiated membership of thirty to forty men and women. One of these covens met in a Chelsea studio. There are in existence four books, a series, simply entitled *Magick*, and printed in Paris. These grimoires give the complete ritual for the celebration of masses, magical litanies, other rites of wizardry, and ceremonial blood sacrifices upon an altar. One rubric runs: "the blood Sacrifice is the critical point of the World Ceremony of the Proclamation of Horus, the Crowned and Conquering Child, as Lord of the Æon". Horus here is but a name, a shamming flamming name. It has nothing at all to do with Horus, the son of Isis, the Lord of the celestial Ladder, the day-god worshipped in ancient Egypt. This "Lord of the Æon", "the Crowned and Conquering Child", the "Elder Brother", as he was fearfully and blasphemously called by the degraded Manichees, is the Power of Evil, Satan.

Another of these books describes a "Gnostic Mass", all filth and wickedness. Well may a word of warning be sounded in these grimoires: "The student, if he attains any success in the following practices, will find himself confronted by things too glorious or too dreadful to be described. It is essential that he remain the master of all that he beholds, hears, or conceives; otherwise he will be the slave of illusion and the prey of madness."

It was about Christmas, 1934, that the manager of a bookshop in Charing Cross Road told a newspaper reporter: "In the past twenty years two of the assistants in our occult book department have committed suicide. We only allow assistants to stay in that department for three months. They read the books in their spare time, and in the past few years several have become mentally unbalanced." (The *Daily Express*, Saturday, 29 December, 1934.)

On 22 June, 1935, there mysteriously disappeared from Saint-Martin-l'Inférieur, a rather remote little hamlet in the Cévennes district, Ardèche, a young cowherd, a lad between seven and eight years old, named Henri Faure. When he did not return home as usual, search was immediately made, but without avail. On the next and several following days the countryside was pretty well explored, yet no signs of the missing boy could be discovered. The police took up the inquiry, and could learn nothing. Madame Chaussineau, a farmer's wife, when in her yard had heard cries of distress about nine o'clock that evening, but they were not repeated, and it was impossible to tell from what direction they had reached her. It seemed as if no clue were forthcoming, and the riddle remained unsolved.

Six weeks later some vagabond tramps from another district, who had, for the sake of poaching, with considerable difficulty climbed to the plateau of Bergwise, which is rather more than a couple of miles from the old château of Pampelonne, discovered there the remains of a boy, and this proved to be the missing Henri Faure. They at once reported their gruesome find to the gendarmerie, and a most unsparing investigation followed. It was proved beyond question that the gaberlunzies themselves could have had nothing to do with the matter.

· That summer it happened there had been a scorching drought, and the body was extremely desiccated by the sun. That the boy should have climbed to the plateau of his own accord was impossible. He had either been carried there or brought in some way by others, probably by two or three persons at the least. What seemed even more curious and significant was that the little corpse had been mutilated in a particularly horrible fashion and certain members were missing.

On 16 April, 1656, Isabelle Cheyné (or Chesnay), who lived at Saint-Martin-l'Inférieur, was examined before the court of Villeneuve-de-Berg on a charge of having overlooked and by her evil charms wasted the Demoiselle of the château of Pampelonne. During the course of the proceedings the wretched woman made a full confession and revealed that the district was infested by a gang of Satanists and witches. She had been initiated into this horrid society by a hag named la Peytière, and together they kidnapped the little son of the village shoemaker, Grandjean. They took the boy to a spur of the mountain range, a place known as le Charnier, where they joined the assemblage of witches under the Grand Master of the locality. Here they killed and mutilated the young Grandjean, some of whose blood was quaffed by the infernal sisterhood, and some carefully preserved for their charms. At another sabbat a lad named Valet was decoyed and murdered in the same way. For a third sabbat a boy named Rouvezier was enticed into a lonely spot and then carried off to le Charnier. The body of Rouvezier was abandoned on the mountain slope. His parents, who were burghers of some means, sought for him in vain for several months and offered a considerable reward.

The witch, Isabelle Cheyné, was burned at the stake in the market-square of Villeneuve-de-Berg. The whole process may be read in the archives and legal registers of the old Vivarais bailiwick.

Now the exact spot known in the seventeenth century as le Charnier, where the sabbat used to be held, is precisely the place where the body of the lad Henri Faure was found in August, 1935. Monsieur Dugas, the *juge d'instruction* of Privas, established this long-since-forgotten fact by means of some contemporary maps and large-scale charts. of the locality. Hence his investigations led him pretty certainly to the conclusion that the plateau of Bergwise, formerly known as le Charnier, was still the rendezvous of Satanists, that the evil tradition of witchcraft had secretly been handed down, and that the unfortunate Henri Faure had been entrapped and done to death by devil-worshippers for their own horrid purposes.

I have said that there is no law against witchcraft in the British Isles, but this statement does not hold good for the British Empire.

Incidentally, it is interesting to note that the last witch to be executed in England by legal authority was Alice Molland, who was found guilty of consuming with her spells Joan Snow, Wilmot Snow, and Agnes Furze, and sentenced by Sir Cresswell Levins at the Exeter Assizes in March, 1685.

Hesketh J. Bell, who spent many years in the British Colonial Service in the West Indies and was subsequently appointed Governor of Mauritius, in his study *Obeah; Witchcraft in the West Indies*, London, 1889, writes: "Before the emancipation, the practice of Obeah was rampant in all the West Indian colonies, and laws and ordinances had to be framed to put it down, and combat its baneful influences." Father Joseph J. Williams, who first visited Jamaica in December, 1906, and, having made three other visits, has passed in all about six years in the island, has deeply studied and is indeed our principal authority on "the Black Man's witchcraft", as he concisely calls it. "The Jamaican term Obeah," he tells us, "is unquestionably derived from the Ashanti word *Obayifo*, which, according to Captain R. Sutherland Rattray, signifies 'a wizard, or more generally a witch'." (For complete clarity's sake we note the modern distinction, wizard, witch, is here made.) Charles Rampini, *Letters from Jamaica*, Edinburgh, 1873, says: "Of all the motive powers which influence the Negro character, by far the most potent, as it is also the most dangerous, is that of Obeah. . . . The Obeah man or woman is one of the great guild or fraternity of crime. Hardly a criminal trial occurs in the colony in which he is not implicated in one way or another. . . . Serpent or devil worship is by no means rare in the country districts; and of its heathen rites the Obeah man is invariably the priest. Many of them keep a stuffed snake in their huts as a domestic god—a practice still common in Africa, from which of course the custom has been derived."

In his Jamaican journal (*Journal of a West India Proprietor*, posthumously published, 1834), under 12 January, 1816, Matthew Gregory Lewis relates how about ten months previously "a negro of very suspicious manners and appearance" was arrested, "and on examination there was found upon him a bag containing a great variety of strange materials for incantations; such as thunder-stones, cat's ears, the feet of various animals, human hair, fish bones, the teeth of alligators, etc.: he was conveyed to Montego Bay; and no sooner was it understood that this old African was in prison, than depositions were poured in from all quarters from negroes who desposed to having seen him exercise his magical arts, and, in particular, to his having sold such and such slaves medicines and charms to deliver them from their enemies; being, in plain English, nothing else than rank poisons. He was convicted of Obeah upon the most indubitable evidence. The good old practice of burning has fallen into disrepute; so he was sentenced to be transported, and was shipped off the island, to the great satisfaction of persons of all colours—white, black, and yellow."

On 25 February, 1818, during his second visit to Jamaica, Lewis gives a long account of a negro, named Adam, who, he writes, "has long been the terror of my whole estate. He was accused of being an Obeah man, and persons notorious for the practice of Obeah had been found concealed from justice in his house, who were afterwards convicted and transported. He was strongly suspected of having poisoned more than twelve negroes", and "no less than three charges of assault, with intent to kill, were preferred against him". "On searching his house, a musket with a plentiful accompaniment of powder and ball was found concealed, as also a considerable quantity of materials for the practice of Obeah: the possession of either of the above articles (if the musket is without the consent of the proprietor) authorises the magistrates to pronounce a sentence of transportation." Adam was immediately committed to gaol; a slave court was summoned, and after a trial of three hours a sentence of transportation was pronounced. The wretch's guilt was so plain, says Lewis, that "the only difficulty was to restrain the verdict to transportation", and "perhaps no offender ever better deserved hanging". In fact had Lewis chosen to press the charges ever so slightly, Adam would have been summarily executed.

Charles Rampini alludes to an Obeah grimoire. The Obeah man "has his cabbalistic book, too, full of strange characters. One of these is now in my possession. It is an old child's copy-book, well thumbed and very dirty. Each page is covered with rude delineations of the human figure, and roughly traced diagrams and devices." The grimoire was also known to Beckford Davis, Clerk of the Peace of St. George's, when, on 26 February, 1866, he was examined under oath by a Royal Commission. Upon being asked whether, in his opinion, "Are these Obeah men still much consulted?" he replied, "Very much indeed." He informed the Commissioners that "grave dirt taken from whence the corpse is buried" was largely used by the Obeah man in confecting evil charms of death. He also testified about one particular Obeah man who was apprehended in his district but was sent to Port Antonio for trial, and he described the contents of his wizard's chest "and a book full of strange characters". From his prominent position and intimate knowledge of Jamaica, the Royal Commission regarded Mr. Davis's evidence as of the first importance.

Father A. J. Emerick, a missionary priest, who voices his opinion after eleven years of experience and close study in some of the most Obeah-infested districts of Jamaica, in his *Obeah and Duppyism in Jamaica*, 1915, says that "Obeah flourishes in Jamaica although the most drastic laws have been passed against it. . . . In witchcraft, we are told, there is involved the idea of a diabolical pact, or at least an appeal to the intervention of evil spirits. In the history and make-up and practice of Obi there is involved the idea of association with the devil. Satan is the invisible head of Obeah."

A French priest, a man of the highest integrity and veracity—indeed, it might be said a man of saintly life—relates the following extraordinary incident, which, seemingly inexplicable, is none the less most certainly true. The period of which he speaks is a good many years ago when the interior of the island of Trinidad, where he was living, was almost completely undeveloped. He was, however, sent by the Archbishop of Port of Spain to take charge of a remote mission. Upon his arrival he found there was no proper presbytery, and that one room of the house which served as such was occupied by an old coloured woman who lived there with a little girl. This hag, who bore a very evil reputation, obviously resented the appearance of a priest, although she made no complaint in words. The neighbours whispered that they hoped "the good Fadder" would drive the sorcerers away. Whilst settling himself in the house the priest was naturally shown the old woman's room. It was largish, and to his surprise it was crammed with that heavily handsome and massive furniture so treasured by the Creoles. There was a huge family four-poster with great pillars, shining like ebony; an enormous wardrobe, mahogany and black as night with age, filled the whole wall space on one side; the other pieces were in proportion. There was one very inconvenient arrangement: the door of this apartment opened into the priest's bedchamber, through which the woman had to pass every time she went out of the house. Besides this there were only two tiny apertures, hardly to be called windows. Orders were given that on the morrow a door was to be made in this room, leading outside. Since there was no help for it, the priest, tired after his long journey, went to bed, having first taken the precaution of securely bolting the partitioning door, and even jamming a stout chair against it. Hardly was his head on the pillow than he heard a curious sing-song chant, not harmonious but monotonous and low, proceeding from the next room. At first he was minded to get up and rap loudly on the wall calling to the woman to cease her crooning, but the strange rhythm acted as a lullaby, and he dropped off asleep. The next morning he rose early and dressed, but noticed that all was perfectly silent in the adjoining chamber. There was something unusual, everything seemed so still. Removing the chair, he unbolted the door and flung it wide, almost fearing an accident had happened. To his amaze the room was absolutely empty, and swept clean. Not a stick of furniture, not a vestige of any person remained. "From that day to this," said the good priest, "neither I nor anyone living in that district have ever seen or heard anything of that woman or of her little girl. How she moved all her bulky furniture out of the room has ever remained an inexplicable mystery.

I would have defied any one man to have shifted the wardrobe alone, and even if the old woman had sufficient strength to carry the furniture away she never could have dragged it through my room without disturbing me. I was not drugged, I awoke fresh and well. These are the facts of the case, and I have never been able to explain them."

An article in *Chambers's Journal*, 11 January, 1902, entitled "Obeah To-day in the West Indies" is very explicit. The writer emphasizes: "In many countries superstitious rites are practised to bring good luck; but that is not the case with *obeah*. Its root idea is the worship and propitiation of the Evil One: it is essentially malevolent. A Negro goes to the obeah-man to harm his neighbour, not to do any good to himself; and that is why the law regards the matter so seriously."

The Jamaican legislation of 1760 very justly enacted that "any Negro or other Slave who shall pretend to any Supernatural Power and be detected in making use of any materials relating to the practice of Obeah or Witchcraft in order to delude or impose upon the Minds of others shall upon Conviction thereof before two Magistrates and three Freeholders suffer Death or Transportation". The filthy materials of Obeah are enumerated as "Blood, feathers, parrots' beaks, dogs' teeth, alligators' teeth, the skins of lizards, broken bottles, grave dirt, rum, egg-shells, hair, chalk", and all kinds of refuse and decay.

A number of cuttings from the Police News in the *Daily Gleaner*, Kingston, serve to show how persistently Obeah is practised. On 24 November, 1933, Vitelleus Brown was charged with Obeah and found guilty. On the following day Alexander Brown was convicted of the same offence. On 14 December, 1933, David Simon was given six months at Spanish Town court; "Six Months for Obeahman" ran the caption. On 9 January, 1934, George Washington Pitt was fined £12 10s. for Obeah. He had boasted that he could cure and he could kill. He escaped imprisonment because of a technical flaw in the indictment. The tale could be almost indefinitely continued.

With reference to the neighbouring island of Cuba, Mr. H. Hamilton Johnston, in his *The Negro in the New World* (1910), states: "The last vestige of noxious witchcraft lingering among the Cuban Negroes is (said to be) the belief that the heart's blood of the heart of a white child will cure certain terrible diseases if consumed by the sufferer. The black practi-tioners who endeavour to procure this wonderful remedy are known as 'Brujos' or 'Brujas' (*i.e.* male or female sorcerers). At the time I was in Cuba (December, 1908) there were four or five Negroes awaiting trial on this charge at Havana. Other cases—said to have been proved beyond a doubt—have occurred in Eastern Cuba within the last two or three years. . . . There is little doubt that occasionally in the low quarters of the old Spanish towns little white girls do disappear." The word "Bruja" is the same as "Bruxa", the Portuguese witch, a Satanist of the vilest and most deadly courses.

Mr. Stephen Bonsal, in *The American Mediterranean* (1912), asserts that in Haiti "children are frequently stolen from their parents and are often put to death with torture and subsequently eaten with pomp at a Voodoo ceremony". He allows that "the cannibalistic feed is only indulged in on rare occasions and at long intervals, and is always shrouded in mystery, and hedged about with every precaution against interlopers"; none the less the cannibalistic feast does take place, and Mr. Mannington, in *The West Indies with British Guiana and British Honduras* (1925), says that it is a notorious fact how at these infernal sabbats the victim's blood is mixed with rum and eagerly drunk in large quantities.

That cannibalism should be practised by these West Indian witches is not in the least surprising. C. G. Seligmann, in *The Melanesians of British New Guinea* (1910), and J. H. Driberg, *The Lango* (Uganda, 1923), relate how Savage Sorcerers disinter dead bodies, and devour them. It is only one more proof that the horrid cult is and ever has been the same the whole world over. In the sixth, seventh, and eighth centuries the tenor of Frankish, Alamannic, and Lombard legislation shows that this murderous foulness was the common custom of the witch in those jurisdictions. Lord Bacon, in his *Natural History*, writes how "divers witches and sorcerers, as well amongst the heathen as amongst the Christians, have fed upon man's flesh, to aid (as it seemeth) their imagination with high and foul vapours". Bodin, also, in his *Demonomanie*, Book IV, Chapter v, enumerates amongst the hideous crimes of witches the fact that they banquet upon human flesh and drink new blood, after murdering little children, whose limbs are supple and tender, to gratify their abominable appetites. He very justly observes that for this alone, if for none other crime, they amply deserve to be put to death, and he instances the case of a pieman at Paris who sold such delicious cates that he attracted crowds of customers to his shop in the Rue des Marmousets. By an accident it was discovered that this wretch made these pasties out of human flesh, which excited such general horror and detestation that he was condemned to the stake, whilst his house was razed to the ground, and it was forbidden to build on so ill-omened a spot. At the trial of Louis Gaufridi, of Accoules (Marseilles), in 1611, many details were forthcoming as to the sabbat banquet, where, although they drank rich malmsey, "the meat they ordinarily eat is the flesh of young children, which they cook and make ready in the Synagogue (i.e. their chief rendezvous), sometimes bringing them thither alive by stealing them from those houses where they have opportunity to come".

A form of witchcraft very prevalent in Jamaica is Myalism, which primarily was the old tribal religion of the Ashanti, although in the course of time and because of changed conditions it has necessarily become very much modified and changed. The name is derived from the Myal dance, which is a great feature of the ritual. An evil and ceremonious dance, as will be noted in detail in the next chapter, frequently formed an important—nay, an integral—feature of the sabbat orgy. The Pueblo Indians of New Mexico and Arizona in their dances actually impersonate supernatural spirits, that is to say, in plain English, demons. Miss Virginia More Roediger, in her study *Ceremonial Costumes of the Pueblo Indians* (1942), describes the dance as "intricate stamping and jumping of perfect poise and hypnotic rhythm, with little posturing and gesturing, but extraordinarily impressive and requiring much vigour and skill".

Moreau de Saint-Méry, in his *Description . . . de la partie Française de l'isle Saint-Dominique* (Philadelphia, 1797–1798), says: "Who will believe that Voodoo inspires something further, something which goes under the name of a dance? . . . To make it even more effective the Negroes mix with the rum, which they swill down while dancing, minutely crushed gunpowder. Onlookers have seen this dance, called 'Dance to Don Pédro', or simply 'Don Pédro', actually kill the Negroes, who have literally danced to death; whilst many of the spectators, hypnotized at the sight of this convulsive and spasmodical exercise, become inebriated by the delirium of the actors, and hasten by the speed and rush of chanting prestissimo their mad measures the orgiastic crisis, which in some mysterious way pulsates and throbs through the whole assembly. It has been found necessary absolutely to forbid dancing Don Pédro under the gravest penalty."

Originally the Myal man was ostensibly in opposition to the Obeah man, in fact he was a kind of "white witch", as the cant phrase goes, who through his charms counteracted the mischief wrought by the rival practitioner. Rampini, however, is able to throw a good deal of light on the subject. He tells us: "The Obeah man must not be confounded with the Myal man, who is to the former what the antidote is to the poison. He professes to undo what the other has done; to cure where the other has injured, but it must be confessed that, both in its operation and its results, the cure is often worse than the disease. In truth, the boundary line between the two classes of professors is oftentimes but a shadowy one." Father Emerick, writing in 1916, says: "Mialism is so mixed up with Obeahism, Duppyism, and other cults of African warp . . . that it is hard to tell which is which and what is what." A duppy is a Jamaica ghost, who sometimes merges into a goblin with poltergeist activities. The negroes, says M. G. Lewis, in his *Journal of a West India Proprietor* (1834, p. 98), are "very much afraid of ghosts, whom they call the *duppy* . . . the duppies of their adversaries are very alarming beings, equally powerful by day as by night, and who not only are spiritually terrific, but who can give very hard substantial knocks on the pate, whenever they see fit occasion, and can find a good opportunity".

Father Emerick continues: "Whatever may have been its origin, Mialism, properly so-called in Jamaica, is a species of Spiritualism. . . . The mysterious operations of Mialism consist in communications with spirits or deaths ('dets', as the Jamaican terms it). The persons who are favoured with communications with spirits are called 'Mial' people. They are said to be 'fo-eyed', that is four-eyed, by which is meant that they can see spirits and converse with them . . . you have mial men and mial women. They are believed to be able to kill or injure anyone by aid of spirits. A mial man and obiman are equally dreaded." In fact, Father Williams points out that at times the two functions are exercised by one and the same individual under a dual rôle. Myalism has not disappeared, as some are inclined to think; it has allied itself with and been absorbed into Obeah, which is a form of devil-worship. They were akin from the first, since Myalism is simply necromancy. "In any case," concludes Father Williams, "the fact remains that actually the forces of Myalism and Obeah today have degenerated into a common form of witchcraft not unfrequently associated with devil worship"—associated, indeed, inevitably and essentially with the foulest demonolatry.

That popular journal the *Church Times* on 21 December, 1928, gave some interesting and significant extracts from the latest number of the Diocesan Magazine of the Bishop of Mauritius (British), who wrote: "I wonder how many people in Mauritius realize what a strong hold sorcery in some form or another has on quite a large number of persons in Mauritius, by no means all of whom are of the uneducated classes, and all of whom profess some form of Christianity. Although prosecutions for witchcraft *qua* witchcraft have ceased, indirectly it is still dealt with under other names by the penal codes of every civilized country. I am assured by those qualified to give accurate information that witchcraft or Petit Albert is practised by many thousands of persons in Mauritius. No one professing the Christian Faith can, withou mortal sin, have anything to do with any form of witchcraft. Petit A lert is nothing less than the cult of the Devil. The petitions are for personal gain or injury to enemies, and are often of an erotic or obscene character. Sacred names and phrases are used in a blasphemous way. These intercessions are accompanied by various ceremonies, in which a skull, a dagger, camphor, and flowers figure. Engravings of Saints have pins stuck in various parts of the figure; I have seen a picture of the Sacred Heart covered with such pins. A crucifix is also frequently used in these blasphemous rites. To take part in such practices, and at the same time to pose as a Christian, is, in my opinion, perilously near committing unforgivable sin."

Every one of these sorceries mentioned by the Bishop and practised in far-off Mauritius, an island in the Indian Ocean, two thousand five hundred miles from Bombay, from Liverpool nine thousand nine hundred and fifty miles, voyaging by sea, can be exactly paralleled in all countries of the world and in all ages.

Le Petit Albert, as we have already seen, is one of the vilest of grimoires. A skull is employed. Necromancy was performed among the Jews by means of the skulls of dead men (*cf.* T. B. Sanhedrin, 65b). In 1324 Lady Alice Kyteler, the notorious Irish witch of Kilkenny, used the brain and clouts of an unbaptized infant with the hair and nails of corpses which she boiled in the skull of a beheaded robber to make evil unguents and drugs. In 1371 a Southwark warlock was brought before Justice Knivet in the King's Bench. The accused was found to have in his possession a book of sorcery "with the head and face of a dead man". The book and head were ordered to be burned.

A dagger is employed. *The Magus* gives "a Dagger" or "a Sword" as one of the "Characters of Evil Spirits". In Chaucer, *The Canterbury Tales*, the Parson speaks of "This horrible swearing of adjuration and conjuration, which these false enchanters or negromancers perform in basons full of water, or in a bright-sword, or in a circle, or in a fire". Roger Bolingbroke, the great wizard who was hanged at Tyburn for high treason under Henry VI, whom he attempted to kill by witchcraft, had among his goetic instruments a curiously painted chair, a magician's robe, a sceptre and four swords or shining daggers. William Stapleton, a priest who had once been a Benedictine, and who busied himself with necro-

mancy between 1527 and 1530, evoking the demons Oberion and Incubus, had magic books, a ring, a plate, a circle, and a sword.

Camphor, the emblem of chastity, is used in protective suffumigations. Francis Barrett says that when an image is made in a silver ring,
being a square table appropriately engraven, it must be perfumed with
musk and camphor, and the ancients affirmed that this gives happy
fortune and every good thing.

Flowers are used in many charms. The Greeks, for example, burned
verbena during invocations and predictions. It attracted good influences
and drove away evil spirits, dissolving many witchcrafts. Grains of black
poppy are thrown upon live coals and from the smoke arising omens are
drawn. This spell, which is in use today, and which is technically named
Captromancy, is mentioned by Dio Cassius the historian, who lived about
A.D. 155–230, and even then it was a very old practice. Future events were
predicted by casting the petals of certain flowers in running water, and
divining from the letters or figures they are supposed to form. Flowers are
often employed in love charms, and some witches professed that they could
cast a spell over a nosegay, which, if presented by a gallant to the woman
who pleased him, would make her comply with his desires and surrender
to his embraces, however virtuous and continent she might be. But this
seems a deceit. The fleur-de-lis in gold, silver, or enamel is much favoured
as an amulet protective against the evil eye. On the darker side witches
use many drugs and poisons such as belladonna, the Deadly Nightshade;
henbane, aconite root or monk's-hood; hemlock.

To desecrate Holy Pictures by piercing them with pins or nails is
fearfully malevolent hoodoo. Here we have sympathetic magic of the
worst and most destructive kind. This falls into the same category as the
moulding of little figures in wax, clay, marl; carving them in wood or
casting them in lead and piercing them with nails, pins, or thorns, sometimes even transfixing the heart with a stiletto. To quote Mr. L'Estrange
Ewen: "Lost in the mists of antiquity is the origin of the practice of
making a small-scale representation of a desired victim, by the mutilation
or ill-treatment of which corresponding suffering could be inflicted upon
the party proposed to be injured. All over the world, among civilized
races as well as aborigines, this curious belief prevailed, and even yet such
homœopathic magic is not dead in the British Isles. Pictures proved to be
as efficacious as more solid effigies." The figurine was generally slowly
melted, or burned, or crumbled away, or even buried in the earth (pre-
ferably in a grave), or drowned in water, and as it wasted and disappeared,
so the victim, having fallen strangely sick, languished, and withered, and
died.

Holy Pictures were used in this magic, the curses uttered as the
sacred likeness was stuck with pins or nails being supposed to light upon
the person named in the malediction. Satanists also slash and cut Holy
Pictures and desecrate the Crucifix out of enmity and malice.

In many country places in England the heart of some animal, a pig
or a sheep, or it may be even an onion or a beetroot, is treated in the same
fashion. In the Somerset County Museum at Taunton, for example, may
be seen shrivelled hearts of pigs, studded with pins, which were discovered

hidden away in old cottages. This was to work harm to the person who lived in the house, or else if a pig or cattle died, and it was thought they had been overlooked, the hearts would be carefully dried and pierced with great pins and thorns, as this would be sure to rack the old witch who had killed the animals with pains and cramps in every joint of her body. In Naples there is the dreaded *Fattura della morte* (death-maker). A large green lemon is selected, and into it are thrust some two dozen or more great nails, about which is most intricately twined a thread of coloured yarn. This is smoked over a brazier by the witches, who at the same time utter their evil incantations. It is considered one of the foulest and most fatal of charms, hideously infective and a sure harbinger of death.

Mention of these wax or clay puppets occurs again and again in English witch trials, and indeed in the records and registers of every country, as in the pages of the demonologists. In an Anglo-Saxon charter, about A.D. 963–975, it is recorded that after a trial a woman was drowned at London Bridge for driving iron nails into the wooden figure of a landowner named Ælsi. The image was discovered in her chamber. It came to my knowledge that scarcely two years ago certain persons at Oxford had fashioned with horrible bans and blasphemy the image in wax of such-a-one who was obnoxious to them, and had pierced it with a bodkin and pins. Old Mother Demdike, the Lancashire witch (1612), said "that the speediest way to take a man's life away by Witchcraft, is to make a Picture of Clay, like unto the shape of the person whom they mean to kill, and dry it thoroughly: and when they would have them to be ill in any one place more than another; then take a Thorn or Pin, and prick it in that part of the Picture you would so have to be ill: and when you would have any part of the Body to consume away, then take that part of the Picture, and burn it. And when they would have the whole body to consume away, then take the remnant of the said Picture, and burn it; and so thereupon by that means, the body shall die".

At Thebes was discovered the small clay figure of a man, tied to a papyrus scroll. The person whose image it was, and who was named in the writing, was thus devoted to destruction. The figure and papyrus may be seen in the Ashmolean Museum, Oxford. In the Pitt Rivers Museum, Oxford, is a clay figure of a man which in 1889 was placed before a house in Glen Urquhart. It was intended to kill the householder.

The Bishop of Mauritius tells us: "It has been known in Mauritius for a newly interred female corpse to be dug up and used for horrible purposes." Remy, in his *Demonolatry*, Book II, Chapter iii (English translation pp. 99–103), explains how "Witches make Evil Use of Human Corpses", and Guazzo, in his *Compendium Maleficarum*, Book II, Chapter ii (English translation pp. 89–90), has as the argument of the chapter "Witches use Human Corpses for the Murder of Men". "In our days," writes Guazzo, "it is the custom of witches to dig up human corpses, for from such horrid material they renew their evil spells." In 1904 three men were executed in Santa Lucia (British island), West Indies, for the murder of a boy. Their motive was to procure his dead hands and heart and head for Obeah.

It may be repeated, and it cannot too often be emphasized, that throughout the centuries in every country of the world we find exactly the same dark practices of evil, the same beliefs, the same rites, the same ceremonies, the same god whom the witches worship in the same way, and the name of that false god is Satan, the prince of hell, the adversary of God and man; Satan, who with his demon hosts is ever interfering in the daily life of mortals, ever—and never more powerfully than now—plotting the ruin and perdition of the human race.

CHAPTER VII

Sympathetic Magic—Wax Images—Figurines—The Covens—The Grand Master—Levitation —The Sabbat—Incubi and Succubae—The Black Mass.

"He observed times, and used enchantments, and used witchcraft, and dealt with a familiar spirit, and with wizards: he wrought much evil in the sight of the Lord."—*II Chronicles* xxxiii, 6.

So ancient, so vast, and so wicked an organization as the world-wide, world-old, supernatural, subversive, secret Society of Witches will necessarily in its method and procedure differ in some obvious details according to country and to century, according to policy and to opportunity, but actually since the aim and ends are invariably the same, since the lord and master of them all from the beginning has been and eternally is himself the same, the fundamental principles, the real activities and calculated operations of the Satanists will be found everywhere and in every age to prove precisely similar and unified, inspired, continued, and energized by essential evil.

History, exploration, oral tradition, written record, bear unimpeachable witness to this truth.

To give one example, we may revert to the image or poppet, the figurine wrought from clay or other material of which we have just spoken, the bedevilment which Mother Demdike declared was "the speediest way to take a man's life away by Witchcraft". This malefic sorcery was practised in Egypt, Assyria, Babylonia, India—see, for the latter, V. Henry, *La Magie dans l'Inde Antique*; for modern India, J. C. Oman, *Cults, Customs and Superstitions of India*, 1908; it is practised in London, Oxford, Cambridge, in Somersetshire, Devon, Dorset, Lancashire, Westmorland, all along the Border Marches; in Northern Africa, see Dr. E. Mauchamp, *La Sorcellerie au Maroc*, 1911; in Nigeria, P. A. Talbot, *The Peoples of Southern Nigeria*, 1926; among the Matabele, L. Decle, *Three Years in Savage Africa*, 1894; in Borneo, C. Hase and W. McDougall, *The Pagan Tribes of Borneo*, 1912; in Malay, Professor W. W. Skeat, *Malay Magic*, 1900; in Australia, A. W. Howitt, *The Native Tribes of South Australia*,

1879; in Mexico, Bolivia, and Peru; in China, J. J. M. De Groot, *The Religious System of China*, 1907; in the Solomon Isles, C. Ribbe, *Zwei Jahre unter den Kannibalen der Salamo-Inseln*, 1903; among the Finns, in Scandinavia, Siberia, Russia, Turkey, Germany, France, Italy—in fact the list with repeated references might be almost indefinitely prolonged. It is hardly an exaggeration to say that the same deadly spell of witch-craft has existed everywhere at all times.

In Italy—and in other countries—the charm is sometimes a little differently worked, the variant being known as "The Spell of the Black Hen". The figure of a hen painted black and stuffed with hair, if possible the hair of the intended victim, or parings of his nails mingled with the hair, is thrown into water to rot away. The black hen may even be knitted of black wool or cut out of black cloth. Black pins are stuck into the stuff, which is buried, or somewhere concealed to perish. There is also the Italian *ghirlanda delle streghe*; the English Witches' Ladder. A cord is knotted at regular intervals and in each knot is tied the feather of a black hen. A curse is laid upon it, and it is considered a fatal talisman of death. In 1886 there was found in the belfry of an English country church an object which seemed so curious that an engraving of it appeared in the *Folk-Lore Journal*. When shown to a very old village woman she at once exclaimed: "Ah! That is a witches' ladder! A bad vile thing!"

In connexion with English rustic witchcraft there is a curious little superstition practised at Kit Knox Hill, Cartridge, Hants. It is said that Kit or Kate Knox was a famous witch three hundred years ago, and so great was (and is) her power that people still visit her grave in a neigh-bouring churchyard to seek advice. The inquirer alone, and, to be more effectual, at midnight, must go to the grave and there solemnly call aloud "Kit Knox; Kit Knox; Kit Knox"; three times. Then listen for the answer, and, it is firmly believed, counsel and guidance will always be given.

We may regard the vast witch organization locally, so to speak, and in a smaller compass. Less than three-quarters of a century after the first settlers had landed at Massachusetts, when the colony was yet young, Cotton Mather drew particular attention to the well systematized and methodical society of the Salem Satanists. He justly regarded it as most significant and ominous that the dark intelligence and power, their leader and lord, should have been able in so short a time to mass and marshal his human agents with such strategy and skill. "'Tis very remarkable," he writes, "to see what an Impious and Impudent *imitation* of Divine Things, is Apishly affected by the Devil", and after showing that the "*Powawes of the Tawnies*", as he terms the native Indian sorcerers, curiously imitate and burlesque in their ceremonies certain incidents of the Biblical narra-tive, he continues: "The Devil which *then* thus imitated what was in the Church of the *Old Testament*, now among *Us* would Imitate the Affairs of the Church in the *New*. The *Witches* do say, that they form themselves much after the manner of *Congregational Churches*; and that they have a *Baptism* and a *Supper*, and Officers among them, abominably Resembling those of our Lord."

This "baptismal" rite on being received into the infernal company is noted by the Dominican Sebastian Michaëlis, who, in his work *Pneumalogie*, 1587, cites a sentence passed upon a gang of witches at Avignon five years before: "You have renounced your most Holy Baptism together with your part in Paradise, and the eternal heritage which our Lord Jesus Christ bought for you and the whole race of men by His death. All these you deny before the said cacodemon in the form of a man, and that blatant devil did baptize you anew with water, and you did change the names given to you at the Holy Font, and so took and received another false name in the guise of baptism." Guazzo remarks how among other initiation ceremonies of witches the demon "bathes them in a new mock baptism". Pierre de Lancre of Bordeaux, in his great work on witchcraft (1610), mentions that a witch, Jeanette d'Abadie, confessed that she had often seen children baptized at the sabbat, and that sorcerers always brought their little sons and daughters to be sprinkled by the devil rather than take them to Church as Christians use. The Scottish witch, Isobel Gowdie, of Auldearne (1662), was marked on the shoulder by the devil, who "sucked out my blood at that mark, and spouted it in his hand, and, sprinkling it on my head, said, 'I baptize thee, Janet, in my own name' ". The Swedish witches (1669) were baptized at Blockula. They added that the devil "caused them to be baptized too by such Priests as he had there, and made them confirm their Baptism with dreadful Oaths and Imprecations". The accounts of the baptisms of the Salem witches, to whom Cotton Mather refers, are most detailed. No less than six of that society were dipped into the water on one occasion.

In the judgement passed at Avignon upon the witches it is said that after their reception by the demon "he branded each of you with his Mark as belonging to him". The Devil's Mark, or Witches' Mark, as it was alternately called, was considered to be the very sign and seal of Satan indelibly imprinted upon the flesh of his servant. Guazzo tells us that at the admission of witches the devil places his mark upon some part or other of their bodies, and the mark is not always of the same description; for at times it is like the footprint of a hare, sometimes like that of a toad, or a spider. Neither does he always mark them upon the same place. When they have been so marked they make solemn vows: that they will profane and insult all holy things; that on certain stated days they will, if they can, fly to the Witches' Sabbat, and zealously take part in its activities; that they will recruit all they can into the service of the devil, and many more horrid blasphemies and wickedness. The Devil's Mark was often quite nondescript in appearance. *The Laws against Witches and Conjurations*, 1645, authoritatively stated that "their said Familiar hath some big or little Teat upon their Body, where he sucketh them: and besides their sucking, the Devil leaveth other marks upon their bodies, sometimes like a Blue-spot, or Red-spot like a flea-biting". Both ecclesiastical and civil Judicature regarded the unnatural mark as the infallible sign of a witch, and Boguet mentions a certain Republic where the magistrates were so scrupulous as to be unwilling to condemn a witch to death unless a mark could be found. But they are very difficult to find, because they are very inconspicuous, and in the most secret parts of the body, often hidden under the natural hair, whence it frequently became necessary to shave the suspect from head to foot. Matthew Hopkins, the notorious "Witch-Finder General", gives a number of indications whereby any bleb or caruncle may be distinguished from the devil's Mark, "a mark whereof no evident Reason in Nature can be given", as Perkins says. Delrio calls the Mark a *Stigma*, and it is given to witches "as is alleged, by a Nip in any part of the Body, and it is blue". "Now, the stamp which imprints these marks is none other but the Devil's claw," writes Sinistrari.

Guazzo has it that the Devil's Mark is sometimes painless and sometimes painful, but with rare exceptions these spots were insensible, and Richard Bernard, vicar of Batcombe, Somerset, in his standard *Guide to Grand Jurymen*, 1627, precisely lays down: "And note, That this mark is *Insensible*, and being prick'd it will not Bleed." Accordingly a test employed again and again was to pierce the mark with a bodkin or long pin, and if the accused felt nothing there was the strongest presumption of guilt. Louis Gaufridi, when in prison under charges of foulest sorcery, was officially visited on 10 March, 1611, by two physicians and two surgeons, who discovered on his body three witches' marks, all of which blemishes when probed with a long medical needle gave neither smart nor pain. No blood or other humour exuded, and on examination the next morning the said spots were neither reddened nor swollen as they must have been in the ordinary course of nature. In Scotland the "prickers", as they were called, experts who examined witches in this way, formed a regular guild.

There are instances upon record and cases can be met with today of the witch who through a sullen preference or on account of circumstances, perhaps, is living solitary and alone, isolated from other members of that dark society. In hamlets and smaller villages there may be dwelling in a quite restricted area some three or four witches. During former years intercommunication was so laborious and difficult as hardly to be conceived of by persons of the present day, the majority of whom have never known anything save the most expeditious and rapid means of locomotion, so that the remotest thorps and most isolated ankerholds can normally be reached with little effort, in easeful comfort, and at the cost of a trifling expenditure of time.

Even without these conveniences—as they are generally thought—the members of the witch society in various districts, however widely scattered, in villages, market towns, great cities, or even in provinces and departments, over the whole countryside, in fact, were linked up in some extraordinary and mysterious way, and a secret correspondence was maintained between them. There is and has ever been an active freemasonry of evil.

As has already been noted, and Guazzo emphasizes, one of the duties imposed upon the Satanist is frequent and unfailing attendance at the midnight assemblies. These conventicles or synagogues or sabbats (as they came somewhat loosely to be known), these "Hellish Randezvouzes", as Cotton Mather aptly terms them, are the gatherings of local companies or sodalities or communities or cells of witches—for they can go under very many names, some seemingly innocent, some grimly significant. The members meet together convened by and under the discipline of certain officials, who were directed by the Master or Grand Master. Attendance at these assemblies was strictly enforced. Isobel Gowdie, the Scottish witch (1662), complained in very feeling terms of the severe punishments inflicted by the local Master of the Auldearne coven. "He would beat and buffet us very sore," she lamented. "We were beaten if we were absent from any gathering, or if we neglected to do anything he had commanded us."

It at once occurs—why did these poor wretches s bmit to this sort of thing? Why did they not boldly break away from the damnable society? Let the devil get his claws into a man, hardly shall he escape. The Satanists had their spies everywhere. The least backsliding was noted, and any lukewarmness in the cause was visited with the cruellest penalties. Thus among the witches of Arras (1460), when one of the coven, Jean Tacquet, a wealthy eschevin, endeavoured to withdraw from their ranks and renounce his allegiance to Satan, the demon fell upon him and beat him unmercifully, compelling him to renew his vows and continue in his servitude. The gang would never have let slip a rich subject. And so the witches, who often feign and profess themselves masters of the devil, are his bond-slaves and most degraded serfs. "There are," says Remy, in his *Demonolatry*, Book I, Chapter xii, "many Faults for which the Demons bring Witches to task with the utmost Severity; such as Failure to attend the Nocturnal Assemblies; Failure to do Evil; dissuading another from Wrongdoing; using their Spells without Success; and very many other Shortcomings of this Kind. For these they are punished with the most Savage Beating, or else they must atone by some Serious Loss of their own Goods." In the days of Remy witches bound themselves by a Solemn Oath, which they were constrained to repeat after the Demon himself, never to betray their Companions in Crime to the Judge. Any such treachery constitutes in the view of the Satanists the gravest offence, and the modern devil-worshippers stick at nothing to silence a traitor. Today many unhappy members of these hellish camorras are only prevented from breaking away through sheer fright. It is a system of terrorism and blackmail. Death is the reward for those who venture to quit their ranks; for, naturally enough, although they seem to grow bolder and viler every year, the Satanists are reluctant that the whole of their dark plot shall be unmasked to the world. Their aim is to bring about universal anarchy, red revolution, and a despotism of evil. Little would they reck of a mere casual murder, or of a dozen murders, for the matter of that. They have at hand subtle instruments, some high-placed and names of note, and can play their game with infinite skill and daring. Many a seeming suicide, many an unsolved mystery, lie to their compt.

The number of members which constitutes a witch-coven is a point that has been much discussed. It is true that Isobel Gowdie of Auldearne in her confession alleged "there are thirteen persons in each coven", and Mr. Alexander Keiler, who has very thoroughly investigated witchcraft in Aberdeenshire and the personnel of the witchcraft covens, writes: "To those unaware of the probable organization of what might be termed the Witch Sect in Europe, in at any rate the sixteenth and seventeenth centuries, it may be explained that the Administrative and Executive Unit of Witchcraft customarily consisted of thirteen persons, and was usually termed a 'Coven' or 'Coeven'." Many examples of the coven of thirteen persons could be cited; on the other hand, an equal number of examples show differing numbers of members in the coven. Ten witches formed the coven of Great Waltham, Stisted, Dagenham, and Sible Hedingham in 1589, of whom four were hanged. The witches of Warboys who killed Lady Cromwell were three in number—Mother Samuel, her husband, and their daughter. They were executed at Huntingdon in 1593. At least thirty-five witches can be traced in connexion with the famous Pendle Forest trials (1613), the first Lancashire witches. Seven witches were concerned in the Fairfax case (1622), and six of these stood their trial at the August Assizes, York. It is uncertain whether they were found guilty or acquitted, as there are conflicting statements. The witch of Edmonton, old Mother Sawyer, hanged at Tyburn in April, 1621, who has given her name to the powerful drama by Dekker, Rowley, and Ford, which was revived in London in 1921 and again in 1936, lived solitary. Anne Bodenham, of Anger, Salisbury, who had been in the service of Dr. Lambe and who learned the black art from that notoriously evil warlock, was married, and ostensibly acted as the village schoolmistress. She was brought to book mainly through the revelations of her maid, Ann Styles, whom she began to instruct in demonianism, but who betrayed her in a sad fright at the terrible mysteries of that awful house. And that in spite of the fact that Mother Bodenham made the wench seal a covenant "not to discover her". There does not appear to have been a coven at Anger or in the Salisbury district. So Mother Bodenham may be considered as a witch who lived alone, and who in the missionary spirit was anxious to pass on the wicked tradition. Today some of the London covens of Satanists are composed of as many as thirty or more members, men and women; some circles, again, are quite small and consist of half a dozen or ten initiates. The Oxford covens are, I believe, all limited in numbers, and rarely admit more than twelve. Here, on account of the conditions of the case, the personnel is continually changing, and the older members before they leave introduce newcomers.

Cotton Mather speaks of *Officers* among the witches. These were in the first place the local Chiefs or Masters of a Coven and their subordinates, above whom ranked the Grand Master of a district, the "head Actor at their hellish Randezvouzes".

This "Head Actor", or President of the Sabbat, was often the Grand Master of the province, and since he was sometimes called "the Devil" by the witches, whilst his satellites and assistants were termed "Devils", some confusion has arisen, and human beings have not been discriminated from malign entities who materialized at these meetings.

Burns Begg (*Proceedings of the Society of Antiquaries of Scotland*, New Series, Edinburgh, Vol. X) remarks that the witches on occasion "seem to have been undoubtedly the victims of unscrupulous and designing knaves who personated Satan". I rather think that the man who personated Satan at these gatherings was not so much an unscrupulous and designing knave as himself a devil-worshipper, who was devoted body and soul to the cult of the demon, and who believing intensely in the force and reality of his own horrible powers, presented himself for the adoration of the witches as the vicegerent of his and their master, and, in the name of the fiend he served, exacted their humblest obedience and exercised a lordship which was as absolute as it was unquestioned.

On the other hand, very often it was indeed some demon of hell, some evil spirit in seemingly corporeal substance and in monstrous shape, who sat upon the throne, there to receive the homage of the children of darkness.

The sabbats of the Neuchâtelois sorcerers were not infrequently presided over and directed by the Grand Master of the district, but a profound scholar, l'abbé Jeanneret, maintains that it is impossible for the unprejudiced historian, in the face of overwhelming evidence, not to believe that upon occasion a fiend was visibly and indeed present at these assemblies. If we are curious to know how these spirits materialized a most satisfactory explanation is given by Pedro Valderama, O.S.A., in his *Histoire Générale du Monde (A Universal History of the World)*, of which this French translation from the Spanish manuscript by the Sieur de la Richardière appeared at Paris in 1619; at least, Volume I is dated 1619, although Volume II is 1617. The book seems to be the first edition of Volume I, and any earlier issue cannot be traced. Valderama, who died in 1611, was engaged upon his work from about 1605 to 1610, but the Spanish original does not appear to have been printed. Our author writes that spirits, when they wish to manifest themselves to human beings, can make bodies for themselves out of inspissated air. He gives as an illustration the fact that water freezes and becomes hard ice, so spirits can solidify air.

One Good Friday when the Louviers coven had met, and their Grand Master the wizard-priest, Mathurin Picard, was performing a horrible mockery of the Last Supper, at the very height of the blasphemy and the foulness a dark familiar appeared suddenly, and during this abominable orgy walked round the table at which the company were seated, crying aloud in a voice hoarse and hot as the breath of Tophet: "*Not one of you shall betray me.*"

Frequently from the admissions of the witches it is possible to identify the name of the Grand Master. In the case of the smaller covens or "sects" and village "knots" or "gangs" the Chief will generally be found to have been an individual of little, if indeed any, historical note, but, as we shall take occasion to remind ourselves, in some instances important political figures and men of high rank were involved.

During the interrogatory in 1481 by the Neuchâtel Ecclesiastical Tribunals of Rollet Croschet, of Boudry, the accused confessed that nearly forty years ago, when hardly in his teens, he had been taken to the Youkke—as the witches' rendezvous was locally known—by a sorcerer named Jaquet DuPlan. This wicked wretch led him before a tall dark man, who (he was told) was the Devil. Evidently the boy recognized this "Devil" as one Robin, a man of quality and grand seigneur, before whom he knelt and at whose dictation, with horrible blasphemies, he renounced God and the Catholic Faith. Robin was saluted as "the Provost". Alice Duke, or Manning, a Wincanton witch (1665), used to summon her familiar by the name of Robin, when he would appear as a man. The demon who served the Irish witch, Lady Alice Kyteler, was called "Robin filius Artis", which may be equivalent to Robin, son of Art. He materialized as a shaggy dog, a cat, and as a black man. He was an incubus.

On another occasion when Croschet attended a sabbat the meeting was held one Thursday in the country lying at the back of the old castle of Valangin—said to be haunted—and a certain "Captain" Hanchemand presided. Now Hanchemand was a citizen of considerable standing in Neuchâtel. In his double rôle of general provisioner and griping extortioner he had amassed abundant wealth and acquired wide influence. He usually employed a young prentice sorcerer, Jaquet DuPasquier, as his intermediary with the witches of the district. DuPasquier used to go round giving notice of the time and place of the next gathering. On one occasion Hanchemand made Rollet Croschet a present of five silver sols, which is roughly about ten shillings of present money with at least five times its spending value.

Hanchemand believed, no doubt, that his fortune and the pressure he was able to bring to bear upon the numerous persons who had fallen into his clutches,—very many good bourgeois; substantial farmers; men of position at Fribourg, Pontarlier, Dombresson, and other towns; and even nobles—would be his safeguard, but when suspicion became too strong he was arrested, and in June, 1439, he was brought to trial before Uldaric de Torrente, a learned Dominican, specially delegated by the Bishop of Lausanne, Messire Jean de Prangins. It was proved beyond all manner of doubt that Hanchemand was chief of the local Sect of witches, and that Jaquet DuPlan was one of the most active and dangerous members of the dark fraternity. Convicted of enormous crimes, both were executed, and in accordance with the law of Neuchâtel their goods were confiscated, two-thirds being forfeit to the city, and one-third being devoted to the service of religion. So vast riches had Hanchemand accumulated that as late as 1455, sixteen years after his death, the courts were collecting various revenues from his estate and adjusting the mischiefs caused by his usuries.

In 1579, at Windsor, the Master of a coven of witches who used to meet "in the Pits" towards the back of Master Dodges' house was old Rosimond, the wise man of Farnham. They had wrought great trouble, and were responsible for the deaths of Master Gallis, mayor of Windsor, of several farmers and servant wenches who offended them in some way. Farnham Common, Bucks, is five and three-quarter miles from Windsor.

The Rev. George Burroughs was the Grand Master of the Salem witches. He used to brag that he was "above the ordinary Rank of Witches", and openly boasted that he had "the promise of being a King in Satan's Kingdom".

A very striking example of a Grand Master of the witches, a notorious revolutionary who employed the Satanists to further his political ends and who was a menace to the kingdom, is found in Francis Bothwell, whose activities have already been described. Other Grand Masters who organized subversive societies, burrowing in secret like moles, were the diabolist Cagliostro; Jacob Falk, "the biggest rogue and villain in all the world", "the Ba'al Shem of London"—a Ba'al Shem, says Margoliouth, being "an operative Cabbalist; in other words, a thaumaturgos and prophet";—Adam Weishaupt, "the Illuminatus", who was inspired by a "fanatical enmity inimical to all authority on earth"; the vile Anarchasis Clootz; and in the nineteenth century Albert Pike, "the Vicegerent of Lucifer", as he has been called, and his successor Adriano Lemmi. There are today several Grand Masters who, although they themselves may not suspect it, are known as Satanists and ardent missionaries of their hideous cult.

The name Sabbat is commonly employed to denote any assembly of devil-worshippers, from the village gathering of perhaps some half a dozen witches meeting in a humble cottage or barn, to the crowded congregation of all classes, who hold their bestial orgies in the mansion of their President, "the Devil", and here they are safe from any espial or interruption. Dr. Fian and his company, of whom Bothwell was the Master, forgathered on All Hallows E'en at the lonely and haunted church of North Berwick. Silvain Nevillon, who was executed at Orleans on 4 February, 1615, during his examination by the Lieutenant-General Justiciar on 20 June, 1614, confessed that he was wont to attend the sabbat in a large house where two hundred persons collected, all of whom save one were masked. At certain sabbats today the Satanists wear masks and are instructed by a witch under the control of a demon. The house which Nevillon described was identified as a great château near Olivet, a village about two and a half miles from Orleans, the seat of a nobleman who was doubtless himself the Grand Master. Here the black mass was celebrated in all its foulness. The Swedish witches (1669–1670) of Mora, on Lake Siljan, met at a house they called Blockula, which was plainly from the accounts they gave, the manor-house or *herrgård*.

When circumstances permitted the witches often met out of doors. The Brocken, commonly known as the Blocksburg, among the Hartz mountains was a notorious rendezvous, especially on Walpurgis Night, the eve of May Day. The Guernsey witches assembled on the sands of Rocquaine Bay. Mother Agar, the Brewham witch, and her company met on Brewham Common, and at Husseys-knap, a coppice hard by the hamlet, which is a very few miles from Bruton, in Somerset. The Neuchâtelois coven came together in the old Jewish cemetery. The Salem witches resorted to "a plain grassy place, by which was a Cart path and sandy ground in the path, in which were the tracks of Horses feet". Upon occasion they met "at a house in the Village, and they had *Red Bread* and *Red Drink*"—the Devil's communion. At the Satanic Mass of blasphemies Madeleine Bavent saw that the host was red. The Abbé Guibourg, in the black masses he said for Madame de Montespan, slit the throat of a little child and mingled the red streaming blood with the chalice.

The Sabbat might be celebrated at any hour, but for obvious reasons of secrecy—unless the rendezvous were very retired—in general night-time was preferred. Boguet says "there is no fixed day for the Sabbat, but the witches go to it whenever Satan so commands". From her experience Madeleine Bavent declared: "There seems to be no fixed day for the assembly."

With many learned arguments and examples Remy demonstrates

"That Witches do often really and in fact Travel to their Nocturnal Synagogues; and sometimes again such journeyings are but an Empty Imagination begotten of Dreams. Further, that these Journeys are performed in Various Manners."

"But it must be known before they go to the sabbat they anoint themselves upon some part of their bodies with an unguent made from various foul and filthy ingredients, but chiefly from murdered children, and so anointed they are carried away on a cowl-staff or a broom, or a reed, or a cleft stick or a distaff, which things they ride." (Guazzo, Book I, Chapter xiii.) The ointment itself has no power or value, but is a mere empty jape of Satan to add ceremony and circumstance to the proceedings. The same may be said of the staff or broom, which is actually an empty symbol.

It is, none the less, very certain that witches can be and are levitated and so transported to the sabbat. The staff or broom is a commonplace object which the devil causes to be used in these mysterious locomotions. Probably the reason for these hellish levitations is an imitative mockery of the ecstasies of the Saints, who have been raised in divine rapture from the ground. So Satan, being the ape of God, will have his juggling shows and his fanfaronades.

In the lives of the Saints the phenomenon of levitation has been recorded again and again, and the evidence is absolutely unimpeachable. St. Francis of Assisi was several times "suspended above the earth, often to a height of three, and often to a height of four cubits". St. Alphonsus Liguori, when preaching in the Church of St. John Baptist at Foggia, was lifted before the eyes of the whole congregation several feet from the ground. St. Gemma Galgani, who died in 1903, was observed to be lifted into the air whilst she was entranced in prayer, and she remained on more than one occasion suspended for an appreciable time at some distance from the floor. Many examples might be cited, the most famous of all being St. Joseph of Cupertino, who again and again rose from the earth in ecstasy. Such crowds followed this humble Franciscan friar that his superiors were obliged to send him to the remotest houses of their province, since the rapture fell upon him and swept him heavenwards, as it were, at almost any and every moment. The learned Görres most aptly remarks that there are a great number of attested instances of Saints who have been levitated, and it is neither impossible nor unlikely that this phenomenon should be imitated by evil powers, as has undoubtedly been the case with certain spiritistic mediums. One example will suffice. Sir William Crookes wrote in the *Quarterly Journal of Science*, January, 1874: "The most striking case of levitation which I have witnessed has been with Mr. Home. On three separate occasions have I seen him raised completely from the floor of the room. There are at least a hundred recorded instances of Mr. Home's rising from the ground." Home, it is said, was first levitated in the house of Ward Cheney, an American manufacturer, at South Manchester, Connecticut. Daniel Dunglas Home was born 1833, and died 1886.

Bovet scores a neat point when he writes: "Transmuting of Shapes, Flying in the Air, and such like are impossible to Natural reason. The more unaccountable these things seem to be in themselves (The real matter of Fact being proved) it ought the more to prevail towards a belief of those extraordinary Agencies, since liars would get as near likelihood as they can and not invent fantastically impossible stories."

We cannot gainsay the common opinion of many profound theologians and the general consensus of the demonologists that witches through the power of the Devil may and indeed do fly through the air at night to their sabbats. The famous jurist, Francesco Pegna, expressly says that this opinion is "most certainly true, since it has been proven by many sound reasons and most apparent signs, by actual fact and experiment". As Henry Boguet remarks, such transvection of witches is rare, but it occurred among the witches of Burgundy and was confessed by Françoise Secretain and others of her coven. Glanvil gives an instance of the levitation of the Somersetshire witch, Julian Cox, who was tried at Taunton before Judge Archer, and hanged in 1663.

The actual ceremonies and conduct of the Sabbat as held in various countries and under various conditions naturally must differ very widely throughout the centuries, but all have two essential features, blazing blasphemy and the most crapulous obscenity.

In the *Pandæmonium* it is justly pointed out how, in spite of divergences and disparity, "those Homages, Offices, and Oblations made to the Devil by his miscreant Hags, and Confederates in their Nocturnal Cabals and Night-Revels have one and the same tendency, and centre in the same miserable and irrevocable point at last".

As a preliminary, the President, who may be the Grand Master of the locality or else the materialization of some evil entity, is adored and worshipped by all present. They pay him homage in the most infamous and beastly manner with prostrations, genuflexions, obeisances, lewd gestures and the reverential kiss of obscenity, *osculum infame*. Sometimes the coven present black candles to their Master. This piece of ritual is found in North Italy, France, Scotland, and the West of England. Guazzo says that the witches carried "pitch black candles", and these burned smokily with a blue flame, as was also observed at North Berwick. This would proceed from the sulphurous matter kneaded with the wax. The candles were, so to speak, mock votive tapers, and further served the practical purpose of giving a dim half-light among those mysterious shades.

The witches then deliver a report of their ill-deeds committed since the last synagogue. Bodin tells us that each sorcerer must render an account of all the evil he has wrought, the mischiefs and murders, the destruction of crops, cattle, barns, byres, and the like, the persons overlooked, lamed, and injured in purse and person. When the Northumberland coven met (1673): "All of them who had done harm gave an account thereof to their protector, who made most of them who did most harm, and beat those who had done no harm."

Next instructions are given to the congregation. Thomas Cooper, sometime vicar of Holy Trinity, Coventry, an Oxford divine highly reputed for his great learning and one who had much experience in cases of witchcraft, in his *The Mystery of Witchcraft*, published in 1617, writes that at these meetings the Devil-President "delivers unto his Proselyte, and so to the rest, *the Rules of his Art*, instructing them in the manner of *hurting* and *helping*, and acquainting them with such *medicines* and *poisons* as are usual hereunto". Spells were taught orally and had to be conned with great care and exactly recited with the correct intonation; the Somersetshire witches of 1665 were instructed in the art of moulding wax images, and they learned where and how and with what words these figurines must be pierced with long thorns or pins; the qualities of drugs and the action of poisons were explained; especially did the witch mid-wives learn how to procure abortion and what emmenagogues were most potent and most pernicious. One witch-midwife of Strassburg confessed that she had procured more miscarriages and killed more children than she could count. The witches were adepts in the horrid art of poisoning, and when charms seemed to be too slow, a tempered draught would often do the trick. Old Simon Forman—"sweet Father Forman", as the Countess of Somerset called him—not only supplied the lady with puppets and talismans but also brewed strange potions in which he mingled phosphorus, subacetate of copper, arsenic, and corrosive sublimate for her enemies to drink. Dr. Lambe, the warlock of Westminster, was famous for his knowledge "of that noble and deepe Science of Physicke", but he "fell to other mysteries". La Voisin, in Paris; Hieronyma Spara, of Rome; La Toffania, of Naples, were at the heads of their profession.

Frequently, and especially was this the case with the larger and more important covens, high politics were and are the principal subject of question and debate at these sabbats, and the powerful gangs of witches strove to decide the destiny of countries and the fate of kings. In 1786 a very secret sabbat or circle was convened at Frankfurt, a meeting of Satanists amongst whom were present Cagliostro; the cabbalist Duchanteau; the "Philallèthes" Savalette de Langes, a traitor "versed in all dark mysteries, complotter in all vile plots", pseudo-Rosicrucian, magician Martiniste; the Illuminatus,* Christian Bode, alias Amelius. It was here that the deaths of Louis XVI of France and Gustavus III of Sweden were decreed. Very similar meetings are held today; very similar murderous resolutions are determined and have been passed into effect. The revolutions that have troubled and vexed peaceful nations, the broils and unrest culminating in the world chaos of an almost universal misery, tyranny, and anarchy, all are fomented, deliberately organized, and energetically assisted by the Black International, the Satanists, who go under a dozen trifling occult names, who mockingly dub themselves political parties. Only too true and of profoundest significance were the words spoken of the holy prophet full three thousand years ago: "Rebellion is as the sin of witchcraft."

When the business of the sabbat had been dispatched it was usual for the whole crew to turn to revelry and feasting of their kind. There were often dances, and these, as it may be supposed, were no graceful and elegant movements, a most pleasing and agreeable recreation, an exquisite art, but the choreography of hell, awkward jiggetings and lewd leapings,

---

* Bishop Horsley, in his *Critical Disquisition* on *Isaiah* xviii, says: "It were easy to trace the pedigree of French Philosophy, Jacobinism, and Bavarian Illumination, up to the first heresies."

the muckibus caperings and bouncings, the loutings and mowings of idiots. Boguet, De Lancre, and several writers have been particular in the descriptions of the witches' dances, as learned from the confessions of these wretches, and the Capuchin Jacques D'Autun speaks of sorcerers, who gyrate hand in hand, and twist and twirl their limbs as driven by maniac frenzy.

The music well suits the movements. As there is an immortal melody and the "perfect Diapason" of Heaven, so is there the horrid cacophony of hell. Music may be potent for evil, unloosing hideous passions and cruelty, as it may be the sphere-born harmony of God,

> That undisturbed Song of pure concent,
> Aye sung before the sapphire-coloured throne
> To Him that sits thereon . . .

It is interesting to remark that in his psychological study *The Germans* (English translation, 1942) Emil Ludwig analyses at length the musical influence of Wagner, whom he calls "the most dangerous of Germans". Wagner's music "is obsessed by sex" and "works upon the nervous system. . . . It is filled with lust for power, inspired by treachery and sex", whilst it "transports the listener into a state of mystical ecstasy".

That certain combinations of sound send out definitely evil vibrations is not to be denied. With shrewd knowledge Toussaint l'Ouverture, the heroic negro chief, when he was appointed Governor of San Domingo, strictly forbade the Voodoo drum with the magic of its monotonous throb and eerie low-pitched call. Bovet tells us that Lapland wizards summoned their familiars by a Magical Drum. He describes one of these which he had examined. "It is marked all over upon the vellum with a sort of *Necromantick* Characters, somewhat like the *Arabick* letters; but doubtless a sort of Orthography taught by the *Black Master* of the Infernal Science. When a Drum is beaten with other magic ceremonies, the Spirit answers out of the drum, and resolves the questions or appoints a rendezvous where he meets the sorcerer." The West Indian Moreau de Saint-Méry, who spent his youth in Martinique, and later became one of the leading legal authorities and a chief magistrate in Haiti, describes the Voodoo dances as performed at the end of the eighteenth century to the boom of the two drums rhythmically struck with wrist and fingers, slowly for one and rapidly for the other. These drums, says Père Labat, writing of the year 1698, are thus used—the larger to beat the time and direct the movements, the smaller being struck much more quickly as an undertone with a higher pitch. Seemingly the one really accompanies the steps, the other arouses and inflames the passions, since the postures and climax of the dance are grossly obscene. A kind of madness falls upon the dancers. They ceaselessly whirl round. They tear off their clothes and bite deep into their own flesh. Some who become senseless and fall to the ground are carried to one side without interrupting the movements, until finally in the darkness promiscuous prostitution holds the most horrible sway.

This might almost exactly serve as a picture of the dancing at the witches' sabbat, only in place of the drums mention is made of various other instruments: violins, tambourines, flutes, rebecks, fifes and drums, hautboys, the bass-horn, a hurdy-gurdy, citterns, the Jew's harp, and (especially in Scotland) the pipes.

The dances of the witch covens had all the frenzy and all the indecency of the Voodoo. So savages dance, and among the North American Indians there is one word to signify both dancing and coitus.

During these frenzied debaucheries witches perform the carnal act with incubus devils, an abomination deeply deplored by Pope Innocent VIII in the great Bull of 1484. "It has come to our knowledge," says that Pontiff, "and stricken are we to the heart to learn it, that many persons of both sexes utterly jeopardizing their souls' salvation are wont to have connexion in horrid venery with evil spirits, both incubi and succubae." The incubus (*one who lies upon* anything, and hence in common phrase, a burden, a heavy task, or trouble) is an evil spirit who assumes a male form; a succuba* (in late Latin, a harlot) is the evil spirit assuming a female form, and since spirits in their own nature have no sex, the famous Dominican, Charles Réné Billuart, in his *Treatise on Angels*, points out that "The same evil spirit may serve as a succuba to a man, and as an incubus to a woman."

St. Albertus Magnus relates how: "The accounts of evil entities, both incubi and succubae, are most exactly true and beyond all dispute. We ourselves know persons who have had actual experience of this, and there are loathly haunted places in which it were perilous for a man to sleep, so molested are they by the visits of the demon succubus" (*Opera*, XV, p. 97). St. Thomas instructs us that although neither good angels nor demons have bodies they can assume material substance, and when they have assumed corporeity these bodies can do what natural living bodies do (*De Potestate*, Q. 6; arts. 6, 7, and 8).

At Bologna, in 1468, a sorcerer was condemned for keeping a common brothel with succubus. John Nider, O.P., Prior of the Strict Dominican house at Basle, in his *Formicarius*, a treatise on Visions and Revelations, written during the Council of Basle, 1435–1437, records (Book V, Chapter ix), how at the time of the Council of Constance, 1414–1417, a succubus residing in that city accumulated immense wealth by her harlotries. Andrew Boorde, the eminent physician of the reign of Henry VIII, in his *Breviary of Health* (1547), says: "*Incubus* doth infest and trouble women, and *Succubus* doth infest men." He further speaks of an anchoress of St. Albans, whom he knew, and who "was infested of such a spirit". This religious woman would probably be the Lady Margaret Smythe, whose enclosure was in St. Michael's Church. The Rev. Robert Kirke, of Aberfoyle, in his *Secret Commonwealth* (1691), denounces as an abomination, "Succubi who trist with men". Swinburne rightly judged that "the singular intervention of a real live succubus" in Middleton's excellent comedy *A Mad World, my Masters*, 4to, 1608, "can hardly seem happy or seasonable". In *The Alchemist*, acted 1610,

---

* Succubus, the masculine figuration, is the more correct and mediaeval form of this word; but for distinction's sake it is customary (when it is required to differentiate) to use the later (Elizabethan) anglicized feminine form succuba, of which terminological liberty I have availed myself here

Sir Epicure Mammon, when indulging in the full flood-tide of his impure yet magnificent dreams, cries:

> I will have all my beds, blown up; not stuffed:
> Down is too hard. And then, mine oval room,
> Fill'd with such pictures, as Tiberius took
> From Elephantis: and dull Aretine
> But coldly imitated. Then, my glasses,
> Cut in more subtill angles, to disperse,
> And multiply the figures, as I walk
> Naked between my *succubae*.

It is curious that in *Bartholomew Fair*, acted in 1614, Ursla, the pig-woman, vehemently abusing her tapster', amongst her Billingsgate should salute him as "thou errant *Incubee*".

Christian Stridtbeckh has a learned philosophical treatise, published at Leipzig in 1690, *On Witches, that is to say Evil Women who have commerce and communion with the Demon*, but on some important points his conclusions must be judged unsound, nor can they be followed. Dr. Johann Friedrich Convinus, in his *Dissertation on the Power of the Devil over the Human Body*, Halle, 1725, whilst flatly denying the power of the devil to propagate in a natural way (p. 19), which is admitted, argues (pp. 41–2) that in a mysterious way from certain plastic substances the devil can build up and energize a human body capable of performing all natural functions. Which resolves itself into a mere quibble, and question of words. The Rector of the University of Wittenberg, Dr. Julius Friedrich Winzer, in his Fourth Commentary on Biblical Demonology, published at Leipzig in 1822, says that in *Genesis* vi, 2, "Angels of God" is a better reading than "Sons of God". (But the Vulgate has "filii Dei".) Dr. Langton, in his *Good and Evil Spirits*, 1942, does not discuss this passage. Dr. Winzer refers to the *Gospel of the Infancy*, vi, 11–12. In the *Book of Job*, ii, 2, the Angels are called "Sons of God". Moreover, the *Book of Tobias* is conclusive, since the devil Asmodeus was jealous of the maiden Sara, and slew her seven husbands.

St. Alphonsus Liguori precisely defines the sin of "congressus cum Daemone", and refers to such great authorities as Busenbaum, Tamburini, Bonacina, Filliucci, Gaetani, Azor, and Vasquez, with many more. Pietro Scavini, Clemens Marc, Martinet, and the more recent theologians follow the great doctor, as also does August Vilmar, who was Professor of Theology at Marburg, 1855–1868.

There are innumerable records of, and references to, these foul incubus lusts, which occur in almost every witch trial. The question involved centres round the problem of materialization, and it is obvious that to perform the essentially carnal acts of coition and generation there must be a very complete and spissated materialization.

Dr. Garth Wilkinson, of whom a notice is given in *The Dictionary of National Biography*, has an account of a séance held with the medium D. D. Home on a July evening in 1855 at Mr. Rymer's house in Ealing. There materialized "a lady's hand of beautiful proportions" and soon the entire arm became plainly visible. The hand, at his request, deliberately placed itself on Dr. Wilkinson's forehead, when the palm was **laid** flat "and remained for several seconds. It was warm and human, and *made of no material but human flesh.*"

On 25 September, 1877, Archdeacon Colley and Dr. Kennedy witnessed a materialization "of exquisite womanhood" through the mediumship of Mr. Monck. "There stood embodied a spirit-form of unutterable loveliness, robed in attire spirit-spun . . . of whiteness truly glistening . . . holding the hand of the spirit-arm that rested on mine. I felt the wrist, palm, fingers and finger-nails; yielding to pressure, having natural weight and substance, and all things pertaining to humanity, but it was damp and stone cold." The succuba often appeared to be entrancingly beautiful. The fact that the spirit-form which was touched by Archdeacon Colley "was damp and stone cold" assumes great significance in the light of the confession of Rebecca West (1645), a witch of Lawford, Essex, who related how the devil came to her "as she was going to bed, and told her, he would marry her, and that she could not deny him; she said he kissed her, but was as cold as clay, and married her that night". The witches of Crichton, which is about six miles from Dalkeith, said that when he embraced them the devil "was cold and his breath was like a damp air" (1678). A Belgian witch, Digna Robert, found that the devil was stone cold all over his body (1565). A lusty young Lorraine sorcerer, Dominic Pétrone, who had been initiated into the sect by his witch mother when he was only twelve years old, declared that, vigorous as he was when he approached his beautiful succuba, Abrahel, her body was so bitterly cold that he felt frozen in every limb. Another of the same gang, called Hennezel, was served by a succuba nicknamed "the Black Chatelaine", who although seemingly a dashing and most lascivious brunette, proved upon touch (as he swore) a body with limbs of arctic ice which rendered him completely impotent and eunuchized.

Sometimes after a while a certain glow seemed to pulse through these corporeal forms, who were extremely amorous in their advances. At a series of sittings in 1861–1865 with Miss Kate Fox, a New York banker of the highest integrity experienced some extraordinary phenomena. This gentleman had lost his wife in 1860, and he was persuaded to join the circle in order to see her again. The lady seemed to appear. "I asked her to kiss me if she could; and to my great astonishment and delight, an arm was placed around my neck, and a real palpable kiss was imprinted on my lips." On another occasion his phantasmal wife came "with the arm bare from the shoulder. I found it as large and as real in weight as a living arm. At first it felt cold, then grew gradually warmer".

Hair has been cut from the head of a materialized form, a beautiful blonde, and under scientific examination proved to be human hair light in colour and silky in texture, altogether different from the hair of any person in the circle. This experiment was tried by Professor Richet.

In some cases the ectoplasmic theory may explain materialization, the "ejection and injection of the psychic stuff or plasma" from the tranced medium. This plasma has been described as a dimly luminous mass of substance, like a sort of transparent gelatine. It may, however, form into a face, which can be recognized, or a hand or some other member, but seldom (if ever) composes the complete human body. This is not to say that the diabolic power may not well be able to cause it to perfect itself, and hence an incubus may be an ectoplasmic form energized by a familiar spirit.

It must now be asked whether children çan be born of the union of the witch with the incubus, and the general opinion of theologians and demonologists is that there have been and are such progeny. Sinistrari holds that it is undoubted by theologians and philosophers that carnal intercourse between mankind and the Demon sometimes gives birth to human beings. Thomas Malvenda, a famous Dominican writer (1566–1628), in his great work *Antichrist*, published at Rome in 1604, writes that "from a natural cause, the children begotten by Incubi are tall, very hardy and bloodily bold, arrogant beyond words, and desperately wicked". This description so exactly fits certain of the prominent figures in the world today that it seems to me the real explanation of much appalling wickedness and of their infinite capacity for evil.

It may be noted that the Evil Spirits, the incorporeal Demons who materialize and copulate with witches, constrain them to the worship of Satan, to the abjuration of the Christian faith, to the practice of enchantments, black magic, and foul crimes, before they will indulge them in this infamous intercourse.

Orgies of carnal obscenities and dances form the commonest occasion among lewd men for celebrations of banquets and junketings. The witches then proceed to the sabbat feast. The Salamanca doctors tell us how these wretches "make a meal from food either furnished by themselves or by the Devil. It is sometimes most delicious and delicate, and sometimes garbage or a pie baked from babies they have slain, or disintered corpses. A suitable grace is said before such a table." The accounts of these feasts differ very widely. The Neuchâtel witches had their fill of good food and good wine, and danced merrily singing *frallalon! frallala!* The Lorraine witches declared that at one sabbat there was no lack of any kind of food, except only salt and bread, save for which two things they sat them down to a regular Lord Mayor's banquet, quaffing the richest and most heady wines to wash down their meat. On another occasion the food was so foul and so filthily served that it would have turned the strongest stomach. The Milanese witches described precisely the same sort of spread. One time the provender set before them was rancid and stank extremely whilst the liquor called wine was black like stale blood and exceedingly nauseous to the taste. At another time there was a most delicious regale with the best wines flowing freely and no stint. Whatever was laid and whatever the beverage, all were expected to eat heartily and carouse and return grateful thanks to their host at the end. Delrio says he had seen an old parchment with the "devil's grace", before and after meat, written out by a sorcerer of long continuance and a frequenter of the sabbat orgies. These formulas were scrolls of frenzied blasphemy.

Cannibalism, as has already been noted in regard to the Obeah orgies, was sometimes practised at these feasts. We have the confession of Dominique Isabelle, a Lorraine witch, who had both seen and tasted the flesh of babes at the devil's banquet. Madeleine Bavent describes how one Good Friday the coven of Louviers performed a horrible mockery of the Last Supper. They brought in the body of a tender infant which had been roasted, and all were compelled to eat of it. Sometimes human meat was swallowed for magical purposes to bind the power of a charm. In 1661, at Forfar, Helen Guthrie and four other ghouls exhumed the body of an unbaptized babe, and cut off great gobbets of the flesh, which they baked in a pie. They believed that by eating of this dish they could never be brought to make avowal of their sorceries. This was technically known as a "mute spell".

At the English sabbats, which seem indeed to have been far simpler in every detail than such orgies as the Biscayan *Aquelarre* or the *Youkke* of Neuchâtel, the food and drink provided for the feasting were of good quality and plentiful, but nothing extraordinary or rare. When old Mother Chattox (or Whittle) was received into the Pendle Forest coven the devil gave the witches for their Banquet, "victuals, viz. Flesh, Butter, Cheese, Bread, and Drink, and bade them eat enough. And after their eating, the Devil called *Fancy*, and the other Spirit calling himself *Tibbe*, carried the remnant away." Some thirty or more years later at the "Feast and solemn meeting at Malking-Tower, of this hellish and devilish band of Witches" on Good Friday, 1612, which was "the great Assembly of the Witches", "with great cheer, merry company, and much conference" they had to their dinners beef, bacon, and roasted mutton. The Somersetshire coven (1665) who met on High Common, near Trister Gate, Wincanton, "all sat down, a white Cloth being spread on the ground, and did drink wine, and eat cakes and meat". The witches of Riding Mill, Northumberland, who met at the house of John Newton (probably the district Grand Master) on 3 April, 1673, were entertained right royally with boiled capons, beef, mutton, plum broth, cheeses and butter, bottles of wine, humming ale, and "a variety of meat" beside. In Scotland the society, as we gather, fared equally well. The Forfar coven (1661) went to Mary Rynd's house, and sat down together at table, "the devil" being present at the head of it, and then they all drank good March ale and brandy. On another occasion "the devil and the said witches did drink together, having flesh, bread, and ale". Once, when a very important meeting of a Renfrew coven was held in an old house near Castle Semple, "a splendid feast was prepared", which indicates that the Grand Master of the old Paisley district was a rich and prominent personage.

The great central act of Christian worship is the Mass, a Sacrifice which can be offered to God alone, and the climax of the sabbat orgies is the horror of the black mass, a sacrifice of mockery, impiety, and blasphemy which is offered to the Devil. Satanists today often meet with the celebration of the black mass as their main object, and it is indeed the culmination and—to use a term of the schools—the very quiddity of devil-worship and the cult of hell. In detail the black mass imitates, so to speak, and foully parodies with every circumstance of crapulous obscenity and contempt the Sacrifice of Calvary.

The black mass today is sometimes celebrated in a cellar, but Satanists have become so audacious and so strong in evil that the largest room in their houses is known to be permanently fitted up for these abominable mysteries. In one case the room is draped with black hangings and the windows are always shuttered with curtains drawn. The fact that the door is furnished with a Yale lock and key arouses no suspicion. Sometimes even a disused chapel is bought by a wealthy Satanist and furnished for the ceremonial of the liturgy of the pit. The Abbé Guignard, a member of the La Voisin coven, chanted Satanic Masses in a cellar over the body of Marianne Charmillon; the Duc de Richelieu (1696–1788), who was, it is said, tutored in black magic by a disciple of the Abbé Guibourg, caused two friars, who were his chaplains, to celebrate black masses in the old deserted chapel of one of his country houses, a remote decaying château. He himself assisted with other devotees. De Sade, in *Justine*, describes the celebration of a black mass in a cloister. Pierre David, Mathurin Picard, and Thomas Boullé, who were attached to St. Louis and St. Elizabeth, at Louviers, celebrated black masses at the sabbats which were held in some house not far from the convent, a rendezvous aptly termed a "den of devils". I know of a black mass celebrated at night in a room at the back of a small squalid shop in the slummiest part of Brighton, not far from Brighton Station. At Merthyr Tydfil the black mass was said or sung in the basement back room of a little house in a poor street, where lived an old man who was reputed to be a "fortune-teller", and who boasted that he belonged "to the oldest religion in the world".

This back room was furnished as a chapel, and the altar, above which was suspended a pair of queer-looking horns, whilst odd objects were ranged on the gradine, blazed with candles. Sometimes the altar is swathed in black velvet, and there are six black candles, three on either side of a crucifix. The crucifix is hideously distorted and caricatured, as J.-K. Huysmans saw at the black mass in the old Ursuline convent near the rue de Vaugirard. Mons. Serge Basset, who was taken to a black mass, observed that in the centre of the altar where a crucifix should be placed was squatting the monstrous figure of a half-human buck-goat, with staring eyes which flickered with red fire, whilst from the tips of its huge horns jetted a dull crimson flame. The altar table itself is generally covered with the three regulation fine linen cloths, overlying the cere-cloth of waxed linen. Sometimes a frontal of brocade or silk is used, and this has been known to be worked with designs of the most obscene esotericism, with many-rayed stars which had men's and women's faces, triangles twined with hissing adders, and the whole heraldry of hell.

In May, 1895, at the Palazzo Borghese, which vast palace had been rented in various suites of apartments, a Satanic chapel was discovered, *Templum Palladicum*. The walls of the room were draped with scarlet and black curtains excluding all light; at the farther end was stretched a huge tapestry depicting "Lucifer Triumphans", the Devil Triumphant, Conqueror of the World, and underneath an altar was erected, in the midst of which between the candles stood a figure of Satan to be adored by his worshippers. The room was furnished with luxurious prie-dieus, with chairs of crimson and gold, with tabourets and fald-stools. It was lit by electricity, so arranged as to glare from an enormous human eye fixed in the middle of the ceiling.

The vestments worn by the hierophant of the eucharist of hell are often of the richest quality and embroidered with the most delicate workmanship, for the Satanists have immense wealth at their command. At the black mass witnessed by Mons. Serge Basset the celebrant was vested in an alb trimmed with richest lace and a cope of flaming scarlet covered with gilt pomegranates and cones. He wore scarlet silk shoes. The Abbé Guibourg was robed in an ample chasuble thickly sewn with occult characters wrought in silver. At a black mass of fairly recent date the priest wore a chasuble of the ordinary shape, but in colour a deep red and on the back was embroidered a huge triangle of some shimmering silk in the midst of which a black goat standing upright butted with his silver horns. There have been described to me, by those who actually saw them, a chasuble of heavy orange satin with a he-goat worked in black; another chasuble was of a peculiar shade of brown, embroidered with a pig and a naked woman in delicate flesh-tint; a third was of a hard glaring scarlet adorned with an enamelled plaque of arsenical green on which were a bear and a weasel devouring the host. There was also a cope of exquisite grey silk on which was woven a female figure with buskined legs, wearing a short sky-blue tunic and the red Phrygian cap. The figure, which in one hand raised aloft a severed head streaming in blood, was surrounded by a garland of oak leaves, and beneath appeared the date "21 Janvier, 1793", the murder of King Louis XVI. The figure represented the Goddess of Reason, who attired in this garb was placed upon the high altar of Notre Dame in the person of a common strumpet, adored by the Revolutionaries and Parisian satanists.

For the order of his service the celebrant of the black mass uses a "missal", which is sometimes a printed book, although more often a manuscript. Some of these "missals" are written in red characters upon vellum. Madeleine Bavent speaks of priests celebrating the black mass, and "reading from the Paper of Blasphemy". These "missals" are by no means the same as, but must be entirely distinguished from, grimoires and books of spells.

The host is generally black. In 1324, when investigation was being made into the sorceries of the famous Kilkenny witch, Alice Kyteler, they found hidden away in the lady's chamber, "a wafer of sacramental bread, having the devil's name stamped thereon instead of Jesus Christ". The devil's host is often of grotesque shape, triangular, with three sharp points as used in the Mass of St. Sécaire, or hexagonal. In colour it is sometimes black, sometimes blood-red. Gentien le Clerc, a young satanist of Orleans, who was executed in 1614, "had often seen the devil's priest elevate the host and the chalice, of which both were black". At Rome there were discovered in a brothel two hosts scrabbled over with letters in human blood. These had been stolen from a church and were to be employed in a love-charm.

The thefts of consecrated Hosts from churches is a fearful profanity which has persisted throughout the ages and was never more common than today. The Host is stolen to be desecrated and abused by the Satanists at their assemblies, or it may be in private, secretly and alone.

Presenting themselves at the altar for Communion, these wretches retain the Host in their mouths and then unseen convey It to a handkerchief or handbag. There is a regular traffic in this kind of thing, and considerable sums of money are paid by those who will actually purchase Hosts secured in this way. Nor is it unknown for the Tabernacle of a church to be rifled during the night. A thief can ask his own price for the Reserved Sacrament, and can always find a ready market in certain occult circles.

This is nothing new. We are continually meeting with these abominations throughout the Middle Ages. Dan Michel, of Kent, writing in 1340, speaks of the abuse of the consecrated Host by witches and evil priests as an atrocious crime, but one unhappily known in former centuries. He also mentions the abuse of chalices which have held the Precious Blood. In 1410, when the Queen-regent Dona Catalina was at Segovia, there was discovered a hideous sacrilege, the maltreatment of the Consecrated Host by a band of Jewish sorcerers. They had also attempted the life of the Bishop of Segovia. The Jewish synagogue was converted into a church of reparation, Corpus Christi, and an annual procession still commemorates these events. In 1507 Martin Plantsch, denouncing witchcraft, deplores the magical masses and the profanation of the Host. In 1532 three Hosts were stolen on Good Friday from a church in Aldgate for black magic, as is recorded in the Chronicle of the Grey Friars. There was a terrible scandal in 1614 regarding the theft of numerous Hosts from the tabernacle of the Cathedral at Porto, and the Inquisitor in Portugal, Manuel Do Valle De Moura, issued particular instructions that the Host must be most securely kept under lock and key lest it be stolen for some hideous blasphemy of witchcraft. In July, 1938, the Vatican published new rulings to protect tabernacles. These laws are most stringent and most detailed. Thus the tabernacle must be immovable, shut on all sides, and of solid material. The key must never be left in the door or on the altar. The employment of safety-alarms is urged to prevent attempts at stealing the Hosts. "World-wide thefts of Sacred Hosts are responsible for the new legislation concerning the safe custody of the Blessed Sacrament. It has been known for many years that attacks upon tabernacles are not inspired by the value of the sacred vessels."

There is cumulative evidence for these thefts and defilements during the past twenty, forty, seventy years. Indeed, so active in wickedness are the Satanists that scarcely a month passes without some such incident, some sacrilege, is reported.

So close is the mimicry of the black mass that, although the ceremony is actually no part of Holy Mass, the *Asperges*, the sprinkling of the clergy and congregation with holy water, is often burlesqued. Boguet tells how "they say mass at the sabbat". He who is to celebrate is clothed in a cope with no cross upon it—or sometimes a broken cross—and the worshippers are sprinkled by the Grand Master holding a black asperge with brackish water or even filthy chamber-lye.

Until modern times the burning of incense at the black mass is rarely noted, although there were mystic suffumigations in conjuring of evil spirits. Silvain Nevillon, a member of the Orleans coven (1615), described in detail a black mass at which he had assisted, when the place—it was held in a house—was thick and foggy with a smoke that smelled abominably, not fragrant and sweet as is the incense burned in churches. The witches brought Hosts which they had kept when feigning to make their Communions at various altars, and the Devil (the Grand Master) fouled the Hosts with fearful blasphemies. Water, or some stinking liquid, was scattered over those present, and the Devil chanted *Asperges Diaboli*. He seemed to read the liturgy from a book which was bound in shaggy skin like the pelt of a wolf. On occasion the Devil preached a sort of sermon, but he spoke in a low gruff voice and it was hard to hear what he was saying.

Today Satanists burn in thuribles and in braziers church incense during their hellish liturgy. They also make a kind of incense from various herbs and spices, the smoke from which is sometimes fetid and stale, sometimes languorous and swooning-sweet.

"Every action of the mass which I saw celebrated at the sabbat," confessed Madeleine Bavent, "was indescribably loathsome."

And so the travesty, the eucharist of hell, proceeds from blasphemy to blasphemy, from obscenity to obscenity, until the canon is reached, or rather the point corresponding to the Canon of the Mass. Then "the Host is really and truly consecrated and offered to the demon". At this moment the celebrant turns his back to the altar.

In some modern assemblies, immediately after the elevation of the chalice there are distributed to the congregation smaller chalices or goblets of wine mingled with some potent aphrodisiac, and before long the scene is a saturnalia of indiscriminate and demented debauchery.

A writer of authority on witchcraft has recently said (1933): "Turning to English accounts, little or nothing of the black mass is to be traced." This, however, on closer inquiry will prove to be only very partially true. Under Queen Elizabeth the saying of Mass was forbidden by law, and the penalty was death. This act continued in force for over two hundred years, but there is evidence that in Protestant England, in Genevan Scotland, and in Puritan Massachusetts the witch covens celebrated a mock-sacrament, which was (in one sense, at any rate) the sorcerers' equivalent.

As we have already noted, the Archdeacon of Lewes required the wife of one Edward Jones to prove "that she did eat the Communion bread and put it not in her glove". This was in 1582, when Elizabeth had been on the throne four and twenty years. On Shear Thursday, 1610, old Mother Demdike instructs her grandson to go to the church to receive the Communion, but not to eat the Bread the minister gave him. This he was to deliver to such a thing (a familiar spirit) as should meet him on his way homewards. This was during the reign of James I.

About mid-August, 1678, "the devil had a great meeting in Lothian, where, among others, was a warlock who had been formerly admitted to the ministry in the presbyterian times, and now he turns a preacher under the devil of hellish doctrine; for the devil at this time preaches to his witches the doctrine of the infernal pit, and in mocking of Christ and His holy ordinance of the sacrament of His Supper he gives the sacrament to them, bidding them eat it and drink it in remembrance of himself. This villain was assisting to Satan in this action, and in preaching." Lord Fountainhall, the famous Scottish lawyer and a strict Calvinist, in recording the same assembly writes that the Devil "adventured to give them the communion or holy sacrament, the bread was like wafers, the drink was sometimes blood, sometimes black moss-water. He preached, and most blasphemously." The villain warlock was identified as Mr. Gideon Penman, who had served the parish of Crichton, some six miles from Dalkeith. He was a man of notoriously defamed and dissolute life, and one who stood high in favour with the devil, by whom he was spoken of as "Mr. Gideon, my chaplain".

Upon the great outbreak of witchcraft in Salem Village, now Danvers, New England, in 1692, "on the 31st of March there was a Public Fast kept at Salem. And Abigail Williams said that the Witches had a *Sacrament* that day at an house in the Village, and that they had *Red Bread* and *Red Drink*. Mary Lewis said, they did eat *Red Bread*, like *Man's Flesh*, and would have had her eat some, but she would not; and said, *I will not Eat, I will not Drink, it is Blood. That is not the Bread of Life; that is not the Water of Life; Christ gives the Bread of Life; I will have none of it!*"

Richard Carrier affirmed to the jury that he saw Mr. George Burroughs at the witch meeting at the village, and saw him administer the sacrament. Mary Lacy affirmed that Mr. George Burroughs was at the witch meetings with witch sacraments. Deliverance Hobbs confessed that she was at a witch meeting at Salem Village. And the said Mr. George Burroughs preached to them, and such a Woman was their Deacon, and there they had a Sacrament. At the trial of Martha Carrier, Mary Lacy testified that she knew the prisoner to be a witch, and to have been at a Diabolical Sacrament.

Mr. George Burroughs had for several years been Pastor at Salem Village, but in 1692 he was a pastor at Wells, Maine. There can be no doubt that he was the Grand Master of the Salem covens. Being found guilty of witchcraft, he was executed on 19 August, 1692.

Throughout the eighteenth century, in spite of the superficial and surface materialism, occult practices and the darker superstitions were rampant amongst all classes of society. More often than not the debauchery of the bucks and bloods, the Mohocks and the Sons of Midnight, the Blasters and Bumpers and Banditti, was demoniacal in the highest degree, their convivial meetings hardly to be distinguished from a sabbat orgy.

There were supernaturalistic impostors of every sort and kind—visionaries, mock mystics, pseudo-prophets, semi-sorcerers, "white" witches, figure-casters, horoscopers, magnetizers, quack healers, convulsionaries, fortune-tellers, canting astrologers, initiates, sibyllas—in fact London and the whole countryside seethed with the cheats and corruptions of these Katerfeltos and Saganas.

In his popular comedy of contemporary life *The Recruiting Officer*, originally given at Drury Lane in April, 1706, Farquhar in quite an ordinary way introduces a scene showing us the sanctum of a Cunning Man—he is a humbug, but his dupes are unaware of that—to whom flock men and women of all classes. In May, 1709, D'Urfey produced at Drury Lane *The Modern Prophets* to expose the frauds and follies of a knot of crazy fanatics, the Camisards, who were making a great noise in the town. In 1726 Mary Tofts, of Godalming, in Surrey, attracted extraordinary attention by pretending that she was delivered of rabbits. The credulous, and even wiser heads, espoused her cause and were loud in their advertisement of this phenomenon. The thing was so talked of and discussed that George I at length sent down one of the royal physicians, Sir Richard Manningham, to examine into so curious a matter, and the cheat was ultimately detected. Hogarth has depicted the lady in all the pangs of labour in his *Credulity, Superstition, and Fanaticism* (1762), an adaptation of his previous design *Enthusiasm Delineated*. To Hogarth also is generally attributed the contemporary satirical print, *Cunicularii, or The Wise Men of Godliman in Consultation* (1726).

And so for more than a hundred years. At the end of the century James Hallett, the Chichester "white" witch and "Curer of all Diseases", has an enormous clientèle. In 1795–1797 he is scattering his handbills far and wide, claiming to be a panaceist, an all-healer. He was consulted by hundreds at his New House, three doors from the Waggon and Lamb, West Gate, Chichester. Special appointments were also given at No. 8 Halfway-House. He was, moreover, ready to wait upon Ladies and Gentlemen "at their own Houses, on the shortest notice". He was reputed to excel in casting Nativities "for the Cure of Witchcraft and other Diseases that are hard to be cured". In fact Hallett differed little, if anything, from the notorious conjurers of the reign of James I. Dr. Simon Reade, of Southwark, who in 1608 received the royal pardon for magical practices and the invocation of unclean spirits; Dr. Simon Forman, of Lambeth, who openly professed warlock arts and was a great favourite with the Court ladies; Dr. John Lambe, an infamous necromancer and much-sought-after vendor of noxious drugs; not to mention the female witch Mrs. Mary Woods, who entertained a familiar spirit, and—although she escaped scot free—was deeply implicated in the plot of the Countess of Essex to poison the Earl.

When such men as James Hallett were openly proclaiming their Ephesian trade and bedevilments one cannot be surprised to find that a serious writer—if in some respects mistaken—addressed in 1821 *Antipas; A Solemn Appeal to the Right Reverend the Archbishops and Bishops of the United Churches of England and Ireland; with reference to Several Bills Passed, or Passing through the Imperial Parliament; especially that concerning Witchcraft and Sorcery.* In very earnest terms he urges that all "defenders of the true faith will be called to contend, even against the 'Ruler of the darkness of this world'; and he has another instrument of assault (the most dangerous, because the least suspected) which a Christian soldier must be prepared to resist, not by weapons of modern philosophy, or modern policy, but by putting on the whole armour of God". "This instrument, my Lords," he continues in his eloquent pleading to the Episcopate, "is Sorcery or Witchcraft. Under the term is comprehended 'all kind of influence' produced by collusion with Satan; all persons who have dealings with Satan, if not actually entered into formal compact with him. That such persons are among men, is abundantly plain from Scripture; and that such practices have been used in all remarkable periods of the Church is testified by the same authority. The Prophets and Evangelists positively declare that such persons will be most numerous and successful in their delusions in the latter days. This sin has ever been marked by the most signal vengeance of Almighty God in the case of individuals; and the permission or encouragement thereof, on the part of governments, has been uniformly followed by national judgements."

The writer then proceeds to quote a number of passages from the Bible, all of which most amply and emphatically bear out his argument. He continues: "Other instances might be adduced; but it may be sufficient to prove from Scripture, that the practice of Witchcraft is the certain mark of a people abandoned to confusion, and popular tumult; and *the permission of it in a government, the positive mark of infatuation.*"

"This abominable delusion of Satan," he truly says, "practised in the first age of the Christian Era, will be prevalent in the last. Witchcraft is expressly . . . classed with other crimes already predominant in *these* latter times—'Adultery, sedition, heresy, and such like' (*Gal.* v, 19-21). All Witchcraft and Sorcery is worship offered to Satan."

The diabolical Societies in which the young Whig lords banded themselves together for the worship of Satan amid every circumstance of profligacy and blasphemy were generically known as "hell-fire clubs". As early as the reign of Queen Anne (1710) Ned Ward tells us that such a club forgathered at a vile tavern in Westminster. By 1721 these abominations had grown to such a height that King George I by an Order in Council, commanded that instant action should be taken for the suppression of these "horrid Impieties". The members of these clubs meet, said the *Gazette*, 29 April, 1721, "and in the most impious and blasphemous Manner, insult the most sacred Principles of our Holy Religion, affront Almighty God Himself", wherefore the King was "resolved to make use of all the Authority committed to him by Almighty God, to punish such enormous Offenders, and to crush such shocking Impieties before they increase and draw down the Vengeance of God upon this Nation". Further discoveries were made. Forty persons belonged to the Hell-Fire Club, which had various rendezvous at Somerset House, in the Strand, at a house in Westminster, and at another house in the fashionable Conduit Street, near Hanover Square. A broadside entitled *A Further and Particular Account of the Hell-Fire Sulphur-Society Clubs* supplies the most shocking details. The President was dubbed King of Hell, and it was common knowledge that the President was Philip, Lord Wharton. A resounding scandal ensued. The writer of this broadside is of opinion that these infamies were largely due to "the Impieties of the late French Prophets", the villains whom D'Urfey exposed in his satirical comedy. Mrs. Delany in her *Autobiography* relates how Dr. Friend, the famous Jacobite physician, told some young persons that he had been present at the fearful deathbed of a Mr. Howe, who had been a member· of this horrible society. The unhappy wretch in the throes of dissolution screamed out with terrific imprecations that he was lost eternally.

Only eight years later, *Hell Upon Earth: Or, The Town in an Uproar*, draws a hideous picture of a Satanic sodality which met in a subterranean cellar. The members for the sake of "wealth and wit" each one made a secret but overt and formal pact with the demon.

In Ireland one of the vilest and most notorious of these demoniac Societies was the Blasters, whose chief officer the authorities discovered to be Peter Lens, a miniature painter, and a professed Satanist, who openly declared himself a votary of the Devil, whose health he had publicly drunk with such horrid execrations as appalled the Select Committee of the Irish House of Lords, which sat to inquire into these flagrant impieti s. A number of persons were examined under oath concerning the dark doings of these "loose and disorderly" reprobates, but Lens seems to have escaped punishment by absconding and swiftly crossing over to England. Profoundly moved and cut to the very heart, Bishop Berkeley penned a trenchant and timely censure upon the *Enormous License and Irreligion of the Times*, in which he emphasized that the blasphemies of the Blasters were no ordinary profanities or oaths uttered in the debauch of drink or the heat of passion, but a studied, deliberate, and public worship of the devil.

There exists, in storage in the National Gallery of Ireland, Dublin, a large canvas painted by James Worsdale between 1735–1738 depicting five prominent members, men of the foulest character, of "The Dublin Hell-Fire Club". This abominable fraternity was founded by Richard Parsons, first Earl of Rosse, who for some reason does not appear in the picture. The Eagle Tavern on Cork Hill was a frequent meeting-place of these diabolists, but the favourite scene of their iniquities was a hunting-lodge on Mount Pelier, near Rathfarnham, which is seven miles south-west of Dublin. This sequestered and out-of-the-way spot was an odd choice for a building. Erected in the 1720s by the Speaker of the House of Commons, William Conolly, and soon deserted by him, it was popularly known as Conolly's Folly. The ground was ill-omened. It had been badly famed as a rendezvous of sorcerers for many a long year past. Even today it is avoided, and many a dark story is still current of strange eerie happenings in this horribly haunted place. The lodge itself is now a mere ruin, hideous, gaping, and bare, but I think that even so those who have visited it must be conscious of the aura of concentrated evil.

Here, then, the Hell-Fire Club was wont to meet. It is recorded that during these orgies there were actually diabolic manifestations, and familiars materialized. It is said that the seat of the vice-chairman was always left empty, and on occasion it was seen to be occupied by a dark shadowy impalpable figure with red fiery eyes.

This "Damnable Cabal", as it was aptly termed, continued—being carried on by new recruits into the infernal society—for more than fifty years. Indeed, there is evidence that about 1770 a black mass was celebrated at the Lodge. In 1779, when Austin Cooper, the antiquary, visited the place he found it in a ruinous condition, but it is believed that during one of the sabbats, not long before, the building had caught fire and was badly damaged. It was said in bitter jest that the votaries of Satan must have deliberately ignited the pile to acclimatize themselves to the eternal furnace, the hell of which they stood in such imminent jeopardy. A wicked sally, but perchance perilously true. At any rate, one is not surprised that even yet the phantoms of the wretched men who revelled there are reported to be doomed and bound to the earthly scene of their devilish crimes, and the spectre of Colonel John St. Leger, not the least infamous of this warlock junto, rides abroad (so folk say) at dark midnight in a coach of flame, whose driver, postilions, and coal-black steeds are all headless, a horrible portent of bale.

In the history of hauntings the phantom coach is a well-known phenomenon, and one generally considered abnormally evil, being connected with demonolatry in some form. It was reported that, after their execution in 1670, that most flagitious warlock Major Thomas Weir and his sister Jean, a terrible harridan, were seen—two hideous shadows—to issue from their house in the Bow Head, Edinburgh, and mount into a hearse-like carriage drawn by sable horses without heads which galloped off in a whirlwind of flame amid piercing shrieks and unearthly howling. Legend has it that Anne Boleyn, the witch, on certain nights of the year, is still driven at a furious pace in a funeral coach drawn by six black horses up the long avenue of Hever Castle. In Westmorland it is believed by many that the rumble of the spectral coach of "the bad Lord Lonsdale" of Lowther Hall is to be heard as it flies across the country behind a team of six jetty phookas whose cloven hoofs are shod with fire. I know of an old château in Normandy the approach to which, a half-mile beneath an avenue of trees, is troubled in much the same way.

As in Ireland, so in Scotland, there were impious clubs. Robert Chambers, the antiquary, in his *Traditions of Edinburgh*, 1824, tells how he had talked with grave elderly people who knew the "last worn-out members of such clubs", miserable wretches who, remorseful and repentant, confessed they had once made pacts with Satan. Chambers was credibly assured that many of the clubs or covens were affiliated to the London and Irish fraternities of evil, and that at one time a high official in these devilries used to travel round and visit each cell or centre to "propagate their vile wickedness". This demonist fell into a deep melancholy and, reflecting upon the horror of his position, went mad, and died raving. The Scotti h clubs had various secret rendezvous in Edinburgh : Allan's Close, Halkerston's Wynd—a wynd is a narrow side-street or passage —and Carrider's Close. The principal scene of their sabbat orgies was in Jack's Close, Canongate. These foul mysteries were celebrated under conditions of almost impenetrable secrecy, and neophytes were obliged to submit to tests of a most horrible and obscene nature before being admitted.

Unfortunately satanism was practised in the two Universities. As early as 1727 reference is made to a Hell-Fire Club at Oxford. Eighteen years later there was a shocking scandal when that notoriously morbid profligate, George Selwyn, was sent down with public ignominy from Hertford College for assisting at the celebration of a mock-communion in a tavern near St. Martin's Church, in High Street. He had mingled the blood from his arm with the contents of the chalice, a piece of witchcraft recalling the infamous eucharist of l'abbé Guibourg in the Palladian chapel of the rue Beauregard.

In spite of the watchfulness of the proctors and other authorities, such is the cunning of diabolism, the foul tradition continued. In the year 1829 a "Hell-Fire Club", consisting of undergraduate members, assembled twice weekly, generally in the rooms of the President in Brasenose College. This College on the north side is bounded by the narrow passage, known as Brasenose Lane, and this connects with Turl Street, the Square wherein stand the Radcliffe Camera and the main entrance of Brasenose, directly facing All Souls. As one goes down towards the Square from the Turl, on the left-hand side is the high garden wall of Exeter; upon the right, the north portion of Lincoln College, which adjoins Brasenose. The windows of Brasenose which give upon the Lane are of a narrow Jacobean order, heavily barred and protected by horizontal as well as perpendicular stanchions. The lower casements, moreover, being nearly on a level with the causeway, are yet further secured by a stoutly meshed wire netting.

One December midnight in 1829 the Rev. T. T. Churton, a Fellow and Tutor of Brasenose, was returning to his rooms, and having crossed out of the Turl had got more than half-way down the Lane, when he saw a tall person, draped in a long black cloak and wearing a large broad-brimmed sombrero pulled down over his face, apparently helping someone to make his exit by means of the window. Most of the rooms were curtained and in darkness, but from this particular corner there streamed a brilliant light. He at once hurried forward to prevent so flagrant a breach of the College regulations, since this room belonged to a wealthy undergraduate, who was strongly suspected of being one of the leading spirits in the Hell-Fire Club. As he advanced he was conscious that a violent struggle was in progress, and that the undergraduate, whose features, distorted with an agonizing spasm of the most ghastly fear, he clearly recognized, was being literally forced through the bars by the superior strength of the mysterious stranger. For a second Dr. Churton caught a glimpse of the latter's countenace, which was so demoniacal and unearthly, so hideous and terrible, that he realized the creature was none other than a fiend of the nether pit. Years after he declared that these appalling lineaments would for ever remain horribly stamped upon his memory. Uttering a prayer for help and strength, he managed to rush past and gained the College gates, upon which he knocked frantically. As the porter opened the door, he collapsed in a deep swoon. At the same moment, with loud cries of wildest alarm and dismay, there trooped out from the rooms immediately to the right of the porter's lodge a crowd of men—the members of the notorious Hell-Fire Club. In the midst of a speech of more than ordinary profanity, with a terrific imprecation upon his lips, the President, who was indeed the owner of these rooms, had fallen dead, and was lying there a convulsed and blackened corpse.

What Dr. Churton had seen was more than sufficiently clear. It may be remembered that the grave Tertullian, in his Fifth Book (Chapter xv), *Against Marcion*, gives it as his opinion that "The soul has a kind of body of a quality peculiar to itself".

The Hell-Fire Club in question never met again. Early in the present century, in 1912, there was, however, a Hell-Fire Club in Oxford, and in 1930 witchcraft and necromancy were being clandestinely practised in the University. It would appear that the evil traditions of Satanism persisted and were handed on, unbroken, from generation to generation of undergraduates. (In 1934 a Hell-Fire Club was meeting in London.) Not many years previously a black mass was celebrated abominably in the ruins of Godstow Nunnery, and it was with difficulty that an open scandal was averted. In more than one village churchyard near Oxford the necromancies of Kelley and Paul Waring have been essayed.

Much the same tale might be told of Cambridge, where, it will be remembered, a number of witches were examined by Dr. Henry More, the famous seventeenth-century Platonizing divine and metaphysician. But it were tedious to repeat these histories of undergraduate warlockry and impieties.

Of all these profligate and satanical fraternities, that coven which has left the most infamous and enduring name is no doubt the sodality known as "The Monks of Medmenham".

Sir Francis Dashwood, Lord Le Despenser, the "Founder and Father" of the Monks, born in 1708, at the age of sixteen inherited vast wealth and estates, including the fair domain of West Wycombe, where his father had built himself a great country house. But the son was by no means content with mere old-fashioned architecture of Vanbrugh's school, however overloaded and grandiose, and he proceeded to turn West Wycombe Park into a mansion, which, even in those days of immense ostentation, ran riot superfluent in a profusion of protuberant porticoes and colonnades, pœciles, loggias, and peristyles, without, all "in the Grecian gusto"; within, most sumptuously Italian, elaborately frescoed, with gaily painted ceilings of amorous foreshortened heroes and gods and goddesses. Gossip has it, be the truth as it may, that of the many gorgeous rooms some few are discreetly kept locked owing to the priapean nature of the decorations and the extraordinary objects of virtu Dashwood collected in his more private cabinets and vitrines.

Only a few miles from West Wycombe Park were the ancient ruins of Medmenham Abbey, an early Cistercian foundation, which, despoliated and desecrate, in the reign of Queen Elizabeth had been purchased from the Crown by the Duffield family, and more or less converted into a dwelling-house or small manor. In 1752 Medmenham was owned by Francis Duffield, a handsome, limber youth who is described as being "of affable disposition, having large dark blue eyes" (A. H. Plaisted, *The Manor and Parish Records of Medmenham*). Unhappily, he had fallen under the evil influence of Dashwood, and became his devoted acolyte.

As early as 1725, when he was but seventeen, Sir Francis Dashwood was known to be a member of a Hell-Fire Club, which met for their lewd orgies in a secret cellar. It was in this same Society that the libertine and "universally hated" Lord Sandwich cut so prominent and foul a figure, an enormous profligate, whose life, according to Lord Chesterfield, most lenient and easy-going of observers, was "one uniform, unblushing course of debauchery and dissipation" from his very teens.

Sir Francis Dashwood, so rumour ran, whilst on the Grand Tour, his first Continental travels, had been initiated into the diabolic cult by a master cabbalist at Venice. Certain it is that he brought back with him from France and Italy a number of grimoires and magical manuals of the most hideous impiety, which could have been obtained in no ordinary way.

To a satanist, such as he, the foundation of a demoniacal fraternity and the celebration of their goetic ritual in the actual sanctuary where once the Holy Sacrifice had been offered day by day and cowled monks had knelt in penance and in prayer gave something of an extra and exquisite titillation of wickedness he hardly hoped to indulge and enjoy.

In 1752–1753 Medmenham Abbey was rented on a long lease from the Duffields, elaborate alterations were made at great expense, and "the Friars of St. Francis", as they were mockingly dubbed, the Brotherhood, were enrolled, Frank Duffield being one of the first novices.

Exactly what these alterations were can well be imagined, and indeed we have contemporary descriptions of the interior of the Abbey. There was a richly ornate withdrawing-room with long lounging sofas covered with green silk damask; a remarkable refectory, for "the cellars were stored with the choicest wines, the larders with the delicacies of every climate"; a library, whose shelves were amply supplied with pornographic volumes and obscene engravings; a number of small, but luxuriously appointed, *cells* or bedchambers for the "friars", "fitted up for all the purposes of lasciviousness, for which proper objects were also provided. As one walked down the corridors spintrian pictures met the eye, paintings of consummate art but of the rankest lubricity. In fine, "there was not a vice for practising which he [Sir Francis] did not make provision".

"Thus far," as Charles Johnstone aptly observes, "the ridicule, however criminal in itself, may seem to have been designed only against those societies of human institution", but the main object was "to attack the very essentials of Religion, acknowledged by every serious person to be divine". The chapel, the secret shrine of the "Friars", was the Sanctum Sanctorum of satanism. This no one was allowed to enter save the Superiors, the inner circle of the elect. "The decorations," Walpole drily observes, "may well be supposed to have contained the quintessence of their mysteries, since it was impenetrable to any but the initiated." That the visitors to Medmenham, and indeed many members of this infamous Society, were lecherous rakehells who assembled for the practice of unbridled lewdness is, of course, a fact beyond question, but it is also certain that among the vile there were viler still, "the elect", or in plain words satanists, devoted to the worship of the fiend.

In the chapel there was an apsidal sanctuary, balustraded with elaborately carved altar-rails, within which upon the foot-pace stood the altar with its candlesticks and furniture, equipped for the celebration of the eucharist of hell. One night the chapel was solemnly dedicated to Satan, in hideous mockery of the Consecration of a Church.

Chiefest among those who formed this "inner group", presided over by "Prior Sir Francis" himself, were young Francis Duffield; Lord Sandwich; "Old Paul" Whitehead, a notorious libertine and something of a satirical poet; George Selwyn, charnelly decadent and debauched; Thomas Potter, a vicious hard cynical wit, to whom with some reason has been assigned that pornographic and profane piece *An Essay on Woman*, with which the name of John Wilkes is so intimately and inextricably connected. Nor without reason, for even if Wilkes himself did not write the wretched thing—"a most scandalous, obscene and impious libel . . . most wicked and blasphemous" the House of Lords justly enough termed it—without a doubt he "enlarged the sketch", and it was he who was responsible for having the type set up and correcting the proofs, although only a dozen copies were intended to have been struck off to be distributed among his cronies, the Friars of Medmenham.

It was to Wilkes, in fact, that the dissolution of the Medmenham sodality was mainly due. It has been truly said that "the Brotherhood of St. Francis, like the Roman Empire, decayed from within", but the disbanding was helped on and hastened from without. "Politics," says Horace Walpole, "no sooner infused themselves amongst these rosy anchorites, than dissensions were kindled, and a false brother [John Wilkes] arose, who divulged the arcana, and exposed the good Prior." Not only were there internecine disputes, but fierce quarrels in the parliamentary arena, when Lord Sandwich in the House of Lords was impeaching Wilkes for blasphemy. The pot calling the kettle black.

At the last meeting of the Friars in June, 1762, only half a dozen members assembled. Not only scandal but indignation was being popularly bruited. The tale of profligacy might be told, but the tale of satanism must not be so much as whispered, cost what it may. Lampoons and caricatures were appearing. One print, entitled *Secrets of the Convent*, seemed to aim perilously near the truth. The diabolical chapel was stripped of its contents, which were hidden away at West Wycombe Park. Books, paintings, furniture followed.

Medmenham Abbey was deserted. Only a twelvemonth after the final rendezvous of the brethren, in 1763, Horace Walpole found the place "very ruinous and bad". Long before the end of the eighteenth century not a vestige of the Sanctum Sanctorum, the mysterious chapel, was left, and then, having been sold in 1777 by Francis Duffield, the Abbey was leased to quite poor folk, who were eager to earn vails from parties of sightseers by showing them the rooms where the Friars had revelled and roared and raked. An extra tip would elicit melodramatic stories of ghosts and imps and devilkins and bugaboos. Picknickers crowded the sloping lawns on hot summer afternoons.

A friend of Wilkes, John Hall Stevenson, the Eugenius of *Tristram Shandy*, the owner of Skelton Castle, near Saltburn, Yorkshire, which he dubbed Crazy Castle, founded a Club, the Demoniacs, which was, perhaps, in some way suggested by the tales he heard of Medmenham convivialities. Today the Demoniacs are remembered through their connexion with Laurence Sterne, but the society seems to have been misnomered. Hall Stevenson was an eccentric whimsical fellow, not without a streak of something very like genius, and Sterne was always his very welcome guest. The other members were Yorkshire neighbours, a hearty coarse bacchanalian crowd, generally speaking, although some were men of parts, and their conversations have been described as full of Attic salt. They were full of English bawdy as well. But the company were not diabolists, and save for their name there was nothing demoniacal about them.

The excursions into occultism of William Beckford were far more refined, and far more serious. It is not surprising that the author of *Vathek* should have been especially interested in Oriental magic, and it is extremely significant that in his early letters to Alexander Cozens we find references to "cabbalistic mirrors wherein Futurity is unveiled", "the Central Fire", and other mysteries. It was Cozens, in the first place, who inspired Beckford with a passion for Persian and Arabic studies, an exoticism upon which his tutor and guardians frowned formidably. Of Cozens' own letters to Beckford, which would doubtless have been very enlightening, nothing remains. But nobody seems to have been aware how powerful was the influence in Beckford's youth of this Anglo-Russian, a fantastic and elusive figure. That black masses were celebrated at Fonthill in December, 1781, and perhaps on other occasions, seems certain. Beckford, moreover, was an ardent collector of grimoires and demonology. In his study, *Beckford* (p. 104), Mr. Guy Chapman says: "Among the items at the famous Beckford Library Sale of 1882-4, there was sold a copy of a book by L. Paulini, in which the late owner had written: 'A book of singular rarity and particularly amusing to amateurs of witchcraft and devildom in general. *Experto crede.*'" The book in question was written by Laurentius Paulinus, Bishop of Strengnäs, and afterwards Archbishop of Upsala. Entitled *Commonefactio de angelicis et pythonicis adparitionibus* (*A Grave and Moral Discourse upon the Appearances of Good and of Evil Spirits*), it was printed at Strengnäs in 1630, having been delivered as a lecture or sermon there on 3 September, 1629. A second edition was published at Upsala in 1646. Beckford assuredly carried his researches into the dark sciences much further than good Archbishop Paulinus would have allowed or approved.

It has been remarked that the black masses of Gilles de Rais at Tiffauges and Machecoul, masses said by the young Florentine sorcerer priest, Francesco Prelati; as also the masses said by the Abbé Cotton, by the Abbé Lemaignan, and by the Abbé Guibourg over the naked body of Madame de Montespan, were murderous as well as sacrilege, but whatever the black mass of the modern Satanist lacks in blood it amply makes up in blasphemy and bestial rut.

Yet, if what is whispered be true, and there seems strong confirmation enough, the shedding of blood is not unknown among the devil-worshippers today in London; in Brighton and Birmingham; in Oxford and Cambridge; in Edinburgh and Glasgow, and in a hundred cities more of the British Isles.

"Certain London cults practise the black mass, where black bread, black wine, and black candles are used, worshippers confess every good deed as a sin, and do penance."—The *Daily Mail*, 14 April, 1934. (The penance being erotic flagellation).

Witchcraft—black magic—Satanism, call it by what name they will, for it is all one, the cult of the Devil is the most terrible power at work in the world today.

Lady Peirse has truly written: "They may call it psychism or occultism; they may learn to cast curses or spells; they may invoke the help of the powers of evil, but it is practically the same thing, and its lure to mankind is as old and mysterious as the wind that blows over the earth, urging them with strange elusive thrills to recapture and use the old powers of the Serpent."

England has repealed the laws against witchcraft.

The Divine Law she cannot repeal. "Thou shalt not suffer a Witch to live."

THE END

INDEX

A CATALOG OF SELECTED
DOVER BOOKS
IN ALL FIELDS OF INTEREST

A CATALOG OF SELECTED DOVER
BOOKS IN ALL FIELDS OF INTEREST

CONCERNING THE SPIRITUAL IN ART, Wassily Kandinsky. Pioneering work by father of abstract art. Thoughts on color theory, nature of art. Analysis of earlier masters. 12 illustrations. 80pp. of text. 5⅜ x 8½. 23411-8 Pa. $4.95

ANIMALS: 1,419 Copyright-Free Illustrations of Mammals, Birds, Fish, Insects, etc., Jim Harter (ed.). Clear wood engravings present, in extremely lifelike poses, over 1,000 species of animals. One of the most extensive pictorial sourcebooks of its kind. Captions. Index. 284pp. 9 x 12. 23766-4 Pa. $14.95

CELTIC ART: The Methods of Construction, George Bain. Simple geometric techniques for making Celtic interlacements, spirals, Kells-type initials, animals, humans, etc. Over 500 illustrations. 160pp. 9 x 12. (USO) 22923-8 Pa. $9.95

AN ATLAS OF ANATOMY FOR ARTISTS, Fritz Schider. Most thorough reference work on art anatomy in the world. Hundreds of illustrations, including selections from works by Vesalius, Leonardo, Goya, Ingres, Michelangelo, others. 593 illustrations. 192pp. 7⅛ x 10¼. 20241-0 Pa. $9.95

CELTIC HAND STROKE-BY-STROKE (Irish Half-Uncial from "The Book of Kells"): An Arthur Baker Calligraphy Manual, Arthur Baker. Complete guide to creating each letter of the alphabet in distinctive Celtic manner. Covers hand position, strokes, pens, inks, paper, more. Illustrated. 48pp. 8¼ x 11. 24336-2 Pa. $3.95

EASY ORIGAMI, John Montroll. Charming collection of 32 projects (hat, cup, pelican, piano, swan, many more) specially designed for the novice origami hobbyist. Clearly illustrated easy-to-follow instructions insure that even beginning papercrafters will achieve successful results. 48pp. 8¼ x 11. 27298-2 Pa. $3.50

THE COMPLETE BOOK OF BIRDHOUSE CONSTRUCTION FOR WOODWORKERS, Scott D. Campbell. Detailed instructions, illustrations, tables. Also data on bird habitat and instinct patterns. Bibliography. 3 tables. 63 illustrations in 15 figures. 48pp. 5¼ x 8½. 24407-5 Pa. $2.50

BLOOMINGDALE'S ILLUSTRATED 1886 CATALOG: Fashions, Dry Goods and Housewares, Bloomingdale Brothers. Famed merchants' extremely rare catalog depicting about 1,700 products: clothing, housewares, firearms, dry goods, jewelry, more. Invaluable for dating, identifying vintage items. Also, copyright-free graphics for artists, designers. Co-published with Henry Ford Museum & Greenfield Village. 160pp. 8¼ x 11. 25780-0 Pa. $10.95

HISTORIC COSTUME IN PICTURES, Braun & Schneider. Over 1,450 costumed figures in clearly detailed engravings–from dawn of civilization to end of 19th century. Captions. Many folk costumes. 256pp. 8⅜ x 11¾. 23150-X Pa. $12.95

CATALOG OF DOVER BOOKS

FRANK LLOYD WRIGHT'S HOLLYHOCK HOUSE, Donald Hoffmann. Lavishly illustrated, carefully documented study of one of Wright's most controversial residential designs. Over 120 photographs, floor plans, elevations, etc. Detailed perceptive text by noted Wright scholar. Index. 128pp. 9¼ x 10¾. 27133-1 Pa. $11.95

THE MALE AND FEMALE FIGURE IN MOTION: 60 Classic Photographic Sequences, Eadweard Muybridge. 60 true-action photographs of men and women walking, running, climbing, bending, turning, etc., reproduced from rare 19th-century masterpiece. vi + 121pp. 9 x 12. 24745-7 Pa. $10.95

1001 QUESTIONS ANSWERED ABOUT THE SEASHORE, N. J. Berrill and Jacquelyn Berrill. Queries answered about dolphins, sea snails, sponges, starfish, fishes, shore birds, many others. Covers appearance, breeding, growth, feeding, much more. 305pp. 5¼ x 8¼. 23366-9 Pa. $9.95

GUIDE TO OWL WATCHING IN NORTH AMERICA, Donald S. Heintzelman. Superb guide offers complete data and descriptions of 19 species: barn owl, screech owl, snowy owl, many more. Expert coverage of owl-watching equipment, conservation, migrations and invasions, etc. Guide to observing sites. 84 illustrations. xiii + 193pp. 5⅜ x 8½. 27344-X Pa. $8.95

MEDICINAL AND OTHER USES OF NORTH AMERICAN PLANTS: A Historical Survey with Special Reference to the Eastern Indian Tribes, Charlotte Erichsen-Brown. Chronological historical citations document 500 years of usage of plants, trees, shrubs native to eastern Canada, northeastern U.S. Also complete identifying information. 343 illustrations. 544pp. 6½ x 9¼. 25951-X Pa. $12.95

STORYBOOK MAZES, Dave Phillips. 23 stories and mazes on two-page spreads: Wizard of Oz, Treasure Island, Robin Hood, etc. Solutions. 64pp. 8¼ x 11. 23628-5 Pa. $2.95

NEGRO FOLK MUSIC, U.S.A., Harold Courlander. Noted folklorist's scholarly yet readable analysis of rich and varied musical tradition. Includes authentic versions of over 40 folk songs. Valuable bibliography and discography. xi + 324pp. 5⅜ x 8½. 27350-4 Pa. $9.95

MOVIE-STAR PORTRAITS OF THE FORTIES, John Kobal (ed.). 163 glamor, studio photos of 106 stars of the 1940s: Rita Hayworth, Ava Gardner, Marlon Brando, Clark Gable, many more. 176pp. 8⅜ x 11¼. 23546-7 Pa. $14.95

BENCHLEY LOST AND FOUND, Robert Benchley. Finest humor from early 30s, about pet peeves, child psychologists, post office and others. Mostly unavailable elsewhere. 73 illustrations by Peter Arno and others. 183pp. 5⅜ x 8½. 22410-4 Pa. $6.95

YEKL and THE IMPORTED BRIDEGROOM AND OTHER STORIES OF YIDDISH NEW YORK, Abraham Cahan. Film Hester Street based on Yekl (1896). Novel, other stories among first about Jewish immigrants on N.Y.'s East Side. 240pp. 5⅜ x 8½. 22427-9 Pa. $6.95

SELECTED POEMS, Walt Whitman. Generous sampling from *Leaves of Grass.* Twenty-four poems include "I Hear America Singing," "Song of the Open Road," "I Sing the Body Electric," "When Lilacs Last in the Dooryard Bloom'd," "O Captain! My Captain!"—all reprinted from an authoritative edition. Lists of titles and first lines. 128pp. 5³⁄₁₆ x 8¼. 26878-0 Pa. $1.00

THE BEST TALES OF HOFFMANN, E. T. A. Hoffmann. 10 of Hoffmann's most important stories: "Nutcracker and the King of Mice," "The Golden Flowerpot," etc. 458pp. 5⅜ x 8½. 21793-0 Pa. $9.95

FROM FETISH TO GOD IN ANCIENT EGYPT, E. A. Wallis Budge. Rich detailed survey of Egyptian conception of "God" and gods, magic, cult of animals, Osiris, more. Also, superb English translations of hymns and legends. 240 illustrations. 545pp. 5⅜ x 8½. 25803-3 Pa. $13.95

FRENCH STORIES/CONTES FRANÇAIS: A Dual-Language Book, Wallace Fowlie. Ten stories by French masters, Voltaire to Camus: "Micromegas" by Voltaire; "The Atheist's Mass" by Balzac; "Minuet" by de Maupassant; "The Guest" by Camus, six more. Excellent English translations on facing pages. Also French-English vocabulary list, exercises, more. 352pp. 5⅜ x 8½. 26443-2 Pa. $9.95

CHICAGO AT THE TURN OF THE CENTURY IN PHOTOGRAPHS: 122 Historic Views from the Collections of the Chicago Historical Society, Larry A. Viskochil. Rare large-format prints offer detailed views of City Hall, State Street, the Loop, Hull House, Union Station, many other landmarks, circa 1904-1913. Introduction. Captions. Maps. 144pp. 9⅜ x 12¼. 24656-6 Pa. $12.95

OLD BROOKLYN IN EARLY PHOTOGRAPHS, 1865-1929, William Lee Younger. Luna Park, Gravesend race track, construction of Grand Army Plaza, moving of Hotel Brighton, etc. 157 previously unpublished photographs. 165pp. 8⅞ x 11¾. 23587-4 Pa. $13.95

THE MYTHS OF THE NORTH AMERICAN INDIANS, Lewis Spence. Rich anthology of the myths and legends of the Algonquins, Iroquois, Pawnees and Sioux, prefaced by an extensive historical and ethnological commentary. 36 illustrations. 480pp. 5⅜ x 8½. 25967-6 Pa. $10.95

AN ENCYCLOPEDIA OF BATTLES: Accounts of Over 1,560 Battles from 1479 B.C. to the Present, David Eggenberger. Essential details of every major battle in recorded history from the first battle of Megiddo in 1479 B.C. to Grenada in 1984. List of Battle Maps. New Appendix covering the years 1967-1984. Index. 99 illustrations. 544pp. 6½ x 9¼. 24913-1 Pa. $16.95

SAILING ALONE AROUND THE WORLD, Captain Joshua Slocum. First man to sail around the world, alone, in small boat. One of great feats of seamanship told in delightful manner. 67 illustrations. 294pp. 5⅜ x 8½. 20326-3 Pa. $6.95

ANARCHISM AND OTHER ESSAYS, Emma Goldman. Powerful, penetrating, prophetic essays on direct action, role of minorities, prison reform, puritan hypocrisy, violence, etc. 271pp. 5⅜ x 8½. 22484-8 Pa. $7.95

MYTHS OF THE HINDUS AND BUDDHISTS, Ananda K. Coomaraswamy and Sister Nivedita. Great stories of the epics; deeds of Krishna, Shiva, taken from puranas, Vedas, folk tales; etc. 32 illustrations. 400pp. 5⅜ x 8½. 21759-0 Pa. $12.95

BEYOND PSYCHOLOGY, Otto Rank. Fear of death, desire of immortality, nature of sexuality, social organization, creativity, according to Rankian system. 291pp. 5⅜ x 8½. 20485-5 Pa. $8.95

A THEOLOGICO-POLITICAL TREATISE, Benedict Spinoza. Also contains unfinished Political Treatise. Great classic on religious liberty, theory of government on common consent. R. Elwes translation. Total of 421pp. 5⅜ x 8½. 20249-6 Pa. $9.95

MY BONDAGE AND MY FREEDOM, Frederick Douglass. Born a slave, Douglass became outspoken force in antislavery movement. The best of Douglass' autobiographies. Graphic description of slave life. 464pp. 5⅜ x 8½. 22457-0 Pa. $8.95

FOLLOWING THE EQUATOR: A Journey Around the World, Mark Twain. Fascinating humorous account of 1897 voyage to Hawaii, Australia, India, New Zealand, etc. Ironic, bemused reports on peoples, customs, climate, flora and fauna, politics, much more. 197 illustrations. 720pp. 5⅜ x 8½. 26113-1 Pa. $15.95

THE PEOPLE CALLED SHAKERS, Edward D. Andrews. Definitive study of Shakers: origins, beliefs, practices, dances, social organization, furniture and crafts, etc. 33 illustrations. 351pp. 5⅜ x 8½. 21081-2 Pa. $8.95

THE MYTHS OF GREECE AND ROME, H. A. Guerber. A classic of mythology, generously illustrated, long prized for its simple, graphic, accurate retelling of the principal myths of Greece and Rome, and for its commentary on their origins and significance. With 64 illustrations by Michelangelo, Raphael, Titian, Rubens, Canova, Bernini and others. 480pp. 5⅜ x 8½. 27584-1 Pa. $9.95

PSYCHOLOGY OF MUSIC, Carl E. Seashore. Classic work discusses music as a medium from psychological viewpoint. Clear treatment of physical acoustics, auditory apparatus, sound perception, development of musical skills, nature of musical feeling, host of other topics. 88 figures. 408pp. 5⅜ x 8½. 21851-1 Pa. $11.95

THE PHILOSOPHY OF HISTORY, Georg W. Hegel. Great classic of Western thought develops concept that history is not chance but rational process, the evolution of freedom. 457pp. 5⅜ x 8½. 20112-0 Pa. $9.95

THE BOOK OF TEA, Kakuzo Okakura. Minor classic of the Orient: entertaining, charming explanation, interpretation of traditional Japanese culture in terms of tea ceremony. 94pp. 5⅜ x 8½. 20070-1 Pa. $3.95

LIFE IN ANCIENT EGYPT, Adolf Erman. Fullest, most thorough, detailed older account with much not in more recent books, domestic life, religion, magic, medicine, commerce, much more. Many illustrations reproduce tomb paintings, carvings, hieroglyphs, etc. 597pp. 5⅜ x 8½. 22632-8 Pa. $12.95

SUNDIALS, Their Theory and Construction, Albert Waugh. Far and away the best, most thorough coverage of ideas, mathematics concerned, types, construction, adjusting anywhere. Simple, nontechnical treatment allows even children to build several of these dials. Over 100 illustrations. 230pp. 5⅜ x 8½. 22947-5 Pa. $8.95

DYNAMICS OF FLUIDS IN POROUS MEDIA, Jacob Bear. For advanced students of ground water hydrology, soil mechanics and physics, drainage and irrigation engineering, and more. 335 illustrations. Exercises, with answers. 784pp. 6⅛ x 9¼. 65675-6 Pa. $19.95

SONGS OF EXPERIENCE: Facsimile Reproduction with 26 Plates in Full Color, William Blake. 26 full-color plates from a rare 1826 edition. Includes "TheTyger," "London," "Holy Thursday," and other poems. Printed text of poems. 48pp. 5¼ x 7. 24636-1 Pa. $4.95

OLD-TIME VIGNETTES IN FULL COLOR, Carol Belanger Grafton (ed.). Over 390 charming, often sentimental illustrations, selected from archives of Victorian graphics—pretty women posing, children playing, food, flowers, kittens and puppies, smiling cherubs, birds and butterflies, much more. All copyright-free. 48pp. 9¼ x 12¼. 27269-9 Pa. $7.95

PERSPECTIVE FOR ARTISTS, Rex Vicat Cole. Depth, perspective of sky and sea, shadows, much more, not usually covered. 391 diagrams, 81 reproductions of drawings and paintings. 279pp. 5⅜ x 8½. 22487-2 Pa. $7.95

DRAWING THE LIVING FIGURE, Joseph Sheppard. Innovative approach to artistic anatomy focuses on specifics of surface anatomy, rather than muscles and bones. Over 170 drawings of live models in front, back and side views, and in widely varying poses. Accompanying diagrams. 177 illustrations. Introduction. Index. 144pp. 8⅜ x11¼. 26723-7 Pa. $8.95

GOTHIC AND OLD ENGLISH ALPHABETS: 100 Complete Fonts, Dan X. Solo. Add power, elegance to posters, signs, other graphics with 100 stunning copyright-free alphabets: Blackstone, Dolbey, Germania, 97 more–including many lower-case, numerals, punctuation marks. 104pp. 8⅛ x 11. 24695-7 Pa. $8.95

HOW TO DO BEADWORK, Mary White. Fundamental book on craft from simple projects to five-bead chains and woven works. 106 illustrations. 142pp. 5⅜ x 8. 20697-1 Pa. $5.95

THE BOOK OF WOOD CARVING, Charles Marshall Sayers. Finest book for beginners discusses fundamentals and offers 34 designs. "Absolutely first rate . . . well thought out and well executed."–E. J. Tangerman. 118pp. 7¾ x 10⅝. 23654-4 Pa. $7.95

ILLUSTRATED CATALOG OF CIVIL WAR MILITARY GOODS: Union Army Weapons, Insignia, Uniform Accessories, and Other Equipment, Schuyler, Hartley, and Graham. Rare, profusely illustrated 1846 catalog includes Union Army uniform and dress regulations, arms and ammunition, coats, insignia, flags, swords, rifles, etc. 226 illustrations. 160pp. 9 x 12. 24939-5 Pa. $10.95

WOMEN'S FASHIONS OF THE EARLY 1900s: An Unabridged Republication of "New York Fashions, 1909," National Cloak & Suit Co. Rare catalog of mail-order fashions documents women's and children's clothing styles shortly after the turn of the century. Captions offer full descriptions, prices. Invaluable resource for fashion, costume historians. Approximately 725 illustrations. 128pp. 8⅜ x 11¼. 27276-1 Pa. $11.95

THE 1912 AND 1915 GUSTAV STICKLEY FURNITURE CATALOGS, Gustav Stickley. With over 200 detailed illustrations and descriptions, these two catalogs are essential reading and reference materials and identification guides for Stickley furniture. Captions cite materials, dimensions and prices. 112pp. 6½ x 9¼. 26676-1 Pa. $9.95

EARLY AMERICAN LOCOMOTIVES, John H. White, Jr. Finest locomotive engravings from early 19th century: historical (1804–74), main-line (after 1870), special, foreign, etc. 147 plates. 142pp. 11⅜ x 8¼. 22772-3 Pa. $10.95

THE TALL SHIPS OF TODAY IN PHOTOGRAPHS, Frank O. Braynard. Lavishly illustrated tribute to nearly 100 majestic contemporary sailing vessels: Amerigo Vespucci, Clearwater, Constitution, Eagle, Mayflower, Sea Cloud, Victory, many more. Authoritative captions provide statistics, background on each ship. 190 black-and-white photographs and illustrations. Introduction. 128pp. 8⅞ x 11¾. 27163-3 Pa. $14.95

EARLY NINETEENTH-CENTURY CRAFTS AND TRADES, Peter Stockham (ed.). Extremely rare 1807 volume describes to youngsters the crafts and trades of the day: brickmaker, weaver, dressmaker, bookbinder, ropemaker, saddler, many more. Quaint prose, charming illustrations for each craft. 20 black-and-white line illustrations. 192pp. 4⅝ x 6. 27293-1 Pa. $4.95

VICTORIAN FASHIONS AND COSTUMES FROM HARPER'S BAZAR, 1867–1898, Stella Blum (ed.). Day costumes, evening wear, sports clothes, shoes, hats, other accessories in over 1,000 detailed engravings. 320pp. 9⅜ x 12¼. 22990-4 Pa. $15.95

GUSTAV STICKLEY, THE CRAFTSMAN, Mary Ann Smith. Superb study surveys broad scope of Stickley's achievement, especially in architecture. Design philosophy, rise and fall of the Craftsman empire, descriptions and floor plans for many Craftsman houses, more. 86 black-and-white halftones. 31 line illustrations. Introduction 208pp. 6½ x 9¼. 27210-9 Pa. $9.95

THE LONG ISLAND RAIL ROAD IN EARLY PHOTOGRAPHS, Ron Ziel. Over 220 rare photos, informative text document origin (1844) and development of rail service on Long Island. Vintage views of early trains, locomotives, stations, passengers, crews, much more. Captions. 8⅞ x 11¾. 26301-0 Pa. $13.95

THE BOOK OF OLD SHIPS: From Egyptian Galleys to Clipper Ships, Henry B. Culver. Superb, authoritative history of sailing vessels, with 80 magnificent line illustrations. Galley, bark, caravel, longship, whaler, many more. Detailed, informative text on each vessel by noted naval historian. Introduction. 256pp. 5⅜ x 8½. 27332-6 Pa. $7.95

TEN BOOKS ON ARCHITECTURE, Vitruvius. The most important book ever written on architecture. Early Roman aesthetics, technology, classical orders, site selection, all other aspects. Morgan translation. 331pp. 5⅜ x 8½. 20645-9 Pa. $8.95

THE HUMAN FIGURE IN MOTION, Eadweard Muybridge. More than 4,500 stopped-action photos, in action series, showing undraped men, women, children jumping, lying down, throwing, sitting, wrestling, carrying, etc. 390pp. 7⅞ x 10⅝. 20204-6 Clothbd. $27.95

TREES OF THE EASTERN AND CENTRAL UNITED STATES AND CANADA, William M. Harlow. Best one-volume guide to 140 trees. Full descriptions, woodlore, range, etc. Over 600 illustrations. Handy size. 288pp. 4½ x 6⅜. 20395-6 Pa. $6.95

SONGS OF WESTERN BIRDS, Dr. Donald J. Borror. Complete song and call repertoire of 60 western species, including flycatchers, juncoes, cactus wrens, many more–includes fully illustrated booklet. Cassette and manual 99913-0 $8.95

GROWING AND USING HERBS AND SPICES, Milo Miloradovich. Versatile handbook provides all the information needed for cultivation and use of all the herbs and spices available in North America. 4 illustrations. Index. Glossary. 236pp. 5⅜ x 8½. 25058-X Pa. $7.95

BIG BOOK OF MAZES AND LABYRINTHS, Walter Shepherd. 50 mazes and labyrinths in all–classical, solid, ripple, and more–in one great volume. Perfect inexpensive puzzler for clever youngsters. Full solutions. 112pp. 8⅛ x 11. 22951-3 Pa. $4.95

CATALOG OF DOVER BOOKS

PIANO TUNING, J. Cree Fischer. Clearest, best book for beginner, amateur. Simple repairs, raising dropped notes, tuning by easy method of flattened fifths. No previous skills needed. 4 illustrations. 201pp. 5⅜ x 8½. 23267-0 Pa. $6.95

A SOURCE BOOK IN THEATRICAL HISTORY, A. M. Nagler. Contemporary observers on acting, directing, make-up, costuming, stage props, machinery, scene design, from Ancient Greece to Chekhov. 611pp. 5⅜ x 8½. 20515-0 Pa. $12.95

THE COMPLETE NONSENSE OF EDWARD LEAR, Edward Lear. All nonsense limericks, zany alphabets, Owl and Pussycat, songs, nonsense botany, etc., illustrated by Lear. Total of 320pp. 5⅜ x 8½. (USO) 20167-8 Pa. $7.95

VICTORIAN PARLOUR POETRY: An Annotated Anthology, Michael R. Turner. 117 gems by Longfellow, Tennyson, Browning, many lesser-known poets. "The Village Blacksmith," "Curfew Must Not Ring Tonight," "Only a Baby Small," dozens more, often difficult to find elsewhere. Index of poets, titles, first lines. xxiii + 325pp. 5⅜ x 8¼. 27044-0 Pa. $8.95

DUBLINERS, James Joyce. Fifteen stories offer vivid, tightly focused observations of the lives of Dublin's poorer classes. At least one, "The Dead," is considered a masterpiece. Reprinted complete and unabridged from standard edition. 160pp. 5³⁄₁₆ x 8¼. 26870-5 Pa. $1.00

THE HAUNTED MONASTERY and THE CHINESE MAZE MURDERS, Robert van Gulik. Two full novels by van Gulik, set in 7th-century China, continue adventures of Judge Dee and his companions. An evil Taoist monastery, seemingly supernatural events; overgrown topiary maze hides strange crimes. 27 illustrations. 328pp. 5⅜ x 8½. 23502-5 Pa. $8.95

THE BOOK OF THE SACRED MAGIC OF ABRAMELIN THE MAGE, translated by S. MacGregor Mathers. Medieval manuscript of ceremonial magic. Basic document in Aleister Crowley, Golden Dawn groups. 268pp. 5⅜ x 8½. 23211-5 Pa. $9.95

NEW RUSSIAN-ENGLISH AND ENGLISH-RUSSIAN DICTIONARY, M. A. O'Brien. This is a remarkably handy Russian dictionary, containing a surprising amount of information, including over 70,000 entries. 366pp. 4½ x 6⅛. 20208-9 Pa. $10.95

HISTORIC HOMES OF THE AMERICAN PRESIDENTS, Second, Revised Edition, Irvin Haas. A traveler's guide to American Presidential homes, most open to the public, depicting and describing homes occupied by every American President from George Washington to George Bush. With visiting hours, admission charges, travel routes. 175 photographs. Index. 160pp. 8¼ x 11. 26751-2 Pa. $11.95

NEW YORK IN THE FORTIES, Andreas Feininger. 162 brilliant photographs by the well-known photographer, formerly with *Life* magazine. Commuters, shoppers, Times Square at night, much else from city at its peak. Captions by John von Hartz. 181pp. 9¼ x 10¾. 23585-8 Pa. $13.95

INDIAN SIGN LANGUAGE, William Tomkins. Over 525 signs developed by Sioux and other tribes. Written instructions and diagrams. Also 290 pictographs. 111pp. 6⅛ x 9¼. 22029-X Pa. $3.95

ANATOMY: A Complete Guide for Artists, Joseph Sheppard. A master of figure drawing shows artists how to render human anatomy convincingly. Over 460 illustrations. 224pp. 8⅜ x 11¼. 27279-6 Pa. $11.95

MEDIEVAL CALLIGRAPHY: Its History and Technique, Marc Drogin. Spirited history, comprehensive instruction manual covers 13 styles (ca. 4th century thru 15th). Excellent photographs; directions for duplicating medieval techniques with modern tools. 224pp. 8⅜ x 11¼. 26142-5 Pa. $12.95

DRIED FLOWERS: How to Prepare Them, Sarah Whitlock and Martha Rankin. Complete instructions on how to use silica gel, meal and borax, perlite aggregate, sand and borax, glycerine and water to create attractive permanent flower arrangements. 12 illustrations. 32pp. 5⅜ x 8½. 21802-3 Pa. $1.00

EASY-TO-MAKE BIRD FEEDERS FOR WOODWORKERS, Scott D. Campbell. Detailed, simple-to-use guide for designing, constructing, caring for and using feeders. Text, illustrations for 12 classic and contemporary designs. 96pp. 5⅜ x 8½. 25847-5 Pa. $3.95

SCOTTISH WONDER TALES FROM MYTH AND LEGEND, Donald A. Mackenzie. 16 lively tales tell of giants rumbling down mountainsides, of a magic wand that turns stone pillars into warriors, of gods and goddesses, evil hags, powerful forces and more. 240pp. 5⅜ x 8½. 29677-6 Pa. $6.95

THE HISTORY OF UNDERCLOTHES, C. Willett Cunnington and Phyllis Cunnington. Fascinating, well-documented survey covering six centuries of English undergarments, enhanced with over 100 illustrations: 12th-century laced-up bodice, footed long drawers (1795), 19th-century bustles, 19th-century corsets for men, Victorian "bust improvers," much more. 272pp. 5⅝ x 8¼. 27124-2 Pa. $9.95

ARTS AND CRAFTS FURNITURE: The Complete Brooks Catalog of 1912, Brooks Manufacturing Co. Photos and detailed descriptions of more than 150 now very collectible furniture designs from the Arts and Crafts movement depict davenports, settees, buffets, desks, tables, chairs, bedsteads, dressers and more, all built of solid, quarter-sawed oak. Invaluable for students and enthusiasts of antiques, Americana and the decorative arts. 80pp. 6½ x 9¼. 27471-3 Pa. $8.95

HOW WE INVENTED THE AIRPLANE: An Illustrated History, Orville Wright. Fascinating firsthand account covers early experiments, construction of planes and motors, first flights, much more. Introduction and commentary by Fred C. Kelly. 76 photographs. 96pp. 8¼ x 11. 25662-6 Pa. $8.95

THE ARTS OF THE SAILOR: Knotting, Splicing and Ropework, Hervey Garrett Smith. Indispensable shipboard reference covers tools, basic knots and useful hitches; handsewing and canvas work, more. Over 100 illustrations. Delightful reading for sea lovers. 256pp. 5⅜ x 8½. 26440-8 Pa. $8.95

FRANK LLOYD WRIGHT'S FALLINGWATER: The House and Its History, Second, Revised Edition, Donald Hoffmann. A total revision–both in text and illustrations–of the standard document on Fallingwater, the boldest, most personal architectural statement of Wright's mature years, updated with valuable new material from the recently opened Frank Lloyd Wright Archives. "Fascinating"–*The New York Times*. 116 illustrations. 128pp. 9¼ x 10¾. 27430-6 Pa. $12.95

AUTOBIOGRAPHY: The Story of My Experiments with Truth, Mohandas K. Gandhi. Boyhood, legal studies, purification, the growth of the Satyagraha (nonviolent protest) movement. Critical, inspiring work of the man responsible for the freedom of India. 480pp. 5⅜ x 8½. (USO) 24593-4 Pa. $8.95

CELTIC MYTHS AND LEGENDS, T. W. Rolleston. Masterful retelling of Irish and Welsh stories and tales. Cuchulain, King Arthur, Deirdre, the Grail, many more. First paperback edition. 58 full-page illustrations. 512pp. 5⅜ x 8½. 26507-2 Pa. $9.95

THE PRINCIPLES OF PSYCHOLOGY, William James. Famous long course complete, unabridged. Stream of thought, time perception, memory, experimental methods; great work decades ahead of its time. 94 figures. 1,391pp. 5⅜ x 8½. 2-vol. set.
Vol. I: 20381-6 Pa. $13.95
Vol. II: 20382-4 Pa. $14.95

THE WORLD AS WILL AND REPRESENTATION, Arthur Schopenhauer. Definitive English translation of Schopenhauer's life work, correcting more than 1,000 errors, omissions in earlier translations. Translated by E. F. J. Payne. Total of 1,269pp. 5⅜ x 8½. 2-vol. set. Vol. 1: 21761-2 Pa. $12.95
Vol. 2: 21762-0 Pa. $12.95

MAGIC AND MYSTERY IN TIBET, Madame Alexandra David-Neel. Experiences among lamas, magicians, sages, sorcerers, Bonpa wizards. A true psychic discovery. 32 illustrations. 321pp. 5⅜ x 8½. (USO) 22682-4 Pa. $9.95

THE EGYPTIAN BOOK OF THE DEAD, E. A. Wallis Budge. Complete reproduction of Ani's papyrus, finest ever found. Full hieroglyphic text, interlinear transliteration, word-for-word translation, smooth translation. 533pp. 6½ x 9¼.
21866-X Pa. $11.95

MATHEMATICS FOR THE NONMATHEMATICIAN, Morris Kline. Detailed, college-level treatment of mathematics in cultural and historical context, with numerous exercises. Recommended Reading Lists. Tables. Numerous figures. 641pp. 5⅜ x 8½.
24823-2 Pa. $11.95

THEORY OF WING SECTIONS: Including a Summary of Airfoil Data, Ira H. Abbott and A. E. von Doenhoff. Concise compilation of subsonic aerodynamic characteristics of NACA wing sections, plus description of theory. 350pp. of tables. 693pp. 5⅜ x 8½. 60586-8 Pa. $14.95

THE RIME OF THE ANCIENT MARINER, Gustave Doré, S. T. Coleridge. Doré's finest work; 34 plates capture moods, subtleties of poem. Flawless full-size reproductions printed on facing pages with authoritative text of poem. "Beautiful. Simply beautiful."–*Publisher's Weekly*. 77pp. 9¼ x 12. 22305-1 Pa. $7.95

NORTH AMERICAN INDIAN DESIGNS FOR ARTISTS AND CRAFTSPEOPLE, Eva Wilson. Over 360 authentic copyright-free designs adapted from Navajo blankets, Hopi pottery, Sioux buffalo hides, more. Geometrics, symbolic figures, plant and animal motifs, etc. 128pp. 8⅜ x 11. (EUK) 25341-4 Pa. $8.95

SCULPTURE: Principles and Practice, Louis Slobodkin. Step-by-step approach to clay, plaster, metals, stone; classical and modern. 253 drawings, photos. 255pp. 8⅛ x 11.
22960-2 Pa. $11.95

THE INFLUENCE OF SEA POWER UPON HISTORY, 1660–1783, A. T. Mahan. Influential classic of naval history and tactics still used as text in war colleges. First paperback edition. 4 maps. 24 battle plans. 640pp. 5⅜ x 8½. 25509-3 Pa. $14.95

THE STORY OF THE TITANIC AS TOLD BY ITS SURVIVORS, Jack Winocour (ed.). What it was really like. Panic, despair, shocking inefficiency, and a little heroism. More thrilling than any fictional account. 26 illustrations. 320pp. 5⅜ x 8½. 20610-6 Pa. $8.95

FAIRY AND FOLK TALES OF THE IRISH PEASANTRY, William Butler Yeats (ed.). Treasury of 64 tales from the twilight world of Celtic myth and legend: "The Soul Cages," "The Kildare Pooka," "King O'Toole and his Goose," many more. Introduction and Notes by W. B. Yeats. 352pp. 5⅜ x 8½. 26941-8 Pa. $8.95

BUDDHIST MAHAYANA TEXTS, E. B. Cowell and Others (eds.). Superb, accurate translations of basic documents in Mahayana Buddhism, highly important in history of religions. The Buddha-karita of Asvaghosha, Larger Sukhavativyuha, more. 448pp. 5⅜ x 8½. 25552-2 Pa. $12.95

ONE TWO THREE . . . INFINITY: Facts and Speculations of Science, George Gamow. Great physicist's fascinating, readable overview of contemporary science: number theory, relativity, fourth dimension, entropy, genes, atomic structure, much more. 128 illustrations. Index. 352pp. 5⅜ x 8½. 25664-2 Pa. $8.95

ENGINEERING IN HISTORY, Richard Shelton Kirby, et al. Broad, nontechnical survey of history's major technological advances: birth of Greek science, industrial revolution, electricity and applied science, 20th-century automation, much more. 181 illustrations. ". . . excellent . . ."–*Isis*. Bibliography. vii + 530pp. 5⅜ x 8¼. 26412-2 Pa. $14.95

DALÍ ON MODERN ART: The Cuckolds of Antiquated Modern Art, Salvador Dalí. Influential painter skewers modern art and its practitioners. Outrageous evaluations of Picasso, Cézanne, Turner, more. 15 renderings of paintings discussed. 44 calligraphic decorations by Dalí. 96pp. 5⅜ x 8½. (USO) 29220-7 Pa. $4.95

ANTIQUE PLAYING CARDS: A Pictorial History, Henry René D'Allemagne. Over 900 elaborate, decorative images from rare playing cards (14th–20th centuries): Bacchus, death, dancing dogs, hunting scenes, royal coats of arms, players cheating, much more. 96pp. 9¼ x 12¼. 29265-7 Pa. $12.95

MAKING FURNITURE MASTERPIECES: 30 Projects with Measured Drawings, Franklin H. Gottshall. Step-by-step instructions, illustrations for constructing handsome, useful pieces, among them a Sheraton desk, Chippendale chair, Spanish desk, Queen Anne table and a William and Mary dressing mirror. 224pp. 8⅛ x 11¼. 29338-6 Pa. $13.95

THE FOSSIL BOOK: A Record of Prehistoric Life, Patricia V. Rich et al. Profusely illustrated definitive guide covers everything from single-celled organisms and dinosaurs to birds and mammals and the interplay between climate and man. Over 1,500 illustrations. 760pp. 7½ x 10⅛. 29371-8 Pa. $29.95

Prices subject to change without notice.

Available at your book dealer or write for free catalog to Dept. GI, Dover Publications, Inc., 31 East 2nd St., Mineola, N.Y. 11501. Dover publishes more than 500 books each year on science, elementary and advanced mathematics, biology, music, art, literary history, social sciences and other areas.